RICHARD WETHERILL:
ANASAZI

RICHARD WETHERILL ANASAZI

Frank McNitt

with maps and drawings
by the author

REVISED EDITION

THE UNIVERSITY OF NEW MEXICO PRESS
ALBUQUERQUE

CONTENTS

III

●

●

ILLUSTRATIONS

PHOTOGRAPHS.

I RETURNED AND SAW UNDER THE SUN, THAT THE RACE IS NOT TO THE SWIFT, NOR THE BATTLE TO THE STRONG, NEITHER YET BREAD TO THE WISE, NOR YET RICHES TO MEN OF UNDERSTANDING, NOR YET FAVOR TO MEN OF SKILL; BUT TIME AND CHANCE HAPPENETH TO THEM ALL. — *Ecclesiastes.*

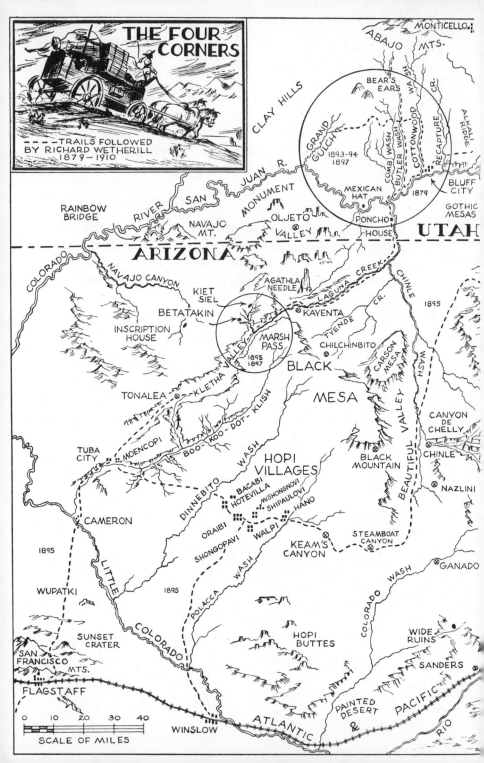

THE FOUR CORNERS

---- TRAILS FOLLOWED
BY RICHARD WETHERILL
1879-1910

MONTICELLO

ABAJO MTS.

CLAY HILLS

BEAR'S EARS

GRAND GULCH 1893-94 1897

COMB WASH

BUTLER WASH

COTTONWOOD WASH

RECAPTURE CR.

ALKALI RIDGE

JUAN R.

SAN

RIVER

MONUMENT

MEXICAN HAT

1879

BLUFF CITY

RAINBOW BRIDGE

COLORADO

NAVAJO MT.

OLJETO VALLEY

PONCHO HOUSE

GOTHIC MESAS

UTAH

ARIZONA

NAVAJO CANYON

KIET SIEL

BETATAKIN

AGATHLA NEEDLE

LAGUNA CREEK

CHINLE

1895

INSCRIPTION HOUSE

MARSH PASS

KAYENTA

TYENDE CR.

1895 1897

KLETHA

BLACK

CHILCHINBITO

CARSON MESA

WASH

CANYON DE CHELLY

TONALEA

BOO- KOO- DOT- KLISH

MESA

BEAUTIFUL VALLEY

CHINLE

NAZLINI

TUBA CITY

MOENCOPI

DINNEBITO

WASH

HOPI VILLAGES

BLACK MOUNTAIN

CAMERON

BACABI HOTEVILLA
MISHONGNOVI
SHIPAULOVI HANO

ORAIBI

WALPI

STEAMBOAT CANYON

1895

SHONGOPAVI

POLACCA

WASH

KEAM'S CANYON

GANADO

LITTLE

1895

WUPATKI

COLORADO

COLORADO WASH

WIDE RUINS

SUNSET CRATER

HOPI BUTTES

SANDERS

SAN FRANCISCO MTS.

PAINTED DESERT

PACIFIC

FLAGSTAFF

&

RIO

0 10 20 30 40

SCALE OF MILES

WINSLOW

ATLANTIC

I

A number of years ago, Jesse Nusbaum and I were exploring cliff dwellings on the west side of Mesa Verde. We saw one that was high up on the canyon wall opposite us, and decided to look into it. But it was a terribly hard climb — up a sheer wall and across a narrow ledge, with a long drop below. But we finally made it. With great elation over our discovery and the successful climb, we peered down through an opening in the rocks at our ruin. And right there before our eyes was an upended slab of stone. On it we read these words: "What fools these mortals be. R. Wetherill."

—ALFRED VINCENT KIDDER.

PROLOGUE

RICHARD WETHERILL was murdered at six o'clock in the evening of June 22, 1910. He died in an ambush in the shadows of a bend in Chaco Canyon half a mile below Pueblo Bonito where a wagon trail, now the road to Farmington, New Mexico, climbs through jumbled rock to the high mesa. Five or six Navajos had gathered there as Wetherill and the cowboy Bill Finn drove a small bunch of cattle down the canyon.

The cattle were the "drags" or drifters from a large herd Sheriff Tom Talle had brought up from Texas. It was a dry year, dryest at Gallup where Sheriff Talle lived, and the grazing was poor even in the Chaco. But Wetherill had the Navajos dig water holes along the Escavada and told the sheriff he could bring his cattle here. They came through the Gap that morning under a rolling cloud of gray dust.

At Rincon del Camino, the place where he died, the road turns to cross the shallow end of a draw among fallen rock and a waist-high covering of spiky, olive-green greasewood. The coloration is such that the eyes, adjusting from a dazzling low sun to the blue shadows, can easily mistake a motionless man or horse for part of the landscape. Erosion has cut the canyon floor so deeply with washes and arroyos that to avoid them the road makes several tortuous bends. For these reasons and probably because the sheriff's cattle were raising a fair dust, Wetherill and the cowboy did not see signs of danger until it was too late.

In the greasewood fringing the draw a Navajo, standing beside his horse, raised his rifle. Two shots and then a third from a .33 caliber Winchester echoed against the canyon walls. The first bullet whined past Bill Finn; the second pierced Richard Wetherill's right hand, entered his chest and killed him instantly. The third bullet was fired at nearly pointblank range after Wetherill slipped from the saddle and lay sprawled in the sand.

There had been a short interval between the second and third shots as the Navajo walked fifty yards to where the body had fallen. He crouched over it muttering.

"Are you sick, Anasazi?"

There was no response. The Navajo pointed the muzzle of his rifle downward. His third shot tore away the right side of Wetherill's head.

At the same moment Finn wheeled his horse. Several other Indians were behind him. He broke through the ambush, exchanged a few shots with the Indians and headed at a run toward Pueblo Bonito. Behind him, outdistanced, came the Navajo Thomas Padilla.

The sound of firing reached the ranch, bringing Marietta Wetherill to a bedroom window. In the doorway of her room in the bunkhouse across the yard appeared the alarmed, inquiring face of Eleanor Quick, the schoolteacher for the Wetherill children. For a brief, still moment the women faced each other across this distance. They heard Finn's horse pounding down the road. Several Mexicans ran toward the wareroom. A string of shrill yelps sounded like a dog or coyote. But these cries were Navajo.

Two Indians who had been waiting under the north cliff near Pueblo Bonito whipped their horses toward the road, riding diagonally to head Finn off before he reached the ranch gate. Marietta and Miss Quick had heard their yelping. Hostine Tso-bakis crossed the cowboy's path first, swinging a quirt or a club down on Finn's shoulders and ignoring the revolver Finn aimed but did not fire. Trailing to one side, armed with a pistol which may or may not have been loaded, was Joe Hostine Yazzie.

Finn's horse had pulled ahead when Finn finally fired four times. Hostine Tso was hit by the fourth bullet in the left side just above the hip. He bent forward in the saddle and his horse slowed as Finn hurdled a wire fence, circled the warehouse and entered the yard. Joe Yazzie meanwhile was finding shelter behind the blacksmith shop. Marietta Wetherill met Finn at the ranchhouse door.

"Where are the children?" he demanded.

"I don't know."

"Get them in quick — hear me? — get them quick. We've had trouble." He started for Wetherill's office, intending to find a rifle. Marietta stopped him.

"Where is Mr. Wetherill?"

"He's down there. . ." Finn shook off the hand holding his arm.

"If there's trouble down there, why aren't you with him?"

"Because they have killed him," Finn told her. And then he went for the rifle.

From her vantage point, Miss Quick observed that "Mrs. Wetherill who had seen the racing from the back door divined that he [Finn] had no cartridges [and] met him just as he jumped from the horse with a six-shooter, and Joe [Yazzie] raised his gun to shoot her but had no cartridges either. Mr. Finn ran through the house, got his Winchester and came out the door, but every Indian had vanished." Soon after, she added, Richard Wetherill's big sorrel horse trotted into the yard, the saddle empty and stirrups swinging.

Richard Wetherill's body was brought to the ranch in a wagon and laid out on the back porch awaiting the arrival of authorities from Farmington. Early the second day a clerk at the Crownpoint agency appeared to inquire about the shooting, saying he represented Superintendent Samuel F. Stacher who had not yet returned from a trip to Oklahoma. This was not really necessary, because Marietta knew him. His name was B. P. Six. The welcome he received, as he later described it to John Charles, a supervisor for the Interior Department, was chilling.

All was quiet in the canyon when he rode up to the ranchhouse at Pueblo Bonito, Six said. Standing in the doorway as though expecting someone, he found Marietta Wetherill. She was pale and watched him with a fixed expression as he approached. Before he could say a word, she spoke in a tight, frozen voice.

"Go to the back porch and see what you have done."

"I hope that you do not connect me with this affair in any way?" Six replied. He was about to say more when Marietta Wetherill interrupted him.

"You and your kind have brought this about."

She then turned and entered the house, Six reported to John Charles, and — with the door between them — he could hear her crying. He did not see her again that day.

ONE

ITS sheer sides of yellow stone rising to a green-capped summit, pierced on eastern approaches by a labyrinth of canyons, the mesa forms a vast valley bastion in southwestern Colorado. A man could wander over it lost for months, traverse its canyon depths and never once cross his own trail. Hard to the east loom the saw-toothed, high La Platas. The eye sweeping westward across sloping land broken only by a few small streams is unhindered for sixty miles, until the flat blue eminence of the Sierra Abajo.

What brought men here and where they came from no one is sure, but a prehistoric people once lived among the clouds on the mesa top. After centuries there they moved into cliff villages that were works of stonemason's art. The villages they built in caves and cavities of the porous rock; their fragile walls, windowed towers and tiers of rooms and terraces were suspended at dizzying heights above the canyon bottoms. Then, faced by a disastrous calamity of nature and perhaps by a hostile enemy, they moved away.

The mesa was abandoned to silence and slow time-change of the seasons. In winter it was dark-visaged, menacing. Snow collared its base in deep drifts and streaked its rocky face on the projecting ridges. In summer the hot sun turned the fingering canyons and the heights above green again. Clouds moving before winds overhead cast giant shadows that drifted west to east across the valley, darkening the verdant mesa top. Piñon pitch was in the air, the bright flash of a bluebird's wing glinted before an empty cave mouth.

Bands of semi-nomadic Utes, dwelling in buffalo skin tipis and shunning the stone cliff houses, were the next people known to inhabit the region. Although they hunted game on the mesa's summit and also prowled the difficult canyons, they preferred to live in the low valleys and make their camps close to river streams. Awed by the majestic mesa, the Utes storied it with supernatural importance. They ringed it with superstitions and myths that were old by the time the first Spaniards penetrated the country.

In the last quarter of the nineteenth century, the first Americans came by wagon into the valley, settled in uneasy contact with the Utes, and listened

RICHARD WETHERILL

to the Indian myths of Mesa Verde. Among the first of these settlers was a family named Wetherill.

THE FIRST WETHERILLS to cross the Atlantic came with other religious refugees from England in the early days of the Colonies, breaking through forests and establishing farms along the eastern seaboard. They were of several faiths but most of those who settled in the good farm country of Pennsylvania were Quakers, living hard, simple lives in the conservative pattern of their religious teaching.

One of this clan, Benjamin Kite Wetherill, was born on Christmas Day, 1831, in Chester County, Pennsylvania. He was a restless fellow who wanted to see the new country far beyond the western hills. At the age of twenty-one he left his father's farm for Wisconsin, moving shortly after to Iowa. On May 22, 1856, he and Marion Tompkins, also a Quaker, were married in the Friends meeting house at Iowa Falls. Benjamin took his wife back to Chester and there, on June 12, 1858, their eldest son, Richard, was born. Other children followed: a daughter, Anna, and then four more sons — Benjamin Alfred, John, Clayton and Winslow. A second daughter, Alice, died as a young girl. None of the children was to have any remembrance of the East for their father refused to stay long in Pennsylvania.

When Richard was a year old his parents moved to Fort Leavenworth, Kansas. From this point Benjamin, short, wiry and always restless, set out on long adventures. During President Grant's administration he was appointed an Indian trail agent, which required his absence from home for unpredictable lengths of time. Riding the Chisholm Trail into Oklahoma Territory and Texas, adjusting land and stock disputes which cattle drives stirred up between Indians and whites, he became known in the prairie towns as an able mediator, a man who could — if not fearlessly, then thoughtfully — placate the angriest nest of hostile Indians.

He may have boasted about this a bit in the places where he stopped, or his ruggedly independent "devil-take-thee" attitude with idlers and meddlers may have irked many who were acquainted with him. In any case he also was regarded as sometimes irascible, usually stiff. With his own family he was a loving husband, if a bit formal, and a good father who taught his boys everything he knew and encouraged them to strike out for themselves.

The family did not attend church regularly. But with Bible-readings and lessons at home the children were reared strictly in the Quaker faith. Marion

Wetherill took the fullest share of this responsibility and to her, probably more than to their father, the boys owed the warp and weft of Quaker principles which so strongly patterned their lives. Marion was a little woman, quiet, self-effacing, yet she ruled her household of growing boys firmly. Her tastes and background were simple enough, coming as she did from a farm family, and she was a good homemaker. Sturdy and plump, with sharp blue eyes, she was the rallying point of the family during her husband's long absences.

Growing up in Fort Leavenworth, always looking forward to his father's new stories of adventure, Richard acquired much of the tough fiber of Benjamin's character and a little of his autocratic disposition; with it he had some of the leavening gentleness of his mother's calm. Even as a youth there was assurance in his dark gaze and in his quiet way of speaking. He had a sense of humor and liked fun; but even as a boy he did not encourage anyone to play a joke on him. When he was eighteen, broad-shouldered but not tall — four inches under six feet — his dark brown hair began to turn gray. He spoke in short, unhurried sentences, his tone quiet but a bit high in register, and he kept his eyes fixed, unblinking and often quizzical, upon those he was addressing. Some of his friends have said they had a nervous feeling that he gazed right into their minds.

In a rugged way he was good looking. He had a sudden, dazzling smile that flashed across a usually serious face, and sometimes a way of holding his head that some thought cocky: chin up and tilted. Equally characteristic was his erect posture. Richard had a straight back. And even as a boy he had big wrists and big, capable hands.

His only formal education he received in the schools at Fort Leavenworth. He learned to speak German with some fluency and retained it always, but later shunned the thundering Germanic epithets for the delicate-sounding expletives of the Navajo tongue. Anglo-Saxon curses he used not at all.

His instructors in Kansas gave Richard a good grounding in mathematics, history and geography. Although he liked books and read a great deal, he never acquired any skill in English composition, or taste for it. His handwriting had a bold, handsome line, but his grammar was faltering and awkward on paper. He spelled fairly well but punctuation bored him; usually he dispensed with it, relying upon a hit-or-miss peppering of dashes.

It was this period at Leavenworth, 1859 to 1876, that shaped his character. His mother worried constantly over her large family, wondering how she would keep her children clothed and fed on her husband's small earnings. As the eldest son, Richard felt it his duty to give what help he could. When he was sixteen he found work at night in the boiler room of a factory. This was one of the memories of his youth he spoke of later without fondness. When he liked what he was doing he gave it the full blaze of his enormous energy. But even in his teens he craved variety, and like his father, he was restless.

As he grew older, Richard assumed many responsibilities of the family, and showed a solicitude for his mother, his brothers and his sister which he continued to feel keenly the rest of his life. At one time or another all of his brothers were to depend upon him temporarily for help, and he encouraged them. There were close bonds between the five brothers and as their leader, Richard rarely failed in what he saw as his part.

The Wetherills moved from Fort Leavenworth to Joplin, Missouri, in 1876. They had been living in Joplin about three years when Benjamin Wetherill, his health and his resources both failing, heard rumors of fortunes in the silver fields of Colorado. Alone, he went to the mining camp at Rico and then almost at once sent for Richard. The prospects appeared good, but the father wanted his son's opinion and his help. Richard, then twenty-one, joined him, and the rest of the family followed soon. Perhaps the Wetherills mined some silver, but if they did it was not long before this became a dispirited effort. If fortunes were being made, they were not being made by anyone the Wetherills knew. In the same year, 1879, they packed their wagons and moved again.

Traveling south through country inhabited only by Utes and Navajos they came upon the San Juan River, close to the Four Corners, and continued westward until they were a short distance above Bluff City, Utah, a tiny Mormon settlement hidden among cottonwood trees on the north bank of the San Juan. Here they hopefully stopped, taking up a small ranch near the river, in a picturesque wilderness of sand and chocolate-colored sandstone bluffs that to this day defies cultivation. They had been here only a few months when one of those cataclysmic downpours, well known to the Southwest, hit their ranch and washed it away. When the sun again emerged and baked the desert dry, it somehow didn't seem worthwhile to rebuild what had been lost.

Leading his family in nearly the same spirit as Moses led the Israelites, Benjamin Wetherill turned eastward again, heading his wagons through McElmo Canyon and then around the long northern walls of Mesa Verde until they rolled through the tall grass of Mancos Valley. The raggedness of their outfit revealed a family that had known hard times. The year was 1880. They decided to stay.

THE TOWN of Mancos and its valley are named from the Rio de Los Mancos, called this by Spanish explorers out of respect for their lame or crippled horses. Journeying westward from Santa Fe the Spaniards had threaded through the La Plata Mountains over ground rough and steep enough to make a devout man beseech the name of his maker in broken monosyllables. For the sweating horses and pack mules, slipping and stumbling across jagged shale and around the spikes of fallen pine, this stage of the expedition had been a bruising ordeal. The small party rested when they had descended out of the mountains, making camp in the cool green valley near the river.

Father Silvestre Vélez de Escalante, one of the travelers, noted the date: August 10, 1776. It appears as a brief entry made along the trail taken by Fathers Francisco Atanasio Domínguez and Vélez de Escalante and their eight companions in their search for a serviceable route from New Mexico to Monterey and the missions along the California coast. Except that the water is cold, even in August, Father Escalante may have found the stream a nice one to wade and to bathe in.

From the valley of the Mancos the Spaniards turned their eyes to Mesa Verde's upthrusting tableland, rising some eight thousand feet above the level of the sea and fifteen hundred feet above their heads. This block of pale yellow sandstone forms a sheer cliff for fifteen miles along the Rio Mancos, while its northern abutment measures some twelve miles from east to west. From the mesa's craggy northern point the Rio Mancos is a twisting thread of blue silk, the green and yellow valley floor a smooth patchwork, a horseman on the Spanish trail a mere pinpoint of toiling motion.

The travelers did not stop to explore the tableland and the myriad canyons thrusting into its dark green heart. An earlier wayfarer, his name uncertain, had called it Mesa Verde. Ute Indians who roamed the region watched this and later parties of Spaniards with suspicion. So long as the Bearded Mouths kept moving, the Utes exacted no more than a burro, an ox or two, or a few horses; they were more interested in maintaining warlike relations with the Navajo and Hopi to the south.

Traveling with the topographical survey party of Capt. J. N. Macomb

RICHARD WETHERILL

as an expert geologist, Prof. J. S. Newberry won distinction as the first white man, so far as is known, to climb to the top of Mesa Verde. This he did near the northern promontory called Point Lookout, in 1859, enjoying the view and the breeze through his beard. But officially he noted only that the mesa's sandstone formation was of the Cretaceous period.

A geologist of sorts himself, John Moss was more a specialist in rock-embedded veins of gold than in ancient masonry. Prospector Moss and his burro ambled into the valley of Mesa Verde in 1873, his object gold — or, failing that, silver. A smarter man than some who followed, John Moss gave a bagful of trinkets to the Utes, assured them his habits were amiable, and in return was granted twenty-five square miles in the foothills of the La Platas where he could search for precious ore without interference.

Apparently the small land grant was unproductive, for Moss soon strayed from it, searching southward through Mancos Valley into the deep gorges of Mancos Canyon. Here he noticed, without much interest, a few small cliff houses clinging to the canyon walls far above. Whatever the importance he attached to it, his discovery of the ancient dwellings became known. In 1874 he agreed to guide the William Henry Jackson party down Mancos Canyon to the cliff houses. Among these was a small ruin high in the west wall which Jackson enthusiastically climbed to, photographed, and named Two-Story House — the first in Mesa Verde to be identified.

Jackson at this time was beginning to win a reputation as the most noted photographer of the unexplored West. He had abandoned his studio in Omaha, Nebraska, four years before to join Ferdinand Vandiveer Hayden, professor of geology at the University of Pennsylvania, in a survey of the Rocky Mountains region financed by the Interior Department. The Rockies were then as unknown to the outside world as the middle of Tibet. Reports of the Hayden party, called the "Geological and Geographical Survey of the Territories," are a landmark in American exploration.

Jackson was accompanied by Ernest Ingersoll — a correspondent for Horace Greeley's *New York Tribune,* two packers, and an acquaintance from Omaha named E. H. Cooper. In September of 1874 Jackson located John Moss at his camp on the Rio La Plata. Combined with his artistry as a photographer, Jackson had a talent for observation, contributing to the 1876 publication of the Hayden Survey the first report of cliff dwellings in the Mesa Verde. This he was able to do after John Moss led his party though Mancos Canyon.

Few men surpassed Jackson for audacity in challenging the roughest trails, the most impregnable heights. But even he found the winding gorge of the Mancos hard going. "The banks," he wrote of the river, "are perpendicular, so that it was an extremely troublesome matter to cross. Added to the difficulties . . . was the thick-matted jungle of undergrowth, tall, reedy grass, willows, and thorny bushes. . . . The current is sluggish, and the water tinged with a milky translucency, gathered from the soil. The bottom is gravelly, but is covered to a depth of two or three feet with a very soft and miry mud. In every turn were deep pools. . . ."

The year following Jackson's trip another member of the Hayden Survey explored the region. W. H. Holmes, a geologist who later became chief of the Smithsonian Institution's Bureau of American Ethnology, reversed Jackson's route in 1875 by working north through Mancos Canyon from a point on the San Juan. He did little more than re-examine the mounds and small cliff dwellings Jackson had reported, but once emerging in Mancos Valley, Holmes swung west around the northern face of Mesa Verde and in McElmo Canyon found a number of large ruins. Among these was a "triple-walled tower . . . situated on a low bench within a mile of the main McElmo, and near a dry wash that enters that stream from the south." Like Jackson, Holmes believed that all prehistoric ruins in Mancos Canyon lay west of the river and that none was to be found in branch canyons to the east.

Jackson also explored this general region a second time in 1875, and Holmes returned in 1876 to search for ruins on the Rio La Plata and San Juan. The next year, Jackson came back for his third and final survey of the area.

Old-timers who settled in Mancos Valley relate that, with John Moss, the earliest pioneers were H. M. Smith and Peter Lindstrom, of Denver, and seven other gold-seekers from California: James Ratliff, A. L. Root, Dick Giles, Harry Lee, Ed Merrick, John Brewer and Fred Franks — all but Moss engaged by a San Francisco banking house to prospect for gold and silver. Not many months passed before these men were joined by a few ranchers and cowboys, lured by the valley's grasslands. They in turn attracted others and the population grew rapidly.

The newcomers planted cleared fields to corn and wheat, built their cabins of squared fir logs in the mountain foothills, and fed well on deer, elk and bear. Winters were bitterly cold with snow sometimes falling to a depth of thirty inches. Spring thaws and rain melting snow off the slopes usually kept the valleys green through the hot months, but not always. Occasionally there were periods of drouth when crops withered and stock grew lean. The earliest settlers diverted water from the Mancos and Dolores rivers into networks of laboriously constructed irrigation ditches.

The greatest concern of the settlers, however, was the increasingly hostile attitude of the Utes. When the whites showed no disposition to move on, the Indians ordered them away. Finally, because the settlers remained, one incident followed another, spreading alarm through the valley. At first it was a cow or steer found dead on the range, only its tongue cut out — or just enough of the hide peeled off for one pair of moccasin soles. Then, as these warnings failed, the Utes contemplated sterner measures. Meanwhile, with very few exceptions, the men of Mancos carried six-shooters and every cabin had a rifle.

Each year brought new families into the valley, the winter of 1876 seeing the arrival of Reese Richards and his wife, the first white woman in Mancos. More women and children followed soon afterwards. Among them were the wife and three children of Andrew Menefee, the wife and three boys of David Willis, Joe Morefield and his wife, and the families of Joe Sheek and Henry Mitchell. They arrived in the summer of 1877. In September of that year the Andrew Menefees, sheltering in a dugout down on the banks of the Mancos, announced the birth of a son, Willie. He was the first white baby born in the settlement, and to celebrate the event some of the ranchers got together and helped Andy Menefee build a log cabin.

After one serious Indian scare, the settlers cut logs in the fall of 1880 for the first schoolhouse and surrounded it with a stockade to which all families in the valley could come in case the Utes should attack. The school was completed in the spring and the stockade was finished soon after. But either the settlers' enthusiasm or their alarm petered out before the stockade was closed with a log gate. The gate was never built; the stockade was never used for defense.

Mancos was without a post office until 1881 and lacked any sort of store until 1883, the settlers in earlier years hauling all supplies by ox wagon or packhorse from Pueblo, the nearest railroad town. By 1878 the rails were extended to Alamosa, shortening the distance but still making it difficult to obtain most of the necessities of life, especially in the winter. Mrs. Clara Ormiston, who came to the valley as a child in July, 1880, said supplies fell short and some people nearly starved during 1883-84 — "the winter of the deep snow." That winter it was all but impossible for a horseman to reach

Alamosa, she said, and "We kids went to school on snowshoes — walked right over the tops of fences buried under the snow."

Some of the privations were relieved by a newcomer named George Bauer, who had left his job as a bricklayer in Del Norte to become the leading merchant of Mancos, eventually becoming wealthy enough to take his family on trips to Europe. After first obtaining a permit to open a post office, he brought in a freight wagon loaded to the axles with general merchandise; before nightfall, his stock all but gone, he realized he was established in business. He built the town's first store in 1883 and in the same room with the post office he opened up a saloon, erecting a partition to separate bar and bottles from the postage stamps.

Bauer's saloon was hailed uproariously by the men, Clara Ormiston recalled, but regarded coldly by their womenfolk. "But nobody said anything because we all wanted a post office so bad. And after all, there was that partition."

LIKE so many other newcomers to the valley, the Wetherills during their first two years had no place of their own. They lived on the ranch of a friendly settler named Coston. Hard work and saving finally made it possible for them to take up a homestead on one hundred and sixty acres of good land at the head of the valley, three miles southwest of the town. Here, in 1882, on a gentle rise above a bend in the Mancos River, the first building of Alamo Ranch was raised: a sturdy cabin of square-hewn logs chinked with white clay and covered with a roof of handsplit shingles. The Wetherills commenced work on the first barn, set out cottonwood trees around the cabin, dug an irrigation ditch diagonally across the front yard, and with a single ox team cultivated twenty acres of land.

When they applied for water claims, the Wetherills were assigned to thirteenth position on the priority list. As long as the Mancos River ran full, each rancher could draw off as much water for irrigation as he needed. In dry spells, when the river level was lowered, water each rancher could draw was reduced according to his priority.

Since their father's health prevented his sharing in hard labor, Richard and his brothers undertook the major work of developing the ranch. Eleven years after the log cabin was built, the Alamo Ranch was one of the most prosperous in the valley and was described by the editor of The *Mancos Times*:

"The Alamo Ranch owned by Mr. B. K. Wetherill, is one of the most beautiful and fertile mountain farms in the West, and Mr. Wetherill and his sons are constantly adding to their acreage. This year they will harvest nearly 200 acres of wheat and 75 acres of oats. . . . With not a dollar at their command they located in this then bleak and barren looking country, overrun with Indians and wild game. . . . They now own 1,000 acres of agricultural lands and have about 300 acres under a high state of cultivation. Their home is large and commodious and is surrounded by good barns, machinery houses, blacksmith shop and numerous tenement houses. They have raised five hearty, hard working and intelligent sons who are perfectly alive to all the issues of the day. Long since the yoke of oxen have been discarded and it is now necessary to employ twenty teams of good horses on the ranch. Mr. Wetherill has two good ditches and has completed a reservoir which when filled will cover from six to eight acres and will be capable of irrigating an extensive scope of ground. This shows what energy and perseverance will accomplish in the West."

By 1885 the original log cabin was but a wing of a low, rambling ranchhouse set in a shady grove of cottonwoods. The house faced east toward the barns, the corrals and the mountains. Several miles to the west, dark as a ship's prow against the sky, loomed the northern point of Mesa Verde. Long rows of white, three-board fences enclosed the nearest pastures and corrals.

Everything in the house spelled simplicity, comfortable use and good cheer. Blue denim strips sewed into one big piece carpeted the floors of the bedrooms, and under these were layers of straw. A girl staying at the ranch one time, and walking barefoot across her room, cried out in delight: "It feels just like walking on moss!"

Most of the furniture was homemade, crude but serviceable, and for each bedstead there was a cornshuck mattress. In the wintertime Marion Wetherill put goose feather ticking over the mattresses, supplied plenty of hand-quilted bedding, and added color by giving each bed a scarlet blanket at the foot. For cold mornings and cold feet, she laid Navajo blankets over the denim carpeting.

Shy in the presence of strangers, Marion Wetherill took little part in the conversation when visitors came to the ranch. She was a solid, warm presence, however, and able with one word or two to create an atmosphere of friendliness. Often, after guests had settled down and were talking easily, someone would notice that Marion had slipped unnoticed from the room. She might be outdoors, fussing over her bed of flowers, or directing the Ute yardman who cut firewood and tended her cows and chickens. More often she would be found in the kitchen, an apron around her ample waist. In the stovelight her features were strikingly similar to her son Richard's: the cheek-bones wide, the firm jawline more square than round. Her hair she wore in tight curls, quite gray, something like a cap.

Several fireplaces heated the ranchhouse, the large stone hearth in Benjamin's room being the favorite family gathering place. This room, sometimes called the den, had bunks along one wall, used by the father and one or two of his sons. It was here that visitors to the ranch were drawn, sometimes unsuspectingly, to listen to old Benjamin's Chisholm Trail stories. These always ended with laments about the illness that now incapacitated him.

Minor clashes — a shooting or knifing, the theft of a cow, jeering oaths from a drunken cowboy — aggravated the relations between Utes and white settlers for several years after the Wetherills began ranching in the valley. There was an ever-present fear that out of some small incident might come a buzzing hornet's nest of Indians, with deaths and burnings before soldiers could be summoned from Fort Lewis, twenty-five miles away. Actually, the Utes probably were in greater danger.

The Wetherill men were among a very few who were on good terms with the Indians. The Utes had nothing to fear from this Quaker family. They learned that the Wetherills desired their friendship, and when they came to the Alamo Ranch on one pretext or another, there was no mistaking the sincerity of their welcome. No Indian was turned away hungry. More than once a sick Indian was taken in by Marion Wetherill and nursed back to health. In return, the Utes permitted the Wetherills, alone among the pioneer ranchers, to run their cattle in the Mancos and branch canyons.

One day in the early 80's a small band of Utes filed into the little Mancos schoolhouse, lined up in a glowering, silent row at the rear of the room. The teacher, who was hardly more than sixteen years old, fought down her panic as long as she could, continuing the lesson in a shaky voice. Under the Utes' watchful stare the young teacher's nerve ebbed away. She dismissed her pupils for the day, hoping that their leaving would not be the signal for some horrible violence. Nothing happened. The frightened youngsters silently walked out and the Utes just as silently departed. It was one of those weird little incidents, so familiar in the valley, which had passed harmlessly.

The worst fright experienced by the people of the valley occurred six years after the Wetherills settled at Mancos. It was remembered afterwards as the Beaver Creek massacre. Clara Ormiston knew two of the ranchers involved but refused to reveal their names.

In early June, 1885, a large encampment of Utes gathered at Ute Mountain, at the western entrance to McElmo Canyon and about a half day's ride from Mancos. From this large gathering one family — a man, his squaws and two children — moved to a camp on Beaver Creek fifteen miles south of the settlement at Dolores. There they rested to allow their five horses and small band of sheep to fatten on the good grass. One early morning soon after, a party of three or four ranchers surrounded the camp. Without warning they opened fire with rifles.

"The way the story was told to me by one who was there," Mrs. Ormiston said years later, "the white men went to Beaver Creek with the sole idea of stealing the Ute's horses. When they fired into the camp they killed the man, one of his two squaws, and then shot one of his children, a little boy. The woman who had not been hit put a buffalo robe over her head and ran for the cliffs. Somehow she managed to climb down the rocks which rise steeply here above the Dolores River. One of the white men rolled stones over the side but they bounced away without hitting her and she swam the river and got away to Ute Mountain, where she told the Indians what had happened."

A war party was formed, setting out through McElmo Canyon in the direction of Mancos. Apparently the first white settlers they came upon were the Guenther (or Guenthnur) family, who lived in a small cabin eight or ten miles west of the Alamo Ranch. Mrs. Ormiston described what occurred:

"The Utes swarmed around the house as night was falling, setting it on fire. When Mr. Guenther came to the door they shot him, but before he died he called to his wife to take the children and get out through another door. Mrs. Guenther was wearing only her nightgown but in the darkness she slipped away. She escaped with her baby in one arm and leading the other child by the hand. A rifle ball had hit her in the shoulder, covering her with blood, and yet she managed to reach the banks of a gulch and hide until morning. When daylight came she saw the Utes had left and she took her children on to the next house, owned by a man named Woolley."

News of the Guenther murder was carried to Fort Lewis, and the troops went to the scene with the agent. "We were just as afraid of the Utes as could be," Mrs. Ormiston said, "but I could see their side of it too. We came in here and fired them out of the country and they had a right to be resentful."

George Menefee, a member of one of the first families to settle in Mancos, has recalled how the Beaver Creek affair and the Guenther murder spread panic through the valley. "Everybody here was afraid of the Utes anyhow, and some of the ranchers sent their families to Durango for a week

ANASAZI   19

or two, until things quieted down. But the Wetherills stayed. Even old B. K. and the boys refused to carry guns. They were very peaceable people."

John Wetherill's wife, Louisa Wade Wetherill, related in *Traders to the Navajos* how old Benjamin, on a winter day, rode into town with a Navajo blanket wrapped around his thin waist and shoulders. A friend warned him he might be shot for a Ute.

"I'd as soon be shot as freeze to death," said Benjamin.

Benjamin Wetherill always relied upon common sense and the lessons of his own Quaker elders who taught him that violence usually begets more violence. He had not worn a six-shooter in Oklahoma Territory and did not propose to start now.

His five sons adopted the same attitude. All were expert marksmen — particularly Richard and Win, who both won trophies for skill in handling a rifle — and many times they brought home deer and wild turkey to add to the family larder. However, unless they were hunting game, Richard and his brothers almost never carried guns.

Henry Honaker, whose family came to Mancos in 1883 when he was thirteen years old, remembered B. K. Wetherill as "kind of a stiff-necked feller . . . who wasn't afraid of Utes any more'n anybody else. He wasn't afraid of nuthin'!" Honaker never saw any of the Wetherill men wearing gun belts, but recalled that they sometimes packed rifles on their saddles.

Several years after the Guenther murder, an exception to this dislike for bearing weapons was related by an Eastern visitor to the Alamo Ranch. Frederick H. Chapin, author and lecturer, was the greenhorn. He noted, on an occasion when Richard Wetherill guided him on a trip through the camps of some Utes who were openly unfriendly, that Richard carried a battered old revolver under his belt. There it remained in spite of Indian threats, and perhaps just as well. Chapin implied that if the gun had been fired, Richard himself probably would have been the victim.

Indians who knew the Wetherills, and in time most of the Utes in the vicinity of Mancos did, realized that in this white family they had staunch friends. One old-time resident recalled a night when a clamor was heard along the Mancos River, close by the Alamo Ranch.

"Some of those damned Utes — drunk and whooping it up," he thought. The Wetherills knew better. Down by the water, in the shelter of the bank, they found three sick Indians, keening their distress in loud tones and one of them all but dead from pneumonia. The Indians were taken back to the ranch, fed and given warm clothing, and in time were nursed back to health.

TWO

WITH every changing season the ranchers of Mancos Valley moved their cattle to get the best grass and water. The Dolores River and Dove Creek country was favored for some of the larger herds during most of the year, but a number of cattle owners wintered their stock as far south as the San Juan. The hard winters always presented a problem. Snow drifted deep in the Mancos and Montezuma valleys, making grazing there impossible; the sheltered slopes and small canyons of the mountains to the east offered a refuge for a few of the ranchers. The Wetherills wintered their cattle in Mancos Canyon and the side canyons of Mesa Verde. Although the Utes regarded this region as their own, they assured the Wetherills that Alamo stock could graze unmolested.

Mancos Canyon was a winding gorge, half a mile wide and fifteen hundred feet deep. The shallow, narrow river twisted through it between deep banks, with towering cliffs of sandstone rising sheer on either side and talus of huge, fallen boulders and sand mounds at their base.

A leaden sky, heavy with snow, could add to or just emphasize the lonely, utter silence. Crows flapped about the cliffs and a hawk circling high, slowly gliding on the air currents, was an occasional hunter. Long-eared rabbits were alert to sudden death from above. A change in the wind's direction caused a sighing among the fir and piñon on the mesa's summit, and from far below brought a faint murmuring of water as the river slipped between ice-frosted banks. At intervals the stillness would be ravelled by the screech of an unseen jaybird.

Time had no beginning and no end. Day turned to night to be succeeded by day again in endless cycle, but time itself was meaningless. Yesterday was the same as tomorrow. Five hundred years ago could have been a moment of yesterday. Only the seasons changed; the cliffs and the canyons were changeless.

A small thing occurred to mar this atmosphere of timelessness. In the river gorge, close to the mouth of Johnson Canyon, Richard in 1884 or 1885 built a cabin, a winter camp, where he and one of his brothers stayed while watching the cattle. They took turns but most often it was a job for Richard and Al. Sometimes John or Clate Wetherill, or Charlie Mason or Jim Ethridge would appear, leading a packhorse with provisions to keep the cabin hands supplied for another month. Whoever came usually stayed for a day or two. Often at such times Richard or Al would ride off into the canyons for hours, searching for mounds and cliff dwellings. They found many, Al making the first discovery of importance — the ruin they called Sandal House.

Charlie Mason, the husband of his sister Anna, was company for Al on a number of these excursions. Once, after finding a cliff house rich with relics, they brought a small collection of pottery and stone implements back to Alamo Ranch. Benjamin Wetherill either sold or gave this collection, the first of which there is any mention, to the wife of a Denver stationer and bookseller named Chain. Years afterward, Al Wetherill wrote of these first discoveries:

"There were six of us [the five brothers and Charlie Mason] actually involved off and on in the explorations of the region. My father never was well enough to give more than moral support and deep interest in the proceedings. Richard, the oldest, was always spokesman for the group, acting in the capacity of head of the household when my father was not able to do so himself. Because we were reared in strict Quaker style, we never questioned Richard's authority."

Standing in the cabin door watching the cattle graze, Richard could look out across the river, and see the mouth of Cliff Canyon nearly opposite. It was one of the deepest and most impenetrable of all in Mesa Verde. Thus he was standing one day when approached by his friend Acowitz. For years the Ute had lived in a hut close by.

The old man's eyes followed the direction of Richard's gaze. Then he spoke. He would tell his friend a secret, he said, a thing unknown to white men. Deep in that canyon and near its head were many houses of "the old people — the ancient ones."

"One of those houses," said Acowitz, "high, high in the rocks, is bigger than all the others. Utes never go there. It is a sacred place."

Richard was intrigued. How would he find it? he demanded. But the Ute shook his head as though he had already said too much.

"I could tell you, but I warn you not to go there. When you disturb the spirits of the dead, then you die too." That is all Acowitz would say.

During the winter of 1887 Richard and Al entertained a visitor at the winter cabin, a Dr. Comfort. The doctor had come from Fort Lewis on the promise he would be shown some of the cliff dwellings. Early one morning Dr. Comfort and Richard rode into Johnson Canyon while Al, alone and on foot, forded the river and started in the opposite direction, into the Mesa Verde. Sixty-one years later, Al described his adventure:

"On this particular day we weren't hunting stray cattle but were on the lookout for ruins. I went up and around and across canyons and mesa tops until nearly dusk. I was about all in, but I thought I'd make just one more climb and across the top to see what there might be in a branch canyon which I passed earlier in the day. By the time I had reached the other canyon, I was through! I was too tired to be interested in new canyons or what they might have in them and besides it was getting dark and I had a long way to go back to join the others. I decided to follow the bed of the branch canyon as being the most direct route to the meeting place."

Al had walked half a mile when, looking up through an opening in the heavy brush and the treetops, he said he was startled to catch a partial glimpse of a cliff dwelling that filled the recesses of an immense cave.

"I stood looking at the ruins in surprised awe. I had hoped to find some unexplored dwellings — but this discovery surpassed my wildest dreams. I gauged the steep walls of the canyon against my tired legs and the ebbing daylight and turned slowly away. They would wait — they had waited for hundreds of years for the moment of discovery.

"I met Dr. Comfort and Richard near the mouth of the fork. They had become anxious and started out to look for me. I told them about the ruins and we intended to return promptly to see how extensive they were. But the pressure of ranch duties once more had the priority rating and we were unable to do anything about the new find at that time."

Al Wetherill was a truthful man, untroubled by hallucinations. Nevertheless his "discovery" when alone and stumbling with fatigue, would be enough to stir up an unending controversy years later.

A year went by. It was winter again and a day of lowering sky. Richard and Charlie Mason were on the top of Mesa Verde tracking strays that had wandered off with a bunch of wild cattle. The men had reached the summit after driving their horses across the icy river and then up a precipitous switchback climb between Navajo and Soda canyons. Now, following the tracks, they found themselves in a place where neither had been before. It was snowing, large, drifting flakes that blurred their vision. Making progress more difficult, a barrier of underbrush scratched and snared the legs of their panting horses. The cattle tracks fanned out or narrowed according to the terrain, sometimes taking the riders closer than they liked to the edge of an abyss. It was December 18, 1888.

Richard and Mason dismounted to rest the horses at a place overlooking a small branch canyon, and then walked out on a windswept point of bare rock. The gulf yawning below them was so deep that a dislodged stone would have plummeted down and struck at last without audible echo. A snow-powdered dark green carpet of treetops ascended the bottom of this gorge into a wider, distant canyon. Suddenly, with an exclamation of astonishment, Richard grasped Mason's arm.

Nearly opposite them, half a mile away and just below the far mesa's brown caprock, was a long, deep opening in the cliff face. Mirage-like in the falling snow and outlined against the cave's darkest shadows, were ghostly traceries of the largest cliff dwelling either had ever seen. The walls rose and fell in broken terraces, pierced here and there by the black, sightless eyes of doorways. Near the center, rising austerely in the afternoon's pale light, a tapering tower of three stories, beautifully round, dominated the entire ruin. It was all as compact, as complete and unreal as a crenelated castle.

The strays were forgotten. Richard and Charlie Mason turned away and started back around the edge of the smaller canyon, keeping the horses as close to the rim as they dared. They broke a fresh trail through the underbrush until they reached a clearing directly opposite the great cave. Here the cliff dropped away abruptly for thirty feet or more, but the problem of descent was quickly solved. Finding several dead trees, they lopped off the limbs to within a foot or so of the trunks, joined the sections together with their lariats and then lowered the whole improvised ladder over the cliff. By this means they reached the bottom.

Now, standing in the silence of the ruin, they could begin to gauge its size. The walls rose in tumbled splendor above them for several levels and to the height of a tall pine — reached into the shadows beyond the round tower for two or three hundred yards. The cabin they had left that morning could be tucked away in a corner of this crowded cave. They moved, scarcely speaking, but their voices magnified in hollow echoes across piles of rubble. Behind them, from one room to the next, they left footprints in dust for centuries undisturbed by any human.

Then, or soon afterward, Richard thought of the name. Cliff Palace. Nothing else would quite do. For several hours he and Charlie Mason explored the ruins with mounting excitement, with the realization they had discovered a prehistoric wonder of architecture undreamed of by their world.

Four hundred people or more once lived here and when they left they took only light possessions that could be carried easily. In the feathery dust of one room the explorers found a stone ax, the heavy blade still lashed securely to the wooden handle. In other rooms were pottery bowls, mugs and large jars for cooking or carrying water, left as though the owners had just set them down and might return at any moment.

The thought occurred: whoever they were, these people had fled after a siege — and there was some evidence to support the idea. Roof beams had been pulled out of almost all of the rooms and not a trace of the timbers remained. That could mean, they reasoned, that attackers had attempted to destroy the village after overcoming its defenders. On the other hand there was little else to suggest there had been siege and violence. They did discover three skeletons in the rubble. After a battle, was that enough?

They left the skeletons as they had found them but took a few pieces of the pottery, eager now to discover if other large ruins were close by. Snow still fell over the mesa and with not too many hours of daylight left, they separated, after agreeing to meet and camp near the place where they had first seen Cliff Palace.

Dusk closed in and they met, first gathering and piling piñon branches for a fire against the oncoming cold. Then, stamping in the snow and flailing his arms over the ruddy glow, Charlie Mason could report nothing more than his nearly frozen hands and feet. Richard had been luckier.

He told of another ruin he had found in the late afternoon, not as large as Cliff Palace but in better condition. After they parted, Richard said, he rode north and then west across the mesa, emerging finally on the rim of a deep canyon. Following its curve he sighted a second large cave and within it a cliff dwelling rising in places to three stories. The light was darkening. Across the front of the cave was a fringe of spruce trees, clinging to a steep slope. One of these, a tree of great height, had sprouted up through an outer retaining wall and for this reason Richard named the ruin Spruce Tree House.

When morning came and they started back for Spruce Tree House they lost their way and presently came to the edge of Navajo Canyon. There, almost at their feet, was a third large cliff dwelling; Richard named it Square Tower House. Built in a curving recess at the base of the cliff, it was smaller

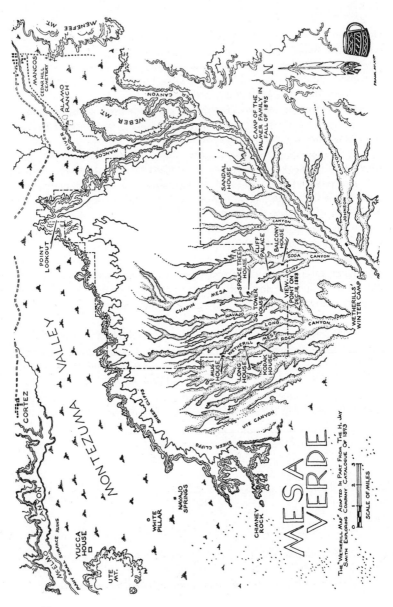

The "Wetherill Map" Adapted In Part From The H. Jay
Smith Exploring Company Catalogue Of 1893

MESA VERDE

SCALE OF MILES

FRANK McNITT

than Spruce Tree House but remarkable for a square tower thrusting four stories high among a cluster of rooms and circular chambers. They inspected it hurriedly and then went on, finding several small ruins in the same vicinity before deciding, after measuring a dwindling supply of food, to turn back toward winter camp in Johnson Canyon.

On their return they encountered the camp of three acquaintances — Charles McLoyd, Howard Graham and Levi Patrick. Richard and Mason stopped long enough for some warming coffee while Richard drew a rough map in the snow showing where they had found Cliff Palace. When he finished, the listening men were determined to see it for themselves; they waited only long enough to be joined by John Wetherill. The four of them packed in on foot with enough food to last several days, while Richard and Charlie Mason continued toward the cabin.

A short time after the McLoyd party returned, the men combined forces for a systematic search, not only of Cliff Palace but of any other ruins they could find in Mesa Verde. For Richard, it was the turning point of his life. Before this, exploring had been a pastime. Now it was to become a passion that consumed his time, his energy and all of his resources. He had discovered a lost civilization.

Many writers have described Cliff Palace but no one has succeeded so well as Willa Cather, who from Richard Wetherill drew a major character for her novel *The Professor's House*, where he appears as Tom Outland. Miss Cather never met Richard Wetherill; he had been dead five years when she visited Mesa Verde, but from one of his brothers she heard how he and Charlie Mason had found Cliff Palace in 1888. Mason also appears in her novel, as Roddy Blake, but even more than Tom Outland he is a character of her imagination.

Miss Cather chose to leave Roddy Blake behind on the day when Tom Outland, alone, discovered the ruin:

> In stopping to take breath, I happened to glance up at the cañon wall. I wish I could tell you what I saw there, just *as* I saw it, on that first morning, through a veil of lightly falling snow. Far up above me, a thousand feet or so, set in a great cavern in a cliff, I saw a little city of stone, asleep. It was as still as sculpture — and something like that. It all hung together, seemed to have a kind of composition: pale little houses of stone nestling close to one another,

perched on top of each other, with flat roofs, narrow windows, straight walls, and in the middle of the group, a round tower.

It was beautifully proportioned, that tower, swelling out to a larger girth a little above the base, then growing slender again. There was something symmetrical and powerful about the swell of the masonry. The tower was the fine thing that held all the jumble of houses together and made them mean something. It was red in colour, even on that grey day. In sunlight it was the colour of winter oak leaves. A fringe of cedars grew along the edge of the cavern, like a garden. They were the only living things. Such silence and stillness and repose — immortal with the calmness of eternity. The falling snowflakes sprinkling the piñons, gave it a special kind of solemnity. It was more like sculpture than anything else. I knew at once that I had come upon the city of some extinct civilization, hidden away in this inaccessible mesa for centuries, preserved in the dry air and almost perpetual sunlight like a fly in amber, guarded by the cliffs and the river and the desert.*

In one particular, the impressions made upon the minds of Al Wetherill, in 1887, and of the fictional Tom Outland are the same: both caught their first glimpse of the ruin from the depths of Cliff Canyon. By having it so in the case of Outland, Miss Cather may have been responding less to a literary device than to her memory of an unusual personal experience.

Miss Cather's most lasting impression of Cliff Palace came from seeing the ruin accidentally and as few have, bathed in moonlight at two o'clock in the morning.

The story has been related by her friend, Edith Lewis, who accompanied her. On their last day in Mesa Verde a guide had taken them down into Soda Canyon. The trail was too precipitous to permit their returning the same way and their guide, looking for another way out, left them at the fork of Cliff and Soda canyons while he explored to the head of the gulch. Night came and the moon rose while the women sat on a flat rock and waited. It was growing late when finally they were rescued — not by their guide, but by two men from the camp of Jesse W. Fewkes, the ethnologist. According to Miss Lewis, the guide had collapsed from exhaustion after reaching Fewkes' camp and their rescuers had been sent back in his place.

* *The Professor's House,* by Willa Cather, by permission of Alfred A. Knopf, Inc., New York.

With the help of the two men, Clint Scarf and Audrey Grey Pearl, the women managed to walk, crawl or scramble up the canyon, finally emerging at Richard's ladder which led them to Fewkes' camp on the mesa. Miss Cather previously had spent the better part of a day in Cliff Palace, on that occasion reaching it by a simple trail cut for tourists. The image she retained most strongly, very likely was the recollection of this night's arduous experience.

As a novelist, Miss Cather never was drawn into the argument which developed, at about the time of her visit, over who first discovered Cliff Palace. Jesse Fewkes of the Smithsonian Institution, who excavated and repaired several of Mesa Verde's cliff dwellings after the Wetherills had left the scene, probably started the controversy in 1910 when, in his report on Cliff Palace, he wrote:

> Efforts to learn the name of the white man who discovered Cliff Palace were not rewarded with great success. According to Nordenskiold it was first seen by Richard Wetherill and Charley Mason on a "December day in 1888." But several residents of the towns of Mancos and Cortez claim to have visited it before that time. One of the first of these visitors was a cattle owner of Mancos, Mr. James Frink, who told the author that he first saw Cliff Palace in 1881, and as several stockmen were with him at the time it is probable that there were others who visited it the same year. We may conclude that Cliff Palace was unknown to scientific men in 1880, and the most we can definitely say is that it was first seen by white men some time in the decade 1880-1890.

Archaeologists who followed Fewkes to Mesa Verde were interested enough to call upon Jim Frink and press him for details. Each time he was asked to describe Cliff Palace as he first saw it, Frink gave conflicting answers. Shortly before his death, he as much as admitted there had been no truth in what he had told Jesse Fewkes.

RICHARD was thirty years old, his hair graying, a young man with responsibilities. The Alamo Ranch appeared to be prospering, but it was burdened with mortgages; it fell to Richard to keep it solvent. Old Benjamin Wetherill still exerted authority as head of the family but success or failure of the ranch depended largely upon Richard. During the winter of 1888-89, therefore, he wrestled with a problem.

ANASAZI

Should he devote all of his time to ranching and let the others explore the great ruins of Mesa Verde, or should he divide his attention and energies between the two? In the end he compromised. Wintertimes he would continue his explorations, from spring to late fall he would attend to the ranch.

The second half of that winter consequently found Richard, John, and Charlie Mason working with McLoyd, Patrick and Graham at Cliff Palace, Spruce Tree House and Square Tower House. Before the snows melted they had a large collection from the cliff dwellings. By spring, with the planting in, they prepared to show the relics in Durango.

Al Wetherill noted:

"The public didn't particularly care about being educated! We opened our exhibit, gave a few lectures about it, decided Durango was too small to be interested in anything but civic betterment activities, and went on to Pueblo. We lived through a short session there, meeting indifference verging on ridicule. We simply couldn't believe it! We were too young and inexperienced to know when we were licked and we were so sure that our mission was worthwhile. So with 'heads bloodied but unbowed,' we decided to take Denver by storm, sure that there we would find enthusiastic audiences. I shudder to think of Denver even now."

In Denver the apathy was as profound as it had been in Pueblo and Durango. Relics of a newly-discovered civilization of Cliff Dwellers? Who cared? Old pots and stuff left by a bunch of primitive savages. No, Denver wasn't interested.

The brothers stayed in the city until they had barely enough money left to eat, settle their modest lodging bill and get back home.

In Mancos, meanwhile, Clayton Wetherill and Charlie Mason had discovered the mummy of a child — the first found in Mesa Verde, according to Mason. They sent it on to Denver in the care of Charles McLoyd. Denver's reaction to the mummy would have made P. T. Barnum click his teeth with envy. Everyone, it seemed, had to see the mummy. And to the Wetherills' pleasure, the interest now extended to the pottery, the articles of clothing, farm implements and weapons.

Among those who came was an emissary of the recently organized Denver Historical Society. The Society would buy the collection if a reasonable price could be agreed upon.

Such unexpected recognition from this quarter melted away the misery caused by previous indifference. But Richard controlled his elation, regarded the emissary coolly, and said he would consult his partners. After a suitable interval he returned with the reply: We-ll, yes. The collection probably was worth much more — but he would be proud to let the Historical Society have it for $3,000.

The Society's annual report for that year and contemporary newspaper files contain no mention of this incident, but The *Colorado Topics* of June 7, 1889, commented that "A wonderful collection of Cliff-dwellers' relics is on exhibition in Denver. An effort is being made to secure them for the State Historical Society." The purchase was consummated the following year.

Officials of the Society believe the funds were raised with the express purpose of preventing the collection from being taken out of the state. Since the Society's treasury could afford only half the cost, three members eventually signed personal notes for the other half. Then, with the collection once moved to the Denver Chamber of Commerce building, the officers reported: "It is one of the largest and most complete collections owned by any institution, far out-reaching the one in the National Museum, at Washington, and one that every resident of the State should be proud of."

During the summer and fall of 1889 Richard attended to the ranch but in December he returned to the cliff dwellings. With his brothers and Charlie Mason he worked steadily until the following spring. They began at Sandal House, then moved down into Johnson Canyon on the east side of the Mancos River and excavated several dwellings there. Of one, which they named Fortified House, John Wetherill wrote:

"Glancing up I noticed a door that had been concealed. . . . I removed a rock and saw that it was the only entrance." Then he removed a section of wall down to floor level, his shovel uncovering pieces of burial matting in the debris.

"While clearing away the rubbish I found a piece of a cinch [or belt]. It was three-colored, red, white, and black. I then broke through the wall on another side. As soon as I dug to the floor I uncovered more matting. I removed some dirt and found an arrow with an agate point on it, the first ever found in a Cliff House in Mancos Cañon." John then called to Mason and together they began excavating the room methodically.

"Charley removed two or three shovelfuls of dirt and dug out a basket. It was 12 inches across the top and 6 inches deep. Henceforward our finds came fast and close together. We found 17 arrows lying across the heads of five bodies. Between the skulls were four bowls. One large skeleton lay on the top of the mat with a bow on one side, a mug and a basket on the other. He had nothing over him; a pair of moccasins on his feet and some feather cloth under his head. Near him lay a hollow stick with both ends wrapped with sinew and with a bonepoint at the end about six inches long. The stick was about twenty inches long.

"Lying alongside of this body were the skeletons of three babies. . . . Two of them had pieces of buckskin with them. After taking them up we found a large mat covering the whole floor. We removed this and found another skeleton and a stick with a loop at the end, that we took for a medicine stick, also two prairie-dog skin pouches. The skeleton was covered with a willow mat. Under the mat were two more made of grass. Under the grass mat was one of feather cloth, after that a buckskin jacket with fringes."

John was doing the best he knew how to record, step by step, the progress of the excavation, and describe what was found in a way that would be useful to scientific men. These were his field notes.

". . . The three baby skeletons were lying on the skeleton with the buckskin jacket. A large mug lay at the head of one of the babies. The three baby skeletons and the one on top lay with their heads up the cañon, while the other had its head down the cañon."

After working through Johnson Canyon, the brothers and Charlie Mason returned again to Cliff Palace. As each relic was uncovered it was marked for identification and put aside to await the next trip by pack mule to the ranch. In late winter and early spring they explored all of the branches of Navajo Canyon and Long and Rock canyons, discovering many more cliff houses. The larger of these included Spring House, Step House, Mug House, Jug House, Kodak House and Long House — the latter nearly as large as Cliff Palace but in an advanced stage of ruin when they found it.

By March, 1890 — fifteen months after the discovery of Cliff Palace — Richard either alone or with his brothers and Mason had found and examined all of the major cliff dwellings in Mesa Verde (by his count, one hundred eighty-two). He had named most of them, he had roughly mapped the entire area explored, and he had painstakingly inspected two hundred fifty miles of the mesa's steep cliffs.

Then followed a period of relative inactivity in the cliff dwellings. It was interrupted only by short excursions to the mesa until the summer of 1891 when Richard, Al and John helped Baron Nordenskiold assemble a collection to take back to Sweden. Their second collection, meanwhile, had been stored in a small barn at the ranch which became a sort of museum; to enlarge it they returned to dig through the winter of 1891-92. In the spring of 1892 the collection was bought by C. D. Hazzard of the H. Jay Smith

Exploring Co. of Jackson Park, Illinois, and exhibited the following year at the Chicago World's Fair.

When the Fair ended, Hazzard stored the collection in a Chicago warehouse. He moved to Los Angeles soon after, leaving the relics crated, and in the spring of 1894 advertised them for sale. No buyer appeared and so in April, 1895, the entire collection of about a thousand specimens was shipped in forty-two boxes, on two years' loan, to the Museum of the University of Pennsylvania. In the following year the collection was bought for the museum by Mrs. Phoebe A. Hearst. A few of the relics which she had taken out for herself she presented, in 1901, to the University of California at Berkeley.

The Wetherills' fourth and last Mesa Verde collection was made in the summer of 1892 for the State of Colorado. The collection was taken to the Chicago Fair as a part of the state's exhibit, which had been financed by a legislative appropriation of $100,000. Of this collection Charlie Mason wrote: "In spite of the fact that all of the Cliff Dwellings had been worked over two or three times we succeeded in making a good showing." When the Fair ended the collection was brought back to Denver and made a part of the Historical Society's original collection of some 1,200 specimens.

Thus the four Wetherill collections from Mesa Verde found their way into public museums: the first being bought by the Denver Historical Society, the second purchased by the H. Jay Smith Exploring Co. and donated finally to the University of Pennsylvania Museum, the third taken to Sweden and later moved to the National Museum in Helsinki, Finland, and the fourth joined with the first and placed eventually in the Colorado State Museum at Denver.

The methods Richard used in excavating the ruins of Mesa Verde were direct, thorough, consistent with the general practice of his time, but — by modern archaeological standards — unscientific. It has been his misfortune that certain scientists have been severe in their criticism of him, if a gentle term may be used, because he failed to employ techniques which were not devised until a generation after his death.

Untutored, unskilled, and with no previous work in their field to guide them, Richard and his brothers went to work with long-handled shovels, digging until they had satisfied themselves they had uncovered everything of significance there was to be found. Indeed, the most bitter of their critics have complained because they were so thorough! When the fine dust of the dry caves blinded and choked them, they tied wet handkerchiefs over their faces and went on digging. When a shovel blade scraped against a fragile piece of pottery, a burial or some other precious find, they would put the shovel aside and scoop away dirt with their hands. The refinements of the trowel, whisk-broom and camel's-hair brush were unknown to them at this time. Likewise, the notes they kept contained no scrupulous record of room measurements or sherd-counts that would identify the development or regression of pottery-making in comparison with that of surrounding areas.

In a ledger they made brief entries, such as those John made in Johnson Canyon, of each relic discovered. With nothing written or known to draw upon for comparison, they considered these efforts sufficient. In addition to the ledger entries, Richard and Al photographed each cliff dwelling where they worked. Their pictures at this stage had more scenic interest perhaps than scientific value, but in any case demonstrated an attempt to document what they found.

Because he concentrated his interest on the larger cliff dwellings, Richard failed to examine thoroughly two earlier and transitional phases of culture. The most obvious signs of these were the low, tumbled walls of small pueblo structures nearly hidden in the underbrush on the mesa's summit, and on the floor of the valleys below. Five of these structures have been excavated since 1950, all in the vicinity of Cliff Palace, and have been dated from 850 to 1075 A.D. Close to the small pueblo ruins there have been found numerous pithouses of the Modified Basket Makers, who are believed to have built and occupied them from about 450 to 750 A.D.

Had Richard excavated the early pueblo sites, there is little doubt that he would have discovered the pithouses because in many cases they lie buried under the walls of later pueblos. No one in Richard's time was able to determine the age of these prehistoric dwellings with any accuracy, but the differences between the Basket Maker and early Pueblo cultures were too sharply marked to have escaped him. And at the same time he then could not have failed to perceive that the cliff dwellings (which flourished from about 1200 to about 1300) showed a third and classic period of the people's development.

Some have said Richard's interest in Mesa Verde was purely mercenary, that he was a professional pothunter. To support this, attention has been called to a statement of Charlie Mason's and to a series of advertisements Richard published one year in The *Mancos Times*.

The offer of the Denver Historical Society to buy the first Wetherill collection, Mason wrote years later, immediately stimulated their efforts. "In

December 1889 we started out to make another collection. This time we went at it in a more businesslike manner, as our previous work had been carried out [more] to satisfy our own curiosity than for any other purpose, but this time it was a business proposition." Richard was no longer living but there is reason to believe he would not have quarreled with Mason's statement. The same motive, no doubt, inspired his advertisement in the Mancos paper, appearing first in September, 1894, and continuing unchanged for about a year:

> Mancos Cañon & the Aztec Cliff Dwellings. Indian Curios, Aztec Relics, Photographs for Sale. Address: Richard Wetherill, Alamo Ranch, Mancos, Colo.

Ten days before this appeared, Richard wrote to an Eastern friend that "Everyone that has been here [at Alamo Ranch] lately wants Cliff Dweller relics or Basket Makers. The mound relics they do not seem to care about except for comparison."

Richard seemed more than just willing to sell the relics which he and his brothers found. About 1890 they had converted a small barn into a museum for the thousands of objects in their growing collection. Visitors who stopped at the ranch, or who came to town and read the local newspaper, were welcome to inspect the museum and no doubt a number of them left with purchases.

Richard, however, was not the first in Mancos to advertise "Aztec" relics for sale — the word Aztec being a conscious misnomer, a concession to a widespread popular belief that the Cliff Dwellers had been Aztecs, which Richard knew they were not. In 1890, four years before he began to offer relics for sale, the Mancos paper printed advertisements reading: *Hildebrand & Bauer, asseyors. Aztec Relics, Ute and Navajo Indian Curios. First Avenue, Mancos, Colorado.*

Such notices appeared each week. As a part of their business in relics, Hildebrand and Bauer grubstaked digging parties to go into the Mesa Verde cliff dwellings and bring back anything that might be saleable. No protest was made at the time, although this was nothing less than subsidized vandalism.

After 1895 Richard recognized the excellent reasons for not selling parts of his collections piecemeal, and ceased to advertise or to sell to tourists or other chance individuals any relics taken from a ruin. From this time forward virtually everything he excavated was maintained intact as part of a collection and was deposited in the American Museum of Natural History in New York.

Censure of Richard, which came years later, has been out of proportion to the number of relics he sold to curious visitors in those earliest years. The practice was not frowned upon at that time. Actually, within limits, it was encouraged by no less a person than the editor of The *Archaeologist,* a magazine to which Richard subscribed and occasionally contributed. The magazine regularly contained a section called The Collector's Department, designed to advise amateurs and professionals alike how and where relics might be purchased. In the February, 1894, issue the question was treated specifically as a problem of ethics by editor Warren K. Moorehead. He took a few licks at "the vandals found in the ranks of collectors" — those who went out to dig but "failed to record their observations" — then continued:

"It might be asked . . . what is permissible? The sale of a whole collection, or part of it, so long as complete finds are not split is always proper. Single specimens, bought of dealers, may be sold with a free conscience, also complete finds. What is really wrong is the destruction of scientific testimony."

Richard Wetherill remained within the professional code which prevailed during the years he was working at Mesa Verde. When he doubted the wisdom of that code he adopted his own, a stricter one. However, he never apologized for having once sold relics, and never attempted to conceal the fact he had done so. Richard and his brothers from the very beginning made every effort to place their collections in museums.

Soon after the discovery of Cliff Palace, Richard wrote to the directors of the Smithsonian Institution and to Harvard's Peabody Museum, requesting that they sponsor himself and his brothers, or send their own scientists to work with them in the ruins. These appeals were rejected.

Although the people in Washington had little interest in Mesa Verde, they would be willing to accept, as a contribution, a Wetherill collection — if it measured up to their requirements. Al Wetherill wrote in 1948, just before his death:

"The reply was, that at that time, they could do nothing themselves, but if we cared to assemble a collection for Smithsonian, they would be glad to accept it. Unfortunately, we lacked financial backing to assemble a collection to meet museum requirements for that worthwhile organization or any other of any size. There would be six of us working on it and we, as other ranchers of that region, had somewhat heavy responsibilities, one of which was an immense mortgage. So, managing for a limited amount of publicity, we commenced into the tourist trade. . . . Within a few years, approximately 1000 people visited the ranch to see the cliff dwellings."

And he added:

"Those who followed us in working the ruins thought of us as vandals. It's been a sore spot with all of us every time we've heard of ourselves referred to in that category. We never destroyed, nor permitted destruction of any of those buildings nor their contents, feeling that we were the custodians of a priceless heritage. Those who came as tourists were aware that we would allow no damage nor wanton pilfering, and not many of them were the type who would."

Referring to the criticism of the Wetherills' methods by some of his colleagues, the late Earl H. Morris, head of the Department of Archaeology for the Carnegie Institution of Washington, wrote:

"As to the 'crimes' of the Wetherills, I am most lenient in my judgment. In their exploration, or exploiting, if one wants to call it that, of the ruins, they did no more, nor differently than I think I would have done under like circumstances. The oft-heard tale of their wanton destruction of walls in the cliff houses was not borne out by the tales which John told me in regard to their early activities."

While the Wetherills were digging in the cliff dwellings of Mesa Verde, a few ethnologists in other parts of the Southwest were beginning the first exploratory research of prehistoric ruins. For the next twenty years no clear distinction would be made in this region between ethnology and archaeology. Not only was there a confusion in terms, but the men in both fields engaged in overlapping functions which properly were outside of their own sphere.

First on the scene was Adolph F. Bandelier, a Swiss-American ethnohistorian who was commissioned by the Archaeological Institute of America "to survey and report upon the living Indians and the ruins of Colorado and New Mexico." Bandelier arrived at Santa Fe in August of 1880 and for the next few years vigorously carried out his assignment. His work was principally among the modern Pueblos of the Rio Grande, but he also inspected a large number of prehistoric pueblo sites, beginning at the then recently-abandoned Pecos Pueblo. He did not excavate any of the ancient ruins, however, but contented himself with taking photographs and measurements of surface remains.

Bandelier's reports attracted such respectful attention that he was made a member of the Hemenway Southwestern Expedition which in 1887 began a series of ethno-archaeological surveys starting in southern Arizona. The expedition was led by an ethnologist noted for his work among the modern Zuñi Indians, Frank H. Cushing, and took the field with a four-fold purpose: to study the ethnological, anthropological, historical and archaeological (in that order) aspects of ruins in the Salt and Gila River valleys.

During the same period other ethnologists, Jesse Walter Fewkes, Frederick W. Hodge, Victor and Cosmos Mindeleff, George A. Dorsey and H. R. Voth were studying the Hopi and Zuñi pueblos. Aside from the Hemenway Expedition's work at Casa Grande, the efforts of these scientists prior to 1908 were centered almost exclusively on the living habits and traditions of modern Indians.

It is against this background that the work of Richard Wetherill may be examined and judged. Even had he stopped with his work at Mesa Verde, his name still would deserve an honorable place in their company.

BARON Gustaf Eric Adolf Nordenskiold, scholarly young son of a Swedish arctic explorer and scientist, when he visited the United States in 1891, stumbled by accident upon the work which was to make him famous. He was passing through Denver in the spring of that year when he saw the Wetherill collection owned by the Denver Historical Society. At once he resolved to find the Wetherill brothers and have them show him the Mesa Verde cliff dwellings.

In June, he arrived by train at Durango. There he rented a buggy and pair to take him across thirty miles of mountain road to Mancos, along the way finding some of the scenery reminiscent of Switzerland. In late evening he drove into the yard of Alamo Ranch and was received, though a stranger, with the warmest sort of welcome. If his English was amusing and at times hard to understand, his bubbling enthusiasm was not, and to the Wetherills his unheralded coming remained a memorable event. Having met nothing but crushing indifference in their overtures to American scientists, they were delighted to have this eager, knowledgeable young foreigner seek them out.

Nordenskiold had expected to remain only a week or two, anticipating nothing more than arduous sightseeing. But he later explained that "On the advice of Richard Wetherill I began these works in a ruin in Cliff Cañon where until then the earth had been barely scratched."

For three days Richard and Al toiled and sweated in the fine dust of a small cliff house, digging first in one of the circular kivas, or ceremonial cham-

RICHARD WETHERILL

bers, at the Swedish scientist's suggestion. The three men presented as unlikely a picture as this canyon had ever seen. In spite of the borrowed leggings and wide-brimmed cowboy hat which he wore, Nordenskiold retained a few refinements of apparel only foreign to this place but in striking contrast to the overalled Wetherill brothers, who looked like a pair of bandits with the bright bandannas tied as masks over their faces to stop at least some of the dust. It appeared strange indeed to find the grizzled Richard Wetherill — who rarely took orders from anyone — meekly following the directions of this stripling. Baron Nordenskiold was twenty-three years old.

The unnamed cliff house nested high on a ledge and could be reached only by a stiff climb from the canyon bottom, first through matted underbrush, then up a sandy, rocky talus. Richard, who had been here once before, had recommended this as a good place to start but had not recommended the alkaline spring near their camp below. The spring was the Baron's first encounter with alkali. The taste, he said, was "nauseous." The site where they worked contained a nine-room house with two small kivas. After they had worked out most of the rooms Nordenskiold called a halt.

"Very good," he had said. "Now you think we should try something ambitious?"

It was early July, a time when the ranch demanded their attention, so Richard and Al retired reluctantly in favor of their brother John who for the remainder of the summer was Nordenskiold's capable foreman. To help him he had at first two, then three, then four laborers hired by the Baron.

For something ambitious Nordenskiold chose Long House, concentrating his effort there for one month "without any particularly good results." His failure to obtain more specimens from Long House was due to the dilapidated condition of the cliff dwelling, with the result that "long labour was necessary to reach the floors, where we might expect to find the most numerous objects."

The Baron was impressed by the fact that Long House was in far more ruinous condition than the other major cliff villages. He offered as a possible explanation for this his theory that Long House might have been sacked and pillaged by an enemy:

"Though the inhabitants . . . were admirably prepared for defense, still there are indications to suggest that they eventually succumbed to their enemies. Human bones — ribs, vertebrae, etc. — are strewn in numbers here and there among the ruins."

In the time remaining, from August 14 to September 14, Nordenskiold worked at Kodak House, Mug House, Step House and Spruce Tree House, likewise investigating a number of smaller ruins. Engaging another laborer to work under John's supervision, he spent two weeks at Kodak House but again was disappointed by the scarcity of material. Only a few days were given to digging at Mug House and Spruce Tree House, but in Step House he was rewarded by finding a large quantity of pottery and a number of burials.

As the digging proceeded Nordenskiold measured the ruins, photographed them, diagrammed the floor plans, and took careful notes on the details of architecture as well as of the relics. In some way he found time, in addition to everything else, to trench the mound of a partially buried surface ruin on a point of the mesa overlooking Cliff Palace, the ruin which Fewkes later excavated and named, ambiguously, Sun Temple.

At Spruce Tree House he anticipated the tree-ring dating method of the American astronomer, A. E. Douglass, by counting one hundred sixty-two annual growth rings on a spruce tree growing through a masonry wall. Thus he came to the conclusion that Spruce Tree House was at least two hundred years old.

An occasional visitor reached Nordenskiold's camp on the mesa between Rock and Long canyons. One of these visitors, an Eastern tourist whom Richard brought in and introduced as Dr. W. R. Birdsall, remained several days after expressing deep interest in the work. A few months after Birdsall's departure the American Geographical Society published a paper written by the doctor which Nordenskiold admitted was "the best description yet published of the ruins of Mesa Verde."

"It was the writer's good fortune," Birdsall wrote, "to visit the region thus briefly described under the guidance of Richard, Alfred and John Wetherill during the summer of 1891, for recreation rather than for the purpose of systematic archaeological study. For several years these men have devoted a great deal of time to the exploration of this region in search of cliff houses and the relics they contain; although not professional archaeologists, they have amassed a very large collection of the remains of the cliff dwellers and are in possession of a vast number of observations and facts concerning them. Indeed, no one knows this part of the Mesa Verde as they do. The upper end of the Mancos Cañon is the usual place which tourists visit to see a few examples of cliff houses, and the hospitable Wetherill ranch is the proper outfitting place."

Baron Nordenskiold reflected appreciation, too. The mesa on which he camped that summer, he named Wetherill Mesa, "after the brothers Wetherill, who have done so much service in the exploration of these regions, and whose knowledge of the Mesa Verde has given me such valuable assistance." Elsewhere he remarked: "During the course of the years Richard and Alfred Wetherill have explored Mesa Verde and its cañons in all directions; they have thus gained a more thorough knowledge of its ruins than anyone."

As his duties at the ranch allowed, Richard carefully observed Nordenskiold's progress and methods, sometimes joining the laborers in digging.

Both men wanted to know where the large population of Cliff Palace, during a century of occupation, had buried its dead. It was here that the question of burial customs first presented itself to Richard. At Cliff Palace and at Step House Richard already had come across a few skeletons of the ancient people with pottery and other grave furnishings laid to rest with them, either buried within the caves or in the trash mounds on the slopes below. But the number found was astonishingly small.

Far back in the cave of Cliff Palace, Richard told Nordenskiold, among the few skeleton burials, he had found human bones of bodies he knew had been cremated, or at least burned. Would that indicate the people of Cliff Palace had practiced cremation on a wide scale? Nordenskiold thought not. If they had, there would be more evidence of it. Down among the rocks below the cave, he said, they probably would find more.

At Step House, Nordenskiold poked into the trash mound south of that cliff village and turned up a crude type of pottery quite unlike the highly finished ware of the Cliff Dwellers. Very possibly the crude vessels belonged to an older race, he said — not realizing how close he was to an important archaeological discovery. "Perhaps they are the work of a people who inhabited Step House Cave before the erection of the cliff village." Afterwards, Richard and his brothers found more of the crude pottery in the same cave. They came to the same tentative conclusion, but turned in another direction without probing further.

A subject of discussion between Richard and his Swedish friend was that of the large, circular rooms, nearly all of them either subterranean or built below floor level, found in all of the cliff dwellings of any size. *Estufas*, Richard called them, using the Spanish word. These circular rooms, built with a firepit in the middle of the floor, sometimes had a low stone bench extending around the wall. The rooms had an average depth of about eight or ten feet and were some eight to twenty feet in diameter. At Mesa Verde there were usually six masonry pilasters, evenly spaced and rising from the circular bench to support a cribbed roof of logs.

Some of the early explorers of prehistoric ruins in the Southwest, applying mistaken logic to an ancient architecture, decided these were tanks, built to catch and store water. In his discussions with Baron Nordenskiold, Richard recognized the circular rooms as earlier counterparts of the same rooms found in modern pueblos: the meeting places reserved, almost without exception, for the village's numerous male clans or societies, and used primarily for ceremonial or religious occasions. Richard referred to them as *estufas,* although before his death the Hopi name, *kiva,* was introduced and in time won preference.

On one occasion Richard's shovel scraped against the side of a pottery bowl. He continued to dig around it, but more carefully. Nordenskiold had been watching, and now stepped forward.

"No, Richard — like this. . ."

With a mason's trowel Nordenskiold picked and scraped gently at the earth impounding the bowl.

"Why waste all of that time?" Richard finally asked.

Intent on what he·was doing, the young archaeologist went on working until the fragile vessel, without a crack marring its surface, stood free. He lifted it, then, as gently as though he were an obstetrician with a newborn baby.

"This way, Richard, you save time. You don't waste."

After that Richard used a mason's trowel.

The relics taken from the cliff dwellings that summer were packed to the Alamo Ranch by burro, and sorted out for crating. Meanwhile, in August, while John and the laborers continued the work, Nordenskiold left with Al Wetherill as his guide for the Hopi pueblos to the south. Accompanied by Roe Ethridge, a cowboy who worked with his brother Jim at the Wetherill ranch, they traveled by horseback to First Mesa for the Snake Dance at Walpi, returning early in September as the cool touches of fall began to be felt in Mancos Valley.

Two weeks later the Baron departed for Durango, this time riding in a Wetherill buckboard and followed by a wagon loaded with relics of the Cliff Dwellers. On his arrival, however, he was served with a warrant by the county sheriff. News of his summer's work had spread. A committee of Durango townspeople, incensed that a foreigner should be taking a wagonload of antiquities out of the country, had protested. The young scientist's boxes were seized, a hearing of the case was set for two weeks ahead, and Nordenskiold returned to the Alamo Ranch wondering if the results of his hard labor were lost. He used the time to take more photographs of the cliff dwellings and enlarge considerably his notes on Cliff Palace.

Nordenskiold appeared in District Court on the day appointed. The lawyer handling the case, after diligent search, had been unable to find any law prohibiting the removal of ancient relics, by anyone, from either the State of Colorado or the territory of the United States. The complaint therefore was dismissed and the Swedish archaeologist was permitted to depart with his boxes. His collection, amounting to some six hundred specimens, was seen on a tour in Europe, later was brought back to Stockholm, and is now in the National Museum of Helsinki, Finland. The Baron's greatest contribution, however, is not the collection but his report on his summer's work, *The Cliff Dwellers of the Mesa Verde*. Published in 1893 at Stockholm, now a collector's item of rare value, the book is the first major record of archaeological work in the United States.

Richard and Baron Nordenskiold corresponded at intervals until the latter's death in 1895 at the age of twenty-six. One of the letters addressed to Richard was written from Stockholm on January 13, 1893, and indicates the cordial relationship which continued to exist between them. It is much shortened here:

My dear Friend,

I just got yours of the 13th December. As you are already on your trip [Richard was then in Grand Gulch, Utah] it will take some time before this reaches you. I wish you success in your trip and would like awfully much to be in the party. . . . I have been in Spain one month and came just a few days ago back to Sweden. As I think I have told you my Mesa Verde collection is exhibited there. I got a gold medal for the collection and the photos. . . .

Among the most interesting things in the exposition was a collection from the Hemenway expedition. It comprised mostly objects from the modern Mokis [Hopi] but also pottery excavated in ruins near the Moki villages. This pottery is of the "transitional" kind but more like the modern than the ancient ware. I do not think there is any "transition" between the modern and ancient pottery but that the modern kind is a new element introduced by some new people . . .

Yours truly,
G. Nordenskiold

p.s. If you would strike some nice Navajo blankets send them to me.

IN THE VANGUARD of an increasing stream of visitors who enjoyed the hospitality of Alamo Ranch, Frederick H. Chapin, Baron Nordenskiold and Dr. Birdsall were among the first to help spread knowledge of Mesa Verde across two continents. Also among these first guests was an Eastern girl who helped to divert Richard's mind from an unrequited love affair (see Appendix G).

Julia Cowing spent a good share of four summers with the Wetherills and became a devoted friend. They met first in the summer of 1891, when Nordenskiold was at work in the cliff dwellings. With her brother and sister-in-law, the James R. Cowings of Brooklyn, New York, she had been touring Yellowstone and the Black Hills of South Dakota. None of them was accustomed to the seamy or rough side of Western life. In Denver a friend, recently moved from the East, insisted they would find Mesa Verde more intriguing than Salt Lake City — the next point on their itinerary. Succumbing to this enthusiasm, knowing nothing of what they might be getting into, they soon found themselves on a dusty tangent, bumpily headed for Mancos.

Stepping off the train at Durango, Julia Cowing knew she was due for an unusual experience. She had traveled far and often from Brooklyn, from one resort to another, rarely having to endure anything less civilized than Denver's Brown Palace Hotel. Now, quite suddenly, all was different. Down the dusty, wide main street, flanked by low brick and frame false-fronts, surrounded on all sides by the high shadowing mountains, she was face to face with a Wild West. The cowboys, grimy miners and bearded prospectors in from the hills and shouldering by, were a dangerous or shaggy breed. She didn't shrink; she was thrilled. Her excitement lasted all during the ride over the mountain road to Mancos where she and her companions were directed to the Alamo Ranch.

She was a tall, slender woman in her early thirties, her medium blonde hair worn in the short, curly bangs then fashionable. Richard and his brothers found her cheerful, curiously different, a small powder charge for any effort they made at conversation. She wasn't really pretty, but engaging.

When Richard suggested he take the Cowings on a three-day pack trip to Cliff Palace it never occurred to him it might prove a painful ordeal for the girl. If Julia Cowing had any misgivings, she kept them to herself and accepted at once. She had assumed that the cliff dwellings, rather like Niagara Falls, were within strolling distance of a comfortable, safe vantage point. Her first glimpse of the mesa's forbidding majesty had chilled her. But she was unwilling now to surrender.

The trip by horseback with two nights out under the stars led to a warm friendship between Richard and the Cowings, but the rough trail so exhausted Julia's strength that for several days after their return she remained in her room. At the end of a week Julia was herself again. She agreed readily when the Wetherills, with casual friendliness, proposed that the visitors remain longer. When James and his wife said they must leave, Julia said she would stay on alone a few weeks longer.

Julia Cowing returned the following summer, at the Wetherills' invitation, accompanied by Lida Harkness, a relative of about her own age, and remained until fall. And in the summer of 1893 she came back again to Alamo Ranch, with her nephew, Herbert Cowing, a boy of fifteen. They remained two months, and returned again the year following for a similar length of time.

A faded photograph, found in an attic in Hamden, Connecticut, shows Richard, Julia and young Herbert Cowing resting on the trail to Cliff Palace. In the foreground there is a skelter of camp gear; in the background, a tent, with tall brush rising all around. This is the place Richard named Soda Springs Camp.

"That a man of Richard's forceful personality would exert a strong attraction is quite natural," Herbert Cowing wrote, more than fifty years after. "That her personality and background would have an equal reaction on him is also to be expected. There is no doubt that such mutual attraction and esteem came to exist."

There was a feeling between Richard and Julia Cowing that extended beyond friendship, of this Herbert Cowing was certain, but it never quite reached the point of an engagement or "understanding." Julia eventually married a New York doctor and settled into quiet, childless domesticity. When a tragic train of circumstance threatened to dishonor Richard Wetherill's name, a long time later, she was one of the first to spring to his defense.

THREE

Today, anyone who carries a running iron is regarded as a cattle thief. Fifty years ago and more, that wasn't so. Every cowpuncher carried a running iron in the cinch loops under his saddle blanket. A running iron is a bar about as thick as a good pencil and two feet long, bent in a curve at one end. A cowboy could heat up a running iron in no time over a small fire of bunch grass and when it was hot it would take only a minute to apply his boss' brand on any unbranded cow or yearling that deserved it.

— JOSEPH SCHMEDDING, 1953.

A CURIOUS legend persists in some parts of the Four Corners region that Richard Wetherill was a cattle rustler of prowess and versatility. The distinction is one which Richard did little or nothing to deserve; it was forced upon him after his death, when he could not deny it.

A search of court records has been made in the five county seats where Richard could have been charged with cattle rustling. It began in the District Court of Montezuma County at Cortez and next moved to the courthouse of Durango in La Plata County, in either of which places actions could have been entered while Richard lived at Mancos. When he moved from the Alamo Ranch to Chaco Canyon in 1898 he was within the jurisdiction of three courts: at Aztec, Gallup and Santa Fe, all in New Mexico. Court records in those towns, therefore, were inspected also, as were contemporary newspaper files in Mancos, Aztec, Farmington, Gallup, Santa Fe and Albuquerque, on the chance that a complaint might have been reported against Richard without ever getting as far as court.

The efforts were almost entirely unrewarding: Richard Wetherill was arrested and indicted once, and then on a charge of stealing one cow. To make it worse, or better — depending on the viewpoint — the jury found him and a co-defendant innocent. The case was thrown out of court, but it had various interesting ramifications.

Richard and a cattleman named Henry F. Mitchell, who had moved to Mancos from Missouri in 1877, were indicted by a grand jury at Cortez in April, 1893, on a charge of grand larceny. The complaint, brought by Mancos rancher Daniel V. Hamilton, accused them of "driving away one neat cattle, valued at $15" and holding the animal in the corral of Benjamin K. Wetherill at Alamo Ranch. This theft, Hamilton asserted, had occurred on September 2, 1892. How the prosecutor justified a charge of grand larceny remains unclear.

When the case came to trial, the jury, composed largely of Mancos men who knew Richard well, returned a verdict of not guilty. Testimony showed that the cow which Hamilton declared was stolen had been butchered a short time after it was driven into the Wetherill corral. Apparently it was unknown to Hamilton, but the hide had been hung over a fence rail to dry out and later was put away. Richard caused a stir in the court when he produced a hide and Hamilton, without hesitation, identified it positively as that of his stolen cow. The case blew up when it was shown that the hide bore only one brand mark, and that not a new one — a brand of the Alamo Ranch.

As customary on a ranch the size of the Alamo, the Wetherills had more than one brand, new brands being acquired as they bought herds of cattle from other ranchers. A story is still told about one of those brands which, some say, the Wetherills "dreamed up" in order to steal the cattle of another Mancos rancher, Charlie Frink. It is a fable only; the facts have faded.

Henry Honaker, who came to the valley in 1883, has told the story as it is recalled in the Mancos area. The Honakers were neighbors of the Wetherills; young Henry helped the Wetherill brothers run their cattle in Moccasin Canyon until 1886, and he remembered them as "right nice people, all easy to get along with." Nevertheless, he did recall that the Alamo Ranch at one time used a cattle brand so curiously similar to Charlie Frink's brand that he believed Frink's occasional complaint that the Wetherills were stealing from his herd. In Henry Honaker's words:

"Charlie Frink's place was down the canyon a piece from the Alamo Ranch and the Frink and Wetherill cattle were running together on the same unfenced range. Now, Frink — he was there first — had a diamond bar brand [◇] and the Wetherills, after they come, a diamond A and bar brand [◇⋀]. Now, anybody can see the resemblance was pretty durn close. Maybe it would be hard to prove it, but the story is the Wetherills took that diamond A and bar brand because it would be so easy to lay on over the Frink brand. I'm not saying they did, but I'm not saying they didn't, either." The fact is they did not. It was a brand they acquired, almost accidentally, from two other ranchers, one of them the same Henry Mitchell who had been accused with Richard in the Hamilton case.

It would have been easy to overlook a public notice in The *Mancos Times* for September 15, 1893, inserted over the names of Richard Wetherill and James Caviness after they had acquired title to a number of cattle in settlement of a bad debt. It announced a public sale of cattle owned by Mitchell and Charles Duff to assure to Richard and Caviness, mortgagees, "the payment of one certain promissory note given for the sum of seven hundred dollars . . . dated the 15th day of September, 1892."

"One certain herd of cattle, owned by Henry F. Mitchell and Charles Duff, and running at large on the public range in Montezuma County and numbering 400 head, more or less . . . [this herd including] all cattle known as Indian cattle ranging on the Mesa Verde, and all cattle branded with the diamond A and bar, [the] OLSAc [brand], running in the Mancos and Dolores ranges; also cattle branded X⇌L, ranging in and near San Juan river . . ."

In short, the Wetherills did not invent the diamond A and bar brand, but Richard acquired it by chance in payment of a debt. Subsequent events showed what little importance he attached to the matter. The sale of the cattle was advertised for October 16, 1893, at the front door of the Mancos post office, a day when Richard planned to be away. He left Mancos in September for the World's Fair in Chicago, not returning until November. A few days following his return, he left Mancos again, on November 29, to be gone until the spring of 1894 on an exploring expedition to Grand Gulch.

The *Mancos Times* did not report the outcome of the October 16 sale and just what happened to the Mitchell-Duff cattle and those brands cannot be determined. For a time at least, some of the stock carrying the diamond A and bar apparently became part of the Alamo Ranch herd. Richard's long absence from Mancos at that particular time indicates a greater preoccupation with prehistoric Anasazi than with "doctored" cattle brands.

Old-timers in Mancos say it was common practice among cowmen during the '80s and after to put a rope on any unbranded strays they found. Belt Dailey and George Menefee, whose families were among the first to arrive in the valley, have testified to this from personal experience. As young men

RICHARD WETHERILL

they were cowpunchers for the Mancos Cow Outfit, a cooperative association of valley ranchers, and heard that Richard Wetherill roped his share of unbranded yearlings:

"He didn't care whose stuff it was . . . but shucks, we did the same — everyone did." And Henry Honaker once said that when he was young "There was a saying that no self-respectin' cattleman et his own beef." This is a truism among the early cattlemen that has been expunged from most of the literature of the West.

Running off branded stock never has been regarded as anything but rustling — reprehensible at all times and a hanging offense often. But before barbed wire fenced the ranges, and when thousands of head of cattle roamed free over public land, any unbranded calf that strayed from its mother generally was considered fair game for a cowpuncher's running iron.

Cattle owners generally were tolerant, figuring that this sort of thing worked out evenly for all, in the end. But sometimes a rancher would take a real grievance to court. One of the more celebrated of these rare cases in the Mancos region involved Richard indirectly. His role in the affair has become so confused that he has been spoken of as one of the defendants, which he was not.

Someone, it seems, had been rustling — not merely abusing the use of the running iron. A group of angry cattlemen, headed by rancher John White, joined in the summer of 1891 to hunt down the thief. From Texas they imported a mysterious individual named, or at least called, George Ivins. In no time at all, Ivins managed to devastate the heart of every unmarried girl in Mancos. Mrs. Clara Ormiston, then in her teens and the daughter of Justice of the Peace Milton T. Morris, once admitted she was one of those smitten.

George Ivins, she said, was an uncommonly handsome young fellow with a "real air" about him. He had turned up in Mancos one autumn day on a fine horse fitted with saddle and bridle that literally dripped silver. "All of the girls tried to date him," said Clara Ormiston, "but he wouldn't date." This merely enhanced his charm. Only John White and a few of the other men knew why Ivins turned down invitations to dances and parties in favor of solitary night rides through the valley.

After these rides, Ivins sometimes appeared at the home of Clara's father. She would be awakened by low voices outside her window, see a flickering lantern, and wonder what her father and the stranger had to talk about at that time of night.

After a few months, the Texan's behavior was explained when John White went to the county courthouse at Cortez and swore out a complaint against two Mancos men, accusing them of stealing thirteen head of cattle. To clinch his charge, White produced a number of cowhides, all bearing his brand. And his chief witness was Ivins, who told the jury he was not a cowpoke but a detective, and that while working as an ordinary range hand he saw the defendants steal the cattle, butcher them, and bury the hides. At night he returned to the places where the hides were buried and after digging them up brought them to the home of Judge Morris. The latter concealed the hides under his house until White felt he had enough evidence to hang the rustlers.

Time plays tricks with memory; shortly before her death in 1953 Clara Ormiston could remember vividly the romantic figure of George Ivins and the horse he rode, flashing with silver. She remembered also, or believed she did, that Richard Wetherill was one of the two men accused of stealing White's cattle. Thus she contributed, innocently, to the legend.

Court records show that on February 25, 1892, John White filed his complaint naming Orville C. Olds and Byron McGeoch, both of Mancos and well-known to all in the valley. When they appeared for arraignment, Judge Peace H. Brigham Jr. ordered each to furnish $400 bond, an amount which neither man had.

Orville Olds, according to Henry Honaker, was a struggling Mancos Valley farmer "who had a big family and never seemed able to get ahead." Byron McGeoch is remembered as a swarthy, handsome young blade, a village Don Juan and a heavy drinker. In his present trouble he turned to his best friend and drinking companion, Ed Caviness. The latter was one of six brothers who had come to this part of Colorado in 1879 with their father, Jim, to settle in Thompson Park, a small valley seven miles east of Mancos.

With the exception of Ed, the Caviness boys and their father were respected by nearly all who knew them. Ed, though, was a maverick. He had no money, but he persuaded his father and his brother Mat to bail McGeoch out of the Cortez calaboose. Richard Wetherill entered the picture only when he and Jim Caviness together furnished bond for Orville Olds; he had no interest in McGeoch. When the case came to trial the defendants were found guilty and ordered to pay penalties and costs which, in McGeoch's case amounted to $532.59, and in Olds', $932.59.

Again, neither man had the money to pay the fine. The court file shows that Jim and Mat Caviness settled Byron McGeoch's fine on October 5, 1892.

Richard and Jim Caviness paid Olds' fine on March 25, 1893. Except for his evident desire to help Olds, Richard had no other connection with the case.

After this experience, Orville Olds apparently settled back into quiet respectability. Byron McGeoch, however, proceeded to get into worse trouble. After fathering a baby girl he separated from the infant's mother and cast his roving eye upon the wife of his friend, the man who had bailed him out of the Cortez jail. The woman responded pliantly and their romance soon became common gossip.

Byron refused to heed repeated warnings and one night while he was drinking at the Buckhorn Saloon, Ed Caviness killed him.

Belt Dailey, who saw the Mancos Lothario stretched out dead with five bullet holes through his body, described the affair nearly sixty years afterward:

"Byron was sitting alone at a table in a corner when Ed Caviness came in. Ed stood at the bar and ordered a whisky. The tone of his voice told the bartender Ed was in a real bad mood. So, to give Byron a chance to get out of there, the bartender went over to where he was sitting and reached up as if to fix an oil lamp hanging from the ceiling. That was a brave thing to do because it put him between Byron and Caviness and gave Byron his chance to bolt for the rear door.

"Byron started to get up, and then rested back in his chair. The bartender thought he had done all a man could do and so he went around behind the bar.

"Ed set his glass down and at the same time turned as if heading for the front door — but he kept on turning, and as he turned he pulled out his gun and fired until it was empty. The first shot hit Byron in the forehead and he fell forward on the table. Then Ed went over and pounded Byron on the back of the head with the butt of his gun. There were a few other men in the saloon but they didn't try to interfere. Ed walked out the back to where he had his horse tied up and lit out, heading east on the mountain road.

"Everyone thought he was going to La Plata, where his wife was staying then, aiming to kill her, too. A posse was formed to get him, but they didn't find him at La Plata. Maybe he knew they would play that hunch. Anyway, he had switched trail and it wasn't until some days later the posse caught up with him. They found Ed Caviness in his camp near Price, Utah. He didn't put up any fight but came back peaceable enough. As I remember it, he was tried and sent up for about ten years."

Richard Wetherill was no hand for riding in a sheriff's posse. The day after Byron was killed he left Mancos for the Hopi country with his brother Clate, Dr. T. Mitchell Prudden, young Bert Cowing, and W. H. "Muldoon" Kelley, publisher of the town's weekly newspaper.

Ed Caviness was found guilty of second degree murder on May 5, 1896. The jury, sitting at Cortez, recommended him to the Court's mercy. This caused The *Mancos Times* to comment, on May 8: "No one in the county has clamored for his life-blood, yet so persistent has he been in his evil career, that not even his manly brothers can find it in their hearts to condemn a long-suffering people for their exultation at his conviction." A short while after, Judge Russell sentenced Caviness to fifteen years in the Cañon City penitentiary.

Byron McGeoch and Clara Ormiston had been schoolmates together. As little children they both had attended the Sunday school taught by Richard's mother, Marion Wetherill. Clara remembered that Byron was killed at just about sundown on the night of a dance that was to be held in the schoolhouse. The young people of Mancos had been looking forward to it. But the shooting put a damper on everyone's spirits and for once the violins of Lafayette Guymon and Clark Brittain, and Fred Farmer's guitar had a melancholy sound.

FOUR

*Grand Gulch drains nearly all the territory southwest of the Elk
Mountain from McComb Wash to the Clay Hills, about 1000
square miles of territory. It is the most tortuous cañon in the whole
of the Southwest, making bends from 200 to 600 yards apart almost
its entire length, or for 50 miles; and each bend means a cave or
overhanging cliff. All of these with an exposure to the sun had been
occupied by either cliff houses or as burial places. The cañon is from
300 to 700 feet deep, and in many places toward the lower end the
bends are cut through by nature making natural bridges.*

—RICHARD WETHERILL, field notes.

THE Alamo Ranch hummed with ac-
tivity in the spring and early summer of 1893. Never before had there been
so much work to be done, never before so many arrivals and departures. The
days were crowded with promise and expectancy. Richard and his brothers
had completed their explorations in Mesa Verde; they returned often, guiding parties of tourists, but their excavating in the cliff houses was at an end.
Now, the visitors arriving nearly every week brought a cheerful, holiday
spirit. Even the bright-blanketed Utes found this mood contagious when they
rode in small bands into the shady yard for a talk or a smoke — or a powwow
over a side of beef down under the cottonwoods by the river.

Summer crops were in and doing well, water flowed deep in the irrigation ditches, the cattle and horses grazed in tall grass and grew fat. Everything
promised a good year. It was almost possible to forget the mortgage on the
ranch, a specter which in leaner months was ever present in the minds of
the brothers and old Benjamin Wetherill.

Late that spring, Richard rode south toward the San Juan, leading a
packhorse through the settlements. By the middle of June he was back again
with the packhorse loaded down under Navajo blankets which he believed
he could sell to Eastern visitors. Benjamin Wetherill was delivering ice to

ranchers throughout the valley. The ice had been cut from his reservoir during the winter, bedded down in sawdust, and he was getting sixty cents a hundredweight for it — a good price.

The Chicago Fair had opened in May, an event of considerable interest to Richard and his brothers since two of their Mesa Verde collections were being exhibited and they were eager to learn the public's reaction.

After stopping off at the Fair for a few days with her nephew Herbert, Julia Cowing came on to Mancos and the Alamo Ranch, arriving late in June. John Wetherill met their carriage down the dusty road a mile or two, whooping and racing his horse toward them until Bert Cowing was sure there would be a collision. Back at the ranch, Richard was waiting to add his greeting. Muldoon Kelley noted in the next issue of his paper:

"Miss Cowing is an enthusiast regarding this portion of Colorado as a summer resort, as this is her third season here. The lady has traveled all over the world, but declines to spend the summer season at any place but Alamo Ranch, where she is always welcomed by the entire Wetherill family." A good friend of the family himself, Muldoon chose his words to allay gossip.

Others came to the Alamo Ranch, drawn by word of the cliff dwellings. A Mr. and Mrs. Wixson of Chicago, who had been so impressed by the Mesa Verde collections at the Fair and wanted to see the prehistoric sites where the relics had been found, came in July. Charlie Mason, now living with Anna in the mountain town of Creede, arrived with a Mr. Crump of London, who was "doing" the Wild West. And at the same time, causing Mother Wetherill to throw up her hands and ask where she could put everybody, came Mr. and Mrs. Robert K. McNeely of Philadelphia in a confusion of baggage, four daughters and one son. A partial solution was found by moving young Win Wetherill and Bert Cowing with bedrolls and beds of straw into the small barn now used as a museum. This tide of visitors and sightseers also brought large numbers of people from Durango, now more interested in Mesa Verde than three years before.

Benjamin Wetherill, remarking tartly that if this kept up they would all be crowded into the trees, secretly enjoyed this company. Next to Julia Cowing, the visitor he liked to talk with most was Richard's friend Charles B. Lang, a young photographer from Pittsburgh who already had explored parts of this region which even Richard had not seen, and who made the Wetherill ranch his headquarters on several occasions. Lang was a quiet man with a bit of the wanderlust and burning ambition to photograph remote corners of the Southwest that motivated William Henry Jackson.

Sometime before 1890, Lang made his way into Utah's forbidding Grand Gulch with a companion named J. B. Neilsen and brought back photographs of cliff and cave dwellings similar to those of Mesa Verde. Possibly a few Mormons had been there in search of stray cattle, but as far as the record shows, Lang and Neilsen were the first white men to enter Grand Gulch.

As a consequence of Lang's discovery, Charles McLoyd and C. C. Graham of Durango explored Grand Gulch in the winter of 1890-91, bringing out a large collection of Cliff Dweller relics. The collection was exhibited in Durango where it was bought by a retired minister from Kentucky, the Rev. C. H. Green. So invigorating was the effect of his purchase that Mr. Green came out of retirement to pack into Grand Gulch himself, add a few relics and photographs to his collection, and then travel about giving lectures on the subject, which he illustrated with lantern slides. When the Colorado exhibit was being assembled for the Chicago Fair, Mr. Green arranged to have his Grand Gulch collection shown at the same time, at the Chicago Art Institute. There it was bought by C. D. Hazzard of the H. Jay Smith Exploring Co., who in turn sold it to the agents for the Phoebe Hearst collection that was given later to the University of Pennsylvania. Meanwhile, John Wetherill had accompanied McLoyd and Graham on their second trip to Grand Gulch, in the fall of 1892.

The stories Richard heard of these prehistoric ruins determined him to see Grand Gulch for himself. But Charles Lang was again in Mancos this summer of 1893 and he and Richard went into business as photographers. With an eye to the tourists flocking to Mesa Verde they inserted an advertisement in The Mancos Times:

> Lang & Witherill, Photographers. Mancos, Colorado. Cliff Dwelling Views a Specialty! Rocky Mt. Views, orders by mail promptly attended to.

As he did so often, Muldoon Kelley misspelled Richard's name. It was a regional tendency, never minded by anyone, and accounted for popular acceptance of the spelling of Weber Canyon and Weber Mountain — both named for the pioneer Webber family.

Toward the end of the summer, Richard was asked to go to Chicago in connection with the Wetherills' Mesa Verde collection. Part of his expenses would be paid by the state, and he would be required only to remain with the exhibit to answer questions.

Richard left Mancos on September 12 accompanied by his friend Harry French, who had come to Mancos from Chicago in 1887. During the time they remained at the Fair they stayed at the home of French's parents.

The first few days were a kaleidoscopic tangle of impressions for Richard, who had not been so far East since his childhood, and never before in a city as large as this. Several times after leaving the fairgrounds he went into the city with Harry French, who still knew his way about, to gaze in wonder at the sights. Lake Michigan's blue expanse, which he tried to compare with the mountain lakes at home, appealed more to him than the tall buildings rising from the business district.

The lights at night, the swirling crowds of people and the noise, the confusion and smells of a big town were an exciting experience. But the baffling network of streets running almost endlessly in all directions made him uneasy and nervous. He confessed to French that he knew, if left on his own, he would be lost in ten minutes. Very quickly the city's novelty wore off and he was content to spend the rest of his time between the fairgrounds and the home of his friend's parents.

The Fair attracted thousands of people from all corners of the country. This was truly a cross-section of America, Richard thought, not realizing that among the jostling swarm of people he stood out as a type. In Denver he had bought a suit of conservative cut; in spite of this, and a white shirt and well-brushed shoes, no one could have mistaken him for other than he was. The leathery skin with wrinkles set deep around his eyes, the level dark gaze, the fierce brush of moustache, his walk — all revealed him as a Westerner much more at ease in a saddle than on hard asphalt.

At the Fair, all of Richard's interest was centered in the Anthropological Building. Prof. Frederic Ward Putnam, director of the Peabody Museum at Harvard University, was in charge of the displays. The huge ground floor was devoted almost exclusively to archaeology and ethnology — some one hundred fifty exhibits in all, including the collections from Mesa Verde and Grand Gulch. The exhibitors for the most part were ethnologists — such men as W. H. Holmes of the Bureau of American Ethnology in Washington, Ernest Volk of Oberlin College and George A. Dorsey of the Field Columbian Museum in Chicago.

The response of the fair-goers pleased Richard enormously. They were curious and he enjoyed answering their questions. Mummies of the Anasazi shown here, as they had been found with their burial garments and pottery grave offerings, attracted the greatest curiosity. The Anasazi, Richard explained gravely, were among the earliest men to inhabit North America about whom anything was known. Natural elements alone had preserved the Anasazi mummies — those shrivelled, leather-hued human beings whose bodies and whose yucca-fiber sandals and feather-cloth robes had defied the decay of centuries by virtue of the dry chemistry of burial in the sand of caves where moisture never penetrated. In their country — his country — the air itself dried and embalmed the dead.

And who were the Anasazi?

Anasazi, said Richard, was a Navajo word. The Navajo used it to describe the ancient people, now vanished, whose ruined dwellings the Navajo found when they migrated into the Four Corners region from the northward. In a loose, vague sense *Anasazi* meant ancient enemies. Richard did not know if this implied that the first of the Navajos had found some of these early ones still in their pueblos and cliff dwellings, and made war upon them.

As to the age of the Anasazi civilization, Richard could not say. He could only explain that the cliff dwellings and pueblos had been built and finally abandoned before the Spaniards arrived in the 1500's. Of this he was sure because no white man's implement had been found in the ruins.

Sometime during the few weeks he spent at the Fair, Richard for the second time met the two young men whose interest in him and in his work was to determine the remaining years of his life: Talbot Hyde and Fred Hyde, Jr., sons of a New York physician and heirs to the Babbitt soap company fortune founded by their grandfather. Their first meeting probably occurred earlier that summer, at the Alamo Ranch.

From these meetings grew the Hyde Exploring Expedition — so named by Richard — and an agreement that Richard would lead an expedition into Grand Gulch during the coming winter. Thus was initiated a chain of events, often misunderstood, widely criticized and ending eventually in Richard's death. Out of their association, however, came pioneering which may be called the cornerstone of Southwestern archaeology.

AT THE TIME of his meeting with Richard in Chicago, Fred Hyde was eighteen years old, a slender six-footer, strikingly handsome and almost painfully reserved. His brother Talbot was two years older, equally tall but heavier, and with an open, friendly manner. Both of the young men regularly received large allowances and in a few years would inherit small fortunes from their grandfather's estate.

Benjamin Babbitt, the grandfather, was the son of a Glens Falls, New York, blacksmith who, after an apprenticeship at his father's forge, came to the city with a new idea and formula for making soap. Within a very few years Babbitt's name was a household word and Babbitt was a millionaire. In the course of his rise to success he married a young woman who has been described by a member of the family as unbending in her own formula — for success in the small world of New York society. Their home was severely correct, a town house on Thirty-Sixth Street in a then fashionable district near Lexington Avenue.

When their daughter Ida Josephine married Frederick E. Hyde, a young physician just beginning his career, Mrs. Babbitt took the couple firmly in hand. It was understood that the doctor and Ida would not set up housekeeping on their own, but would live with the Babbitts. Further, it was agreed, in return for a generous allowance, young Dr. Hyde would confine his practice to families of good social standing and thus avoid bringing the diseases of "common people" into the Babbitt home. Nothing very much was heard from the doctor after that, except in time he and Ida Josephine became the parents of two sons, Benjamin Talbot Babbitt Hyde and Frederick Erastus Hyde, Jr.

Neither was distinguished as a student, although Fred is said to have displayed flashes of brilliance at Harvard, where he attended classes more or less regularly for four years but never was graduated. Even at college Fred remembered his father's early warning that women were dangerous, predatory creatures to be treated always with cold reserve. And sex, it was impressed on the boy, was an impure weakness, animal-like in all of its manifestations, to be condoned only occasionally and then in the married state. These ideas haunted the youngster. At college, in what was almost frantic rebellion, he periodically disappeared from his classes for days at a time, returning unappeased, nervous, convinced he was a monstrous, unnatural sinner.

Talbot Hyde, meanwhile, had grown to maturity as a thoroughly uncomplicated person. Lacking his younger brother's erratic streaks of brilliance and perverse humor, Talbot was temperamentally placid and easygoing. He was determined to do his best in meeting his grandfather's expectations: that he carry forward the fortunes of the Babbitt company and perpetuate the family name.

Talbot had just started working for the company, in 1896, when his grandfather died — to be followed in death six months later by Ida Josephine, the boys' mother. Half of Benjamin Babbitt's estate went to his wife and the

RICHARD WETHERILL

remainder in equal shares to Dr. Hyde and the two sons. Besides an immediate inheritance of about five hundred thousand dollars each, Dr. Hyde, Talbot and Fred also received large stock holdings which paid substantial dividends. This money, derived from a universally popular soap, now called Bab-O, financed Richard Wetherill's work and subsidized the Hyde Exploring Expedition from 1893 until 1903, when the partnership between Richard and the Hyde brothers was dissolved.

For seventeen years Talbot remained with the Babbitt company, resigning after he had become president, in 1913. Then only forty years old, he retired to a life which interested him more. Although married twice he had no children of his own, which must have grieved him because he was devoted to children. He was much interested in the Boy Scout movement while he was still living in the East, and he organized, after moving to Santa Fe in 1927, the Children's Nature Foundation on a large ranch near Tesuque.

Snakes had a fascination for Talbot and he was known to argue that the snake — not the dog — truly was man's best friend. This feeling was unshakable, even though he was struck by rattlesnakes twice, on one occasion so severely he almost died. When he recovered he regarded the incident impersonally — it had been an experiment to gauge the audio-sensitivity of a giant diamondback rattler — and continued to carry poisonous as well as non-poisonous snakes with him when he lectured to Boy Scout groups. The problem of transporting the snakes he solved by dropping them into a pillowcase, which he stuffed into a leather traveling bag.

From the beginning of their association until its end, Talbot's relations with Richard seem to have never changed: each for his own reasons respected the other and there was a feeling of common purpose between them, but it was a feeling quite impersonal which never grew into a close friendship. Although he was the older of the two by fifteen years, Richard always addressed Talbot formally, as "Mr. Hyde" or, in his letters, "Dear Friend Hyde." With Fred a much warmer relationship existed, a fond relationship approaching that between a father and son. There were times when Fred's unpredictable ways were a clear annoyance to Richard, but even then, as always, there was a strong bond and understanding between them.

BLUFF CITY was on the verge of a boom when Richard made it the headquarters of his expedition to Grand Gulch in the winter of 1893. A small migrant army of gold-seekers had arrived and were at work, their tents and shacks lining the San Juan's banks for several miles. Newcomers staked out claims with each sunrise. Few of them brought their women, but for a mining camp life was quiet: the Mormon townspeople — good, quiet God-fearing citizens — had nailed the lid down.

Enough gold was sluiced out of the placer mines to keep the boom alive for three or four years, and to maintain the wistful illusions of a lonely desert village that wanted to become a city in more than name. No one troubled to make a count of noses in 1893 or later at the peak of the boom — but the population of Bluff may have reached a thousand.

The old Mormon trail from upstate Utah descended through a gap in the rock bluffs just east of town, bringing all kinds of wayfarers besides the prospectors: emigrant families in search of greener land, bands of Utes or Navajos, cowboys on the prod, Indian traders in from the desert to replenish their supplies and spend a night or two soaking up human companionship — and assorted, unclassified types of callings various or none at all.

Unable or unwilling to foresee a day when their prosperity would evaporate like morning mist from the river, the Mormons built their town solidly, for the future. They used stone instead of lumber and built a fine church, a large schoolhouse, neat homes set back from the rows of cottonwoods which they planted along the town's one S-curving main street. There were several stores, a harness shop and a big livery stable — but almost no place where a tired man could buy a shot of whisky.

It was an almost dry oasis, man-built, bravely planned — and in the center of nowhere. A green spot in a beautiful wide river canyon surrounded by vividly-colored sandstone.

Richard Wetherill knew the town from harsh experience. He knew it in its best and most hopeful years, but he was there again to see the placer miners drift away, the traffic over the emigrant trail thin to nothing, the town wither and all but die.

For four years more, until he moved to Chaco Canyon, Bluff City was as familiar to Richard as the creases in his hand, the place where he outfitted for trips through the entire Four Corners region. He knew the river valley here as level, nearly two miles broad, walled on either side by chocolate and taffy-colored sandstone bluffs. Grass grows tall, violently green in the damp of the river edges, and the river flows, not deep but wide and swift and muddy.

Half a mile west the valley opens out still more and there is a mile-wide gap in the northern cliffs. This is the entrance to Cottonwood Wash — not shady as its name implies, but wide and bare, a naked stretch of white sand and clay parched by the sun, the surface crackled and curling from dried-up moisture, dotted with sagebrush. In the rainy season the wash sometimes carries a foam-flecked runoff flood from the northern slopes into the San Juan.

This was the route Richard took in his attack on Grand Gulch, following Cottonwood Wash almost to its head, then cutting west when he had the twin rounding peaks of the Bear's Ears in range.

Few places in the world are so cut off from civilization as Grand Gulch. In four centuries only a handful of white men have explored its depths, yet in prehistoric times it was one of the most populous centers of Anasazi culture. No road, not even a trail or wagon rut leads to it from any direction. Nels C. Nelson of the American Museum of Natural History, who retraced Richard's ground in 1920, accompanied by John Wetherill as guide, Talbot Hyde and several others, mapped the gorge as best he could from horseback, located eighty cave and cliff dwellings and photographed a few of them. Upon his return to New York he jotted down these impressions for a preface to his unpublished report:

". . . One of the least frequented and probably also one of the most inaccessible parts of the United States. A great rift in the earth, tortuous and fantastic, with mushroom or toadstool rocks, monuments of standing, seated, and bust figures, hats atilt, and every conceivable form and shape on which imagination seizes or turns into semblance of life. . . . The general course is northwest to southwest, but a hot sun makes me aware that we face in turn every point of the compass. . ."

The area is so bewildering to the eye that it is no wonder Richard lacked precision in locating the sites where he worked. Nels Nelson was bewildered, too, when he retraced Richard's progress through Grand Gulch and attempted to identify the ruins Richard had described in his field notes. Two of those he did locate, however, were near the head of the gorge: Richard's camp and Cave No. 1, and Cave No. 2 — the latter sheltering a small cliff dwelling of twelve or thirteen rooms, two kivas of the Mesa Verde type, all perched precariously a hundred feet above the bed of the gulch. Only a short distance beyond, Nelson noted on his map:

"Canyon closed to pack animals. Cliff walls three hundred feet high and only fifty-six feet apart, and a high talus, one hundred feet in front."

Richard laid the groundwork for this expedition while visting Julia Cowing at her brother James' home in Brooklyn, sometime after the middle of October, 1893. In an undated letter to Talbot Hyde, who was then hardly farther away than the other end of the Brooklyn Bridge, Richard proposed the methods of work which he would use:

> I arrived here night before last and will commence on Monday to outfit with such articles as cannot be procured at Durango. I send a form of work [a record sheet twelve by thirteen inches and ruled off in squares] that will meet all requirements unless something else occurs to you that would be of special interest. I find there are none printed but I can do as heretofore, secure blanks and mark them myself in this manner — viz.:

1 number of house or ruin	2 number of article	3 name of article	4 number of room
5 number of section	6 depth	7 number of floors if any	8 remarks

> Every article to be numbered with India ink and fine pen or with tube paints white, red or black. Plan of all houses & sections to be made on paper or book to be ruled both ways. Drawing of article to be made on paper with numbers and name. Photograph each house before touched, then each room or section and every important article as found.
>
> I think you will find this will meet all the requirements of the most scientific but if you have any suggestions whatever I will act upon them. This whole subject . . . is in its infancy and the work we do must stand the most rigid inspection, and we do not want to do it in such a manner that anyone in the future can pick flaws in it.

Richard knew that whatever he brought out of Grand Gulch would be given by the Hyde brothers to the American Museum of Natural History. The value of the collection would depend entirely upon his ability to document every phase of his work. He recognized that he was entering a new field untouched by the ethnologists. This was archaeology. Richard was a groping, untutored but ardent pioneer. He had nothing but his own past experience and his ingenuity to guide him. He knew his limitations, his lack of scientific training or education, but he hoped that his work would stand "the most rigid inspection" of the scientific men who had not yet ventured out into his country.

His stay with the Cowings lasted no more than a week and was a pleasant, final interlude in the only vacation he is known to have allowed himself. After leaving Chicago, he had come East by way of Niagara Falls and Saratoga Springs, drawn to that fashionable resort and racing town more by his interest in horses than in stylish women. An impression has existed that during this same trip he went to Washington to interest officials at the Smithsonian Institution in further work at Mesa Verde. Tom Outland, Willa Cather's fictional counterpart of Richard, did go to Washington for exactly that purpose, and Outland's failure to arouse even a glow of interest makes a moving passage in Miss Cather's novel. Her version correctly projects the blank wall of indifference Richard met, but the truth is he never made a pilgrimage to Washington. The Smithsonian he never saw — his only contact with officials there was by letter.

From Brooklyn Richard returned directly to the Alamo Ranch, arriving there early in November and eager to get on with the winter's expedition. The weather was unusually favorable.

He left Mancos on November 29, his party including his brothers Al and John, their friend Charles Lang (the photographer), Harry French and Jim Ethridge. From Cortez they entered McElmo Canyon and then crossed the high, southward sloping tableland above the San Juan where there is nothing but sand and bunch grass to resist the knife edge of a November wind, and came down finally into Bluff City. Here they were joined by Bob Allen, a Mormon and native of that town, and a Denver man named Wirt Jenks Billings.

Besides the horses they rode, Richard had brought from the home ranch three pack mules, but now he hired more horses and mules. Supplies to last a month were bought and, on the day of departure, lashed in two-hundred pound packs on the mules.

As leader of the expedition, Richard assigned each man to specific tasks: his brothers John and Al were named mule wrangler and cook, respectively. Ethridge and French would scout ahead to locate ruins that might be worth investigating. Lang, of course, with Richard, would take photographs and also, with Billings, help Richard with measurements, cataloging and notes. Bob Allen and any other man who could be spared was to make periodic trips back to Bluff City, packing out the material excavated and loading the mules for the return with fresh supplies. All of the men were given shovels, and would dig.

The party was in the field four months. At the end of this time the result of Richard's organization and planning was a collection weighing well over one ton and numbering 1,216 specimens, including 96 skeletons. Not all of the collection, however, was from Grand Gulch. Richard filled fifty-two large pages with field notes, these showing that the first 428 specimens were found in Cottonwood Wash. Later in the season (at just what stage is uncertain) the party moved south across the San Juan to the Chinle Wash — which Richard knew and referred to as "the Chelle." Working down the Chinle for eight or nine miles they came to a large cliff dwelling which Richard named Long House, noting that "The house is 537 feet long — about 75 feet above the creek bed at the foot of a cliff . . ." Evidently they remained here several days, gaining an additional 71 relics. S. J. Guernsey later made a more thorough excavation of the same cliff dwelling and named it Poncho House.

Richard was aware of a curious observation McLoyd and Graham had made during their work in Grand Gulch in 1890-91. They noted in a catalog for the collection that some of the mummies, baskets and sandals belonged to a primitive culture that somehow was "different" from that of the Cliff Dwellers. They had not excavated very deeply in any of the ruins, and the specimens in which they traced evidence of a different race had not been found in sufficient quantity to lead to more positive conclusions.

Richard's party had proceeded no farther than the ruins of Cottonwood Wash when he began to find proof of a people which had used the caves before the arrival of the Cliff Dwellers. Far below the floor level of the cliff dwellings he uncovered burial remains which in most respects were foreign to anything he had ever seen before. These remains he found in burial pits, round or oval cysts which in some cases had been used previously for storing food. As the digging continued, Richard observed sharp contrasts:

These people made beautiful, and sometimes very large baskets. But they had no pottery. The large baskets, some four or five feet in diameter, usually were found covering a burial.

They were slightly taller people than the Cliff Dwellers.

Their skulls for the most part were long and rather narrow, and in all cases were of normal, undeformed shape. The heads of Cliff Dwellers always were flattened at the rear, thus making them appear shorter and broader. This flattening of the occipital bone was caused by the use of cradle boards.

Sandals of these ancient ones were rounded or squared at the toe, without indentation. Cliff Dweller sandals were indented at the little toe.

These ancients had no knowledge of the bow and arrow — the most common weapon of the Cliff Dwellers. Instead, they used a dart or spear with a throwing stick called an *atlatl*.

There was no doubt in Richard's mind that he had made a significant discovery, when he wrote from his camp on Cottonwood Wash to Talbot Hyde one evening in December, 1893:

"Our success has surpassed all expectations. . . . In the cave we are now working we have taken 28 skeletons and two more in sight and curious to tell, and a thing that will surprise the archaeologists of the country is the fact of our finding them at a depth of five and six feet in a cave in which there are cliff dwellings and we find the bodies under the ruins, three feet below any cliff dweller sign. They are a different race from anything I have ever seen. They had feather cloth and baskets, no pottery — six of the bodies had stone spear heads in them . . ." The letter was addressed from "First Valley Cottonwood Creek 30 miles North Bluff City" and on the back of one page Richard had scribbled "Excuse sand in this letter — we are in a sandy place."

Talbot Hyde asked Richard for specific information. In reply, Richard for the first time referred to "the Basket People" to distinguish the older people from the Cliff Dwellers. He said he could "now easily separate the two classes of people and their belongings," and added: "I named the cliff dwellers, and you should have the honor at least of naming these, since it is your expedition." In the same letter, dated February 4, 1894, from Bluff City, Richard wrote:

The baskets have nothing attached to them for carrying them unless it would be the very large ones, but I think they are a head cover. They are made from willow the same as any Indian basket work. Yucca is also used a great deal . . .

The rock of the caves could easily disintegrate, and would in time form a foundation for the cliff dwellers to build upon, but this is not always the case. When the Basket People dug out their bottle-shaped rooms the tops, of course, were all on a level with the surface, and they covered them in such a way that they could not be detected. The C.D. [Cliff Dwellers], in some cases, built over them not knowing they were there. In others that were open, the C.D. used to throw rubbish . . . The hair is black, neither straight nor curly. The Basket People and the C.D. both made feather cloth. . .

The feathers are from the turkey. The B. P. used the caves more as a burial ground than anything else. Some of the caves have evidence of being temporary camping places for these people. . . They are a larger race than the cliff dwellers. I have measured none of them, but I know from comparison, as I have now handled more than one hundred of each. I intend to write something for the Archaeologist [magazine], but will wait for you. . .

In the absence of other evidence, Richard's claim to having named the Cliff Dwellers has to be taken on faith. The name was not used by Jackson or Holmes in writing for the Hayden Surveys, but it does appear in a letter written by S. E. Osborn, a prospector, to The *Denver Tribune-Republican* in 1886. Osborn, who had worked in the canyons of Mesa Verde and was writing of ruins he had found there, could have adopted the name after hearing it used by Richard or his brothers. Richard was given to understatement, especially when referring to himself or his work.

Talbot Hyde followed Richard's suggestion that he name Richard's "Basket People," replying he thought they might be called Basket Makers. This Richard accepted and then tactfully added, without elaborating, that he had certain reservations. He wrote Hyde in March that "The Basket Makers, as you called them before is more distinctive than anything I could have thought [of] for a name but it does not convey an idea."

Possibly Richard had in mind that the Cliff Dwellers and Pueblo Indians were identified by their type of dwellings rather than by their most common handicraft (pottery), and the term Basket Makers might confuse these Anasazi with modern Indian tribes who still made baskets. However, he proposed no alternative name but continued to use "Basket People."

Many of the Basket Makers' salient characteristics Richard observed closely and recorded in his field notes or in letters to Talbot Hyde and Dr. T. Mitchell Prudden. The field notes have been preserved but a number of the letters are lost. Richard's analysis of the material he found has not been contradicted in any important respect by archaeologists who have worked in this field since. Although additional knowledge of the Basket Makers has been gained in the last forty years, his original discovery laid firm groundwork for those who followed him. Nevertheless, during the remaining sixteen years of his life he received no recognition for his contribution and few archaeologists at the time accepted the Basket Makers as more than Richard's fanciful invention.

The Basket Makers were treated seriously in a popular article Dr. Prudden wrote for the June, 1897, issue of *Harper's Monthly*. It was titled "An Elder Brother to the Cliff Dwellers" and based entirely upon information which Richard supplied to his friend. A somewhat more scientific treatment was given in 1902 in a pamphlet written for the American Museum of Natural History *Journal* by George H. Pepper — but this, too, was based largely upon Richard's notes and was illustrated with photographs from the Wetherill-Hyde and the McLoyd-Graham collections. So far as the archaeologists of that day were concerned, Prudden's article and Pepper's summary of others' findings only inspired more condemnation of Richard as a charlatan.

Alfred Vincent Kidder, the first archaeologist to offer proof of Richard's discovery, has recalled that when he was a student at Harvard, a professor in one of his classes spoke scornfully of the Basket Makers as a hoax conceived by Richard Wetherill. The professor told the students that Richard "had taken his undeformed skulls, baskets and sandals and had segregated them from the rest of his Grand Gulch collection to create a myth of 'an early basket race.' " In that way, the students were told, "Richard Wetherill had increased the sales value of his collection if not its credibility."

This attitude of scornful disbelief changed suddenly, a few years later, when Kidder went into northeastern Arizona to work with S. J. Guernsey.

"As soon as Guernsey and I got into the caves of the Monuments area and Marsh Pass we found exactly the same sort of Basket Maker remains Wetherill had described," Dr. Kidder has recalled. They reported their findings at White Dog Cave and elsewhere and their colleagues took respectful notice. "That immediately changed everything. Faith was restored and Basket Makers ceased to be a myth after 1914."

RICHARD told Dr. Prudden that his first discovery of the Basket Makers was in a cave in Cottonwood Wash (rather than in nearby Butler Wash, as some writers have said). And in writing of the discovery to Moorehead of The *Archaeologist*, Richard said:

"Two feet below the lowest remains of the Cliff Dwellers, we have found remains of quite a different tribe. . ."

In other ways, too, it was a startling discovery. Ninety-two skeletons were found in mass burials, the broken bones mute evidence of a prehistoric massacre by some stronger band. The skulls of most had been crushed, but whether before or after death in some cases was uncertain because stone projectile points were found among the ribs and embedded in the backbones. An atlatl point was buried in the top of one skull, protruding at an angle which indicated the shaft had penetrated the victim's throat under the chin. Driven through the pelvis of another skeleton Richard found a huge obsidian blade transfixing and pinning the hip bones together like a skewer. Richard marveled at the force revealed by that fatal thrust.

More evidence of violence was found when Richard reached Grand Gulch and in one cave uncovered nine mummies. One of these was a very old man, nearly six feet tall. He had been slashed, apparently with a stone knife, across the full width of his back and also across his lower abdomen. The ragged wound had been sewed up with cord of braided human hair an eighth of an inch thick, the stitches spaced roughly half an inch apart — as rudely as one might mend a gunny sack. The body was unusually well preserved: head tilted up and back as though the old man suffered unendurable pain at the time of death, the left hand clutching the right wrist and the right hand gripping the wound on the abdomen, both legs flexed, the knees drawn up tightly.

Richard studied the poor fellow carefully. And then to Talbot Hyde he wrote, "Whether it is a specimen of surgery or not, I have not yet determined. It seems most horrible to me. The face seems to indicate pain. . ."

In the same grave were other grisly remains: a pair of feet and legs cut off at the knees, and with them a pair of hands and arms amputated at the elbows. The rest of the body was missing. Buried with the old man and the dismembered limbs he found an oddly carved piece of wood, canoe-shaped, eighteen inches long by four inches wide and two inches deep. In the space where it had been hollowed out he found two pouches made from the skin of a mountain sheep. One of the pouches contained a stone knife blade still attached to its wood handle, a bone awl and some loose spear points. Tied up in the other pouch were smaller bags filled with lumps of coloring matter. The nature of these articles and their presence in the grave told nothing. Such burial offerings were found frequently in Basket Maker graves.

Richard was an engaging conversationalist, expressing his thoughts or ideas with ease and often with humor. When he gripped a pen, however, the wells of expression dried up and his style resolved into awkward sentences. He was conscious of this and mentioned it at the end of this letter to Dr. Prudden, giving his friend requested information about the Basket Makers. The letter was written after the first Hyde Exploring Expedition trip to Grand Gulch and at a time when the doctor was completing his article for *Harper's Monthly*:

I meant for you to use my notes and photos and take from them, whatever you wished to use. I did not understand that you would get out a dry scientific paper.

You already understand what we call the Caves — apparently at one time there was a smooth dirt floor in them several feet in thickness. (It is not likely that they were used as places of residence at all.)

In these floors egg shaped holes were dug in cases where the sand was soft [and] they were walled up and plastered. But the majority were merely finished with plaster, smoothing the interior. . . Many of these are found in one cave . . . Originally they may have been intended for caches since both the Pah Ute and the Navajo use the same thing for the storing of grain — near their fields, by digging into some high spot where the water will all drain away.

I believe it is the custom of the present Indians to build a fire inside and pretty thoroughly bake the linings of the cache. This of course would drive out all the moisture and make a safe granary.

The Basket People, as we call them, seem to be confined to a very small area. How far West they may extend we do not know, but the Cottonwood [Wash] seems to be the Eastern limit and the Elk Mt., the Northern. Canon de Chelle, at the mouth, is the Southern on this side of the Colorado. What may be [found] on the other side I do not know . . . [but] I have a faint suspicion that if the Pah Ute country was well prospected the result would be similar. . . .

In these pot holes or caches are found the bodies of all ages and sexes — sandals upon the feet — human hair, gee string, cedar bark breech cloth. Beads around their necks. All wrapped in a blanket made of rabbit fur — of a weave similar to the feather cloth. Then they are [found] in a mummy cloth or sack such as the Peruvians used. This is made from yucca fiber and good cloth it is. Over the head is a small basket — flat — about 20 inches in diameter, usually found in good condition; Apaches make a similar one today.

Along the arms are scattered spear points, fine bone awls, all long ones . . . All have a hook on one end. ⌐━━━━
. . . Never a stone axe has been found. Small baskets containing corn and seeds with ornaments [are] usually near the head. Wherever an Atlatl has been found it was broken and was on top [of the body] . . . The pipes are usually in small baskets near the head. Over all is the large basket. Nearly always two bodies have been found in one grave. No pottery has been found in one of these pot holes. The skulls are all natural — long and narrow.

We have made our greatest finds in caves where there were no Cliff Dwelling ruins. . . The sandals were not all square toed but differed from the Cliff Dwellers in this way (see diagram). 1. Basket Maker, and much finer than the usual C. D. 2. Cliff Dweller. See hook for little toe.

The letter shows Richard as a keen observer, not only of objects found and their relationship to other prehistoric and modern tribes — but of objects missing. Every archaeologist knows the importance of this. The object missing can be as significant, in the science of reconstructing ancient history, as the object present. Here, as in every other place where he worked, Richard was conscious of this; and that is why he emphasized that in these Basket Maker sites he had found no pottery, bows and arrows or stone axes — and that the caves probably were not "used as places of residence at all."

At the conclusion of this letter Richard expressed in one brief paragraph his aspirations, and admitted his gravest handicap:

I want to make myself thoroughly acquainted with the whole Southwest. Some time in the future I hope to do something in the way of putting my work in book form. But first I must be educated. This is rather a slow process.

Richard did become acquainted with a large part of the Southwest but never was able to publish anything in book form. Largely for that reason his pioneering work generally has failed to receive recognition. There are a few notable exceptions. John Otis Brew, director of Harvard University's Peabody Museum, has written that the work of Richard and his brothers "can be argued as the most far-reaching single event in Southwestern archaeology." Remarking on Richard's failure to publish the results of his findings, Brew added that "Although the influence of the work and deductions of the Wetherills has been widely felt, it has come to us mainly from the pens of others and through collections of artifacts in various museums. Most of their operations have not been described in print."

In his article for *Harper's Monthly*, Dr. Prudden generously acknowledged the help Richard had given him and concluded on a wry note:

"Will none of our great universities realize before it is too late that the treasure house of folk-lore among the Pueblo Indians is crumbling fast and that these fields of American archaeology in the Southwest are wide and fruitful?"

The appeal would go unheeded until a later generation, beginning with Kidder and Guernsey and Nelson, took the field about 1914 — four years after Richard's death.

Fortunately, the winter of 1893 was mild, without the sub-zero temperatures at night and the snowstorms which usually at this time of year close upon Grand Gulch with icy grip. Richard and his companions worked steadily in the sand and rubble of the caves. At Christmas there was a week's interruption, when all of the men rode into Bluff City for a celebration arranged by elders of the Mormon church. Their invitation had come through Bob Allen. By early March they were digging in the vicinity of the natural bridges — graceful stone arches formed by erosion. These they encountered where the gulch narrows to an impassable gap before dropping off into the San Juan River. The men were thirty miles below Graham Canyon, where they had entered Grand Gulch, and had worked out more than a hundred caves.

The methods of excavation Richard used in Cottonwood Wash and Grand Gulch — digging through the Cliff Dweller level of human remains to the older Basket Maker level, and drawing conclusions about the relative place in prehistory of both by comparison of what he found — were a simple application of the modern stratigraphic technique.

Stratigraphy is based on the principle that the oldest remains of a civilization, by a process of time and accumulation, will be found buried deepest under the ground's surface. Each layer of debris above the bottom progressively indicates a later period in the life of any village, the top layer of refuse naturally being the last before the site was abandoned or destroyed. By comparison of these successive layers of debris, and their relationship in time with findings in other localities, archaeologists have been able to piece together many parts of the puzzle of how people of the past have lived.

The thoroughness of his work, combined with shrewd observation, brought Richard close to the basic methods of modern stratigraphic excavation. In the refuse mound of San Cristóbal ruin of Galisteo Basin, Nels C. Nelson first developed the technique in 1914, and so effectively that Alfred Vincent Kidder immediately afterward employed the same methods at Pecos Pueblo. Both men have acknowledged the importance of Richard's contribution, and John C. McGregor, in his *Southwestern Archaeology*, observed:

"So far as is known at present, Richard Wetherill . . . was the first to make use of natural stratigraphy as applied to archaeological problems in the Southwest. From his work in the western San Juan he established the Basket Maker Culture stage as distinct from, and earlier than, that of the later Pueblo people." *

RICHARD had intended to extend his work to the vicinity of Navajo Mountain, several days' to the southwest, but approaching spring made this plan impractical. His notes show that some work was done in Allen Canyon, high in the foothills of the Abajo Mountains, and down through Butler Wash which runs parallel to and just west of the Cottonwood. As in the case of Long House (Poncho House) on the Chinle, his notes do not tell at what stage he and his party reached these places. No help is supplied, either, in determining the route of the expedition by the cataloging of the collection, since the artifacts were not numbered entirely in the order of their discovery. It is certain, however, that Richard did not get as far south as Marsh Pass and Tsegi Canyon, as some have believed.

After four months in the field, Richard disbanded his party at Bluff City in March. The 1,216 relics packed out by mule train had been stored temporarily in Bluff and now were loaded on wagons and taken to the Alamo Ranch. When he reached there, Richard spent two months working over the collection, sorting out and cataloging the material before crating it for shipment by

---

* Quoted with the permission of John Wiley and Sons, Inc., New York.

rail from Durango to New York. In the fall of 1895 the collection was presented by Talbot and Fred Hyde to the American Museum of Natural History. Most of these relics now lie uncrated and in storage, but a number are displayed in the Southwest Hall as the First Wetherill Collection "made by Richard Wetherill about 1890."

Just how much the expedition cost the Hyde brothers is not certain, although $3,000 would be a reasonable estimate. Early in the season Richard had reported that the January bills for wages and materials totalled only $450. Expenses for March, he told Hyde, "will be less, for all extra men you are paying at the rate of twenty dollars per month each and board, and you may rest assured they are working for it."

The extra men were Indians; two were the most engaged at one time, so the party never numbered more than ten men. The other men received somewhat more than the $20 paid to the Indians, while Richard received about $25 a week — but never more than $100 a month. He tried to keep expenses down, even furnishing three pack mules of his own and horses for all of the men.

"Tell me how much you want to put into this work," he wrote Talbot, "as I will work accordingly. I mean this, that I want to get you the largest collection possible in the time allowed, with the money you have for that purpose."

Talbot Hyde made no complaint, but he was so slow in forwarding checks that Richard had to remind him several times that his men were working without pay, and the expedition was badly in debt. Eventually the money arrived, but not before Richard was driven into quiet frenzy over how he could keep going and settle bills for supplies bought "on expectation."

Thus he wrote to Talbot on February 4: "The check reached the ranch, but did not get here [Bluff City]. I wish, if you can, you would send to the First National Bank at Durango, one hundred and fifty dollars ($150), to be placed to my credit; the balance, if you can, place to the credit of B. K. Wetherill." This might indicate that Richard had to borrow from his father to meet his payments. And on March 20, again from Bluff: "I have now laid the most of the outfit off until I hear from you."

Bluff was booming with gold fever, Richard informed Hyde. While his men were waiting to be paid they staked claims along the San Juan and tried their luck at placer mining. A hard day's work, but no harder than working in the caves of Grand Gulch, produced gold dust worth five dollars over the counter, or five times as much as they had been earning. Catching some of

ANASAZI   73

the fever himself, Richard suggested to Hyde that, "If you care for a claim I will locate one for you and do the assessment work."

Hyde finally sent a check and Richard wrote on March 28: "Yours rec'd. As I wrote you before I had laid the boys off until I heard about funds. I am very glad to have received the money just now as I was getting in desperate circumstances. I would not have felt it so much but we lost $2500 last fall [at the ranch], or rather didn't make it on account of early frost — but I don't grieve over it.

"I am in the field where I like to work and have no thought for anything else, but it is necessary to have supplies . . . I now have paid up so my credit is restored. I had over $300 to pay off here in Bluff."

A rancher digging a well in Montezuma Valley, not far from Mancos, stumbled accidentally upon a cache of human bones. It happened just in time to provide an unexpected climax to the first season of the Hyde Exploring Expedition. The rancher, named Snider, started digging in what appeared to be a natural depression in the ground. The hole reached a depth of two feet when Snider's shovel churned up a human bone. Continuing to dig, Snider went through another two feet of earth and more bones, and then realized he had struck a mass burial pit. He stopped work on the well and wrote to Richard, whom he knew to be in or near Bluff, describing what he had found. Richard replied he would be passing that way within a short time and asked Snider to wait for his arrival.

The ranch was southwest of Aztec Springs near the Yucca House group of ruins. When Richard and his brothers, Al and John, reached Snider's place about the first of April they saw at once that the "natural" depression chosen for the well actually indicated one of the kivas associated with the ancient pueblo.

By tracing the kiva's perimeter, Richard and his brothers marked off a circle twenty-one feet in diameter and began digging within that area. Nothing but a few pottery sherds was found until they reached a depth of eight feet. At that level the top of the kiva's buried masonry wall was encountered. From this point on the Wetherills proceeded even more cautiously, so that their shovels would not damage the thin layers of adobe plaster still adhering to the inner wall surfaces.

Seven thicknesses of the plaster were peeled off, one at a time, revealing four layers that had been painted in different colors: the first color an earth red, the second white, the third green, and the fourth red ochre. In following the wall's contour they uncovered eight masonry pilasters spaced at equal intervals and resting on a masonry bench encircling the room a few feet above floor level. Architecturally, it was similar to the kivas they had examined before in the cliff dwellings of Mesa Verde. Otherwise, however, it was unusual for being one of the first painted kivas found anywhere in the San Juan region. All of these details Richard described in a letter two months later to Moorehead of The *Archaeologist*, adding that,

"At a depth of ten feet we came upon a mass of skeletons that had originally been thrown into the room in a haphazard manner. All of the skulls saved had each a hole in it such as would be made by striking it with a stone axe. Of twenty-five specimens examined, all proved to be of the cliff dwellers' type, having the perpendicular flattening at the back of the head.

"The skulls from the regular burial mounds in the vicinity have the oblique flattening upon the back of the head, showing there must be some distinction made between the races.

"We infer from this discovery that these skeletons must have been prisoners or captives killed and thrown in this estufa."

The four months of Richard's work for the Hyde brothers would not begin to replace the losses the Alamo Ranch had suffered the previous fall from frost damage. And yet he had had the opportunity to be "in the field where I like to work and have no thought for anything else." Besides, he had discovered the Basket Makers, and added immeasurably to the knowledge which would be useful to him in the next few years.

FIVE

THROUGH the spring and early summer, 1894, Richard again gave most of his attention to the ranch. In May a letter came from Talbot Hyde saying that he and Fred would like to see the country where Richard had worked the previous winter. Richard invited them to come out, and to make the Alamo Ranch their home during their stay. He promised them they might also enjoy some hunting in the mountains, and recommended the trout to be found in the mountain streams.

When the Hydes arrived two weeks later they were prepared to spend the rest of June at the ranch. At the end of the month Richard began outfitting for their trip, and on the fifth of July, with Clayton accompanying them, they started for Bluff City and Grand Gulch. A number of years afterward Talbot recalled their experiences, by a slip of memory referring to the time as the summer of 1895.

"By doing a bit of excavating ourselves," he said, "we learned something of the great difficulties encountered upon turning over the cave floors often covered with a layer of bat droppings [or, more likely, turkey droppings] and an impalpable dust, the deposit of centuries. We took many photographs.

"After resting at Bluff City we followed up Cottonwood Canon and then heading the canons and washes to the West, struck out directly for Elk Mt. and made the Bear's Ears . . . It took all of one day to break trail up Elk Mt. and we made camp near an excellent spring for four days [where] our burros mixed with a bunch of wild colts and were not so easily found . . . After visiting the caves and cliff houses we returned to Bluff and retraced our way to Mancos."

When he and Fred returned East, Talbot added, they took with them the negatives, maps and all of the records Richard had made during the winter expedition. Richard's field notes survive, but the maps and negatives have not been found. This material may have been turned over a few years afterward to George H. Pepper, then on the staff of the American Museum of Natural History, since the only early photographic prints of the 1893-94 expedition known to exist are in the collection now owned by Pepper's daughter, Mrs. James Cameron. No data whatever relating to the Hyde Exploring Expedition have been preserved or can be accounted for by the widows of the Hyde brothers.

Once more at Mancos, at the end of July, they found that Julia and Bert Cowing had arrived at the Alamo Ranch for the summer, and other guests were expected. Meanwhile, there was a little flurry of excitement when Clayton was kicked in the chest and sent sprawling by a burro that resented Clate's efforts to throw a pack over his back. The wind was knocked out of him, but no bones were broken. A short time afterward Richard was kicked in the face while breaking a red-eyed bronco. After making sure his nose was still where it ought to be, bent but not shattered, Richard went on bronco-breaking with nothing worse than a split lip.

A distinguished gentleman from Ohio was among the visitors at the ranch that summer. Judge Charles Candee Baldwin of Cleveland, a presiding judge of the Ohio Circuit Court, had first come to Mancos the year before and now was back with his brother to enjoy the Wetherills' hospitality. Judge Baldwin had a lively interest in the cliff dwellings and contributed a small amount of money to add to funds supplied by Talbot Hyde and a man named McNeely for the excavation of the painted kiva on Snider's ranch in Montezuma Valley. Although Judge Baldwin was considerably older than Richard, a firm friendship developed between them, Bert Cowing once hearing the judge speak of Richard as "a king among men."

Talbot and Fred Hyde also were at the ranch at this time and may have been members of the party when Richard took Judge Baldwin and his brother onto the mesa to explore and photograph the cliff dwellings. In any case, the Hydes left shortly afterward, on August 8, for New York. They were impressed with the Grand Gulch collection and let Richard understand that his first expedition was merely the beginning of their association. Nevertheless, when they left Mancos no definite plan had been agreed upon for the coming winter, when Richard could best afford to be away.

By the middle of October Richard realized that the ranch was in serious trouble. He wrote to Talbot Hyde on the sixteenth, explaining how the summer's dry spell had ruined nearly all of the crops, leaving only enough wheat for feed, flour for the family's needs, and seed for the next year. He added that the misfortune "has put me in such shape that I will have to borrow $6,000.00."

Would Talbot help him, providing Richard offered sufficient security? "If I get it for 6% per annum, giving 640 acres of land and improvements as security, we can make it in one good crop but I would require 5 yrs. time to pay it easily. I have not yet made an application for a loan [but] if you have any funds to invest in that way you may do so as you know it is Gilt Edge security . . ." And from this Richard went on to a discussion of other matters so as not to seem to press too hard in his appeal.

Hyde replied that he did not have the money to spare. It is uncertain just how or from whom Richard finally succeeded in raising the loan. But from this point on the Alamo Ranch was operated under crushing debt and for the next four years, until he turned his back on Mancos and left the ranch in Al Wetherill's care, Richard was oppressed with constant worry.

Once the discouraging fall harvest was in and all other duties attended to, Richard's thoughts dwelt on that winter, and finding another collection for the Hydes. He held his own counsel, not writing again to Talbot Hyde until the following June, but a week or so after Hyde had declined his appeal, he began outfitting for another trip. This time he had no positive objective but to explore new country.

Unfortunately — since this winter found him doing some of his most interesting work — Richard either made no field notes or they have been lost. Only an incomplete, undetailed record exists to show that in November he was looking for ruins in New Mexico, perhaps along the Animas and the San Juan. It is uncertain whether he was alone or had companions with him. But in December he was heading north again into Utah where he saw the year out in a lonely wilderness of mesas and deep canyons. Apparently he found nothing there to hold him long, for once again he turned south.

One chilly day in January, 1895, Richard, now accompanied by his brother Al and Charlie Mason, crossed the San Juan below Bluff City and entered the slag-heap wasteland which offers the only northern approach to the unearthly beauty of Monument Valley. For the next four months the men lived on whatever game they could shoot, or food they could obtain in barter at some isolated hogan. From here south to Marsh Pass and beyond there were no trading posts, no white men. They met only drifting bands of sheep and occasionally a few Indians. It was country trackless and uncharted, filled with danger for three white men traveling with desirable horses and burros.

IN the deepest recesses of the Tsegi's three main canyons, noisy jays lord it over the smaller birds, their scolding cries shattering an otherwise profound silence. During the warmer time of year there is the added hum of honeybees thrusting into the purple blossoms of the beeplant which grows here in profusion, or hovering in the patches of wild roses among the scrub oak against the canyon walls; at night the thin, steady trill of crickets threads the stillness. But in March the only sounds are those of the jays and the rustle of running water.

Small springs bubble up a cold, clear water at the head of each canyon. The streams thus formed gradually widen and become cloudy with sand as they flow on a twisting, shallow course downward to where the three forks of the Tsegi open into one broad canyon six hundred feet deep. Here the streams converge into one, becoming Laguna Creek which flows eastward along the floor of the sandstone chasm to the mouth of the Tsegi at Marsh Pass. At this point the stream abruptly turns off in a northerly direction until it eventually joins with the Chinle Wash.

Marsh Pass is a narrow gap, about half a mile long, between Mesa de la Vaca on the east, and a nameless, tilting shelf of pink sandstone on the west which rises to a high tableland thickly carpeted with dark green juniper and piñon. Skeleton Mesa and Agathla Needle lie roughly to the north, the wide Chinle Valley off to the east. Below the pass, opening gently, is the Kletha Valley, descending steadily for some fifty miles to Moencopi Wash and the westernmost of the Hopi villages. Several miles north and south of Marsh Pass there are found, high on the western side, a number of small cliff dwellings and, scattered out below them against the edge of the valley, the ruins of small pueblos abandoned by the Anasazi more than six hundred years ago. Since then the Navajos have claimed the valley as exclusively theirs. This makes the Navajos practically newcomers, because the first known inhabitants, the Basket Makers, moved in nearly two thousand years ago. From that time forward the region has been occupied more or less continuously.

It was here that Richard, Al Wetherill and Charlie Mason worked during the first two months of 1895, probing through the high caves and the pueblo sites until at last they turned up Laguna Creek and followed its winding course into Tsegi Canyon. Their progress was leisurely, as they halted often to work in small surface ruins which were scarcely more than mounds of sand and rubble littered with thousands of fragments of pottery. When they came finally to the great opening of the Tsegi where the canyons spread out like fingers from the palm of a hand, Richard chose to turn off to the right and follow the center branch to its head. Had they continued straight onward another mile or two into one of the smaller gorges, they would have discovered the immense cave and the shadowy ruin of Betatakin — which was found fourteen years later by John Wetherill and Byron Cummings.

Their choice made, they proceeded first across a broad sandflat and then between the deep, zig-zagging banks of an arroyo, riding single file and crossing and re-crossing the shallow stream. Above the arroyo, perpendicular cliffs of red sandstone closed in on them from either side, blotting out all but a band of March sky.

They had not traveled far when the sides of the arroyo widened out and then dropped off into a narrow little valley perhaps several hundred yards long. In the center of this was a pond fed at the north end by a waterfall spilling over a stone ledge from a higher level of the canyon floor. This was the first of five such waterfalls and "lagoons" Richard later said he and the others found loosely linked over a distance of not more than eight miles. On one or more of the lagoons they saw wild ducks floating among the reeds and tall grasses.

Following the stream bed on a constantly rising, twisting course, the men were conscious always of the red cliffs towering to the left and right of them but opening now to a wider stretch of sky. They emerged finally onto a high, grassy plain, perhaps a quarter of a mile across and sheltered along its borders by clumps of pin oak. A few giant Douglas firs grew in niches of the cliffs above the canyon floor.

Up to this point they had failed to detect the faintest trace of human life, but now, just around a shallow bend of the west cliff and one hundred feet above them, was the high arc of a cave — not deep but long and overhanging the rubble of a tumbled Anasazi dwelling. The cave's arch was as lofty as a cathedral spire, the prehistoric dwelling it shelters a humble abode.

Neephi, his lead mule, was a veteran of many hundreds of bone-sore miles. During periods of recuperation at the Alamo Ranch, Richard described Neephi as "fat and rolicky." Now, at some camp site between the mouth and head of the canyon the men were following, and while they were asleep, Neephi broke his hobbles and ambled off. A common enough occurrence, but one Richard found sufficiently interesting to mention in a letter to Talbot Hyde. He tracked the mule and found him. In such a place, in such circumstances, it is probable the broken hobble was responsible for Richard's finding something of greater interest.

Richard first glimpsed Kiet Siel when he rounded a turn in the canyon.

It came into view suddenly, without warning hint of potsherds scattered on the canyon floor. Above him on the left, buried deeply and airily supported on the curved lip of rock forty feet above the tops of the thick pin oak, the mammoth, elliptical cave stared back at Richard like a giant eye fixed immovably and low in a forehead of red sandstone cliff. Reaching across its deep shadows and from corner to corner was the largest cliff dwelling in Arizona: three long tiers of rooms and fallen walls, pale gold in the morning light.

Dense undergrowth of oak fanned out under the lower rim of the cave, obstructing approach. Once through this the cliff dwelling loomed above, nearly a half of it built upon a deeply undercut and vaulting span of tawny rock. Otherwise, across the cave's opening, the first tier of rooms could be reached by scrambling up a bare stretch of sandstone tilted at an angle of forty-five degrees. A massive retaining wall, now badly broken and fallen outward, extended from one side of the cave to the other; at approximately the center was a wide opening bridged by a ponderous log more than two feet thick at its butt end and thirty-five feet long.

How such a log had been raised to such a height puzzled Richard and his companions as they climbed to it by using toeholds which had been chipped in the stone by the Anasazi centuries before. On reaching the great tree trunk its purpose for being there, at least, became clear. Grooves worn or burned over the log's upper surface indicated where long ropes of yucca fiber once bit into the wood as the Anasazi hauled up heavy loads of stone and adobe for building their village.

In common with all Cliff Dwellers, the people of Kiet Siel had tossed their refuse over the lip of the cave, making a sizable mound of debris forty feet below and on the one avenue of approach. Over this mound Richard and Al and Charlie Mason crunched through a mass of broken potsherds, some of it suggestive of the black-on-white pottery they had found at Mesa Verde.

Most of it, though, later was to be known as polychrome — the predominant colors being orange, red, white and a black that sometimes fired blue — or the gray corrugated ware of cooking pots, liberally blackened with soot. Mixed in with the sherds were layers of gray ash, chunks of charcoal, worn-out sandals, flakes and discarded knobs of stone used in making knives, axes, hammers and weapons, also fragments of animal bones, corncobs and squash rinds — this whole conglomerate mass indicating not only a good deal about the eating and living habits of Kiet Siel, but the fact this village had supported a large population over a long number of years.

The terraces and small courts of the cliff dwelling itself also were littered with fragments of shattered pots, but it was not Richard who gave the village its name. Kiet Siel in Navajo means broken pottery; he called it Long House. As he did in some of the other major ruins he discovered, Richard scrawled his initial and surname with a fire-blackened stick — "R. Wetherill" — at the far central rear of the cave. Under it he wrote the date, but this has been crossed out. Near the place where he left his name, some prehistoric artist had painted three turkeys on the cave ceiling. The birds were perched gravely, with inscrutable symbolism, on the heads of three men. The turkeys were painted in profile, their human perches in full-face view. Had Richard looked for subtleties of form and detail he would have found none. The faces of the three male figures were featureless blanks. Their flat arms dangled straight down from broad square shoulders, their feet were spread wide and planted firmly.

Close by but cheerfully unconcerned with the turkeys, *Kokopelli*, the hump-backed flute player of renowned sexual prowess, was outlined in white paint. His figure is found on cliff and cave walls through the whole San Juan region. For once the old boy was relaxing instead of playing on his pipe in his usually tense squatting posture — and obviously enjoying it. Stretched out indolently on his back, his flute raised to his mouth, this *Kokopelli* had one leg crossed casually over the other knee. For just this once he didn't seem to care if the girls were listening or not.

Slightly smaller than Cliff Palace, Kiet Siel possesses qualities that, in the eyes of some, lend it greater charm and interest. The imagination of its builders, for one, who conceived the daring plan of constructing the walls of a teeming village partly on the fragile crown of an arcing span of stone, partly on a buttressed and filled-in tilt of rock. Built in a remote place that remains relatively inaccessible, Kiet Siel occupies the head of a canyon of running water and lush greens below great walls of perpendicular, deep red sandstone. Finally, it holds a place of preeminent interest because it was the focal center of an Anasazi culture that co-existed with and yet differed from such other major centers of the time as Chaco Canyon and Mesa Verde.

In the three or four days Richard and his companions worked in Kiet Siel on this trip, Richard counted 115 rooms — missing, perhaps, as many as 40 or 45 buried beyond immediate reach under fallen debris. Six of the rooms he found were circular kivas, somewhat similar to the kivas at Mesa Verde, but lacking masonry pilasters for supporting the roof as well as the stone bench encircling the circumference of the chamber.

Elsewhere in Kiet Siel, however, he found a number of small rooms, roughly rectangular, which were entered through a doorway and might be considered ordinary living rooms except that they contained the ceremonial features of a kiva fireplace and stone air deflector between fireplace and doorway.

Had Richard then had the benefit of greater experience this circumstance would have appeared more significant, for in just such peculiarities archaeologists later traced important tribal and regional influences. At Betatakin, in 1909, John Wetherill and Byron Cummings found no circular kivas at all, but rectangular surface rooms with kiva features — an architectural deviation that, among other things, indicates the people of Kiet Siel were of different stock and perhaps spoke a different language.

Tree-ring dating, a nearly-exact science introduced after Richard's death, shows that Kiet Siel was occupied, approximately, from 1116 to 1286 A.D. There was little or no evidence of the mayhem and massacre Richard found in some of the caves of Cottonwood Wash and Grand Gulch, and even at Snider's Well. Many of the rooms in Kiet Siel that he and Al and Charlie Mason opened up had been deliberately sealed by the departing inhabitants. Unbroken pots and other utensils too heavy to carry away had been left behind; in one room they found a great pile of corncobs and broken melon or squash rinds — sure sign of food edible enough when the departing people cached it. An invasion of the region by raiding enemies cannot be ruled out, but most evidence pointed to an orderly, peaceful, planned withdrawal. Abandonment of the cliff village may have been caused by the Southwest's most severe drouth of prehistoric times, between 1276 and 1299.

Following his return to Mancos, Richard wrote to Hyde on June 3, 1895, telling how he had spent the early part of the past winter in New Mexico and Utah, "and all this year in Arizona at the head of the Rio de Chelle." The latter was Richard's name for Chinle Wash, and at this time he made the mistake of believing that the Chinle's main source was Laguna Creek, heading in Tsegi Canyon, instead of in Canyon de Chelly. Thinking, then, of the Tsegi, he added: "I have just returned from there [and] met with good success." Neglecting to point out he had discovered the second largest cliff dwelling in the Southwest, he went on to say:

"We dug from one burial mound 400 pieces of pottery — very fine. At least one-half of it is red [polychrome] — this is by all odds the finest collection of pottery that I have seen. . . .

"That is the best place to get a collection I ever saw — it requires work but the results are very satisfactory.

ANASAZI

"The best cliff houses that I have seen are in that country and not one has been dug into — one house in particular [Kiet Siel] containing 115 rooms. 75 are as perfect as though just left. The rooms are clean — roofs all one — altogether it is the place to study the subject."

The following January, when it appeared that the Hyde brothers would have Richard lead an expedition to the Marsh Pass area in the coming summer, Richard compared the relative difficulties and cost of work in Canyon de Chelly and Tsegi Canyon, advising that from the standpoint of expense, the Tsegi would prove more costly but its cliff dwellings would yield better relics for a collection. His own preference for working once more in Kiet Siel and its neighboring ruins is expressed in a letter to Talbot Hyde dated January 6, 1896:

"I think I wrote you of the ruins of Cañon Du Cheusne [de Chelly]. If not, the cost of getting to and from them will be slightly less than going to the head of the Chelle — which is the best place I have ever yet found to find Relics . . . at least 20 articles will be found per day per man — for instance we dug in 4 days last year what it took 20 days to get out.

"It is 90 miles to Bluff [from Mancos] and 80 miles from there to the forks of the Chelle [in Tsegi Canyon]. This is a hot country as you well know but we can work easily and late. Sufficient water can be had as the springs are numerous but none of them run off very far from their source on account of being swallowed up in the sand — It is safe to say it will take 8 or 9 days to travel to this vicinity."

This letter contains one of the few references to Canyon de Chelly which has been found in Richard's correspondence. This would indicate he had only slight knowledge of the region. When he visited Canyon de Chelly is uncertain; probably it was in the spring of 1893 when he and his brothers Al and John traveled as far as the Hopi Mesas to gather objects of modern Indian life for the Colorado exhibit at the Chicago World's Fair.

What became of the collection made in Tsegi Canyon in the spring of 1895? It is the one major collection Richard made which has not been traced.

SIX

Benjamin WETHERILL, sixty-three years old — ailing, but unwilling to admit it, heard stories coming from the San Juan and succumbed to gold fever. In January, 1895, he left the Alamo Ranch for Bluff City, once more hoping to make his fortune. Richard had disappeared somewhere in the Marsh Pass region, along with Al and Charlie Mason and so was of no help to him. Win was at school in Denver. Old Benjamin was joined in this newest adventure by John and Clayton. Together they worked their claim during the rest of the winter, but with little success.

For a time they each managed to take out an ounce or so of gold a day, but stormy weather and floods on the San Juan constantly interrupted their work. Nevertheless they stuck it out until approaching spring weather drove them back to the ranch.

Muldoon Kelley observed in his paper on May 3: "B. K. Wetherill is home from the San Juan placer fields after an absence of some months. He did not bring in a wagon load of gold."

The spring planting was well in the ground when Richard and his companions rode into Mancos, ragged and weary. Their shaggy hair and beards and the condition of their clothes told eloquently of the many weeks they had been gone, the hardships they had endured.

Neephi and the four or five other mules that had become gaunt under travel rations and heavy loads of pottery brought back from Tsegi Canyon, were turned out to fatten and rollick in a clover patch. Richard and Al shaved off their beards. Their mother mended the rents in their clothing. The collection of relics, remarkably unharmed, was stored in the little museum. Richard again turned his hand to ranch duties, and to guiding the increasing number of tourists to the ruins of Mesa Verde.

Among scores of visitors this season were Miss Alice Eastwood of San Francisco, and Dr. T. Mitchell Prudden of New York. Both came in July, drawn to Mancos for quite different reasons, and each found a warm welcome at the Wetherill home.

ANASAZI

Miss Eastwood then was thirty-seven and already started on a career that made her internationally known as a botanist. She had joined the staff of the California Academy of Sciences in 1892. Her work took her all over the world, collecting thousands of plant specimens for her herbarium, and she came to Mancos with this purpose in mind. Richard, however, took her up on the mesa to see Cliff Palace before she left, a week afterward, on a ten days' trip with Al Wetherill to collect desert plants in southeastern Utah. It was the first of several visits Miss Eastwood made to the Alamo Ranch. Each time she was most particularly welcomed by Al, who shared a sincere interest in her work.

Dr. Prudden was on one of the first of his summer trips to the Southwest, seeking relief on the windswept, sunny plateaus from his regular duties in the laboratory and lecture rooms at Columbia University. His arrival was the beginning of a long, close friendship between the scholarly pathologist and the Wetherill brothers. During these years, and usually with Clayton as his guide, Dr. Prudden explored nearly every corner of the 120,000 square miles of Indian country and came to know it as intimately as he knew Manhattan Island or his native New Haven.

A tall, lean, sad-faced man with a long, thin head and a prominent nose above a drooping moustache, he had about him an air that almost at once commanded the confidence of frontiersmen in this region, as well as of the Navajos who usually were slow in showing approval of any white man. A bachelor, he was a man with a quiet voice and a gentle manner.

As his knowledge of the region increased, his interest in the modern Indians and their ancient forbears deepened proportionately. Of formal training in ethnology or archaeology, he had none, but his grasp of these sciences was remarkable for a man so dedicated to an unrelated science: medicine. His enormous vitality found an outlet, first, in solving some of the mysteries of the Anasazi, and then in writing about his trips and discoveries. From his pen — and he wrote with a pen — came a number of semi-technical articles, notably "Prehistoric Ruins of the San Juan Watershed" which was published in The *American Anthropologist* in 1903 and belongs with the Hayden Surveys as one of the first reports of this kind in print.

In a lighter vein, for laymen, he wrote other articles and one book of lasting, popular interest. For *Harper's Monthly* he wrote "A Summer Among the Cliff Dwellings," "Under the Spell of the Grand Canyon," and "An Elder Brother to the Cliff Dwellers." His book, *On the Great American*

Plateau, which appeared in 1904, synthesizes everything he knew and felt about the Southwest.

Dr. Prudden obtained all available maps of this wild, largely unknown region and when he found that each was inaccurate or lacking in the detail he wanted, he made a map of his own. Published with his report on the San Juan ruins, this map shows the course of rivers and their tributaries, mountain ranges and the more important trading posts and towns of the Four Corners region, as well as the approximate location of most of the ancient ruins throughout the area. Despite certain inaccuracies it was the best archaeological map of the country up to that time.

After his first visit to the Alamo Ranch, Dr. Prudden arranged in advance for Clayton or one of the other brothers to meet him — at Albuquerque, Gallup or Durango, depending upon the plan of exploration for that season. The brother who met him, and usually it was Clate, always had a fully outfitted pack train waiting so no time would be lost in getting started.

Aside from his contribution to the public's knowledge of the region, Dr. Prudden's most important achievement in this field was his special research into the little-known, small unit-type pueblo which flourished throughout the San Juan Basin about a thousand years ago. In simplest terms, the unit-type pueblo which he named was a communal dwelling, consisting usually of one story and from three or four rooms to fifteen or slightly more. In the smallest of these dwellings the rooms were laid out in a single straight row; as they became larger, wings were added at both ends to form an open rectangle. In each case the pueblo almost invariably faced south, overlooking one or more detached kivas and, generally farther to the south, a communal refuse mound.

Dr. Prudden largely confined his research to surface exploration until 1913, when he partially excavated four unit-type structures in and near Montezuma Valley. Two years later, before illness forced him to remain in the East, he excavated at three more sites in the same general vicinity. Although his digging uncovered not more than twenty-five rooms and four kivas, his work is significant because it was the first to focus attention upon the small, transitional period of Pueblo life and architecture rather than on the more spectacular dwellings of the so-called Classic period.

On his first visit to the Alamo Ranch, Dr. Prudden was a guest of the Wetherills for most of July, 1895. In August it was proposed that a party be made up to go to the Snake Dance being given that year at Walpi. The group included Richard and Clayton, Dr. Prudden, young Bert Cowing — who was spending his last summer at the ranch, and Muldoon Kelley.

Bert Cowing kept a journal of the party's experiences, a lively and observant account written for the benefit of his family. Muldoon Kelley, presumably the one qualified writer of the expedition, glumly remained silent and did not send his paper one line.

Richard thought it advisable, time being short, to take a guide who would know where they could find water and good grass. A Navajo of his acquaintance named Jim Joe, or Te-hah-ah-ne, who lived near Bluff City, seemed to meet his requirements and was engaged.

Following a branch of the Chinle, which Bert Cowing understood Richard to pronounce "Chilla-lee," they spent their fourth night in the vicinity of Marsh Pass. Then, favored with good, hot weather and none of August's cloudbursts, they descended through Kletha Valley to the sandy plateau overlooking Moencopi Wash. From there Jim Joe took them eastward across a high, open desert broken here and there by wide, deep canyons, where the only trees were patches of cedar dotting the highest mesas. They crossed Dinnebito Wash, dry as a whitened bone, and after some two hundred miles and six days on horseback, came to the wide valley below Walpi. Here they parted company with their guide.

The bare rock mesa was now between them and the afternoon sun, rising darkly from the desert like the hull of some gigantic sailing vessel which had foundered in a dun-colored sea. Even to Richard's experienced gaze, the rows of houses lining the summit to the very edge of the cliff were indistinguishably a part of the color and substance of their remote setting. The mesa's rocky cap blended so perfectly with the low, uneven outline of the stone and adobe village that the deceptive mingling of the two was nearly perfect; mesa and crowning pueblo knit into one. Gradually, as they adjusted their eyes to the heights above, they could make out three distinct villages: Walpi on the prow of the mesa, then, connected with Walpi by a narrow gap, the pueblos of Sichomovi and Hano.

A faint throb of a drum was the only sound that came to them. Their first impression was that the entire mesa was deserted by all except the unseen drummer. But as they rode up the steep switchback trail leading to the summit, they caught sight of burros corraled in the rocks, naked Hopi children skittering in play among the ledges, and blanketed women moving intently along a web of foot-trails.

When they reached the top and turned into the narrow streets of Hano, Richard and his companions were met by the neutral gaze of Hopi eyes watching from doorways, windows and rooftops. As they proceeded on to the plaza, however, a small band of children and dogs formed a procession in their wake. They sensed there was nothing unfriendly in this reception and they were not regarded as unwelcome intruders.

Richard and Clayton left the others in the plaza's baking sunlight and buzz of flies to inquire for a place to stay. A wizened old grandfather paused in his unloading of juniper branches from a burro to hear their questions. After a short palaver that was a mixture of gestures and a few words in Navajo and English, the old fellow limped off with a motion for them to follow. He led them back the way they had come to a house close to the head of the trail. His knock brought an immediate response and he left them there, with a short, middle-aged man and his plump, smiling wife.

From the dim interior the wide-eyed bashful gaze of several small children was fastened upon them. And while their host was giving smiling assurances of welcome, Richard could see that the family's quarters, already crowded, hardly could take five more bedrolls. Bert Cowing explained how the problem was solved:

"Our house was right on the top of the trail. It was very nice and clean, considering, but nevertheless we preferred to sleep outdoors [on the rooftop]. During several nights the wind blew pretty hard and blew considerable sand into our beds . . . We stayed at the house of a certain Tom Polyke [probably Polaka, the son of Hano's chief] who is known as one of the most progressive of the Moquis. He is one who favors schools and such modern institutions. Our landlady makes the best pottery in town or in fact in any of the towns so far as I know."

This description would fit the famous potter of the Tewan village of Hano, Nampeyo, who revived this degenerating art after she saw a number of superb prehistoric pots excavated from nearby Sikyatki and other ruins, and used these as models. Besides setting other Hopi women to following her example, Nampeyo made bowls and jars which frequently found their way into museums.

On the morning after their arrival, Richard and the others explored the three villages. In the narrow passageways between the houses of Walpi they heard occasionally the chants that came from the subterranean chambers of the Snake and Antelope clans. The Hopi villagers moved quietly about their affairs as though oblivious to the ceremony which soon now, on the ninth day, would reach its culmination in the narrow open plaza. Every so often a blanketed Snake clan priest would emerge from his kiva and hurry off on some mysterious errand, holding one corner of his blanket before his bowed head. Almost instinctively the people of Walpi sensed his approach and turned their backs or averted their eyes so they would not observe his passage.

During the next three days of waiting the hours passed quickly for everyone except Muldoon Kelley, whose interest flagged after the first tour of the villages. Each evening they returned to the house of Tom Polyke carrying the few things they had purchased or bartered for that day.

Under a tarpaulin against a sheltering wall they amassed their growing collection: pieces of pottery chosen carefully in the three villages, but most of them from the home where they stayed; katchinas, carved from cottonwood and brightly painted, representing the Hopi deities said to dwell among the peaks of the distant San Francisco Mountains. They collected belts woven beautifully in designs of green, red and black and reminiscent of the fragments of weaving Richard had found in the caves of Butler Wash and Grand Gulch. A finely-loomed blanket or two was bought, and a woman's dress of black-dyed wool, designed to be worn with the left shoulder bare, and caught at the waist with one of the colorful belts.

In the afternoon and evening before the final, public ceremony, the villages of Walpi, Sichomovi and Hano became crowded with new arrivals: Hopi families from the mesas to the west and from as far as Moencopi; groups of Navajo who silently, proudly kept apart by themselves; and a scattering of white people, about seventy in all — traders, Government men and ranchers for the most part, but also a few tourists who had braved the trip by carriage or wagon from the nearest railroad town, Winslow.

Contrasted with the bright velvets of the heavily jewelled Navajo women and colored head-shawls of the Hopi, the dress of the four or five white women was conspicuous by its very conservatism: prim shirtwaists stiffly starched and high-collared, high-buttoned shoes and long skirts which swept the ground.

Further emphasizing their own tribal apartness from their bareheaded Navajo sisters, the white women sought protection from the hot sun under big black umbrellas. In this high, windswept setting the umbrellas bobbed about, drab accents in a scene otherwise drenched with color.

When the sunlight faded from the rooftop of Top Polyke's house, Richard and his companions were among the first to be aware that something strange was happening. Sounds coming from the mesa trail indicated the villages were about to be attacked in force. A curious crowd gathered.

Out of the darkness emerged the forms of a weird procession. A milling cluster of Hopi men, staggering under their burden, were toiling up the steep path bearing on their shoulders a long ladder taken from some adobe dwelling. Riding the center of the ladder, maintaining an uncertain balance, was the figure of a very large person who was interspersing alarmed imprecations with sharp commands. Someone in the waiting crowd seized a torch and in its flaring light the caravan struggling upward sprang into bright relief against the darkness.

"Easy now — careful!" cried the figure on the ladder. "Don't let me fall, damn it all!"

The angry voice was a woman's. Fascinated by the spectacle, Bert Cowing wrote in his journal that all of the commotion "was found to be nothing more nor less than a certain Mrs. Low, who weighed well on toward 250 pounds and was short and square, being carried up by about sixteen natives." She was, it turned out, a rather well-known newspaper writer.

Standing off at one side of the rooftop, watching, Richard smiled and afterward remembered Mrs. Low. There was logic in the manner of her conveyance that appealed strongly to him. As he described the scene later, only his eyes betrayed amusement:

"It was inevitable because she was so heavy — there just wasn't any other way for her to get up that steep trail."

On one of these three days on First Mesa, Richard met Dr. Jesse Walter Fewkes of the Smithsonian, who the year before had published a report on the Snake Dance ceremonies at Walpi in 1891 and 1893. Bert Cowing only recorded that the two men met, making no note of their conversation. Evidently the encounter made no particular impression upon Richard, as it might have had he known how Fewkes would later refer to his work at Mesa Verde. Instead, his attention centered on the color and life of the pueblo and the ritual upon which the Hopi placed so much dependence for rain.

Like every Indian pueblo, Walpi had its share of dogs. These animals had one remarkable trait, or at least so it seemed to Richard. If they were below and wanted to go up, the ladders by which the Hopi climbed to the second and third terraces of their village were no barrier: the dogs negotiated them — up or down — in one mad scramble.

Another aspect of the mesa dwellers, which Bert Cowing observed, was a custom the Hopi sometimes used to punish burros that wandered astray.

"A great number of the burros," he wrote, "had their ears clipped or entirely cut off. We learned that there was a law that a burro found in a cornfield was entitled to have its ear clipped for the first offence, the other one clipped for the second, and the first one entirely cut off for the third, etc. When the ears give out, they hunt up the owner and make him pay for damages. I guess it doesn't hurt the burros much, and it probably lessens their value, so the owner is punished as well as the burros."

Richard's keenest interest was in discovering similarities between the arts and crafts of these Hopi and those left behind by the Anasazi of Mesa Verde and Tsegi Canyon. As stonemasons the Hopi were definitely less skilled, or more careless; as potters, most of them were inferior; but as weavers and farmers they were probably more than the equal of the old people of Kiet Siel. However, more important, Richard remarked to Clayton and Dr. Prudden, was the astonishingly close relationship in crafts and customs between these modern mesa dwellers and the ancient Cliff Dwellers.

If he saw any of the ceremonies in the kivas of the Snake and Antelope clans, it escaped Bert Cowing's notice. As to his reaction in the tiny plaza when the dancers gathered about Snake Rock and eighty reptiles — many of them rattlesnakes — were released, Cowing has since written: "I do not recall any special comment by him, but am sure that we all expressed in one way or another how much we felt the serious spirit of the Hopis about the ceremony, in contrast to the rather fantastic effect some of it had upon the whites."

The opening part of the ceremony when the priests of the two clans faced each other before the *kisi* or shelter of green branches where the snakes were hidden, moved Richard and the others quite as much as the succeeding stage when the Snake priests circled the plaza in shuffling dance step, the twisting reptiles held between their lips, the tails of the larger snakes dragging in the dust.

This part of the ceremony had no lack of drama. But the opening chant of the Snake priests, their bodies daubed with black soot, kilted in buckskin and foxtails and wearing a spread of red-dyed eagle feathers in their loose hair, had an equally powerful effect.

Chanting while they bent forward, swaying with arms interlocked before the *kisi* and the facing line of Antelope priests, the rhythm of their slow movement was nearly hypnotic and in itself somehow snake-like. Nuances of tone in this singular deep-chested Hopi Snake chant, sung only to the dry swish of gourd rattles and stamp of moccasined feet, were deeply moving.

Bert Cowing was fascinated as he watched the brief final phase of the ceremony. Hardly noticed by the throng of onlookers, the chief of the Snake clan had outlined a circle with corn meal at one corner of the plaza opposite the *kisi* where the Antelope priests still stood in line shaking their rattles. As the outline was completed several old women stepped forward and filled in the circle with more of the white meal.

Quite suddenly the dancers moved forward and dropped their snakes into the circle of corn meal, burying it under this writhing, tangled mass. Then each in turn plunged his arms fearlessly into the swarm to clutch as many of the snakes as his hands could grasp.

Snatched thus until the circle was cleared, the snakes were carried on the run out of the plaza, down from the mesa and to the four sacred directions on the desert below. There the snakes were released, it being understood that on their return to the underworld they would tell how well they had been treated by their Hopi sons, and carry with them the prayers for rain and a good harvest.

On this occasion the prayers were not answered immediately, nor for some days afterward. A wind of gale force, whistling across the mesa during the final moments of the ceremony, filled the sky with ominous clouds. But when the sun went down two hours later it was still dry in the streets of Walpi and the evening star glittered brightly. The visitors who had made such a stir with their arrival now moved quietly about their departure. All but a few were gone by the time the moon came up. Walpi faded back on its rock into the night. Richard and his friends remained, stretched out in their bedrolls on Tom Polyke's rooftop. Only a few points of light here and there proved that the villages were not entirely asleep or deserted.

THE PUEBLO OF ORAIBI, on Third Mesa, was the oldest and largest of the seven Hopi villages, with a population of nearly eight hundred. Because the pueblo was built well back from the rim of the mesa it was not convenient for the women of Oraibi to toss all of their refuse and sweepings over the cliff. Instead, they used several refuse dumps just beyond the outer tier of houses — or, failing that, an abandoned room or kiva. For this reason the smells of Oraibi were more pungent, the flies more numerous than in any of the other villages.

Richard's party rode into Oraibi on the day following the Snake Dance and in a short time secured a room, not to sleep in but as a place for storing the packs and saddles. The late August nights were still warm enough to make an open rooftop inviting.

Early the next day Richard and Clayton left with Dr. Prudden, whose work now called him back to New York. They took him to the railroad stop at Winslow, some sixty miles across sandy desert.

Richard and Clayton returned three days later and as a streak of gold rimmed the sky on the morning following, they left the sleeping pueblo with only a drowsy dog or two to notice their departure. Once the wagon road leading down from the mesa was behind them they prodded their horses to a lope, anxious to travel as far as possible in the cool early hours.

At Keam's Canyon they stopped in the shade of a cottonwood beside the store of the well-known English trader who had given his name to the place, Thomas V. Keam, while Richard inquired about hiring a guide. He found a young Navajo who said he knew all of the country well and would, on one condition, take them by way of the Chinle valley to within a short distance of where the Mancos River flows into the San Juan. The Indian gravely said his white man's name was George Washington, and then explained that if he were to go, his wife must be permitted to go with them.

The Navajo woman proved to be an excellent companion, if a silent one during the long ride. A slender girl with a flashing white smile, she gave no sign of tiring and, in fact, sometimes set a pace herself that had Muldoon Kelley muttering through clenched teeth. In her attitude toward her husband, and his toward her, there was something that puzzled Richard and then made him smile because these two showed none of the reserve Navajo couples usually assume among strangers. Also noticing this, Bert Cowing wrote that the pair "were very loving . . . I mean they acted more like a newly married couple than would be expected at that stage of the proceedings. He handed her onto her horse every time in the politest possible manner."

Toward evening of the second day they were in close range of the Carriso Mountains and a trading post in the foothills, when the Navajo said the hogan of his father was only a short distance off. He asked them to go there with him and stop for the night. Richard and the others readily agreed, Muldoon Kelley expressing particular pleasure at the idea of parting from his saddle. When they rode up to the hogan George Washington and his wife were greeted warmly by his mother and two sisters, who then turned to welcome the four white men. The father was not there but Bert Cowing told what happened on the old man's return:

"George Washington had been away from home for five years . . . When we had been sitting in the hogan for some time, the father came in.

George Washington was seated by his squaw on the ground, and as his father came in both their faces brightened up and the father advanced and took his hand and sat down on the right side of him, putting his arm affectionately around his neck.

"The squaw meantime came around on the other side of the old man and he put his arm around her neck and for a moment they remained silent, the father apparently saying a blessing, all of them having their heads bowed. It was all very quietly done but it was done in a way to remove all doubt about the Indians having natural affection."

They were sitting in this manner when a howling windstorm swept down upon them, driving the sand in a thick brown curtain. The storm's fury caught them unawares, Cowing said. "We hardly had time to fix our packs and saddles before we were covered with sand. As soon as possible we crawled into the hogan . . . This one was pretty spacious but it got pretty close after a while in spite of the hole for a chimney. For over an hour it blew to beat everything . . . When the sand stopped it began to rain and that lasted for half an hour or more."

Darkness having followed closely on the rain, the women set about building a fire and preparing food. After they had eaten, Cowing wrote, " . . . the girls roasted corn on the coals for us and I assure you it was very fine. But they made the queerest compound . . . When they got through with their fire in there they pushed the coals aside and on the warm sand and beneath they laid green corn leaves smoothed out and overlapping each other a little . . . On this the old woman laid a sort of mush which was merely soft, fresh corn ground into meal just like the ground corn. It made a cake about two feet by ten inches square and an inch or a little more thick. Over this she put more corn leaves and over them sand and on top of it hot coals." The bread was left to bake in the coals all night.

Richard and his companions started on the last stage of their journey early the next morning, crossing several dry washes skirting the slopes of the Carrisos and then riding in merciless noon heat through the grotesque formations of Redrock Valley until they came finally to Nolan's trading post on the San Juan.

Sweat plastered the shirts to their backs and was running in rivulets from their dust-caked faces, when they dismounted in front of Nolan's and walked through the doorway into the store's cool darkness. On the counter was the usual communal water bucket and dipper. But Muldoon Kelley's eyes had lighted thoughtfully on a pile of watermelons off in one corner. He would have one of them he thought. He did, and then another, and perhaps a third. He was a man of great thirst.

The ride from Nolan's store to the Alamo Ranch was a nightmare for the editor. Either the watermelons had not quite ripened, or Muldoon had been too greedy. In any case his complexion soon matched the color of the discarded melon rinds. At some point during the afternoon Mr. Kelley could ride no farther. They stopped at a ranch where the Wetherill brothers knew the people and hired a rig. Groaning, but still game, Muldoon was boosted into the carriage seat, the reins were put in his hands, and the journey proceeded relentlessly into the gathering dusk.

The massive outline of Mesa Verde was only darker than the sky when the riders finally entered Mancos Valley. That day they had covered a distance of sixty miles.

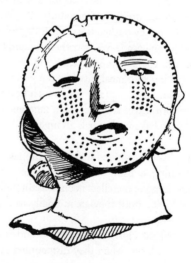

I hope in that time to learn a little about this region that may be of value to some one who will know how to use it.
—RICHARD WETHERILL, in a letter
to Talbot Hyde, January, 1903.

SEVEN

Dick Wetherill is now in Arizona, but failed in his invoice of "Notes of Travel" for this issue . . . The Apaches are on the Warpath in New Mexico and Arizona. Dick Wetherill had better head the band wagon towards the Ute reservation.
—THE MANCOS TIMES, January 17, 1896.

ON a late summer day in 1895 a wagon bearing the dust of hard travel pulled up at a store on the main street of Mancos. The arrival attracted more curiosity than the usual stranger's rig. Something about its lines and loading was different. This one combined the serviceable qualities of a heavy-duty ranch wagon with the grace of a stylish passenger vehicle. Its outline was high and rectangular. For stormy weather it carried thin cedar panels which could be fastened along the sides and rear to shut out the rain.

At the moment, with the noon sun nearly overhead, the wagon was open to any chance breeze. This allowed passersby and loiterers to observe that the family of five sitting in the vehicle was rather out of the ordinary too. On the front seat with the father, his frail wife was folding a sealskin coat in her lap. She had worn the fur against the morning chill coming over the mountain road from Durango. Behind the parents, seated in the main part of the wagon in the bored attitude of those who have been riding a great distance were a girl of eighteen and a small boy and girl. Under his arm the boy held a silvery object of valves and coils half as big as himself, a musical horn distantly related to the tuba. On this, not long before, he had been practicing his scales.

Twisting the reins around the brake handle, the father stepped down and went into the store. To the man he found behind a counter he said:

"My name is S. L. Palmer — from Burdett, Kansas. Would you be so kind as to tell me how I can find the Wetherill place?"

The clerk came around the counter dusting his palms on the seat of his pants, and led Palmer back to the door.

"Lots of folks have been coming to look at Mesa Verde since the Wetherill boys started digging up there," he observed in a general way.

"I've just brought my family seven hundred miles for that reason," Palmer said.

After a slow, speculative stare at the stranger's rig and its occupants, the clerk raised an arm and pointing finger. "Take the turn there at the postoffice and go down that road until you come to the church," he said. "Then turn sharp right again and follow straight along the river. The Alamo Ranch is down that road and you can't miss it — the house sets in a cottonwood grove off to the left a piece, on a little bend. You'll see four or five barns and sheds there too."

"Thank you, friend," Palmer nodded.

"It's three miles," the clerk said.

The clerk stood in the doorway watching until the wagon was out of sight and then ambled back into his store. "This town's gettin' to be a regular resort place," he muttered to a tiger cat dozing in the window.

Sidney LaVern Palmer and Elizabeth Ann, his wife, were Quakers. They had met some twenty years before when she was a student at the New England Conservatory of Music in Boston and he was touring the East as a member of John Philip Sousa's Band. Even when they moved to Illinois after their marriage and he put away his cornet, for a while, to become a telegraph operator for a railroad, music remained an important part of their lives. They taught each of their children to play a variety of musical instruments, starting them early. As time went on, and after moving to Kansas, they spent much of each year traveling about the country giving family concerts or "entertainments" in the towns and lonely settlements wherever they chanced to stop. The concerts helped to pay their expenses and at the same time brought music and gaiety to small, remote communities that were hungry for both.

The eldest daughter, Marietta, had her mother's large brown eyes and small stature. But she was plump, had her father's vitality and his features with certain refinements: the mouth firm, full and tending to smile; the forehead rising rather high and broad. She was born in Serena, Illinois, October 5, 1876. Six years later her father moved to Scott City, Kansas, and after a few months to Burdett, twelve miles from Fort Larned — Great Plains country only recently wrested from the Cheyenne and Sioux. Here, LaVern Jr.

RICHARD WETHERILL

and Edna were born, and the family settled on a wheat farm that also boasted a small fruit orchard. Marietta had a pleasing soprano voice and while she could play a number of musical instruments quite well, she preferred the harp and the guitar.

Her father was less than average height but he was powerfully built and had a large, handsome head. Although most of his acquaintances wore beards, or at least a moustache, Sidney LaVern Palmer was uncompromising with the razor: he had neither. His Kansas neighbors remarked that for a farmer he did precious little farming. He was fastidious about his clothes, preferring suits of dark cloth and city tailoring to the workaday garments of provincial life, liking a shine on his high black shoes even when all the dust of Kansas conspired against this. More remarkable still, he wore a derby hat when farm business took him to town.

The fact is, Marietta's father owned a Kansas farm but the farm in no sense ever owned him. It was not long after he moved to Kansas that he began taking his family on "concert tours" which each year somehow ended in longer absences from the home at Burdett.

One year, when Marietta was quite small and they were traveling in the Deep South, they met and joined forces with a patent medicine drummer who gave tent shows. The drummer, as they did, rode from one town to the next in a wagon, but his was painted gorgeously in red and gilt. When the Palmers first encountered him, quite by accident in a town where they were giving a concert, they were charmed to discover that his chief patent remedy was a concoction he put up in little brown bottles and called a "blood purifier" — guaranteed to cure anything, from bowel disturbances to morning vapors.

Combining the talents of the musical Palmers and the patent medicine was to their mutual advantage. For a short time, until Sidney LaVern Palmer decided to take his wife and children to Florida, the arrangement provided gratifying rewards.

About a year later the Palmers made their first journey overland by wagon into the Southwest; the country appealed to them so strongly they returned each summer.

The wagon Palmer designed for these Western trips was built to withstand a knocking about on the roughest trails, and at the same time afford some comfort.

Constructed on a conventional Studebaker running gear, the wagon was built out over the wheels, with two seats placed lengthwise along each side of the body and separated from the front seat by floor-to-top cabinets. At the back were more cabinets to carry clothing, bedding, dishes and cooking utensils, and provisions enough to keep a family of five for a week at a time. The seats were upholstered with light tan leather. Above them, and at the back just under the roof, were cases lined with blue plush and fitted with glass doors.

It was here that the musical instruments were stored when the family was traveling. A collapsible table let down from the top, for meals, but otherwise was folded out of the way; at night the seats could be arranged into comfortable beds. There was space reserved for Palmer's photographic equipment. He was a good amateur photographer with some interest in archaeology. At the ruins he visited in the Southwest he took photographs and collected prehistoric relics. These last found their way eventually into several museums, but the best of the relics were given by his children, after his death, to the museum at Mesa Verde.

When Sidney Palmer brought his family to Mancos and the Alamo Ranch he had not met the Wetherills but he knew of their work in the cliff dwellings. Because other visitors had come ahead of them, there was not room enough for the Palmers in the ranchhouse, so they were invited to set up camp in a juniper and piñon grove on a knoll close by and to stay as long as they liked.

Richard was at the Hopi Snake Dance, but was expected to return any day. Marietta's father had expressed a wish that Richard be their guide when they explored the mesa. Meanwhile, with John or Al or Win for company, he made short excursions down the valley and into Weber Canyon. There were enough surface mounds here, marked by low tumbled walls and fragments of pottery to occupy his interest for some time.

Occasionally in the early September evenings the Palmers went to the house for a few hours around the big stone fireplace in Benjamin Wetherill's room. The good company and warmth of the fire encouraged yarn-spinning. Al and John were good story tellers. So was their father, whose memories of frontier days on the Great Plains seemed inexhaustible.

As Benjamin Wetherill talked of old times his voice mellowed, losing a bit of its tart rasp. Something in his slight, spare frame belied his age. His figure was youthful, at odds with his big head and gnarled hands with the restless thumbs he clasped across his vest. In the firelight, he reminded Marietta of a Roman senator with the body of a puckish gnome; his close-cropped thatch of hair, the ruddy cheeks and button-bright eyes and the square white beard were from a steel engraving of the Roman Forum.

Marietta heard how Richard and Charlie Mason had found Cliff Palace. The Wetherills told also of one terrible winter when a blizzard buried the Mancos Valley to depths so great that the Mormon families living in Weber Canyon were marooned. Richard realized their plight, killed a cow and with Al's help managed to get the meat to the stranded people through the deep drifts.

In these and other stories Richard appeared in dramatic roles which might impress a more romantic girl, but Marietta scarcely listened. Her interest was centered on young Win, so nearly her own age, handsome, and a gay companion who paid her much attention. The stories about Richard registered only vaguely in the back of her mind.

Marietta Palmer was not impressed, either, on the evening when she first met Richard. It was dark around the barns when those in the ranchhouse heard the horses outside, then the squeak of saddle leather, a few short words of tired men, and the thud-thud as heavy packs were loosened and dropped to the ground. A voice was heard asking for a light. Someone went out from the ranchhouse with an oil lamp. There were just three of them: Richard, Clayton and Bert Cowing. Muldoon Kelley had not turned in at the gate, but continued on home in the borrowed rig.

Richard, like the others, was well caked with red dust and a cloud of it lifted as he beat his hat against one leg. His hair was tangled and a heavy beard covered his face. Short, broad through the chest and shoulders, with a round, strong-featured head set on a powerful neck, in this poor light he might have been mistaken for Ulysses S. Grant, worn and haggard after the Wilderness campaign. Tired as he was, his motions were swift as he took care of the horses and with Clate and Bert Cowing turned them into the corral and then forked in hay.

Afterwards there had been the briefest exchange of greetings, Richard saying hello to the girl and then, with the two others, disappearing into the house. The Palmers went back to their camp on the knoll.

"They did not look like much to me," Marietta later wrote of this meeting, but "Mother Wetherill sent word to our camp that because the boys had been gone on this Arizona trip so long she was going to give a dinner to celebrate the homecoming, and would we join them? We did, and what a big difference there was!"

It was the night following the return when they all gathered at the supper table. Except for Richard's quiet, black gaze and Clate's laugh and ready smile, she would not have recognized them. During the day they had scrubbed themselves in the river. Now, freshly dressed and free of villainous beards, they appeared far less formidable. Marietta began to notice flashes of humor in Richard's manner. But in repose there were creases and a weather-beaten look that made him appear older than he really was. She observed with surprise, because Richard then was just thirty-seven, that his hair was quite gray.

Later that evening, again around the fire in Benjamin Wetherill's room, the conversation turned to the mesa and its cliff dwellings. When Marietta's father spoke of Cliff Palace, Richard offered to take them there — the next day, if they wished. He began to tell of the many strange things he and his brothers had found in the canyons of the dark mesa and as he talked the images he created of a vanished civilization caused Marietta to lose all sense of time.

After the Palmers had been to Cliff Palace and several other cliff dwellings, Richard found them a camp site in a box elder grove near Sandal House in Mancos Canyon. With their wagon brought up to the trees and the pair of mules put out to graze, they remained two weeks. The isolation would have been complete except for Richard's occasional appearances, always unannounced but always as casual as he could make them. These visits, he assured them each time, were only by chance and were accidental.

"I was just riding by," he would say breezily. "And being so close I thought I would stop and see how you folks are fixed. Is everything all right?"

Marietta and her parents always said they were just fine, and then suggested he stay a bit and rest his horses. For on these visits Richard had a pack-horse with him and in spite of his lame excuse of being headed in some other direction, the packs always contained more food than one man could eat in a month. Accepting the Palmers' invitation as though doubtfully, Richard would unhitch the packs and then, opening them, drop the pretense that the food was for anyone but these friends. His explanations were always gravely received. And after letting a little time pass, Marietta's mother might propose that it was getting late, and Richard should stay for supper.

Richard stayed. Afterward, around the campfire when the sky was darkening and the stars beginning to appear, Marietta's father would say:

"Why don't you take your bedroll off that horse, Richard, and spend the night? We will have an early breakfast and you can get started then. You couldn't go far tonight anyway."

Richard's visits to the Palmers' camp did not escape notice, as Marietta learned when she rode back to the Alamo Ranch one day with her father to have the mules re-shod. In the blacksmith shop they encountered a tall, slender young man who eyed them quizzically. This was Jim Ethridge, a cowboy who lived on the ranch with his brother Roe. Marietta came to know him well, and once described him:

"He was a very blond young man and although I once saw his hair clean and it was what is now called platinum, it always looked gray like the dust. His eyes were very light, like boiled gooseberries, and his eyebrows and lashes whitish; his complexion was sand color. He was quiet, extremely bashful, and seldom had much to say."

On this occasion he overcame his shyness, and as the girl stood waiting for her father, he asked in a drawl, "Where did you say you come from?"

"I didn't say," Marietta smiled. "But it's from Pawnee County in Kansas, and a town I bet you never heard of."

"Well now," Ethridge said with a grin, " — from Pawnee County. You know, you're the first girl I ever knew who Richard Wetherill would ride from here to yonder to see."

Marietta looked Jim Ethridge in the eye. "Mr. Wetherill and my folks are good friends," she said. "And I guess we enjoy seeing him anytime at all when he can come."

And Ethridge laughed and said, "All right, we'll see who likes who — but you don't fool me none."

Nights around the fire below Sandal House became occasions to look forward to and remember. Richard had the gift of all true story weavers and could make the images of his enthusiasm come alive in the flickering light and shadows. On these nights particularly, with Marietta listening, he was very talkative. One story that he told of the Cliff Dwellers moved the girl deeply because it was a tragedy for which he had no explanation.

Richard and his brothers and Charlie Mason had been working through a large ruin in a fork of Johnson Canyon when they opened up a kiva. In it and lying on the floor they had found skeletons of four people — a man, a woman, a small child about young Vern's age, and a little baby. All had died violently. For centuries the bodies lay just as they had fallen in death.

The man had fallen backward, his legs stretching upward into a narrow ventilator shaft through which he may have attempted to escape. Across one of his outflung arms were the remains of the boy — his son, no doubt — and close by were the woman and infant.

ANASAZI 105

The skulls of the parents and the boy had been crushed, each by one blow of a stone ax. Whoever used this weapon had dropped it and left it there. Richard found the stone blade on the kiva floor. It fitted perfectly the holes in the skulls. The baby's head was so badly shattered that only fragments of it were recovered.

Nowhere else in the dim, silent cliff dwelling had they found any other trace of violence. Then why in one room — and a kiva? If the village had been attacked by enemies, wouldn't they have found more of the dead? To Richard and his brothers it appeared that this family had been murdered by their own people. But why?

As the sparks and piñon smoke curled away, the conversation turned to other places, to desert, canyon and high mountain country known only to Navajos, and to ancient ruins never explored that were said to equal or surpass even the cliff dwellings of Mesa Verde. They spoke of Pueblo Bonito in Chaco Canyon, which neither Richard nor Sidney Palmer had seen and knew of only from hearsay.

About ten years before, Palmer said, he had brought his wife and Marietta to the modern pueblos along the Rio Grande, stopping at Santa Fe and Albuquerque and asking everywhere for directions to Bonito and the other great villages of the Chaco. Almost everyone he questioned either had never heard of that region or was unable to tell him where the Chaco was. All anyone seemed to know was that Chaco Canyon lay somewhere off to the northwest, far on the other side of the Jemez Mountains.

A few warned him against trying to go there. He would have to cross miles of desert where there was no water, they said, and enter a country inhabited only by hostile Navajos who would kill him, his wife and his daughter if they were not lucky enough to die of thirst. Several well-armed men experienced in desert travel, in the ways of Indians and finding hidden springs, might succeed in reaching the Chaco and be able to return safely. But for an unarmed Kansan to attempt it in the company of a woman and small child — it would be certain death. He had reluctantly given up the idea, Palmer said, but someday he might still undertake it.

Richard rubbed his chin. He knew the hazards Palmer spoke of were exaggerated, that a few white men had found the Chaco without serious trouble and had not been molested. "There will be nothing to do at the ranch this winter that Al and John couldn't handle," he said after a moment. "From what I have heard, the Navajos down there wouldn't harm anyone. Would you like me to take you?"

"We have made no other plans — we would like to," Palmer said. As easily as this, Richard's future again was shaped.

IT WAS early fall, 1895, and Richard wrote Talbot Hyde: "I am going into New Mexico for a little while to see if I cannot find some more accessible ruins where I can put in this winter and find a different character of relics."

Richard and the Palmers left the Alamo Ranch on a frosty October morning, outfitting in Durango with supplies for two months: boxes and bags of food weighing a thousand pounds and an equal weight of hay and grain for their animals. Of these there were seven: two big mules, Tender and True, drawing the Palmers' wagon; two other mules, Mesa and Cañon, harnessed to Richard's spring wagon which was to carry the bulk of the load; and three saddle horses responding to the names Nocki, Whiskers and Rats. They carried no tents, but Richard took several heavy tarpaulins and his own bedroll. The Palmers, as usual, would sleep in their wagon. As important as anything else were the barrels lashed to both wagons which were for water and could be refilled when they left the settlements on the San Juan.

For six days they traveled, at first following the gorge of the Animas and then climbing out onto the high, flat plateau stretching off southward in a gradual, steady descent. The peaks and then the foothills of the La Plata Mountains lay to the west until the country on both sides opened up into a broad valley as they approached the San Juan. They forded that river a short distance east of Farmington on the fourth day and spent that night near the trading post of Dick Simpson, an Englishman who, like Tom Keam, had come to this part of the country seeking adventure, married a Navajo girl, and stayed. One surviving fragment from a diary Marietta kept at the time tells of the day following:

We next drove to Swires trading store. We felt we were in unexplored country. Old man Swires very old [and living] with brother. Small stock — very dirty much pawn. Road little used. No Indian wagons — one wagon at store to bring in freight. Secured guide here to take us on into unknown. No road except the old unknown road [used] by early explorers to San Juan from Santa Fe. Many places so grass grown we could not find it. Other places entirely washed out. First day to Tsaya no water. Spring found next morning.

The "road" amounted to no more than faint wagon wheel ruts meandering off into sand and bunch grass. Their guide was a Navajo who was engaged to take them as far as Pueblo Bonito and then leave them.

About noon Richard called the Palmers' attention to the landmark of the three jutting peaks of El Huerfano, some thirty miles to the east. Almost due south of those peaks another thirty miles, they would find the Chaco.

Since crossing the San Juan they had seen many signs of Navajos: flocks of sheep moving in slow white patches through the pale-green sagebrush, smoke rising on cold air in straight plumes from far-off hogans, and now and then two or three blanketed riders, men and women both, who rarely came close but from a distance stopped and stared curiously at the white strangers. Some of the men carried guns across their saddles and Marietta had a twinge of certainty the guns were not loaded for small game alone. But then, glancing toward the man in the spring wagon, she drew reassurance because in Richard's attitude there was no trace of concern.

She was riding Nocki, a bay mare Richard had let her choose from the Alamo Ranch, and as the horse trotted on the flanks or in advance of the small caravan Marietta was conscious that Richard's eyes were upon her as often as they studied the landscape. The shyness she had first felt in his presence was disappearing. More and more she reined in her horse to keep pace with his wagon and she and Richard found so much to talk about that the miles fell away unnoticed.

Her ideas about him were changing rapidly. He was not at all as old or so stern as she had thought. She discovered she could make him smile, and even laugh.

On the morning of the sixth day they crossed an expanse of sandy desert, reaching the Chaco Wash several miles west of where the Escavada comes into it at an angle from the northeast. Both stream beds, however, were absolutely dry. This indeed was a wilderness, Marietta thought, with no trees anywhere and not even a bird's cry to break the silence. A few hogans had been seen, a few poor cornfields, but these Indians had few horses and no wagons at all so the country they were traveling was trackless and desolate.

Their guide had turned off to the left and now was leading them along the north side of Chaco arroyo and toward a wide, low gap between two mesas which showed across their horizons only outcroppings of stone and scattered clumps of dwarf juniper. Now the ground was firmer and less dragging under the wagon wheels and they entered the canyon. It was quite wide, perhaps half a mile, the Chaco Wash cutting through it in a deep, twisting bed worn by years of erosion. The floor over which they were riding was a chalky color, dotted with clumps of grass and greasewood, nearly flat but rising almost imperceptibly to the east. As they progressed farther the canyon deepened, its tawny walls now rising 200 feet between the occasional out-jutting *rincóns*. On the mesa to the right, outlined against the sky, Richard saw the dark brown walls of a ruin — Peñasco Blanco. Soon after, they passed close by two smaller ruins on the canyon floor and finally were in sight of the great pueblo ruin which had brought them here. Pueblo Bonito! The beautiful village.

They unhitched the wagons and made camp under the dark north wall of Bonito where the heavy masonry tapers gradually upward to a height of four stories. For once, Richard's usual gravity deserted him. Golden light of the late October afternoon slanted down through the canyon, burnishing the sandstone cliffs. Before the sun sank behind the Lukachukais he had climbed through the vast arc of tumbled masonry and high crumbling walls that was Bonito. He quickly inspected Pueblo del Arroyo a few hundred yards to the west — and Bonito's twin giant — Chetro Ketl, a quarter of a mile to the east — and returning, he discovered behind Bonito the ancient stairs and toeholds the Anasazi had cut through a chimney in the canyon wall. Climbing these he had emerged on a bare rim of rock that was now scoured by a driving wind.

Spread out directly below him was the immense half moon of Pueblo Bonito, shadowy in the fading light, its outer walls reaching in open-armed embrace toward the canyon. Far on the other side of the arroyo were mounds which he knew meant the presence of other ruins. It was a moment of intense inward emotion for Richard. All that he was looking down upon far surpassed anything he had imagined. These great pueblos dwarfed everything he had seen before. Cliff Palace or Kiet Siel could be lost in one curving wing of this giant called Bonito.

Only a cold wind whipping at his sheepskin jacket reminded him of his responsibility to the family waiting for him. But his excitement increased as he descended from the top of the mesa. Untold treasures of a vanished civilization lay buried here. Where was a man to start?

For a month they remained in the Chaco. Although the days and nights turned bitterly cold and wind funneling through the canyon blackened the sky with sand, blinded them, choked them, Richard took little notice. With Marietta's father he explored the canyon from Peñasco Blanco to Pueblo Pintado. He marveled over the towering walls and the banded, massive effect of pueblo masonry that had resisted the elements for a thousand years. He stood at the talus base of Fahada Butte, 400 feet high, and promised himself that someday he would climb its sheer, broken sides to the top.

He rode over the windswept north mesa in search of the Navajos he knew were there from seeing their cornfields and a few bands of sheep in the canyon. And when he found the lonely hogans he dismounted at a short distance and waited as the shaggy Indian dogs came out barking and showing their teeth, the man and the dogs both observing the proprieties of a stranger's approach in the Indian country. The snarling dogs usually brought a Navajo to the door. Then the sheepskins or hides covering the doorway were brushed aside and Richard was asked to enter. In the dim smoky light of the hogan he spoke with the Indians in their language and the strangeness between them soon disappeared.

The Navajos were threadbare-poor. They had few sheep and horses, miserable clothing, scarcely any silver or turquoise. After a suitable time had passed Richard was asked, with the greatest indirection, where he had come from and the purpose that brought him here. He replied that with Hostine Bitzeal (Strong Man) and the two women and children he had come from the mountains far to the north to see the stone pueblos of the Anasazi.

And then he would ask the older men what they knew of these abandoned villages. They all told him the same thing: their ancestors had found the broken pueblos, just as they appeared now, when they arrived in the canyon many generations ago. At that time there were more cedar trees on the mesas, and more grass. The Chaco Wash had more water in it then and the stream flowed at the surface of the canyon floor clearer than now — not muddy and far down between eroded banks of an arroyo. But the Anasazi were gone even then, leaving no trace to tell where.

Richard was aware that such legends are not infallible, that the accuracy of Indian folklore wears thin after several generations. In any case, as later research would show, the main channel of Chaco arroyo filled with sedimentation, about the year 1860, and changed its twisting course. In the process, the water level at some stage naturally would have had to have been higher.

Marietta sometimes rode out with Richard. Several times she was hurt when he seemed so withdrawn that her sallies left him solemn and unresponsive. Once or twice he failed to hear her at all when she spoke to him. He was a different person from the man she had come to like so well on the long ride from Mancos. But soon she perceived that Richard's abstraction reflected no fault he found in her; his mind simply was wrestling with the mysteries locked up in this once densely populated region.

Richard revealed his true feeling for Marietta one particularly cold night when an accident nearly took their lives. She and the children had built a huge bonfire under a projecting angle of the cliff near their camp. Supper was over and to enjoy the fire's warmth in greater comfort Richard pulled the seat out of his spring wagon and tossed it on the sand, inviting the Palmers to use it. Marietta's father said the wooden box he was sitting on was comfortable enough, so Richard sat with her mother on the wagon seat while Marietta and the two children stretched out on a blanket nearer the flames.

Suddenly, with no more warning than the crack of a pistol shot, a ton of rock detached itself from the cliff over their heads and fell in crashing chunks toward the fire. Richard and Mrs. Palmer tumbled backward off the wagon seat and at the same moment flaming faggots of the fire were tossed in every direction, plunging the camp into darkness. For a few seconds after the rumble of falling stone had subsided there was silence. Then Richard shouted:

"Marietta — where are you? Are you hurt?"

A dazed voice answered. "I — I'm here."

Scrambling to his feet, Richard found the children and Marietta in the debris, bruised, bleeding from a few cuts but not badly hurt. The parents were not injured. Richard picked Marietta up, his arms lingering to steady her.

"What a fool I was!" he exclaimed.

Marietta's voice trembled. "Why — how, Mr. Wetherill? It wasn't your fault."

"I should have known better," he muttered. "We were too near that rotten rock and had too big a fire. If anything had happened to you . . ." and his voice trailed off. To Marietta it sounded like ". . . I don't know what I would have done."

During the remaining days they did some digging, a little at Pueblo Bonito but most of it across the Chaco Wash in mounds near the opening in the mesa known as South Gap. Here they found a number of burials with offerings of pottery. Then, toward the middle of November, they broke camp and rode eastward out of the canyon toward the towns along the Rio Grande, about a hundred miles away.

They went first to the pueblo of Jemez and then over a rough mountain road through a pine forest that led them down to Cochiti Pueblo in the valley, and finally to several other Indian villages on or close to the big river. At Santa Fe they stopped for several days and might have remained longer if Richard's restlessness in the old town had not hurried them along.

For Marietta the lights at night, and the crowds of people strolling about the plaza were a welcome change from the desert's solitude. She drank in the sounds, the pungent smells of the narrow streets with avid delight. With sidelong glances she noted critically what the señoritas and American ladies of the old Spanish city considered stylish in hats, bodices and hemlines. The comparison gave her no feeling of disadvantage. Before starting on this trip she and her mother had ordered liberally in Denver stores and now wore high-necked, long-sleeved shirtwaists with lace at the throat and wrists. Marietta's divided skirt was sand colored, her mother's brown; both buttoned across the front for town wear. Each wore high walking boots laced up the front — the lacing a trifle uncomfortable because it pinched Marietta's ankles where it crossed over the hooks.

Santa Fe's churches and old adobe buildings cradled in the lower slopes of the Sangre de Cristos were immensely appealing to the impressionable young girl from Kansas. But cities and towns, even if they were beautiful or unusual, did not appeal to Richard. In the future he avoided Santa Fe, returning there only the few times urgent business made it necessary. He had little interest in the Spanish history of this territory and was not curious about the colonists who had moved up the Rio Grande with Don Juan de Oñate in 1598. His abiding interest was in the Anasazi, the settlers who had preceded the Spaniards by centuries.

From Santa Fe, Richard and the Palmers turned one morning late in November onto the sparsely traveled wagon road descending toward the Sandia Mountains and little Mexican settlement of Bernalillo. They stayed for a day or two in Albuquerque, a growing mercantile and railroad town where mud in the main streets froze in ruts two feet deep and saloons still outnumbered churches and schools. On Christmas Day they were in Socorro, leaving there before the new year to travel westward into Arizona.

Before leaving Albuquerque, Richard wrote a letter to Talbot Hyde which was to have future significance. In this and following letters Richard spoke so enthusiastically of Chaco Canyon that he kindled Hyde's curiosity and fired his determination to attempt at least one summer's excavation of the Chaco ruins. Thus a chain of events ending finally with Richard's murder had its beginning — and Richard wrote on the first day of December, 1895:

112   RICHARD WETHERILL

Not having anything important on hand this winter I have taken the opportunity to visit the ruins of New Mexico. Those of Chaco Cañon being the greatest in New Mexico and almost unknown — every one so far having tried to get Relics there making a total failure of it — for that reason more than any other I wished to examine them — I was successful after a few days search in finding relics in quantity — the ruins there are enormous — there are 11 of the large Pueblos or houses containing from one hundred to 500 rooms each and numerous small ones — how many I do not know but there must be more than 100. I stayed there until I had gotten 40 pieces of pottery . . . Grass and water is plenty — wood is scarce. A wagon can be driven to the Ruins in 5 or six days from our Ranch.

Richard mentioned visiting the Rio Grande pueblos — some antics of a Koshare dance he had found repelling — and then said he had been to Santa Fe "but was much disappointed in my visit there as they had nothing that I expected." He said he planned to return to Mancos by way of Arizona "and visit every ruin known of by the Indians — if I can possibly do so — and get back in time to go with your expedition." The expedition was planned for the following spring, to the region of Marsh Pass and Tsegi Canyon.

He promised Talbot a map of the country he and the Palmers traveled through, pointing out areas where it might be worthwhile for the Hyde Exploring Expedition to work. Richard referred again to the coming spring expedition, however, and added: "I am saving specimens from all over this region for comparative study. I have voluminous notes of this trip, a copy of which I will send you." These notes and letters demanded the change of plans which sent Richard back to Chaco Canyon instead of into Arizona the next spring.

"So far," said Richard, "I am like Schlatter the healer. I started from home dead broke and am still that way but have not yet missed a meal. I love the work and the research and for that reason I can stand almost anything." Francis Schlatter, a noted religious fanatic of the day, wandered penniless through the Southwest clad in sandals and a long robe.

RICHARD and the Palmers arrived in the valley of the Verde River, explored Montezuma's Castle and other ruins of Arizona, and then headed north for Oak Creek Canyon and Flagstaff. In many of the places where they stopped, the Palmers gave impromptu musical performances, played for dances and sometimes gave a stereopticon show in a church or public hall. Some of the tunes he heard almost nightly began to run through Richard's head, but when he tried to hum them he couldn't. Music he liked, but carrying a melody was beyond him and the best he could do was whistle a few notes of his favorites.

As for Marietta, who sang or played the guitar, no one had more fun than she. The young men who came to these affairs always were eager to dance with her, Richard noticed. As soon as someone else could be found to take her place she would be out on the floor swirling and laughing in the arms of a stranger. For her it was pleasant and innocent enough. But Richard, after watching for a while from his post at the door, would disappear. Once when this happened Marietta's mother went looking for him and found him wandering about outside in the darkness.

"Richard," she said, "I have noticed that whenever someone plays for Marietta and she dances, you leave the hall. Does her dancing seem wrong to you?"

Gruffly he replied that he saw nothing wrong in Marietta's dancing — it had been hot and noisy and he had just come out for some air. Mrs. Palmer wondered, but said no more. A few days later Richard told her, out of a clear sky, "You know, I never realized how much I have missed by not being allowed to dance, or to learn."

The snow was beginning to melt from the open valleys and southern slopes when they reached Flagstaff, the lumber town perched high in a shoulder of the San Francisco Mountains. After replenishing their supplies they started on again, soon crossing the Little Colorado and turning eastward at the greening oasis of Tuba City to visit the Hopi villages. It was April by the time Richard took them through Marsh Pass, across the red sands south of the Chinle and once more into the valley of the San Juan. Now swollen with melting snow from the western ranges of the Continental Divide, the river was a brawling obstacle to their progress.

Their provisions were exhausted. For two days they had eaten nothing but dried peaches and chocolate. With the San Juan boiling high and no sign within miles of even a Navajo hogan, the situation looked serious.

Frequently during the recent weeks, Marietta had tied her horse to the tailboard of Richard's wagon, accepting his invitation to ride with him. Sharing his company made the long hours pass quickly. Thus it happened she was riding in the spring wagon when they came to the San Juan. At the river bank Richard reined in the mules and jumping down he paced the water's edge, studying the current. The Palmers and the children, meanwhile, had come alongside. Marietta's father joined Richard and for a time they stood talking in low tones, Richard now and then shaking his head as if in doubt. Marietta overheard the last part of their conversation.

"Can we make it without the wagons tipping over?" her father asked.

"There is nothing to do but try," Richard answered. "I don't know of a better ford than this within miles of here. Since your outfit is topheavy I will go first and if I get across I'll go on to Bluff for help. A strong team hitched on with your mules should get you over."

Then he turned to where Marietta sat waiting. "I'm going to try it," he told her, swinging into the seat. "Do you want to stay here with your folks?" He expected her to stay.

"I am going with you," she smiled.

Richard started to answer, then saw she was determined, and changed his mind. Before either of the Palmers could protest he yelled at the mules and the spring wagon lurched down the sandy bank and into the river. Marietta clutched the seat with all her strength as the wheels bounced crazily over stones and then sank in sand and water to the hubs. Before she knew it the river was up to the wagon bed, the current had swung the tailboard sharply downstream and the two mules were plunging forward, now swimming, now scrabbling for a footing when they touched bottom. They made headway but it was slow, and Marietta could see they were being carried on the muddy tide. Near midstream Richard swung toward her and yelled: "Are you afraid?"

"Sure I am — I'm scared to death!" Marietta shouted back. But she was smiling and her brown eyes were sparkling with excitement.

"Hold tight," he ordered " — the worst is coming." And a moment later: "If the wagon begins to tip or the current really takes it, I'm going to cut the team loose. If I do, you jump for it. Grab the nearest mule by the tail — understand? He'll get you to shore."

Marietta nodded that she heard.

For a minute or two, in the swiftest channel of the river, wagon and mules were swept helplessly downstream. Then, with redoubled fury in response to Richard's roaring encouragement, the mules swam diagonally against the current and began to narrow the distance to the north bank. As the animals at last gained a sure footing Richard climbed out on the wagon tongue clutching a coil of rope, and leaped into water up to his waist. He staggered ashore, wheeled, and roped the smaller of the mules around the neck. Then he dug his heels into the steep bank and tugged. Mules and wagon, Marietta swaying on top, came dripping onto dry sand.

Recalling the experience more than fifty years afterward, Marietta Wetherill said: "Maybe those mules deserve some credit. But I was sure then, just as I am now that no man but Mr. Wetherill could have gotten us across that river."

Something in her eyes at the time must have told him how she felt because Richard suddenly discarded a little speech, painfully prepared, which he had been saving for later.

"Is there anything you are afraid of?"

"Oh, I guess not." She didn't quite know what to answer.

"Tell me, what do you do with your fear?"

"Well, Mr. Wetherill, I don't know. I suppose I just swallow it."

There was a pause. Then: Will you marry me?"

Marietta was taken by surprise. She knew she liked Richard very much, that she respected him, but again he seemed so much older than she. Finally she answered.

"I will have to think about it."

Richard would not be put off. "I have been thinking about it for a long while. Marietta — will you marry me?"

After another pause Marietta, hoping this was right, said quietly: "Yes, I will marry you."

The Palmers, meanwhile, had been watching from the far side of the river. "We called back to them that we would go and get help, but doubted they could hear us for the noise of the river," Marietta recalled long after. "We drove away and got up to Butler Wash and found that the road was so washed out that we could not possibly take the wagon any further. As only one of the mules was broke to ride, Mr. Wetherill tied the other to the wagon and told me I would have to stay there until he came back."

He found a small cave high in the rocks where she could hide and left her there with the warning to make no sound if Indians appeared on the road below — even if they should steal the tethered mule and burn the wagon. She waited for him eight hours but saw no sign of an Indian. Richard's warning, however, had not been an idle one. Only a few months before, within a short distance of this place, a tenderfoot from Boston, traveling alone, had been murdered by a band of Navajos after resisting their demands that he give them his food. The tenderfoot had made the mistake of reaching for his rifle. Also in the same vicinity, Indians recently had attacked the Barton brothers' trading post, killing the two men and burning their bodies.

In Bluff, Richard was able to hire a wagon and team of strong horses. He bought a few provisions and then started back on a circuitous route with several Mormon friends who had offered to help. Marietta recalled that when they again reached the river ". . . it was daylight but my parents were anxiously waiting by a campfire they had kept burning all night. The water was down, as always in the morning, and the Mormons put their heavy team on with the mules and made an easy crossing."

Richard parted with Marietta and her family a few days afterward, in Monticello, Utah. The wedding was planned for the following fall when Richard was to join the Palmers in California. In the months between, the Palmers continued northward to the Yellowstone and then to the Pacific Northwest. Richard returned to Mancos and began outfitting for the summer's work for the Hyde brothers.

From Talbot Hyde came word that Frederic Ward Putnam of the Peabody Museum and American Museum of Natural History would be associated with the Hyde Expedition the following spring. He informed Richard:

We have decided to continue the work (with you under Prof. Putnam's supervision) in your country to make a comparative study of the various branches of the Uto-Aztecan stock as represented. To do this we feel it is essential to have your co-operation. This is the plan: That if we undertake the work Prof. Putnam will detail a man to superintend the field work and work up the result during the next winter.

EIGHT

Of such character are the ruins of the Pueblo Bonito, *in the direction of Navajo, on the borders of the Cordilleras, the houses being generally built of slabs of fine-grit sandstone, a material utterly unknown in the present architecture of the north. Although some of these structures are very massive and spacious, they are generally cut up into small, irregular rooms, many of which yet remain entire, being still covered with the* vigas, *or joists, remaining nearly sound under the* azoteas *of earth; and yet their age is such that there is no tradition which gives any account of their origin.*

—JOSIAH GREGG, "Commerce
of the Prairies," 1844.

TWO years before Richard Wetherill brought the Palmer family into Chaco Canyon the large trash mounds of Pueblo Bonito were searched for burial remains by Scott N. Morris of Farmington, the father of archaeologist Earl H. Morris. He found nothing he thought worth taking away. Others had been there before him, a scientist or two, sheepherders and cowboys, members of two military expeditions against the Navajo, and a few chance explorers and writers.

Random pitting of Bonito's mounds uncovered neither burials nor other loot. Until Richard and Sidney LaVern Palmer dug near the small house mounds on the south side of the canyon in 1895 it is doubtful if anyone found much in the ruins — which archaeologists refer to as the greatest on this continent, north of Mexico.

No one knows who, after the Navajo, was the first to discover the canyon's ruins. Indians from Jemez and other pueblos near the Rio Grande, traveling with trade wares to the west, probably were well-acquainted with the Chaco. Governor José Antonio Vizcarra led troops through the canyon in 1823, during a Navajo campaign, and in his journal referred only to *"Pueblo del Raton"* — Pueblo Pintado. Rafael Carravahal, native of San

Ysidro, near Jemez, explored the Chaco in the early 1840's or before and gave to the major ruins the names by which they were known to Richard.

Josiah Gregg, that early chronicler of New Mexico, made the first printed reference to Pueblo Bonito in the passage quoted at the chapter heading, but Gregg never claimed to have visited the Chaco. There are reasons for believing his report was hearsay and that the ruin he called Bonito actually was Pueblo Pintado.

During the turbulent period of the Spanish Conquest and afterward, Franciscan priests and small companies of armored horsemen blazed desert trails north and south of the Chaco, but none reported having entered that isolated region. This is interesting, since from the Spanish settlements of Cuba and Cabezon one wishing to travel west would find an accessible route leading through Chaco and avoiding the hillier terrain to the north the Spaniards actually preferred.

Miera y Pacheco, a captain of engineers and one of those in the 1776 expedition of Fathers Domínguez and Escalante, rendered a crude but partially accurate map on which, in the "Provincia de Nabajoo" the name "Chaca" appears for the first time. The map locates ancient ruins far to the north, where the Rio de las Animas enters the San Juan, but shows none at all in the vicinity of "Chaca" — nothing, in fact, but oven-like symbols of Navajo hogans.

Truthfully, Pacheco designated the region from Chaco to Canyon Largo, to the north, as the first historically known stronghold of the Navajo. The fact it was known as densely occupied by Navajo might explain why priests and soldiers avoided it. They knew well that warriors of that tribe, unlike the peaceable Pueblos, would exact fearfully more in Spanish blood than it was worth to detour around them.

Carravahal of San Ysidro may well have been one of the first to spread word of Chaco Canyon's great ruins among settlements along the Rio Grande, and thus bring the Chaco to the attention of authorities at Santa Fe. In any case, Carravahal was chosen as guide on the second recorded expedition by white men to the canyon, which would mean he had been there at least once previously. This was in 1849 — the same year the first regular mail stage was established between Independence, Missouri, and Santa Fe and only three years after the Territory of New Mexico was seized by the United States in the war with Mexico and came under American rule. The expedition was commanded by Brevet Lt.-Col. John M. Washington, military governor of New Mexico, and its purpose was to march against the Navajo wherever they might be found, and convince them that the American authorities would stand for no more looting and murdering in the Spanish-American settlements.

Narbona, a Navajo chief, and six of his band were killed by the troops in Chuska Valley. This encounter and a subsequent treaty made with the Indians at Canyon de Chelly are described in a report of the journey written by a young first lieutenant of the topographical engineers, James H. Simpson. With this report Simpson included the first authentic map of the Chaco and a firsthand account of its ruins.

Simpson neglected to tell more of the guide Carravahal than to say, when they came to Pueblo Pintado, that he "probably knows more about it than anyone else" when a dispute arose between the Mexican and Hosta, a Jemez Indian also attached to the command as a guide. Hosta was an engaging, talkative fellow who won Simpson's good opinion while slyly answering the lieutenant's questions with the Jemez equivalent of a Baron Munchausen. Like Carravahal, Hosta was familiar with this country but his stories about it were as tall as the butte now bearing his name.

Simpson quoted Hosta as saying that the people of his pueblo called this easternmost ruin of the Chaco the Pueblo de Montezuma, adding that he, personally, preferred Pueblo de Ratones. Then, warming to his subject, he related that the pueblo had been built by Montezuma and his followers (the Aztecs), convincing Simpson "that, after living here and in the vicinity for a while, they dispersed, some of them going east and settling on the Rio Grande, and others south into Old Mexico."

When asked his opinion, Carravahal shrugged that he knew nothing, Señor, about the glorious legend of Montezuma; that the name by which he called the ruin was . . . Pueblo Pintado — Painted Village. Had he been a more glamorous fellow and embroidered his stories a bit his name, as Hosta's, might now appear on maps.

Simpson did, however, adopt Carravahal's name for this pueblo as well as for the others the Mexican identified as they progressed through the canyon: Wijiji (Greasewood), Una Vida (One Life), Hungo Pavie and Chetro Ketl (derivation and meanings uncertain), Pueblo Bonito, Pueblo del Arroyo and Peñasco Blanco (White Bluff).

While the rest of the command pressed forward, Lieutenant Simpson and several companions remained for two days in Chaco Canyon while Simpson examined the ruins, measured some of them and jotted down observations that were remarkably perceptive. Trained as a soldier, his attentiveness to archaeological detail was surprising. Probably because Pintado was the first of the great ruins encountered he gave it a major share of attention, finding "in the masonry a combination of science and art which can only be referred to a higher stage of civilization than is discoverable in the works of Mexicans or Pueblos of the present day."

After "partaking of some refreshments" he settled down to his notes. "In the outer face of the buildings," he wrote, "there are no signs of mortar, the intervals between the beds being chinked with stones of the minutest thinness. The filling and backing are done in rubble masonry, the mortar presenting no indications of the presence of lime. The thickness of the main wall at base is within an inch or two of three feet; higher up, it is less — diminishing every story by retreating jogs . . ."

It is apparent from his report that the canyon and its ruins appeared almost exactly to him in 1849 as they did to Richard Wetherill in 1895. The only difference of consequence was the depth and course of the Chaco arroyo. Of Pueblo Bonito he wrote:

"The circuit of its walls is about thirteen hundred feet. Its present elevation shows that it has had at least four stories of apartments. The number of rooms on the ground floor at present discernible is one hundred and thirty-nine." Hazarding a guess, he said Bonito's rising tiers probably once numbered six hundred and forty-one rooms — somewhat short of today's estimate of eight hundred.

In remarking upon the canyon's appearance Simpson noticed what Richard observed in 1895: scrub cedars, thinly scattered, on the mesas, patches of grama grass dotting the canyon floor. "The country," he said, "presented one wide expanse of barren waste." The water in the Chaco Wash (this was at the end of August) "can only be relied upon with certainty during the wet season."

Wind and snow, sun and rain beat down and washed over the Chaco but had wrought only imperceptible changes when, in the spring of 1877, William Henry Jackson came through with three companions, all riding burros. The yarn-spinner, Hosta, now about eighty years old and relying upon the grandson he brought with him "for his eyes," was Jackson's guide. The fourth member of the party was a Mr. Beaumont, an interpreter, of the same village as the Mexican Carravahal.

It was in the dry season of May, the bed of the Chaco was hot sand. They dug wells to bring up nauseous alkali water and their throats rebelled while their tongues thickened with thirst. They remained for a week and in that time Jackson made notes and a map so painstaking that their usefulness survives.

One pack burro carried all of their supplies and equipment. To save weight, Jackson had brought along a quantity of new, experimental English photographic film for his 8 x 10 camera. In Santa Fe he had awaited its arrival by mail; it came so late he had started without testing the film's capacities. He took almost four hundred exposures, the first photographs ever made in the Chaco. But when he returned to his darkroom in Washington not one of his exposures would develop; the new film was a complete failure.

But Hosta, in spite of his age and oncoming blindness, was the same old Hosta. On the summit of the north mesa above Pueblo Bonito, Jackson discovered the tumbled walls of an immense ruin which, because of its elevation and sweeping view of the canyon, he named Pueblo Alto. Then, as Simpson in his innocence had done, the veteran explorer and photographer turned to Hosta and asked the old man what he knew of it. At first, said Jackson in relating the incident, Hosta "protested entire ignorance of its existence, and said that none of his people or any of the Navajos knew anything of it. A day or two afterwards, however, while on the way home, he modified this statement by saying that there was a tradition among his people, of one pueblo among the others that was above them all, not only in position but in strength and influence, and was called El Capitan or El Jugador. He explains the latter name by saying that among his people the gambler was regarded as a type of superior people."

Jackson had his doubts. Not taking the bait, he observed dryly that Hosta's story might have been "gotten up for the occasion, to explain something he knew nothing of." It was Jackson's unvarnished candor which made him the valuable commentator that he was.

Deep in the exposed bank of the Chaco Wash, near Pueblo del Arroyo, Jackson removed a skull and with it fragments of human bones and potsherds. Imbedded with these he found traces of masonry walls. They were fourteen feet below the canyon's surface. He read the story they told correctly.

"This deposit," he noted, "represents the ancient surface of the grounds about the pueblo, and was probably the sloping bank of the stream, which during the occupancy of this pueblo may have been a considerable river. Since the desertion of this region the old bed has become filled to the depth of at least 14 feet, and through this the arroyo has made its present channel."

It is questionable if the Chaco Wash ever had been "a considerable river"

RICHARD WETHERILL

although possibly it once carried a more constant flow of water. Jackson was the first, though, to observe an ancient, deeper level of civilization occupying the canyon. In Richard Wetherill's time and later, masonry walls were found twelve feet beneath the court level of Pueblo Bonito, fourteen feet below present surface level of Chetro Ketl's long north wall. In the canyon below Shabik'eshchee, near Wijiji, remains of a pithouse were discovered twelve feet below the ground's surface.

Jackson made notes and drew ground plans of twelve of the canyon's most important ruins, observing three distinct types of wall masonry which he correctly believed indicated different periods of occupation and different stages of construction. Pueblo Bonito, he found, was "the largest and in some respects the most remarkable of all. Its length is 544 feet and its width 314 feet . . . A marked feature is the difference in the manner of construction, as shown in the character of the masonry and of the ground plan. It was not built with the unity of purpose so evident in the pueblo of Chettro Kettle and some others . . . The masonry, as exhibited in the construction of the walls, is quite dissimilar in the different portions, showing clearly that it was either built at different periods, or that it had once been partially demolished and then rebuilt."

In one short week Jackson covered an astonishing amount of ground, discovered a hitherto unknown major ruin, and observed some of the most significant aspects of the Chaco. With more time he would have come upon the multitude of smaller ruins on the south side of the canyon and its remarkable place of Anasazi religious gathering — Casa Rinconada. As it was, like Simpson, he directed all of his attention to the north side of the Chaco Wash, except in the one case of Peñasco Blanco.

Others who visited the Chaco in the years immediately before and just after Jackson contributed less to an understanding of the region. A professor, Dr. Oscar Loew, in 1874 ventured as far as Pueblo Pintado, mistook it for Pueblo Bonito, and was convinced that it had been built by the Aztecs. He concluded that the kivas were "temples, in which the sun was worshipped," a romantic notion but inaccurate since Pueblo Indians do not — and probably never did — "worship" the sun. A year later, Lt. C. C. Morrison of the 6th U. S. Cavalry, during a 4,427-mile territorial survey, rode through the canyon making accurate observations but adding little to the information already reported by Simpson. Possibly he noticed that before him (in 1858) a company of mounted riflemen had passed this way in search of raiding Navajo, camped for one night near the talus east of Chetro Ketl and whiled away the cold

November evening carving their names and a few pictures on the tumbled sandstone boulders. That, however, was the sum of their literary contribution. Victor Mindeleff, the ethnologist, and author Charles Lummis both briefly visited the Chaco in 1888, and in 1890 another writer, F. T. Bickford, spent eight days there. Bickford searched for burials, found only a few fragments of skulls at Peñasco Blanco, and decided that the kivas were ingenious "tanks" for the capture and storage of rain water.

All of those who came and wrote of the ruins referred to them by the names that Carravahal gave to Lieutenant Simpson. No one since Simpson, however, has given that estimable fellow any credit or even troubled to mention him, although — after the Indians — he could well have been the discoverer of Chaco Canyon.

MANY YEARS AGO, perhaps as many as fifteen or twenty millions, the Chaco was deep at the bottom of a salty sea. When the waters finally receded, the nearly flat mesa tops were strewn with sharks' teeth and shells which had fossilized were embedded in the soft Cretaceous sandstone. The Chaco's average elevation above sea level is now 6,500 feet.

Before the region was thoroughly dried out, however, a population of enormous animals took over, dominating lesser creatures that included an ancestor of the crocodile. Their bones have been found at Ojo Alamo a few miles northwest of the Chaco where the Hyde Exploring Expedition established a trading post.

When the first human beings wandered into the Chaco is entirely conjectural: nothing yet has been found to date their arrival earlier than about 700 A.D. — the Late Basket Maker period. The Grand Gulch and northern San Juan area, then, was a major population center several centuries or more while, so far as known, the Chaco still remained uninhabited.

The Indians who first settled in the Chaco possibly were related to the early Basket Makers of the San Juan region where Richard discovered the first traces of them in burial or storage cysts sheltered within caves. The relationship appears to have been one of nearly direct descent, perhaps from several mixed racial strains. In the interval of centuries between the Grand Gulch Basket Maker period and Chaco's Classic Pueblo period there seems to have been a progressive development toward a fairly well unified group of people in the San Juan Basin referred to now as the Anasazi. Certain differences among them there were — in the overall pattern of architecture and of arts and crafts. Common to all, however, and indicating their close relationship, were basic practices. For one, they were primarily farmers rather than warriors. A style of pottery (while others were developed) was typical of the region: a white slip polished or otherwise and decorated with designs painted in black. Burial customs were much the same, and the skeletons of the dead indicate a close resemblance.

The Chaco Anasazi belonged to a flourishing people who were doing just about the same things in the same way about the same time in southwestern Colorado, southeastern Utah and large parts of Arizona and New Mexico. Although farming engaged most of their time they were superb stone masons and proficient hunters, but warriors only in case of necessity.

The discovery, by Frank H. H. Roberts, of Shabik'eshchee Village — a group of eighteen pithouses and a prototype of the Great Kiva, on the rim of Chacra Mesa nearly opposite the pueblo of Wijiji — came sixteen years after Richard's death. Remains of other pithouses were found in the canyon, most of them on the canyon's south side and usually buried eight feet or more below the canyon's surface. It is doubtful that Richard had any knowledge of the presence of Late Basket Makers in Chaco Canyon or knew that in some cases the first, small Chaco pueblos were built on top of pithouse foundations. Concentrating upon Pueblo Bonito, he might have traced, but probably did not, the humble beginnings of pueblo life in the canyon. Bonito was in effect an enormous apartment house which had evolved slowly and by constant additions, beginning with a pithouse site that progressed to one or perhaps several tiny pueblos before all were buried under the sprawling community village.

Only one of the developmental pueblos marking the transition from pithouse to large, communal pueblo has been excavated in the Chaco. Situated in a low *rincón* a trifle south and due west of Fahada Butte, it was brought to light in the final days of the Civilian Conservation Corps and therefore named the Three-C Site by Gordon Vivian, its discoverer. The tiny building provided what every archaeologist wants most to find — a hitherto unknown link or chain of continuity between two known periods of civilization.

The nine small rooms of the Three-C Site had been built in a two-tiered rectangle rising to a height of only one story. Adjoining the pueblo but separated from it were two small kivas. The structural materials included, progressively, the post-Basket Maker slabs of sandstone set in the ground vertically and a holdover from pithouse architecture, then adobe "turtlebacks" or molded blocks of clay, and finally a rough-coursed masonry associated with

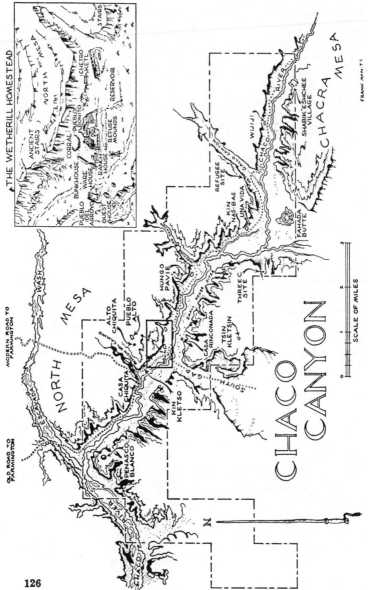

THE WETHERILL HOMESTEAD

NORTH MESA

ANCIENT STAIRS
PUEBLO BONITO
CORRAL
BUNKHOUSE
PUEBLO DEL ARROYO
WARE HOUSE
GUEST HOUSE
RANCH HOUSE
CHETRO KETL
STAIRS
RESERVOIR
REFUSE MOUNDS

CHACRA MESA

CHACO RIVER
SHABIK'ESHCHEE VILLAGE

WIJIJI
REFUGEE SITE
KIN NAS-BAS
UNA VIDA
FAJADA BUTTE

NORTH MESA

MODERN ROAD TO FARMINGTON
OLD ROAD TO FARMINGTON
ESCAVADA WASH

ALTO CHIQUITA
PUEBLO ALTO
HUNGO PAVIE
THREE-C SITE

CASA CHIQUITA
CASA RINCONADA
TSIN KLETSIN

KIN KLETSO
PEÑASCO BLANCO

CHACO CANYON

N

SCALE OF MILES

FRANK M·N·T·T

the earliest pueblos. Other vestiges of life here, but principally pottery, are positive evidence of the continuity of habitation of the Chaco by the same people, from the rude earth dwellings of Shabik'eshchee to the more elaborate of the pueblos.

Some time has been spent by a few archaeologists in trying to prove that there was no continuity of life in Chaco Canyon between the occupation of Shabik'eshchee Village and the Pueblo period in its changing phases up to 1000 A.D. — and thus the Chaco Culture as we know it was not indigenous but imported. Harold S. Gladwin, who is one of this belief, writes in *A History of the Ancient Southwest* (1957) that Shabik'eshchee was the only Basket Maker site in the Chaco during the eighth century. He says he failed to find a single site of any kind representing the period 850 to 1000, and that there is no evidence prior to 1000 of a communal building in the Chaco intended to house more than one family. He argues that the Chaco was an empty pocket after 850 until, about 1000, descending Navajo marauders chased a lot of peace-loving Anasazi into the canyon. He places advent of the first Navajo scouts at 850 or just after, which may be possible but for the present is not provable.

Here, possibly, in Gladwin's failure to find what he was looking for, is a case where an archaeologist's negative findings signify nothing more than bad luck. For Chaco Canyon and its approaches abound with Basket Maker sites contemporaneous with Shabik'eshchee. A group of such sites is found a few yards east of the road entering the canyon from the south and a few miles south of the present monument boundary; there is another site on the summit of the first *rincón* east of Peñasco Blanco; still another, and quite large, is found on the southeast slope of the unnamed mesa rising just south of the Escavada Wash and half a mile east of the present Chaco Canyon trading post. There are many, many more.

The Three-C Site, similar in nearly all respects to what Prudden defined as a unit-type pueblo, was occupied in the tenth century (perhaps even before), and the number of rooms, two kivas, and sixteen burials found there indicate it may have housed three families over a considerable period of time. Other small pueblos on the south side of the canyon, designated as Bc sites when excavated in the 1930s by the University of New Mexico, offer ample evidence — by masonry and pottery and burials, if not by tree-ring dates — of occupation long before 1000. Masonry of the earliest sections of Pueblo Bonito and Una Vida, to mention just two of the large pueblos, indicate they were small but growing communal villages in the tenth century.

127

The importance of the Three-C Site mainly lies in its clear evidence which refutes all such notions that the transitional and the Classic Pueblo builders were entirely unrelated to the Chaco pithouse dwellers. It does not, however, answer questions which must have plagued Richard Wetherill: Where did the people go? Why did they leave?

Few places in the world where crumbling walls tell of "lost" civilizations give such mute testimony as Chaco Canyon does to man's bitter, losing struggle against the forces of nature. In the silence of the Chaco, melancholy because of the manifold evidence of once-great accomplishment, it is this sense of ancient struggle, of a multitude presence among the hundreds of mounds and broken ruins, that excites the imagination.

Richard was one, and there have been many more, who was drawn irresistibly to this arid, even desolate canyon for these mysterious reasons. Other places he had been to and left were far more beautiful, a thousand times more practical for homesteading.

He saw it first much as Lieutenant Simpson and Carravahal saw it: a canyon eighteen miles long, nowhere more than a mile wide, the mesas dotted with juniper, the broken cliff walls of yellow sandstone at most rising three hundred feet, the canyon bottom dry sand through which erosion cut deep washes — the deepest and widest of them being the usually dry Chaco arroyo. To the people of Shabik'eshchee Village and to the builders of the great and less-great neighboring pueblos, the canyon must have looked far different, far more inviting.

In wet seasons, as always, the river rises in the slopes of the Continental Divide, about thirty miles east of the Chaco, and then flows west and then north for one hundred twenty-five miles until it meets the San Juan near Shiprock. Twelve centuries ago the river probably ran between shallow banks on the surface of the canyon floor, willows and cottonwoods lining its course, colonies of frogs in the shaded places and where the stream widened into pools. Even then the semi-desert sand must have covered much of the region, but tall pines and Douglas firs mingled with the juniper and piñon on the mesas. The stump of one giant fir tree was excavated from the west court of Pueblo Bonito when Neil M. Judd worked there for the National Geographic Society in the 1920's. Literally thousands of pine logs, some as great as two feet thick, were used as ceiling beams and for kiva roof supports. Quantities of pine charcoal have been found in ancient fireplaces. This prodigal use of a timber now extinct in the Chaco suggests that the fringes of a forest once reached into the canyon, and must be weighed with new evidence that per-haps many of the Chaco's heavy roof timbers were carried or dragged from the distant Lukachukai Mountains.

With water enough and timber available, the Chaco attracted a large and ever-increasing population. Game was plentiful: antelope, elk, deer and bighorn sheep, bears and lynx and mountain lions, beavers, badgers and coyotes, foxes and porcupines. Bones of all of these animals have been found in the ruins as well as those of dogs and wild turkeys, although whether the turkey was used for food is uncertain.

Slight traces of irrigation ditches and dams have been found and al-though rainfall and snow probably was not much heavier then than now (annually, about nine inches), it is reasonable to picture the canyon as once being planted richly with corn, beans, squash and pumpkins to support the growing Anasazi population.

Tree rings from Chaco roof timbers — some of them so well preserved in the deep dry rooms that they might appear to have been cut yesterday — show the region suffered a six-year drouth beginning in 1035. Instead of causing a widespread exodus, however, the drouth marked a period of even greater ex-pansion, an ambitious flowering of new construction. The people of Bonito remained, adding new rooms as old ones were abandoned, improving the workmanship of their masonry even though the beautiful banded effects they achieved — quite similar to the banded masonry of Pompeii — was to be covered immediately under adobe plaster. The same situation prevailed in some of the other pueblos.

No one will ever know how many pueblos were occupied at the peak of the Chaco's golden period. As compared with such other centers as Mesa Verde and the Marsh Pass-Tsegi Canyon region, the number of the Chaco's inhabitants must have been large. Some have estimated the population to have been ten thousand, but that is no more than a guess. Again with a margin for error, it has been estimated that Pueblo Bonito once numbered eight-hundred rooms. A few score of these rooms would either have been abandoned completely or used only for storage, making it unlikely that more than one thousand persons ever lived in Bonito at one time.

When Richard brought the Hyde Exploring Expedition to Chaco Can-yon a general survey was made of the major ruins, but the first serious effort to map all of the sites was made in 1947 when Lloyd M. Pierson, a student at the University of New Mexico, undertook a comprehensive survey. (In 1922 an excellent topographical map of part of the canyon was made by

Robert P. Anderson, showing the location of a few of the ruins.) Pierson's map, which includes only those ruins within the boundaries of Chaco Canyon National Monument and admittedly is incomplete, shows one hundred twenty-five sites on the south side of the canyon and eighty-five north of the Chaco arroyo, a total of two hundred and ten. This number represents surface sites only. Excavation from one end of the canyon to the other, a task of impossible magnitude, might double or triple Pierson's total.

As any metropolis always does, the Chaco drew, from all points of the compass, "foreigners" and outlanders by the scores — clans and family groups of distant relationship to the Chacoans, even small villages of entirely separate tribal identity. The latter, it is believed, largely settled along the slopes of the southern cliffs, from Peñasco Blanco to the Gap and then on to Fahada, bringing with them different customs and dialects strange to the older inhabitants north of the river. In short, eleventh century Chaco Canyon was a primitive Athens of America, the largest, the most thriving and progressive center of human life on the continent north of Mexico. Concurrent with this period of growth, tentacles of Chaco influence spread north to the Ackmen-Lowry region of Colorado and as far south as Zuñi.

The jewellers of Bonito, meanwhile, worked with remarkable craftsmanship, turning out pendants, necklaces and pieces of mosaic from rough chunks of that most highly prized, semi-precious stone: turquoise. It was little matter that turquoise was not to be found in the vicinity of the Chaco; traders and Bonitoans themselves carried it out by the ton, raw, from Los Cerillos in the Galisteo Basin below modern Santa Fe. Transparent obsidian, to be used for knife blades and arrow points, was found in the Jemez Mountains. Salt was brought from the salt lakes south of Zuñi, and seashells, for ornaments, were carried over hundreds of miles from the Pacific Coast.

Clan priests, who probably had more to say than anyone about how the communal life of Pueblo Bonito would be conducted, imported macaws and parrots from regions far to the south. These birds of rainbow-hued plumage may have been regarded as sacred, or at least of special significance to one or more of the clans, since objects of wood used in elaborate kiva ceremonials were carved and painted in their image. When he excavated Room 38 in the very old north-central section of the pueblo, Richard Wetherill found — among other objects suggesting this had been a clan's ceremonial chamber — the skeletons of fourteen macaws. Two of the birds had been buried "with great care" in circular cavities "carefully formed, filled with adobe" about a foot below floor level and then covered over so carefully as to leave no sign of their existence. Remains of the other twelve macaws were found in the floor debris of the room, leading Richard and his associates to believe they had been held captive there either in cages or on perches.

A type of pottery unique to the Chaco was developed, its frets and hatchured designs being applied with a black mineral paint to a white slip; large cylindrical jars measuring as much as twenty inches tall and tapering gently to six or eight inches across the mouth were found in quantity — but hardly ever outside the boundaries of the Chaco. These and human effigy vases were developed to a high form of art. "Corrugated" culinary ware of a gray, unpainted paste abounded, as did the more usual forms of bowls, pitchers and hand ladles of black-on-white design. More scarce was the black-on-red pottery, while polychromes were not introduced until the post-Bonito or historic period when small bands of Rio Grande Pueblos fled to the Chaco during the Spanish reconquest.

Toward the end of the eleventh century, variants of the Chaco's banded masonry began to turn up in strange, far places. It was found at the Village of the Great Kivas in Nutria Canyon, sixteen miles northeast of Zuñi; at the small pueblo of Lowry in Colorado, thirty-two miles northwest of Cortez; at Kintiel in Arizona, twenty-two miles south of Ganado; at Ridge Ruin near Flagstaff, and elsewhere.

Writing to Dr. Prudden in 1897, Richard commented that " . . . on the high mesa East and North of Navajo Mt. — are ruins similar to those in Chaco, N. M."

A diffusion such as this indicates a definite Chaco influence, a small exodus of Chaco people to new locations, or both. None of the outlying sites, however, shows the degree of Chaco influence as found at Aztec Pueblo, sixty-five miles to the northwest. Closely resembling Chetro Ketl in size and general architecture, Aztec appears to have been built in the first two decades of the twelfth century although there were earlier inhabitants in that area. Soon afterwards, approximately at the same time as a gradual exodus from the Chaco began, Aztec was abandoned — part of it to be occupied at a later date by people moving southward from Mesa Verde.

The reason for Aztec's construction poses a question: was it the result of friction or strife in the Chaco, to the end that a dissident group of Chacoans broke away to begin life again in a new community? Or could it mean that by 1100 the Chaco, with its resources nearly exhausted, was unable to accommodate any further increase in population and thus Aztec became the center of a natural overflow? Either answer — and there might be a better one — would be difficult to prove.

A single, one-story row of rooms divides the inner court of Pueblo Bonito into two plazas of equal size. The south end of this dividing structure terminates at a square fallen wall that once enclosed a Great Kiva. This, a ceremonial gathering place for the entire pueblo, for some unaccountable reason was not touched during the five years of excavation by the Hyde Exploring Expedition. Nor was a second Great Kiva, somewhat smaller and situated in the north end of the west plaza, which was uncovered by Neil M. Judd's party. The remnants of a third — probably much older and simpler in design than the other two — were partially disclosed at the same time by Frank Roberts, in the subsurface of the west court.

The Great Kivas of the Anasazi have been compared, insofar as significance to their builders is concerned, to the medieval cathedrals of Europe. Indeed, there is some parallel because to Indian and to Christian each form represented the supreme achievement — architecturally and in their own spheres — of man's religious expression.

Otherwise, except for the religious exuberance revealed by this cementing of art and architecture with the toil and sweat of nearly the whole community, there is obviously no comparison. On the one hand we have the great spires and flying buttresses resulting from the Creation story when, after God's gentle touch and from Adam's rib, Eve was the issue. On the other, architectural features of the Great Kiva or ceremonies performed therein resulted from the Anasazi's concept of not one but many deities, and of their own Origin legend.

Puebloans traditionally have believed their ancestors were confined to dark, damp regions far below the earth's surface. By propitiating their deities the more fortunate ones finally emerged into the sun's light after many successive and arduous stages — through a small opening or hole in the ground.

Always, much importance has been attached to that opening, as the means by which the ancestors moved from the dark underworld to a favored place of light and warmth on earth. From Basket Maker times until the present, first in the partially subsurface pithouse and later in the small kivas which developed from them, that opening has been preserved symbolically as a small round hole in the clay floor, now known by the Hopi name "sipapu."

In the Chaco, the pithouses of Shabik'eshchee had the sipapu; later, the

RICHARD WETHERILL

little kivas of the developmental pueblos had them. And later still they were found in the Great Kivas — not all but in some. Even where the sipapu was not present there were often facilities, as at Casa Rinconada, for dramatizing in most vivid fashion the emergence of the people from the depths of the earth.

The evolution of the Great Kiva, which probably had its modest origin north of the San Juan about 700 A.D. and reached its greatest stage of development in Chaco Canyon four hundred years later, is still conjectural. So far as known, it began as a large circular structure, partly below the ground's surface and without any special ceremonial features of design to indicate it was more than a village gathering place. One such structure, forty feet in diameter, was excavated by Dr. Roberts at Shabik'eshchee. Other prototypes of the Great Kiva of the same approximate period have been found in the La Plata district of Colorado, at Alkali Ridge and at the Ackmen-Lowry sites in the same state, and at Red Rock Valley, Arizona.

In the Chaco's flowering eleventh century a wave of religious fervor swept the canyon that was never equalled in other regions of the Southwest. A dominant factor in the tremendous building activity that came at the same time, this religious zeal found its expression in the costumed, intricately ritualistic ceremonies conducted in the massive Great Kivas. The largest of the pueblos had them, the one in the center of Bonito's plaza measuring sixty feet in diameter. Neighboring Chetro Ketl had two: the larger of the two, measuring sixty-two and a half feet in diameter after several phases of development, was excavated in 1921 by students of the University of New Mexico under the supervision of Edgar L. Hewett. The second resembled more closely the smaller kivas of Chetro Ketl. Since backfilled, it was excavated by two sisters named Woods, working with the University of New Mexico field school in the 1930s.

Jackson, in 1877, found surface evidence of Great Kivas at Una Vida and Hungo Pavie, at Peñasco Blanco and Pueblo Alto. He overlooked a smaller, detached sanctuary, Kin Nas-bas, which occupies the summit of a *rincón* just west of Una Vida.

The builders of Aztec Pueblo held their communal ceremonies in a Great Kiva of slightly more than forty-eight feet in diameter. Down in the Zuñi country, in Nutria Canyon, two Chaco-type Great Kivas dominated a tiny pueblo and inspired the name: Village of the Great Kivas. One measured fifty-one feet, the other seventy-eight feet in diameter — the largest of the Classic Pueblo period yet found. On Whitewater Creek in Arizona, just south of the Rio Puerco, where there is another Classic Pueblo site showing Chaco influence, there are two more. There is still another at Allantown, Arizona.

Some, but not all of the Great Kivas had adjoining outer rooms apparently used by clan priests and other participants in the ceremonies. Otherwise their features were much the same: partially subsurface with entrance down a flight of stairs; a masonry bench for spectators running the inner circumference of the wall; a masonry firebox, flanked by long masonry vaults which are believed to have been covered with boards to serve as "drum" platforms for the stamping feet of dancers. In some there were evenly spaced wall niches, those of Chetro Ketl yielding fabulous deposits of bead necklaces and turquoise pendants. Methods of supporting the roof over such a large area varied. At Bonito, Chetro Ketl and Casa Rinconada, four massive beams rising from each end of the floor vaults supported a roof which, except for a center smoke hole opening, enclosed the entire sanctuary. At Aztec the roof supports were masonry pillars.

When he was exploring small mounds on the south side of the canyon in search of burials in 1895 and again in 1896, Richard examined and photographed but did not attempt to excavate the Chaco's largest Great Kiva. Now known as Casa Rinconada and probably the most elaborate of its kind ever built, it is seventy-two feet in diameter and located apart from other structures on the top of a low hill, nearly opposite Bonito and overlooking several miles of canyon floor. Presumably it served as a great sanctuary for the small pueblo villages in the vicinity on the south side of the river, possibly for the entire Chaco population.

Features which make Rinconada unique began to emerge with excavation by the University of New Mexico in 1931 and became clearer five years later, when Gordon Vivian, discoverer of the Three-C Site returned and in the course of stabilizing the ruin carried the excavation a step farther. From one of two antechambers at the north side of the sanctuary, he found a flight of steps leading to an underground passageway which emerged in a circular structure built into the kiva's floor. By using this passageway, unobserved by spectators seated on the Great Kiva's encircling bench, clan priests or other performers could enter the vast firelit chamber, and make their appearance — quite literally in the spirit of the Origin legend — from the very bowels of the earth.

In other respects, Rinconada is quite remarkable. Its depth from roof to floor was about twenty feet, it walls four feet thick at the base. Without crowding it could comfortably take several hundred spectators besides a score or so of costumed performers. The ponderous beams supporting the roof, Vivian found, had rested on four huge disks of sandstone, each four feet across, fifteen inches thick and weighing about one thousand pounds. Similar stones were found in the Great Kiva at Chetro Ketl. When it is remembered the Chacoans had no metal tools but relied only upon stone mauls and hammers and knew nothing of the block and tackle, the tireless devotion they brought to the construction of Casa Rinconada compares with the building of Egypt's pyramids.

Why did the Chacoans abandon their great pueblos, their canyon and its mesas? And where did they go? These questions were constantly in Richard Wetherill's mind. Half a century of patient, scientific research after Richard's death has provided some tentative answers.

Were the Anasazi of Chaco wiped out by enemies? Almost certainly they were not. Despite certain fortress-like characteristics of Bonito — such as the sealing of the few outer-wall doorways while the pueblo was still occupied — there is no evidence that the Chacoans in over four hundred years of occupation suffered more than minor raids. The positive signs of violent death which Richard found in the canyons north of the San Juan are entirely absent in the Chaco. North of the San Juan, fratricidal war among the early Basket Makers seems to have been fairly common. No Cut-in-Two, no lanced pelvis, no mass grave such as the one found at Snider's Well, has been found in the Chaco. Apaches and Navajo would have raided, stormed and looted the Chaco had they come upon it in time, but there is evidence they came one hundred and fifty years or more too late.

Were they decimated by plague, as their villages became overcrowded? The surprisingly few burials that have been found, except in the vicinity of a few "immigrant" small house sites on the south side of the canyon — where these outlanders introduced their own burial customs — does not indicate a major epidemic although it would be arbitrary to rule this out as a possibility.

The most probable explanation of the Chaco's decline might be found in a combination of factors. To begin with, the Chaco never was fertile "green" country with a high annual precipitation, but at best a region that was semi-arid, favored with a scant forest fringe and a river which could be depended upon from day to day but rarely carried much water. The complete deforestation of the area, with a resultant soil erosion and lowering of the water table could have had a serious effect upon the canyon's corn and bean fields. Wild game that may have been abundant in the earliest days no doubt withdrew before the expanding population and the retreating edge of timber land. Surviving the seven-year drouth of 1035-41, the Chacoans may have experienced a succession of moderately dry years in which crop yields became progressively smaller and their hunters had to travel farther each year to find any game at all.

A slowly diminishing supply of food and fuel for an expanding population, instead of a severe drouth such as the critical one of 1276-99 which caused the gradual abandonment of Mesa Verde and the Tsegi Canyon areas, may thus be the most dependable answer.

By tradition we are conditioned, in our thinking on such things, to recall Noah and the Great Flood, to consider the mass exodus of the Jews from Egypt, with appropriate visions of bleak desolation left in the wake of the fleeing legions. Dramatically, this is splendid. Historically, for the Chaco, the mass exodus concept may be all wrong and it probably is.

The Anasazi were a tough, tenacious little people, accustomed to hardship, slow to panic, and not given to kiting off in droves when adversity descended upon them. The courageous stamina of their modern descendants is proof enough of this. All evidence available points to the conclusion there was no mass exodus of the Chaco, of Mesa Verde, or of Tsegi Canyon's cliff houses. Rather, it appears, that there was a gradual wearing away of these populations by nature's slow attrition, a movement by clans and village units to new and more favorable locations. Also, it appears that when the last of them were gone and their fields stood nearly empty, there was little noticeable change in the appearance of the canyon to explain their departure. A lowered water table is hard to see.

Tree-ring dates indicate that major construction in most of the large Chaco pueblos halted early in the twelfth century or a few decades before. The beam found in Pueblo Bonito which shows the latest cutting date was brought down in 1130; the last cutting date at Chetro Ketl was 1116; at Del Arroyo, 1103. These dates give some evidence, but no proof, that the Chacoans may have started to abandon the canyon sometime before 1150.

But tree-ring dates can be deceptive and "prove" several conflicting things at once. Over in the Hopi country, as an example, archaeologists have found no roof or kiva beam at Old Oraibi that was cut later than the year 1760. If one were to assume that Pueblo Bonito was deserted by 1150 because its last beam was cut in 1130, it would be consistent to say that Old Oraibi was abandoned about 1780. Consistency here becomes troublesome since Oraibi was still thriving at the turn of this century and only now is going into its decline because of political strife which divided Oraibi fifty years ago.

But for other reasons and better evidence than tree-ring dating, it is possible to believe that if the Chacoans were not gone by 1150, only a few of them remained in the canyon and these few were dominated by or assimilated into a small new group of migrant Anasazi from the north.

People from the Mesa Verde — McElmo Canyon region began filtering southward across the San Juan in the tenth and eleventh centuries, bringing with them their own ideas of architecture, masonry and pottery. A few early arrivals settled on the south side of the Chaco. The Chaco people who built Aztec remained only twenty years or so when they moved out, sometime after 1113, and the Mesa Verde people moved in, staying on through the thirteenth century. Meanwhile, other people from the Mesa Verde region continued migrating south to the Chaco, occupying parts of Pueblo Bonito and other pueblos in the near vicinity, building a few new sites of their own.

Richard Wetherill first found unmistakable evidence of this Mesa Verde occupation while excavating rooms in Pueblo Bonito in 1897 and coming upon typical Mesa Verde pottery in such large quantity as to eliminate any possibility it might be trade ware brought in by footloose transients.

Only a few years ago, while excavating Pueblo del Arroyo, Gordon Vivian found at the immediate rear of that village a circular, tri-walled structure seventy-three feet in diameter and similar in many respects to ruins of that kind found in 1876 in McElmo Canyon and vicinity by William H. Holmes. At Del Arroyo the circular inner room contained no floor features ordinarily found in a kiva. Surrounding it were sixteen rooms arranged in two concentric circles, six rooms in the inner circle, ten in the outer one. Adjoining this tri-walled structure on the south was a contemporaneous pueblo of possibly seventy to eighty rooms. Where the tri-walled structure was joined to the rear wall of Pueblo del Arroyo the joint was bonded, a method of construction foreign to Chaco architecture. Generally speaking, the masonry was of the Chaco type but cruder in workmanship. Vivian came to the conclusion this structure was built early in the 1100's, and in his report commented:

> It seems definite that there was a Mesa Verde occupation of the Chaco, but the question of its extent has not been resolved . . . It would appear that this occupation was rather extensive, but that it

did not center primarily in the re-use of the large Chaco pueblos as was the case in the east ruin at Aztec. Rather, it appears to have been confined to scattered groups who, while re-using some rooms as those cited for Bonito . . . also constructed small dwellings along the north side of the canyon floor.

Early in 1954, Vivian was excavating another tri-walled structure, the Hubbard Mound at Aztec, sixty-two feet in outside diameter, showing three or four stages of occupation at the same site. As nearly as he could determine the ceremonial tri-walled structure, built over earlier house walls, was constructed later than the one at Pueblo del Arroyo. Commenting upon this in a letter, he wrote:

"I'd say definitely that the people who built both were carriers of the same tradition if not practically the same people. But I suspect that Del Arroyo was built first, probably about one hundred years earlier, before the advent of the Classic Mesa Verde pottery."

The Great Kiva and the ceremonial tri-walled structure both appear to have originated north of the San Juan and later been imported into the Chaco. Here the former was elevated from a crude, enlarged pithouse used as a communal meeting place to a massive, complex affair representing the highest peak of Anasazi religious fanaticism. There may have been some distant relationship between the two structures at one time, the tri-walled structure being a later offshoot, never changing radically in its design and never achieving the monumental proportions of the Great Kiva, although outlasting it in actual use.

Many mysteries of the Chaco have been solved since Richard and the Hyde brothers pioneered the first scientific excavation in that area. Richard was one of the first to be baffled by the question of where the Chacoans disposed of the thousands of their dead. That is still a mystery.

The Mesa Verde people who mingled with and outstayed most of the last diehard Chacoans probably were gone from the canyon by the late 1200s, as the low water table sank still lower and food became harder to produce for even their small numbers. The latest tree-ring date found in the Chaco, 1178, was turned up when Gordon Vivian and Tom Mathews were excavating Kin Kletso, a pueblo to the west of Del Arroyo with indications of an early Mesa Verde or San Juan occupation.

From 1200 to about 1400, a handful of Chaco people apparently lived in small, defensive sites, some of them located for protection against invading Navajo on narrow ledges half way up the sides of Fahada butte. Then, following the Pueblo Revolt of 1680, a small wave of refugees moved into the Chaco — Pueblo Indians from the Rio Grande fleeing from the revengeful Spanish soldiers. On the south side of Chaco Wash, in the vicinity of Wijiji and eastward, the Rio Grande refugees climbed to the heights of Chacra Mesa and built small, temporary stone hovels. They may have remained until as late as 1750, apparently getting along harmoniously with the Navajo who overran the region and who, during this period, adopted a number of Pueblo crafts and ceremonial traits.

Historically, after the Rio Grande refugees departed, few if any but Navajo entered the canyon — the Spanish prudently staying away — while the ancient ruins crumbled slowly and sank deeper under blowing sand. For another hundred years there was little to break the deep silence. When, exactly, Carravahal came upon the ruins and under what circumstances, is not known. Possibly he came alone, or perhaps in the company of one or two others from his village of San Ysidro, having heard of this place from the Indians of Jemez.

Where, Carravahal must have asked himself, as so many others have done since, did the ancients who built these pueblos go?

At best there are only a few clues. The Chacoans' craftsmanship and individuality as potters and masons already had degenerated before they left the canyon. Those who left after privation and duress, most likely after serious erosion of their self-esteem, no doubt were ready to adopt the customs and art-forms of the regions where they settled. In any event it has been difficult to trace them with absolute assurance. The best evidence is that some went east to the Rio Grande and Galisteo Basin — others, perhaps, toward Acoma — still others to the country near Zuñi.

NINE

WHEN the decision was made to excavate Pueblo Bonito, Richard Wetherill was somewhere in Arizona with the Palmer family. His letters reporting his unusual discoveries in Chaco Canyon had persuaded Talbot Hyde to postpone their plans for work that summer in the Marsh Pass region. In New York, with Fred Hyde an acquiescent partner, Talbot laid the groundwork for the Pueblo Bonito expedition.

Talbot took his project to Frederic Ward Putnam, who in 1894 had been appointed curator of anthropology at the American Museum of Natural History. Putnam also was curator of the Peabody Museum at Harvard and was regarded as the leading figure and one of the founding fathers of American archaeology. Asked by Hyde to direct the expedition in the field, Professor Putnam expressed keen interest but said his other duties prevented his leaving the East. He recommended that Talbot engage in his place a talented young student doing special work under his tutelage at Cambridge. The student's name was George Hubbard Pepper. Dr. Putnam felt certain that, with his occasional counsel, Pepper could handle the assignment creditably.

Thus it was that Richard, who by long habit and preference was accustomed to go where and as he pleased, answering only to himself, found that in the work he had initiated he would be subject to the orders of another man. Work-hardened, the most knowledgeable explorer in the Four Corners region, Richard was approaching his thirty-eighth year. George Pepper had never been in the Southwest and his only experience of the country and its Indians was what he had gained in the classroom. Pepper was twenty-three years old.

The two men met at the Alamo Ranch in April, soon after Richard left Marietta Palmer at Monticello. Pepper had arrived in Mancos with two cameras, a small trunk filled with stationery and notebooks, the kindly instructions of Professor Putnam, and his own determination to make a name for himself. No taller than Richard, he was of slight frame, had a firm jaw and graceful, long-fingered hands. His hair, raven-black and fine, received his attention; he

RICHARD WETHERILL

allowed it to grow long but never disorderly. His conversation was brisk, witty, and radiated optimism.

Not quick to draw conclusions about a man, Richard delayed forming any now and if anything his manner was merely a shade more polite than usual. If he resented his demotion he was determined not to show it to Pepper. Meanwhile, he busied himself outfitting for the trip to Chaco Canyon. This meant, besides securing horses to ride, supplies had to be loaded six feet deep in the bed of a freight wagon, including barrels of water, tents, tarpaulins, ropes, chains, bedrolls, oil lamps and oil, axes, pickaxes and a dozen long-handled shovels, and half a ton of grain and baled hay. Along with the rest were boxes of food staples, bags of flour and sugar, crates of canned coffee, a side or two of beef, and slabs of bacon and salt pork.

The valley of the Mancos was just turning green as the party set out for the Chaco, one hundred and fifty miles to the south by way of Durango. With Richard and George Pepper went Clayton Wetherill, engaged for two months as cook and general helper; tall, drawling, hot-tempered Orian Buck of McElmo Canyon, as freighter between Bonito and Mancos; and E. C. Cushman, a valley cowhand whose duties were unspecified. Possibly Talbot Hyde also was a member of the party; in any case he was in the Chaco for about a week as an observer during the opening stage of the expedition.

Of Cushman, little is known other than the fact he hired on for a month. Orian Buck, though, was a man no one could fail to notice at once, and remember. For some reason Pepper referred to Buck in the early months as "Oscar" — a slip no doubt, and lamentable because it overlooked the point that the constellation Orion, for whom Buck seems to have been named, is within the orbit of Taurus the Bull.

Ordinarily taciturn, the gangling Buck had a volcanic temper that seized him in fits and without warning. If one of the horses or mules in his charge failed to move fast enough, Buck flew into a frenzy of swearing. When oaths failed to blister the beast into action, Buck would fling his hat to the ground in cursing disgust, and stamp on it. If the rage really was upon him, Buck then would seize the harness in his teeth and bite it, sometimes even bite the side of the wagon.

Richard paid little attention. He knew Orian Buck and his tantrums from a long time back and knew they were over with as suddenly and harmlessly as they started. Even as the air crackled with oaths, any horse or mule that knew Buck knew the man would never beat him.

As their horses jogged ahead of the top-heavy freight wagon, Richard had an opportunity to become better acquainted with the young man who was to be his boss. Pepper told him, bit by bit, of his background. Before they had ferried the San Juan near Bloomfield, the river high and dangerous because of quicksand, Richard had this much of Pepper's story pieced together: He was the son of David Joline and Alice Sophia (Hubbard) Pepper, born at Tottenville, Staten Island, on February 2, 1873 . . . His father was a postman . . . There were doctors in the family and perhaps from them young George inherited some of his analytical, scientific bent . . . One of his grandfathers (on the Hubbard side) was a well-known, well-to-do surgeon . . . The grandfather once wrote to the boy saying that he would like to adopt him and if George would change his name to Hubbard, he would pay his expenses through medical school and make a great surgeon of him. The boy thought about it, and refused . . . Instead, he went on collecting arrowheads and other curious relics of the Staten Island Indians . . . He didn't have enough money to go to college (his father couldn't send him), but he was ambitious . . . After finishing high school he went to the Museum of Natural History and became a student in a museum course in anthropology.

Call it what you like — aptitude, if you wish, and hard work — whatever it was it made a strong impression on F. W. Putnam. Under the Professor's fatherly eye George Pepper made remarkable progress and, just the year before, at the Professor's suggestion, had enrolled as a special student at the Peabody Museum in Cambridge.

And while they were riding south, and as though preparing himself for the challenging tasks ahead, Pepper jotted down notes:

DISTANCE FROM MANCOS, COLO. TO CHACO CANON, N. M.

	Miles
Webers	3.4
East Cañon Bottom	8.0
To foot of Hill	9.0
To top of Hill	11.3
Dale's [Sam Daler's] Ranch	29.50
Dale's to Aztec, main road	22.00
Aztec to Bloomfield P. O.	9.3
Bloomfield to Solomon's Place	3.3
Ferry Bloomfield — Simpson's	13.8
Simpsons to Walling's Store	18.6
Walling's Store to Chaco	21.2

It added up to 149.4 miles. They made their camp in the lee of Pueblo Bonito's high north wall, pitching a tent among the big fallen rocks back against the cliff. The chuck box was pulled off the rear of the wagon and set up against Bonito's back wall as a pantry. Next to it they placed a small iron stove, and next to that a barrel of water. For drinking only. If you have to wash — try digging in the arroyo. This was a thirsty place and for the long hot months ahead it would be their home.

Stray sheepherders, cowboys and soldiers who had passed this way in years before had added damage to time's erosion by tearing gaping holes in the pueblo's massive base, seeking entrance to the small dark rooms. Three of the rooms that had been breached this way, Richard put to use — one of them still smoothly plastered and the adobe showing where Lt. James H. Simpson had scratched his name and the date, August 27, 1849. One of the rooms was used as a storeroom, another as a photographic darkroom, and in the third the food supplies were kept. A side of beef was swung from a projecting roof timber overhead.

As field director it was Pepper's responsibility to hire Navajos who would do the greater part of the digging, but since he knew nothing of their language, and they had no interpreter, he relied upon Richard's help. Talbot Hyde had cautioned Pepper that expenses must be kept low or the summer's work would be cut short. For this reason, possibly, only one Indian was signed on in the first month — a strong young fellow named Agovita Tensia. But as word got about that as much as fifteen dollars a month might be earned by digging in the great ruin, hungry Navajos from miles around descended upon Richard clamoring to be put to work.

During the first month — work having started on the fifth of May — the two refuse mounds directly south of Bonito were trenched. From previous experience with such mounds Richard was confident he would find hundreds of burials with rich funerary offerings of turquoise and pottery.

When he wasn't observing the digging or offering suggestions, Pepper spent much of the time in his tent where a rude desk had been built from boxes, anxiously awaiting developments. With the help of Clate, Orian Buck, Cushman and the one Navajo, Richard first uncovered a masonry wall forming a rectangular enclosure about the mounds, then dug several test trenches laterally in the east mound toward the center. Occasionally he stopped work to carry whatever had been found to Pepper's tent for cataloging. Finally, a main trench bisecting the largest mound through the center was dug to a depth of eight or ten feet.

To the extent of its encompassing thoroughness this method of trenching was new to Richard, and apparently was undertaken at the suggestion of Dr. Putnam. Beyond that, however, no attempt was made at layer-by-layer analysis of the material turned up. That was a procedure still unknown.

And the results? From Richard's point of view, and Pepper's, the work amounted to absolutely nothing. Nothing Richard had found was considered of importance: worn-out sandals, flakes of stone, thousands of pottery fragments, pieces of animal bone, bits of charcoal, remnants of cloth and fine-braided twine or rope of yucca fiber — the sweepings of rubbish which had accumulated for two or three centuries. And mingled with this debris were tons of loose building stone thrown here when the Bonitoans repaired or built additions to the pueblo.

Not one burial was found. Viewed with other evidence, this was astonishing and upset a popular notion that the Anasazi unvaryingly buried many of their dead in a pueblo's trash mound, intending no disrespect for the departed.

It was baffling, since Bonito's inhabitants had numbered in the thousands over the years of the pueblo's occupation. What had happened to them? Richard eventually entertained a theory that with a few exceptions the dead were cremated. This belief or suspicion he never offered as a certainty since the evidence was almost entirely negative. He based it largely on one circumstance: the discovery of scores of deep cylindrical pottery jars buried in some of Bonito's rooms. Such jars were unique to Chaco — so far as the Southwest is concerned — and apparently of ceremonial rather than utilitarian use. Although none of the jars was found to contain ashes, Richard believed it possible they might have been used for this purpose until the ashes were disposed of later.

The mystery was only heightened when, on the first of June, Pepper had Richard shift his operations to mounds on the south side of the canyon in the vicinity of Casa Rinconada, and then west about half a mile to the western slope of the Gap where he and Sidney Palmer had done some digging the previous November. Here, either below level canyon floor or in small mounds, buried at depths of from several inches to four feet, Richard and the men with him uncovered thirty skeletons. This was a relatively small number, but enough to indicate a sharp difference in burial customs between the large pueblos north of the Chaco Wash and the smaller ones strung along the south side.

Occasionally Richard paused in his digging to take photographs or to jot down notes. He was working in Mound 3 of the Gap when a shovel turned up an oddly-shaped piece of pottery. It was unlike anything he had seen before. "Quien Sabe — ?" he wrote in the notebook, entering a number and description of the object as well as a rough sketch: three jars joined together in a triangular cluster. A canteen, he thought, left in the grave to quench the departed one's thirst on his long journey. But it was not Chaco pottery, he was certain — more likely some trade ware brought in from the south.

Before the Hyde Expedition's work in Chaco Canyon was brought to an end, eighteen skeletons were found in rooms of Pueblo Bonito in addition to the thirty burials found on the south side of the wash. Other excavators following Richard and the Hydes encountered similar, baffling circumstances. Today, after many of the Chaco ruins have been excavated, only 302 burials have been found in the Chaco.

June heat and the sun's unbroken rays bore down relentlessly, with the temperature rising a few points above 100°. After the first day of working in the mounds the two Indians Pepper now employed refused to continue. Was it the heat or something else? It was not the heat, the Navajos said earnestly, it was "the sickness" they feared. Richard believed them, knowing well the reluctance of a Navajo to approach or have anything to do with the dead.

This confronted Pepper with a problem. Orian Buck was leaving for Mancos to freight in supplies and he was taking Cushman, who had quit, with him. Buck would be gone for three weeks, which left the Hyde Exploring Expedition shorthanded. On June 12, Pepper conveyed his troubles to Talbot Hyde:

"Mr. Buck started Monday morning for provisions and we expect him back a week from next Monday. Since then I have been working in the trench with Richard. It is rather hard work being that I have never been accustomed to it, and especially so as the thermometer registers 150 degrees at midday; but the work must go on and, as I am unable to get Indians, I intend to use the spade until Buck gets back."

Other matters besides heat and blistered hands troubled Pepper. He was worried about an agreement Talbot Hyde had made with Richard, assuring Richard of six months' work at $110 a month. Pepper was anxious to make every possible economy and suggested there might be a way to reduce Richard's salary to Hyde's advantage.

Talbot Hyde replied at once that his agreement with Richard must not be broken. He suggested that Pepper find other ways to economize.

And now it was July, and thirteen Navajos had been added to the payroll and were working in the great ruin with Richard and Clayton. Although the Indians had been signed on at only fifty cents a day, their wages were mounting up; a plan was devised to pay some of the Navajos with coffee or provisions. Pepper thought he could persuade those who demanded silver dollars to take less than the $15 promised — and considerably less than the $20 a month he told Hyde they were getting:

"For instance," Pepper wrote on July 27, "we can get the Indians to do the work, as well as white men could do it at the rate of $13 per month, which would be a saving of $7 per month on your lowest rate, per man." Hyde's response is not known. Possibly he thought it would be unfair to cut the Navajos' wages to forty-four cents a day. Pepper's account book shows the Indians who were not paid off with provisions continued to get fifty cents a day for the remainder of the summer.

July was a month of intensive work in the ruin and a month of visitors. Dr. Jacob L. Wortman, assistant curator of mammalian paleontology at the American Museum of Natural History, spent several days in the Chaco about the time Pepper was wrestling with the problem of what he should pay the Navajos. This was the first and apparently only meeting of Richard and the New York scientist, but in these few days a friendship started which Richard later felt justified his giving Wortman's name as witness to his work in Bonito. Soon after Wortman's departure, Clate Wetherill, who had made a trip back to the Alamo Ranch, returned with his brother Al and Dr. Prudden. The doctor stayed for about a week and Richard in his free time showed him what had been done in the excavations and took him to other ruins in the canyon.

Also with July came the seasonal rains. For two weeks the rain fell nearly every day, and frequently in blinding torrents. A wall of muddy water one morning swept down the dry arroyo, while the runoff from the mesas channeled into streams, merged, and swelled to small rivers that cascaded in waterfalls over the cliffs. Previously Richard had dug two wells in the arroyo, surrounding them with a barbed wire fence to keep away the Navajos' horses. On the morning when the Chaco River flooded he found everything had been carried away — the wells, the posts, the barbed wire. At this point, just below Pueblo del Arroyo, the rushing stream was at least thirty feet wide and several feet deep; obviously it would be some time before the wells could be restored. For several days afterward, therefore, the Hyde Expedition depended on rain water in the natural "tanks" or recesses in the cliffs above Bonito.

The natural recesses were present in the time of the Bonitoans and without doubt had been used by them as gratefully as Richard used them now.

In spite of the rains, work progressed remarkably well. Excavation had begun in the old north central section of the pueblo where eighteen rooms and one large kiva were cleared. Perhaps the selection of this area for starting work in the ruin was accidental — perhaps not. Almost as if by design, however, Richard methodically excavated those rooms which, combined, represented the oldest unit of Pueblo Bonito. Here the walls had no rubble core and facing of masonry, but were the thinness of one course of stone, often strengthened with stout stakes. Such walls could not have supported more than a third level of rooms. Arcing behind them, however, as the wings of the old village were extended gradually on both sides, the much later walls at ground level were more than two feet thick, rose at the rear to some forty feet high, and encompassed an outer four- or possibly five-story tier of rooms.

After a series of rooms had been thoroughly cleared, the excavations were backfilled. This was done principally because any other method of disposing of the sand and rubble would have consumed too much time and money.

On an average working day, Richard and Clayton were up at five-thirty with the first streak of dawn, Clate firing up the stove to get breakfast while Richard attended to various odd chores before the Navajo diggers arrived at seven. About this hour Pepper would be out of his blankets, pulling on shirt and pants and washing the sleep out of his eyes from a pail of water. Then in the cool morning air he would amble over to the cookstove and eat before getting down to work with his notebooks. As field director he divided his time between his tent, which also served as headquarters and office, and visits to the scene of that day's operations.

Richard was out on the ruin all day with the Navajos — until they quit at six o'clock — watching and supervising as they worked their way down through layers of debris, working in groups of three or four and in several rooms at a time.

On his periodic forays from the tent, Pepper carried with him a large roll of tape and, with Richard's help, made perhaps the most exhaustive measurements of objects and room dimensions in all the annals of archaeology. Not only were the dimensions of every room measured and recorded, but all features within each room were measured to the last centimeter. Altogether, it was a prodigious effort, a staggering record of size and relationship *in situ* of one thing to another. To make the record complete, photographs were taken of each room, sometimes a dozen negatives being exposed to show a room in various stages of excavation. There is reason to believe, while Pepper and Richard both used the cameras, that most of the photographs were made by Richard.

None of the rooms failed to produce something of interest but late in August, while excavating a tiny room situated close to a large kiva in the north-central area, Richard and the Navajos struck one of the largest deposits of pottery ever found in the Southwest.

After clearing away a few clumps of greasewood and digging through the covering layer of drift sand, the Indians came to the top of the buried walls. Two feet below the ground's surface a few pieces of turquoise were found. Going a foot deeper, the shovels turned up a scattering of potsherds. Presently, charred beams and brick-red adobe wall plastering were uncovered, showing that the room had been destroyed by fire. The outlook for finding anything not burned was poor.

But then, farther still under the sand and in one corner of the room, the digging revealed a cache of some twenty cylindrical jars and bowls — all perfect, all found as though stored there purposefully. The work then proceeded with tense expectancy for two days more, the sand which had filled the lower part of the room being all but spooned out in order not to miss or break anything. At the end, they had 114 cylindrical jars, 22 bowls and 21 sandstone jar covers. Among other objects were scores of turquoise beads and a dozen turquoise pendants.

The summer's work was drawing to a close when, immediately adjacent to the pottery cache, two connecting rooms were excavated with results that were even more rewarding. The first of these rooms, so small that a six-foot man could hardly spread himself out on the floor, was the sealed burial place of an obviously important personage. Water had seeped in through a break in the walls, scattering the bones of the skeleton, but many of the objects placed in the room at the time of interment had escaped damage. These included a quiver containing eighty-one arrows, a bird effigy of hematite, its tail inlaid with turquoise and pieces of shells, and —thrusting out of the sand — more than three hundred wands or staffs of wood, curiously carved at the projecting handle ends. Pottery offerings also had been left with the burial, including several mugs that bore a distinct resemblance to mugs Richard had found in the cliff houses of Mesa Verde.

Noting with his usual care the exact distance between objects, Pepper in effect sniffed out a mouse and missed a mountain. The ribs of the skeleton, he noted, were "in the southwest corner . . . 1 foot 6 inches north of the

The Wetherill brothers, photographed about 1893 at the Alamo Ranch. From left to right: Al, Win, Richard, Clayton, and John. Usually, during this period, Richard allowed a moustache only; the presence of a beard indicates he may have just returned from one of his long trips into the Four Corners wilderness. The three older brothers are seated while the younger two stand.

The Wetherills' original log cabin at Mancos appears at the right, forming a small wing of the Alamo ranchhouse. Benjamin Kite Wetherill and Julia Cowing, who visited here several times between 1891 and 1894, are seated in front of the porch. The woman standing is unidentified.

Richard and Benjamin Kite Wetherill are shown, left, at what may be a Ute wedding party in 1891 or 1892 at Mancos. Elmer Coston is fourth from the left. Al Wetherill, center, looks over the shoulders of a young Ute couple. Orian Buck, right, towers over a Ute known as Indian Jim.

Basket Maker remains, discovered in Cave 7 during Richard Wetherill's 1897 Grand Gulch expedition. Mingled with undeformed skulls of the Basket Makers are ollas or culinary pots of the later Cliff Dwellers, who built houses above the burial cysts of the earlier people.

Marietta Wetherill is the central figure in this group picture of the 1897 Grand Gulch expedition. Dutch ovens steam over hot coals in the foreground.

Kiet Siel ruin in Arizona, approximately as Richard Wetherill found it. *Courtesy of the American Museum of Natural History*

A quiet evening at Pueblo Bonito after the Navajo fiesta. The date is September 4, 1899. Dr. Prudden, George Pepper, and Clate Wetherill are playing cards. Mary Phelps of Farmington, a hired girl, dandles young Richard while his parents relax at the right.

Navajos gather at Pueblo Bonito for the fiesta. Bonito's southwest corner appears at left and the Wetherill house in the center. Near the tents is wood hauled in for the cook-fires. Horses' shadows indicate it is about 10 A.M. South Gap appears at upper right.

A foot race enlivens the Chaco fiesta. Some of the Navajos wear bandoliers and six-shooters and at least two brag eagle feathers in their hats. Pepper, as race official, is partly visible in the clearing. Above left is the Wetherill house, and beyond that the ruins of Pueblo Bonito.

Fragments from Richard Wetherill's field notes of Cave 9 and his description of Cliff Dweller relics found there. Later notations in pencil or blacker ink were made by Nels C. Nelson of the American Museum of Natural History.

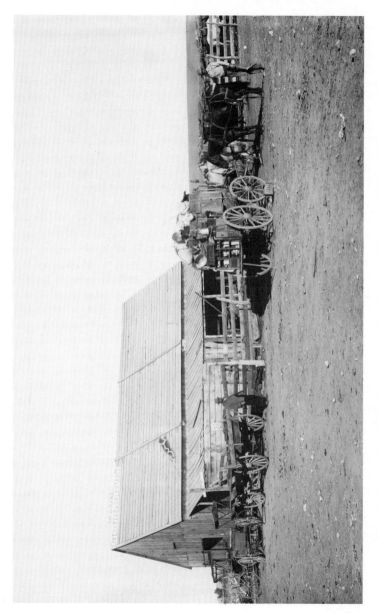

The Hyde Expedition's freight wagon, midway between Mancos and Chaco Canyon, stops at Frank B. Allen's Grand Livery Stable in Farmington, later the corner of Main and Allen streets. Allen himself stands at the left, Orian Buck, Richard's freighter, at the right.

Bend of the road at Rincon del Camino, Chaco Canyon, where Richard Wetherill was murdered. He left the trail at the bend, blinded by the evening sun, and rode into the grease-wood after Talle's stray cattle. A moment later the Navajo carefully aimed his rifle and fired.

Richard Wetherill, as he appeared in the only known portrait made of him. It was taken at the St. Louis Fair, 1904, in a time of many worries after the liquidation of the Hyde Expedition.

The musical Palmer family paused long enough for a photographer to pose them against a painted backdrop. It was somewhere in the West, probably in 1895, the year when Marietta Palmer first met and was not entranced by Richard Wetherill. She stands at the right with her mother and father, Elizabeth Ann and Sidney LaVern Palmer. Sister Edna and brother LaVern Junior hold still in chairs.

Indian fiesta, Chaco Canyon, September 4, 1899. The tall man, center, probably is Black Horse—not a chief, but one of the tribe's influential men in the 1885-1910 period. For reference, compare this photo with 1911 J. B. Moore catalog photo of Black Horse. *Mrs. James Cameron collection*

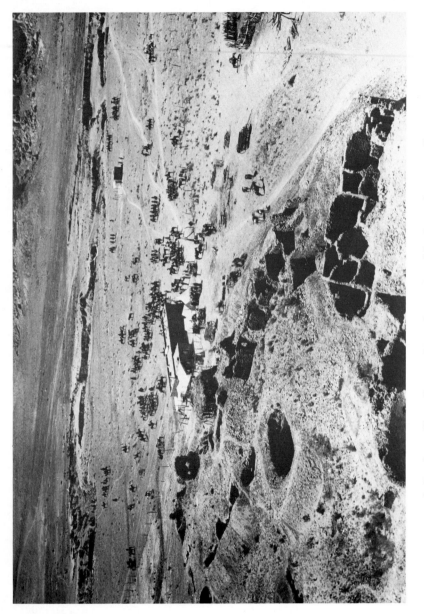

Indian fiesta, Chaco Canyon, September 4, 1899. *Mrs. James Cameron collection*

southern wall and 1 foot west of the doorway . . . A little west of the ribs and 3 feet from the south wall, the right clavicle was found; a little west of this at a distance of 2 feet 9 inches from the southern wall, the left femur was located; and a few inches north of this a scapula. Near the femur mentioned, the main portion of the vertebral column was located."

Exciting stuff this, on a high academic plane. Very nearly all of the poor fellow's bones were named and accounted for by tape measure. Spoiling the total effect, though, was the fact the bones had been washed about by water penetrating the burial room — making the ultimate disposition of remains as significant as debris washed up on a beach. In measuring the findables, Pepper overlooked or failed to mention one detail: the skull of the honored dead. Was this important personage buried with his head, or without it? Pepper neglected to say.

In the second connecting room, which was even smaller than the first, a mass grave was found containing fourteen skeletons, the bones again scattered by water. Two, however, were relatively undisturbed and also gave evidence that these had been men who once enjoyed high station, one of them especially since his wrists and ankles were encircled with massive bands of turquoise beads and pendants, and around his neck and at his abdomen were two pendants of more than four thousand pieces of turquoise.

The proximity of the two burial rooms to the large kiva suggests the possibility that the individuals laid to rest here may have been priests and members of an important clan. An interesting point evidently not determined when the rooms were excavated is whether all met death and were buried at approximately the same time, or over a long period of years.

With the fourteen skeletons of the second room, Richard and Pepper found the usual pottery offerings, six flageolets carved from wood, stone effigies of frogs and tadpoles (which some modern Pueblo Indians believe play beneficial roles in the filling of dry stream beds), and a curious cylindrical basket six inches deep and encrusted on its exterior with a solid mosaic of turquoise. As he lifted this object to inspect it, Richard discovered it was surprisingly heavy — and no wonder. When the contents were sifted and counted they were found to number 2,150 disk-shaped turquoise beads, 152 small turquoise pendants, 22 large turquoise pendants and 3,317 shell beads and small pendants.

Throughout August, Pepper employed eighteen Indians in the excavation and then let all but five go during the final month. By the time work ended for the season on September 24, thirty-seven rooms had been cleared and a collection of artifacts that would fill one freight car had been transported to Durango to be shipped by rail to the museum in New York.

After their return to the Alamo Ranch in October, Pepper used his influence as a representative of the museum to secure preferential freight rates from the Denver & Rio Grande Railroad. Also, he wrote to Talbot Hyde asking for more money. Against a balance of $31.97 in the Hyde Expedition's bank account, he explained, there were debts including unpaid salary amounting to $175 owed to Richard and $123 due Orian Buck. A check for $400 would settle everything, Pepper believed. Talbot Hyde may have winced, but actually the summer's work had been accomplished at astonishingly low cost. A fairly close estimate, based on Pepper's notes and account book, would be about $3,500.

Richard's earnings for half a year's work — $660 — failed to offset his losses, but he was well satisfied and grateful to the Hydes for the opportunity to "labor in my favorite work." During his absence from Mancos, affairs at the ranch had deteriorated and he had been compelled to sell all of his holdings to meet notes and mortgage payments.

He took as cheerful a view of this as possible, writing Talbot Hyde that "My circumstances are now such that I am free to work [at Bonito and elsewhere], as I have lost all the property I had and this work is now all that I am fitted for. It has been the cause of loss but I can build up a better reputation for careful honest work. I shall refer you to Dr. Wortman of the American Museum or to Dr. T. M. Prudden of Columbia College for a report upon the work in Chaco Cañon."

Richard revealed for the first time that there was friction between himself and his young associate. His remarks show how strong that feeling was.

"Mr. P's [Pepper's] records are O.K. also but I know the man better than you ever will, therefore I know I will receive no credit from him unless I were in his presence. Since he is the head of the expedition I ought not to expect it of course but it is my right just the same. As far as I know everything is pleasant with him — and O.K. — and I wish it to remain so. But I wish to say that if we go into the field together again that you could put me on a different footing — I think that you would find that it would result in the saving of much money, and greater results would follow though this collection is one worthy your name.

"Nothing whatever was accomplished this year until I mutinied (unfortunately I can not express myself in such beautiful language as to bring tears to your eyes or I might be tempted to try). But Mr. P. soon saw that it was the proper way to change the method and everything went along as fine as could be."

Richard's observation that he would receive no credit from Pepper for his part in the excavation of Pueblo Bonito was prophetic. It is customary, in archaeological reports, for a field director to name those who assisted him and at least mention the nature of their contribution to the overall effort. Pepper rather carefully did not refer to Richard at all when, twenty-four years afterward, he published his report on Pueblo Bonito. He did not mention, either, Frederic Ward Putnam, who had secured his position as field director, guided such of his efforts as were beyond Richard's experience, and was the supervisory director of the project. Only in a brief foreword written by Clark Wissler of the museum staff does it appear that Richard Wetherill and his brothers and Dr. Putnam were associated with Pepper. Consequently the impression has been given that the work of the Hyde Exploring Expedition in Chaco Canyon was virtually the achievement of one man — Pepper.

The reference in Richard's letter to his "mutiny" and the subsequent change in methods received no further clarification at the time and it is uncertain what Richard meant. It is known that Pepper, for the first two months of the summer, confined the work to searching for burials. Possibly Richard felt that valuable time was slipping away with little to show for it. In any case, the work was shifted early in July to Bonito's most ancient rooms.

In the same letter, Richard mentioned his approaching marriage to Marietta Palmer whom he was to meet in California. While he was there he said he would try to interest the San Francisco Academy of Sciences in sponsoring a winter expedition. Before returning home, he hoped to take his bride to Mexico City. As it turned out, there was no Academy-sponsored expedition and no honeymoon in old Mexico.

RICHARD WETHERILL and Marietta Palmer were married by a justice of the peace on December 12, 1896, in Sacramento. It was a simple ceremony witnessed only by members of the Palmer family and a friendly couple they had met, while vacationing through the Northwest, somewhere on the road south from Oregon. After the wedding Richard took his bride to San Francisco and to a hotel on one of the hills overlooking the bay crowded with steam vessels, masted schooners and fishing boats. After a week here, they made a leisurely return to Mancos by way of New Mexico, arriving at the Alamo Ranch the morning of December 30.

ANASAZI   151

On the day following his return Richard wrote to George Pepper and presently received a reply. The letters strikingly contrast two personalities:

> Yesterday we returned from New Mexico after our trip through Cal — we gave up our Mexican trip until some future time. But I hope to start on the expedition into southern Utah in about 10 days. I[t] did me much good to know that Prof. Putnam and Mr. Hyde were pleased with your work. That means much for you in the future.
>
> It is a grand opportunity you have in visiting Cambridge and seeing those rare old specimens. Don't fail to see the jewelled frog if there is any possible chance of your having the opportunity.
>
> The California collection[s] that I saw were very unsatisfactory and hardly worthy of notice since most of them had no data. Therefore were mere rubbish.
>
> I presume your time is fully occupied between your studies and the girls and theaters.
>
> There are a couple of young men here at the present time who seem to be much interested in the work and I feel now that they will take it up where we left off if we give them a little inducement. The younger one spent $1400 last year in pleasure and seems to have unlimited means . . .
>
> Mr. Buck wrote me that the Columbian Museum had put an outfit in the lower canons. We can work alongside them if in no other way . . .

The California collections Richard referred to probably included relics found by McLoyd, Graham and Patrick and bought by Mrs. Phoebe Hearst. His suggestion that Pepper not overlook seeing a jewelled frog in the Peabody collection raises a point of doubt. Possibly the frog effigy was from Chaco Canyon; one apparently similar, in any event, was found in Pueblo Bonito early the next spring.

Pepper replied, in part:

> I received your "at home" in due time but have neglected to pen a formal reply — however as formalities are generally the result of habit or a strict regard for etiquette and fashionable form, the words are as shallow and as meaningless as are the people who are the de-

voters that bow at the shrine of fashion's god, therefore I will throw form to the winds and congratulate you from the depths of my heart upon the step you have taken — may your life from this time forth be filled with joy and happiness — and should the road become rough it will merely be an occasion to prove the true worth of God's greatest gift to men.

I shall be more than pleased to meet your wife — and will look forward with happy anticipation to the time when I can see the Alamo Ranch in reality as I now see it in imagination . . .

And now with hearty congratulations and wishing for a happy present and if possible a still brighter future I beg to remain . . .

Richard's plans for a winter expedition had been made under curious circumstances. His friend, Charles Lang, had appeared at the ranch late in the fall. He brought word that the Field Columbian Museum of Chicago was organizing a party to survey the Grand Gulch region. Much concerned that others intended to enter a field where he felt he and the Hydes had prior interests, Richard sent an urgent message to Talbot, suggesting that the Hyde Expedition get back into the Basket Maker country as quickly as possible. He regarded the Field Museum's reported plans as an encroachment.

Talbot failed to share either Richard's interest or his anxiety. He and his brother Fred were unable to afford a winter expedition and would not be able to give Richard even token assistance in outfitting a small party.

In the meantime there were two developments. First, it was learned that the Field Museum was not going into Grand Gulch after all, but would send a group of men to explore other canyons of the San Juan region. Secondly — and this really was a windfall — a rich young Harvard student and his tutor had turned up in what Richard must have regarded as his darkest hour. George Bowles, the student, and C. E. Whitmore, the tutor, arrived in Mancos with money to spend and adventure their object. They were agreeable to suggestion.

Richard proposed that they finance an expedition to Grand Gulch, of which he would be the leader. The plan was accepted enthusiastically and it was decided to take to the field early in the following month — January. Richard's young bride brushed aside his objections and insisted that she be allowed to accompany him.

TEN

*Finally, we wish to state explicitly that no censure of earlier ex-
cavators is to be construed in this critical examination . . . The
Grand Gulch material is a case in point. The Wetherill brothers,
so often maligned, were far from being ruthless vandals . . . The
fact that hundreds of baskets, pots and other objects collected by the
Wetherills prior to 1900 are recorded by localities, and in many instances according to sites, testifies to the care with which the field
work was done. In the case of the Grand Gulch material it seems to
us that the cliff dwellers themselves were the chief offenders
in so disturbing stratified remains that no positive archaeological
evidence of age could be obtained.*

— EARL H. MORRIS and ROBERT F. BURGH,
Anasazi Basketry, 1941.

JANUARY, 1897, was bitterly cold.
The skies were sullen; the winds carried streamers of sand through the canyons. Clayton Wetherill was on the San Juan with the Alamo horses, restive to
get away and join his brother's expedition. Orian Buck was in McElmo Canyon breaking horses for the trip which the bad weather was delaying. Heavy
snow forced postponement of the departure until the eighteenth.

Then from Bluff City, where he hired extra horses and loaded the pack
animals with supplies, Richard led his party to the head of Cottonwood Wash
and cut west to the place where the Bear's Ears mark one of the few entrances
to Grand Gulch. Buttoned to the chin in a heavy sheepskin jacket, Richard's
bride shuddered when she saw the treacherous trail falling away before them.

"It was so crooked," Marietta said, "that even a rattlesnake would have
a hard time getting down without breaking its back."

Richard had supplied the expedition with more than forty horses but
was to find this number insufficient. "We had several extra ones on the way
down to use in case of accidents which proved of frequent occurrence," he

noted in his report. "One animal fell off of a bridge and broke its neck. Another fell off the trail where it wound about a ledge going into the cañon and was killed instantly. Another fell off of a cliff with the same result. Two gave out completely and were abandoned . . ." In all, nine horses were lost.

Marietta watched with horror as one of the pack animals lost its footing and plunged over a two-hundred foot cliff. At the bottom the packs exploded on the rocks, littering the ground like snow with the contents of several cracker boxes. Luckily, Whitmore and Bowles, who had put up about eighteen hundred dollars for the trip and found this part of it more than they had bargained for, managed the descent without accident.

In its planning and details of organization the expedition followed the lines laid down by Richard for his first trip into Grand Gulch. But now the party was larger and better equipped: thirteen men and one woman as compared with eight men in the winter of 1893-94. Another difference was Richard's certainty this time of accomplishing a specific objective. Having discovered the Basket Makers, he intended now to document the discovery.

To match the money provided by the Eastern men, his share of interest in the expedition, apart from his unsalaried leadership, included supplying some of the horses and pack animals from the Alamo Ranch stables. He explained, now, how the party was assigned to regular duties, in an introduction to his field notes:

> C. E. Whitmore and George Bowles furnished the money to carry on the work and each took an active part doing all in their power to make a success, Hal Heaton was a visiting member but proved to be a very useful, at first in the work of excavation and later as chief assistant in the culinary department.
>
> Levi Carson and E. C. Cushman had charge of the pack train after camp was located in Grand Gulch. Making weekly trips for supplies and horse feed to Bluff City which was the base of supplies. Here we had a commissary tent in charge of C. M. Tomkins [Clayton Tompkins, Richard's uncle and brother of Marion Wetherill] whose sole business it was to take care of and store the relics as they came in and issue goods to the packers.
>
> Clayton Wetherill and G. Bowles looked after the riding stock and pack animals not in use, looked up fresh workings and kept the camp in fresh meat. At odd times [they] would help in excavating and always in moving camp.

George Hangrove had charge of the kitchen and found the duties very onerous as he had to be up at 4 a.m. to get the morning meal in time. Storms and frequent movings did not tend to lighten the work. Jas. Ethridge, O. H. Buck, C. C. Mason, Bert Hindman and R. Wetherill were in the excavation continuously, and all others whenever other duties pertaining to the work did not interfere. Mrs. R. Wetherill kept the notes and records and helped much in the measurements, etc. [Another member of the party, William Henderson, Richard forgot or failed to mention.]

More than 40 animals were used. 27 to 30 were packed all the time with from 100 to 250 [pounds] each. Each member of the party had a saddle animal except C. Wetherill and Bowles who had two each.

No grass whatever was found. The animals subsisted on the grain fed them with the tops of brush which they picked. Before leaving there many were weak and thin . . .

And then Richard added these remarks about the general nature of Grand Gulch:

Ingress or egress is very difficult, there being not more than 5 or 6 places where even footmen can get in or out of the cañon.

Wherever there are slopes, a sparse growth of piñon and cedar occurs; about the springs are cottonwood, willows and box elder. In the shaded side cañons are mountain ash and hackberry. The usual brush of the cañon is scrub oak. Canes or rushes cover the bottom lands in the vicinity of the water.

To enter the cañon a party must be equipped with suitable pack animals and expect to spend 3 days on the road from Bluff to reach it.

Richard and his party remained in Grand Gulch for about a month, working out of six main camps which they set up, one after the other, under the sheltering cliffs and close to firewood when that could be found. Since there was little or no water flowing in the canyon bottom they had to depend on melted snow, of which there was more than they otherwise might have wished.

The bitterness of the weather and constant threat of heavy snowstorms which could have cut off their retreat, filled Richard with anxiety. Their horses would have made poor eating. He concealed such thoughts but was conscious of the value of each short hour of daylight, rousing his men in the cold blackness before dawn so they might start working in the caves long before the pale sun appeared through morning fog. They worked until darkness made them stop. After supper, around a warming fire, they turned in early to get what rest they could before the cook's voice awakened them to another cold morning.

Richard pressed them hard, almost as though this was the most arduous of military campaigns. He was sympathetic when weariness and gloom descended upon them, offering encouragement; but he was aware always of the perils a blizzard might bring. Marietta saw him hardly at all except at night, since he was always out where there was digging and she was in camp keeping notes on the Basket Maker and Cliff Dweller relics brought in. Sometimes, for relief, she helped the cook by baking hot biscuits for the men's supper.

Washing himself free of the caking dust with melted snow, Richard at night was a rough-appearing bridegroom to a girl of nineteen. But in a brusque way he let the others become aware of his devotion; he treated her tenderly and called her by a Navajo name, Asthanne — Little Woman — when they rolled into their blankets.

One night it snowed softly for several hours and with it there was something that Marietta always remembered as a part of her honeymoon. By her side in the darkness she felt him stir and then sit up.

"It's snowing," Richard said.

Marietta mumbled a few syllables and shrugged deeper into the blankets. Maybe if it snowed hard enough they wouldn't have to get up so early in the morning.

"Those mummies," Richard said. This made little sense to his bride but she sighed agreeably. "They'll get wet," said her husband. And suddenly he was out of their bed and Marietta was asleep again.

This night, as almost always, they had been sleeping under the protective ledge of a cave. Dimly, through her sleep, Marietta could hear footsteps, coming and going, and then there was Richard's voice, sounding pleased.

"They're all here. Where would you like them — at the head of the bed or at the foot?"

Marietta started up, sleep gone, and wide-eyed. There was Richard beside their bedroll, crouching, both arms circled about in supporting embrace two of the withered Ancients he had carried in out of the snow. Several others he had propped up close by. The mummies stared back at her sightlessly and gape-jawed, the long wild hair of one streaming down across a wizened, tobacco colored face. Out of a dry throat Marietta finally answered:

"At the foot, Mr. Wetherill. At the foot of the bed."

It was there, at the foot, that what seemed to Marietta an unholy host leaned or reclined in frozen postures for the remainder of the night.

Snow and howling winds that filled the canyon air with stinging red sand slowed their progress but did not stop it. Under the sandstone and adobe walls of the houses built in caves level with the canyon floor or a little above it, Richard's party dug into the ancient cysts and brought out the burials of the Anasazi with their cone-shaped baskets large enough to contain or to cover a large man. Robes covering some of the dead, still in fair preservation though a thousand years old, were woven from strips of fur. The square- or rounded-toe sandals covering the withered feet were woven in geometric designs of red and black much like the designs the later Cliff Dwellers and early Pueblos of the region used on their pottery.

From the head of Grand Gulch where they had entered, Richard probed innumerable small sites as well as the ruins of eleven large caves on a southward course of thirty-four miles. He had worked in some of the same places three years before, some had been rudely excavated before his time by Mc-Loyd, Graham and Patrick. Cliff Dweller remains were not shunned if found in excellent condition, but the effort always was in digging deeper to expose what was left of the Basket Makers.

Richard was seriously handicapped in his attempt to keep a photographic record of his work. He was using a large camera mounted on a heavy tripod, and 5 x 7 glass plates. The extreme cold made it difficult to mix his chemicals. One night the temperature dropped far below freezing and all of his negatives for that day were ruined. On another occasion, when he had used up his glass plates, he could not find an accessible cave or cliff house room dark enough, even with the use of blankets, to renew his supply. And almost always there was fog or the dim light from an overcast February sky to make picture-taking nearly impossible. With Marietta's help, however, he kept pages of notes on the more than five hundred and fifty specimens found, and diagrammed each of the major caves where the work was done, numbering everything.

Most of the caves they explored were close to the bottom of the canyon and therefore easily reached; a few, however, were high in the cliffs, and these gave trouble. To reach the high dwellings Richard resorted to methods he and his brothers had used in their early explorations of Mesa Verde.

One cliff house, five hundred feet above the canyon floor and perched in its cave some fifteen or twenty feet below the rimrock, was reached from above by means of a rope dropped from the top with its end dangling in space. With a second rope tied around his waist and paid out slowly by others on the rim, one man lowered himself into the cave on the free-hanging rope. It was a hazardous undertaking and resulted in the finding of only a few specimens of minor interest.

At other times the trunks of dead trees were lashed together, butt to top, to form a crude ladder. In such a manner the men were able to scale heights of a hundred feet or more and to reach the long ledges or shallow caves where the Anasazi, with the patient toil of mud wasps, built their high, clinging homes. Nearly always, the toe and hand holds pecked in the cliff surface by the Ancients as their means of access, were too worn by time and erosion to be safe.

On both faces of the canyon as they worked south, Richard found painted figures or clusters of hands in red, black or green. At some places, mingling with these, and pecked into the stone, were formalized figures of mountain sheep, turkeys, snakes and scrolls. Near the lower end of the canyon wind, sand and water had formed a succession of natural bridges. "Under these bridges," Richard observed, "in some cases are houses and here are the pictographs in the greatest profusion. The painted ones of the Basket Maker with the later ones of the Cliff Dweller cut or incised in the rock . . . "

On one of his trips from Bluff City, Levi Carson brought Richard a letter from Talbot Hyde, the first since the previous spring when he was working in Chaco Canyon. With the next pack train to Bluff, Richard sent his reply, dated the fifteenth of February:

> Yours just rec'd. We are doing our work here carefully and thoroughly since the value of these things consist[s] largely in the scientific data procured . . .
>
> I was somewhat surprised to hear from you at this late date as I had written two or three times and not heard a word since last spring when you were here, (you may have said something in your letters to Pepper), so I did not know whether or not my work [at Pueblo Bonito] met with your approval. I fancied it had not . . .

Not much material of the Basket Makers has been found yet. Our next move will take us to their burial places.

We hope soon to cross the San Juan and visit Mysterious Cañon in which are many great ruins. We will finish this cañon first. By that time we will have burros and mules enough to move with. Here we are are using horses, having forty head. It takes a good many with such a large party, there being fourteen of us. My wife is in the party doing the work Pepper did last summer.

The severity of the weather and the weakened condition of the horses made Richard change his plans as the work in Grand Gulch came to an end. Instead of the entire party enduring the unrelieved hardships of a trip to Mysterious Canyon, some fifty miles west of Grand Gulch and south of Navajo Mountain, he sent only Orian Buck and Charlie Mason accompanied by George Bowles. These three departed with the strongest of the horses. With the rest of the party he returned to Bluff City and rested there for a few days while outfitting the next stage of the expedition.

Then, with ten pack animals and enough supplies to last a month, Clate Wetherill, with William Henderson and Jim Ethridge, started for Moqui Canyon, due west of Grand Gulch and emptying into the Colorado River above Hall's Ferry. Clate's task was to explore the large caves there for Basket Maker material. He found the caves without trouble and in them many of the now familiar and oddly-shaped cysts, but others had come before him and the cysts were empty.

In the meantime, Richard left Marietta with his friends the Allens, in Bluff City, and with the remainder of the party headed down the Chinle Wash toward Marsh Pass, stopping on the way to dig once more in the large ruin now called Poncho House. In Marsh Pass, according to plan, his group would be met in several weeks by the two parties working in the other canyons.

Many ruins he had not seen on his previous trips were discovered now by Richard's party, in the region where his brother John later was to build a trading post for the Navajos and where the little settlement of Kayenta would spring up in the red sand hills. They worked in the vicinity of Agathla Needle or El Capitan, the giant volcanic shaft of rock that rises from the desert north of Kayenta, and at Moqui Rock just north and west of Black Mesa. Of this last place Richard remarked:

"The Rock is so called on account of the great ruin upon the top, at the present time in ruins and the material of which it had been made lies strewn on the ground beneath. It was quite easy of access as the slope of the rock on the south is so easy one can walk up. The height is not above 150 feet. The base of the Rock will perhaps occupy 3 or 4 acres, while the apex is not 100 ft. sq. Burial places are situated all around in regular burial mound within a ¼ of a mile of the rock."

Presently Moqui Rock would figure again in the story, but now Richard was traveling once more into Tsegi Canyon. Exactly two years after his discovery of Kiet Siel, he was returning to that great cliff house, promising Teddy Whitmore that they would find more pottery than their horses and burros could carry out. On this occasion he took measurements of Kiet Siel and diagrammed its floor plan, but his drawing later was separated from his field notes and has been lost. His description of Kiet Siel and its neighboring ruins survives:

The Great Ruin or cliff dwelling is in the head of the 2nd right hand fork going up on the west side. Not many feet above the bottom of the Cañon, about 50 ft., in the bottom against the cliff are a few rooms that we failed to measure. They were filled up with debris from the house above. Our time being limited we attended strictly to the Main Ruin (for description see ground plan and measurement of Cliff house, Laguna Creek).

Our camp was made on the opposite side of the Cañon in a cave which had been used as a sheep corral by the Navajos. This one at one time contained a building of several rooms. With burials on the slope in front, since we found several skulls sticking out. This cave we did not work. Could not stand the filth and dust raised by shoveling. The fifth right hand cañon on the way up has two lagoons filling the cañon from cliff to cliff one mile apart and each one a mile long and about 300 yards wide. The depth is unknown. At the season we were there a narrow sandy beach was exposed making it easy for us to go up the Cañon. Ducks are plenty on these lakes. A cliff house was found above the upper lake in which a set of weaving implements were dug up from the floor of one of the rooms. Valley ruins with a great deal of the gray and red pottery with the black decorations are found on all of the untillable low points in all of these cañons. The cliff houses seem generally to be fortifications for these valley people.

This passage, the one existing fragment in which the discoverer of Kiet Siel mentions that great cliff village, shows Richard at his worst. Clear enough in his own mind was what he meant when he wrote "the second right hand fork going up on the west side" and "the fifth right hand cañon on the way up." Between the mind and the paper, unfortunately, the thread of meaning was all but lost.

The work of the expedition was nearly at an end; the whole party — with the exception of Marietta who was still waiting in Bluff City — united again in Marsh Pass. Then all was thrown suddenly into confusion. Teddy Whitmore and young Bowles were missing from the camp. While a search for them was carried on through the maze of canyons where the most experienced of them might easily have lost his way, an Indian came to Richard with a message.

The wealthy Harvard student and his tutor had been kidnaped and were being held for ransom. The messenger (whether he was a Paiute or Navajo is uncertain) named the amount demanded — several hundred silver dollars — and dropped a few frightening hints of what would happen if the money was not supplied pronto.

Nothing is known of Richard's reaction to this. He may have attempted persuasion and a threat of reprisal unless the two men were freed at once; that would have been in character, from what is known of him. In any case the kidnapers were determined to carry the thing through. Since the few dollars in the pockets of all the men came to only a fraction of the money demanded, Richard sent a rider to Bluff City with a message he hoped would be believed and honored with silver.

Several days passed before the rider returned. He had been successful and the money was turned over to the Indian who had been acting as intermediary. Taking the heavy sack of coin in a firm grip, the Indian quirted his pony into a run and soon disappeared through the pass. Some hours later, haggard from their experience but otherwise unharmed, Whitmore and Bowles rode into camp. Their Indian abductors had held them for three days and four bone-chilling nights as prisoners on the top of Moqui Rock.

After an absence of three months, Richard's party headed toward home, returning to Bluff City in April, where Marietta and Uncle Clate Tompkins were waiting. There the men disbanded. Nearly two thousand relics, weighing a little less than one ton, had been brought in by the pack animals. Richard persuaded some Mormons to haul the collection in wagons to the Alamo Ranch, the price agreed upon being a quarter of a cent per pound. Teddy Whitmore and Bowles, with Richard's assurances that their half share of the collection would be held for them until they sent for it, went on to Durango and boarded a train for the East.

Richard had been home only a week when he began outfitting for the second season's work for the Hyde Exploring Expedition in Chaco Canyon. On May 7 he wrote Talbot Hyde that his winter trip had been a great success, so much so that the Cliff Dweller and Basket Maker material of the region where he had worked was now "practically exhausted."

The collection remained unopened at the ranch until the following October when Richard, again home from Pueblo Bonito, wrote the first of a number of letters to Hyde offering, with the agreement of Bowles and Whitmore, the entire collection at the price of $5,500. If Hyde accepted the proposal, Richard would receive half of that amount.

"I am willing to do the fair thing," Richard said, "by giving you all the time you may desire for it . . . Photos and data are as complete as we can make them except the fine one hundred and twenty four room house in Laguna Creek, Arizona [Kiet Siel]. This house has had about all the measurements made for reproduction. It was thoroughly excavated and all the material is in this collection."

Talbot Hyde was interested, knowing what an important addition it would make to the collection already given to the American Museum of Natural History, but felt the price Richard asked was too high. Although Richard was badly in need of money to pay debts on the Alamo Ranch, he and the others finally agreed to Hyde's offer of $3,000. In January, 1898, the collection was shipped to New York. With it went a short note to Hyde, with this rather poignant postscript:

"My interest in this collection is to be paid to Mrs. R. Wetherill except $100.00 which you can have sent to me by express . . .

"You see, I am horribly in Debt here through my efforts to help all. The result is I am thrown now entirely on my own resources which are nil. I am obldged to make a move which I think will be in the San Juan [region] at first . . . "

ELEVEN

MARIETTA was only twenty years old and Richard was thirty-eight when he brought her back to Chaco Canyon in the spring of 1897. After a honeymoon in the cold wilderness of Grand Gulch the girl's first home as Richard's wife was a wall tent under the high cliff back of Pueblo Bonito.

Most brides would have found this less than alluring. For Marietta, accustomed to years of wandering travel with her parents, there was little cause for dismay. She was in love with the hard-working, often silent man whom she still called "Mr. Wetherill," and fitted herself cheerfully into the simple rough ways and routine of the Hyde Exploring Expedition.

Since Clayton was not a member of the party his duties of the previous summer as cook fell to her and to an Indian named Juan. Presiding over a small iron wood-stove set on stones against Bonito's back wall, she and Juan cooked for the members of the expedition and sometimes for the Navajo workmen, with whom she was soon on excellent terms. In her free time she helped Richard when he needed her and otherwise wandered alone on horseback through the canyon or began to brush up acquaintances with Navajo families living near the Escavada.

A few of the Indians adopted Richard's pet name for her, Asthanne, Little Woman, finding it appropriate. All of them, meanwhile, had agreed on their own name for Richard: to them, because of his work, he quite naturally became "Anasazi." On his frequent visits to the Chaco, Dr. Prudden heard the Indians speak of Richard by this name with mingled humor and respect; the nickname stayed.

The youthful George Pepper at first had also addressed Richard as "Mr. Wetherill" and then, after an interval of calling him by no name at all, used "Richard" and found it more comfortable. Perhaps he thought it unusual, but he rarely heard anyone speak of "Dick" Wetherill. The Navajos, quickly perceiving Pepper's interest in snakes and fearless handling of them, called him, among themselves, Hostine Klish, Snake Man.

Starting at the end of the third week in May, work in the great ruin this second season progressed more rapidly than before. To meet the expedition's expenses, Talbot Hyde had deposited more than $3,000 in the bank at Durango, but two months later the funds were gone and Pepper had to request Richard not to cash a check of $255 for salary until Hyde could be prevailed upon to deposit more money. This still left the expedition owing Richard $444 in unpaid salary, with an additional $110 owed to Orian Buck and $152 to the Indians.

Overlooking a number of essential expenditures that as field director he would have to make, Pepper had employed twenty Indians to work in the ruin. At the same time, apparently without asking too closely about the cost of supplies, he ran up large bills in Farmington and Durango. In estimating his expenses he neglected to allow anything at all for hay and grain for the horses until the middle of July when Orian Buck, returning from one of his periodic trips with the freight wagon, told Pepper that various merchants were demanding payment.

If they didn't pay up soon, the blasted sheriff would be down handing out processes, the teamster warned Pepper solemnly.

Pepper found it hard to cope with these problems, all foreign to his experience. Marking in his time-book the hours put in by each Navajo was a boring chore. He gave it up completely in September. The small intricacies of a large payroll and the price of hay interested him far less than the dimensions of a hematite bird or diagramming the layout of a room.

Someone, however, had to be responsible for these unpleasant details. With no funds in the bank, with salaries and wages long overdue, and with numerous creditors setting up a clamor every time Buck came to town, Pepper turned to Richard for advice. He received a practical suggestion.

"It would be handy," Richard said quietly, "if you were to make yourself scarce when the sheriff comes. Maybe he won't come. But if he does, you might just disappear for a few hours. Perhaps I could talk him out of serving claims on us until Mr. Hyde puts more money in the bank."

He and Orian Buck would wait for their pay, Richard said. The Navajos would not. While the money had lasted Pepper paid them with checks, which the Indians accepted reluctantly — much preferring silver dollars. Now some other means of keeping them at work would have to be found. Pepper began paying off many of the Indians with coffee and supplies at prevailing trading post prices. Since the wholesale price paid for the supplies was well under the traders' prices, this might be regarded as a sharp transaction. Actually, aside from the traders' mark-up for profit, the arrangement was not entirely unfair. Just as the traders did, the Hyde Expedition had to figure on the cost of hauling the supplies many miles into the Chaco.

Without troubling to explain the complexities of the problem, Richard and Pepper both informed Hyde about this, the latter appealing for more money to meet the expedition's debts. "We have sold nearly three boxes of coffee to the Indians since we have reached camp," Pepper said, and " . . . this means quite a saving as there is a profit of over eight dollars on each box."

Quite as candidly, Richard informed Hyde: "A good share of the groceries bought this year went to pay labor bills. That is a good way to do since the item of coffee costing you 12½ cents per pound brought you twenty five cents readily." For other food items used thus in trade the profit was much less or non-existent.

The Navajos were satisfied with the arrangement since it saved them riding thirty or forty miles to the nearest trading post. But the impatient merchants of Farmington were harder to satisfy. For the first time the ancient canyon was invaded by bill collectors. When they came, Pepper disappeared into the ruins of Chetro Ketl while Richard reasoned and argued and in the end won an extension of time.

And so, with some moments of anxiety, the summer's work continued. In early August the heat became so intense that Marietta, in the early stages of her first pregnancy, begged Richard to take her some place cooler. He took her to the Alamo Ranch, making the round trip of three hundred miles in a little more than a week. While in Mancos he learned the Snake Dance was to be given at Walpi on August 19 and so consequently hurried back with this information, knowing that Pepper was eager to see the Hopi ceremony.

On his arrival at Pueblo Bonito he found that a Mr. Robinson of the American Museum of Natural History had come out to inspect their work. Robinson was as anxious as Pepper to see the Snake Dance. To Richard's dismay, they took the one good camera used for photographing the work in the ruin and departed, with instructions to Richard to carry on. They were gone eleven days.

By nature and tradition, Richard's Indian friends were acquisitive. There was nothing morally wrong, they thought, if they "captured" anything of value in or about the ruin that was not nailed down. When Anasazi rebuked them for this they wore the look of injured innocence. No real sense of guilt was felt.

The summer before, one of the Navajos had attempted to liberate the expedition's iron cook stove, heavy but not bolted to anything solid. Richard had intervened. The stove was returned and the Indian received a mild reprimand. There were no bad feelings on either side. "The one who intended to take the stove," Richard later told Dr. Prudden, "was very submissive and made a good hand after."

Of more serious concern was the Navajos' inclination to pocket any object of desirable turquoise turned up in their digging. To meet this problem, Richard reported to Hyde, he arranged for at least two Indians to work together in one room "or as many as could to advantage, because there were so many more eyes to see, and less likelihood of their stealing. So much rivalry existed that they would tell upon each other if anything was taken." Even with these precautions, some relics were stolen.

The object of the most celebrated theft — a crouching frog carved from jet with eyes and a collar of inlaid turquoise — now reposes safely in a glass case in the American Museum of Natural History. Seeing it there, no one would guess its history.

The jewelled frog was found early in the summer during the excavation of Room 38 in the central north portion of the pueblo. Other interesting things had been turned up in the same room, including a square tablet of jet inlaid at each corner with round turquoise stones, bone scrapers inlaid with a mosaic of turquoise and jet, and the skeletons of fourteen macaws.

Soon after the discovery of these objects, the jet frog with the jewelled eyes disappeared. Richard questioned all of the Navajos, receiving only denials or blank expressions of innocence.

"Most likely it will turn up this winter," he finally wrote Hyde, knowing that the jet frog was such a rare, valuable object that its possessor would boast about it.

Months later he traced the ornament to the store of an Indian trader on the San Juan, near Farmington. Diplomatically, Richard did not mention that the frog with the turquoise eyes had been stolen, but merely asked the trader his price for it. The trader mentioned a figure. It was too much, Richard said. Sitting with their feet on the fender of the stove the two men discussed the weather (dry), the price of wool (low), the price of saddles (high), and then the weather again. As he was leaving, Richard ransomed the jewelled frog for about half the amount the trader had asked, and for what Richard considered a fair price — fifty dollars.

Sifting sand from Rooms 39 and 48, two of the Navajos found a number of fine arrowpoints at the bottom of their wire screen. Someone observed them stooping to pick them up and then pocketing them. Again with diplomacy, Richard said nothing — since he had not seen it himself — but sent Marietta to the Indians a day or so later to ask if they had any arrowpoints they would care to sell. For a small sum the arrowpoints changed hands.

Hosaleepa, whom Richard regarded as the best Navajo he had, captured one of the finest turquoise pendants ever found in Bonito. Richard puzzled over the best course to follow, and finally did nothing about it. A man of rare intelligence and rarer sensibilities, Hosaleepa would know that Richard knew the pendant came from Pueblo Bonito. Even if Richard were to broach the matter indirectly there would be a tacit accusation of theft. This case was exceptionally delicate and the only one of its kind involving Hosaleepa.

"I explained to Mr. Robinson why I did not get the pendant from Hosaleepa," Richard told Hyde, hoping that Talbot would understand.

But in other respects Hosaleepa did not always require such careful treatment. He turned up late for work one morning, something unusual for him, and Richard told him to take the rest of the week off and really rest. Hosaleepa was not offended and after that turned up on time.

Out of his experience in working with Indians, Richard weighed the question of Hosaleepa's integrity, while advising Hyde about practical matters to consider for the following year:

" . . . you will find him more honest than a white man," he said. And then: "In the light of past experience I should say work not more than six men beside the cook. He should be a white man; a Navajo has too many friends."

Richard knew the Indians well, but he could be strict if he thought the occasion demanded. Sometimes he indulged in horseplay which now might be easily misunderstood. One story in particular gained currency after Richard's death when told by several Indian agents, none of whom claimed more than hearsay knowledge of it. Navajos who met his displeasure, according to this story, he locked up overnight in a dark room of Pueblo Bonito. Knowing their fear of chindees, or spirits of the dead, he supposedly closed them in with four or five skulls of Anasazi taken from the ruin. And to add a bizarre touch of horror to the punishment, it was said, he lighted the skulls with candles.

The story has been disputed by men who, like the Indian agents, had no personal knowledge of such an incident but did know Richard well and have said it was the sort of thing he was incapable of doing. There is another version of the story that has the ring of truth to it.

Four or five of his Indians got roaring drunk one night on bad whisky they had bought from Mexican sheepherders who were passing through the canyon. Early the next morning Richard found the Navajos sleeping off the effects of their jag in one of the rooms they had been excavating. Taking a shovel, Richard covered them partially with a few inches of loose dirt. Then on the edge of the bank above the room he lined up a row of grinning skulls recently found in one of the pueblo's burial rooms.

The reaction of the Navajos, when they finally awoke, was all that Richard had anticipated, and more. Thomas Padilla, the first to emerge from his befogged slumber, quaked through the various stages of terror and then calmed down when he recognized the skulls for what they were. It occurred to him to carry the prank a step further. Shaking his companions, and bringing them staggering to their feet, he pointed dramatically to the skulls and cried out:

"Murderers! See there, the heads of the Mexicans you killed last night!"

Marietta Wetherill, in recalling this episode, said the red-eyed Navajos grinned sheepishly when they gathered around Juan, the cook, to beg for coffee. As each in turn told of his paralyzing fright, first at confronting the grinning skulls and then at the thought of murders committed in the daze of alcohol, they doubled up with laughter and soon had the whole camp laughing with them. The story was told many times later, Marietta said, to entertain visitors who came to Pueblo Bonito.

RELATIONS between Richard and George Pepper grew cooler as the summer wore on. When the time came in September to break camp and return to Mancos, the two men were trying to preserve some pretense of good feeling. Neither spoke openly to the other of what was in his mind, either then or later, but both knew they could continue working together only with great difficulty.

If Pepper confided his feelings to Talbot Hyde at this time, he must have done so verbally because his letters of this period contain no complaint against Richard. Hyde was, however, well informed of Richard's attitude toward Pepper. Richard was not a domineering person but unquestionably he was aggressive, filled with a fiery energy and a desire to get things done. He was critical of Pepper's scientific methods, and — where Putnam's influence entered in — unduly so; he was certainly impatient with the young field director's candid dislike for manual work and his boredom with the financial affairs of the expedition.

Possibly the greatest point of friction, and one for which Pepper cannot be blamed, was Talbot Hyde's decision to place Richard under the young archaeologist's general field supervision. Any Easterner of Pepper's years and limited experience, regardless of his abilities — and Pepper's were considerable — undoubtedly would have found it hard to win the veteran Wetherill's respect.

These aspects troubled Richard when, at the end of the summer of 1897, he wrote Talbot Hyde summarizing the season and suggesting certain changes for the next year:

> Yours received, and will answer to the best of my ability . . .
>
> We arrived at Pueblo Bonito about the 22nd [of May]. Work continued steadily until Mr. Robinson's arrival. In the early part of August, I made a trip home, and found that the snake dance at Hualpi would take place on the 19th. I hurried back to camp and arrived in time to get Mr. Pepper and Mr. Robinson off to see it.
>
> The camera episode you know of.
>
> The taking away of it prevented the completion of the work in hand by me. As I know well that material without positive proof has little scientific value . . .
>
> Seven o'clock in the morning every man [Navajo] was at his place, when I was in camp. They worked until noon, nooned one and a half hours, then worked until six p.m. . . .
>
> Most of all the workmen we had were pretty bright fellows, and considered the work a good thing for them, as long as they could cash their checks readily, (but cash at all times would have been a great saving). I found that in many cases they had to discount their checks to get money for them.
>
> Checks mean a great waste of time as well.
>
> The work I should consider systematic, at least while I was there. I knew at all times what to expect in certain rooms, and was on hand to photograph and number.
>
> You see, I placed room numbers upon articles found, and then sent them to Pepper's tent for him to catalogue and number.
>
> Each one knew what was expected of him, and where and how

to work; failure in this meant the loss of their job, as also being late more than two mornings.

The majority of the workmen camped with us, so there was little trouble on that score . . .

You paid me for my time, but did not outline my duties, but I felt that the success of the expedition depended upon my efforts. Therefore, every moment I had was spent with them giving instructions and placing room numbers upon articles, except when doing Photograph work, trading for mutton, etc. I measured nearly all the rooms, and gave all finds personal attention. My rule was to be up at five-thirty every morning except Sundays . . .

Richard then mentioned the thefts of ornaments referred to earlier. He concluded with recommendations for improving the expedition's work the following summer:

A live man who has fondness for the work to take charge, or at least one who has conscientious scruples; one whose sole aim is not the almighty dollar. One who is not lazy; one who can get up in the morning and put his shoulder to the wheel; an able bodied person who does not need a valet; somebody worthy of confidence and trust and who realizes the importance of the work. A man of this kind can do all the work that Pepper and I both did . . .

Get mules. They are good anywhere either for teaming or packing, and can pick their own living except in the settlements. There will be a big saving in feed. Then get a cheaper driver, one for twenty or twenty five dollars per month at most. You can easily see that fifty dollars per month can be saved on feed, twenty on a driver, as by giving him more time he can cook his own meals. The place that I hold will be unnecessary as a good manager can see to all that. A saving can be had by having the white cook, since he can make his own wages trading . . .

Don't furnish such bountiful supplies of stationery to haul over the road. Limit the outfit to necessities.

Pound saved in hauling means a great deal of labor saved in taking care of material afterwards . . .

If Richard hoped Hyde would relieve Pepper of his duties and put him in charge of the expedition, he was disappointed; Talbot made no changes in their positions and ignored all of Richard's practical suggestions. Two days later, as an afterthought, Richard wrote again:

> I forgot to mention that very little work was done after the first of August. I made the trip home with my wife and took back $100.00 in silver with which to pay up outstanding obligations.
> Then the eleven days while Mr. Robinson & Mr. Pepper were at the Snake dance little could be done —
> While they were away I found that there was no money in Bank and that Pepper was liable to prosecution by the Angry holders of his checks —
> It would have cost him very much trouble had any of them gotten him — As it was I volunteered to come to Mancos & telegraph any message he might write for funds
> I made the trip from Chaco to

There the page of the letter turned and the remainder of it is missing from the file of correspondence Hyde originally gave to the museum. In the upper left corner of the first page is the pencilled notation: "Part copied 6-10-02 G.H.P." A number of the other letters in the same file bear the same notation. If Richard had been successful in concealing his feelings about Pepper during their daily association at Pueblo Bonito, Pepper had no reason for doubt when he came upon this file on June 10, 1902. Thereafter, and George Pepper let it be known quite openly, he and Richard Wetherill were enemies.

TWELVE

HE had been back at the Alamo Ranch only a few days in October, 1897, when Richard conceived a plan which would lead the Hyde Exploring Expedition along an entirely new course and affect, in some degree, nearly every Navajo living in Arizona and New Mexico. His plan was to open a trading post at Pueblo Bonito.

During the first two seasons in Chaco Canyon, Richard had become aware that the Indians needed and would welcome a store close to the operations of the expedition. At his suggestion, his brothers Al and Clayton, and Orian Buck left Mancos in October to spend four months in the Chaco, building a small store and establishing trade with the Navajos of that region.

It was a modest start. Against the rear north wall of Bonito, where their kitchen formerly had been, Al and Clate erected a one-story appendage to the ruin, some fifteen or twenty feet square and opening from the inside into three or four of Bonito's cleared-out rooms. Since Buck was away most of the time with the freight wagon hauling in supplies from Farmington, the brothers had only a team of burros to help in dragging stone and barrels of water used in mixing adobe mortar. Early in the new year, however, the walls were up and covered with a brush and adobe roof resting on beams taken from the ruin. It was tight, snug and small and crowded with the dry goods, harness, galvanized ironware and rope, the boxed, bagged or canned food supplies, the axes, chains, lamps and fuel oil, and a few of the novel "sundries" and an assortment of candy which the Indians would want in bartering their wool and blankets or in pawning their jewelry. The Wetherills, for the first time, were in trading business with the Navajo.

Al still found time to dig in the big ruin. Hopeful of finding something valuable, unaware that this might be contrary to the interests of the Hydes, he wondered if Dr. Prudden in New York knew of a "philanthropist" who might be interested in buying a few relics. Dr. Prudden replied that he did not and chided Al mildly for making such a proposal. He suggested that anything of interest taken from Pueblo Bonito ought to be retained in one collection — implying of course the Hyde collection for the American Museum of Natural History.

Al had no need of a philanthropist since his digging produced practically nothing. "Al has $10.00 worth of material, at least he asks that for it," Richard informed Talbot Hyde on his brothers' return to Mancos. Richard said he felt Al and Clate had wasted their time and the winter, so far as they were concerned, was a failure. In this he was quite wrong, not realizing then how important the little store they had built would become.

The trading post at Pueblo Bonito was a "regular" store, Al wrote Dr. Prudden in March, 1898. It had enjoyed brisk trade from the moment it opened. Buck had stayed on to run it, when Al and Clate departed. When Richard arrived in the Chaco in May for the third season's work in Pueblo Bonito, the amount of business transacted in the store would open his eyes.

Unless there was a shooting in one of the saloons or a robbery of a station agent on the Denver & Rio Grande, Muldoon Kelley reserved space on the front page of The Mancos Times for advertising and for state news and political notes largely clipped from other newspapers. Since the local news rarely was either gruesome or sensational enough to excite attention, readers of The Times would start with the back page to read about the recent social doings of the town.

Muldoon departed from usual custom for the March 11, 1898, issue to give a column or so on his front page to a story written by Al Wetherill, just returned home, describing the mysteries of Chaco Canyon. Contributions of this sort were rare but gratefully received. One week later more news of the Wetherill family appeared, this among the "personals" on the back page:

A nine and a half pound boy came to the home of Mr. and Mrs. Richard Wetherill on Thursday last, and 'Papa Dick' has not regained his ruddy color, although insisting that his nerves are unshaken.

Marietta named her first son Richard, for his father. Happiness at the Alamo Ranch over the baby's arrival was shadowed by overtones of quiet desperation. Approaching his fortieth birthday, his hair now more gray than brown, Richard found himself backed against a wall. Benjamin Wetherill was critically ill, the ranch was mortgaged to the hub of the last wagon, other debts had accumulated, Richard had exhausted his last source of credit and the creditors were pressing him hard for payment. On top of it all was the conflict with George Pepper and Richard's doubt that Talbot Hyde would have any further need of him.

In this despairing mood, less than two weeks after his son's birth, Richard told Hyde "I have lived in uncertainty all winter and it drives me wild almost — You see, I have turned off everything I had to pay up all obligations I had leaving not a thing except teams and what is in your hands — making me so horribly dependent upon you . . . "

April came before there was any answer from Hyde. Then on the eleventh Richard acknowledged Hyde's letter of assurance that he would be wanted again for the work at Pueblo Bonito, the letter coming "to hand yesterday with the result that it removed any distress of mind as well as circumstances — Thank you very much — "

There is nothing more definite to indicate what Richard was thinking of or how he was determining to resolve his problems than his next letter to Hyde, written from Chaco Canyon on July 3, when he said he had left Mancos and the Alamo Ranch "for good." Perhaps by then he realized that the winter months Al and Clate had put in at Bonito had not been wasted after all — that the little trading post, while in itself no answer, was a promise of what might be done in the future.

Early in May, with a freight wagon loaded with supplies and belongings, and after what he thought was a last farewell to friends in Mancos, he resolutely turned southward again toward the San Juan with the intention of making a new home for himself and his family in Chaco Canyon. With him in the wagon were Marietta, still pale from her recent confinement, and their two-months-old boy.

For two summers the Richard Wetherill home in Chaco Canyon had been a wall tent; now in July of 1898 it was a single room in a three-room structure shaped like an elongated shoebox and built within a few yards of Bonito's western wing. Perhaps because wood in the canyon was scarce, it had no fireplace.

Thomacito, Cocinero, Tin Head and Joe Perraly — Navajos who ordinarily were employed to dig in the ruin — were engaged by Richard as stonemasons and carpenters on his arrival in the canyon in May. Stone for the building's walls was brought from a tumbled prehistoric wall just east of Bonito. Water for mixing mortar was dragged from the arroyo well in a barrel lashed on top of a sled of parallel runners formed by two logs; the adobe clay they found as the Anasazi had — by digging a hole a few feet from the building site and wetting down the loose earth with water.

Ancient ceiling beams found during the excavation of Pueblo Bonito were used (to the infinite displeasure of later archaeologists) to support the roof. When finished it was not a handsome building but it was solid and tight, relatively cool under the hot sun, and offered protection against the canyon's winds and frequent sandstorms. In the years following, as his family grew and he found time for it, Richard added rooms until the original space was doubled. The store, at the west end, eventually became his office and another wing was built for a new and considerably larger store.

George Pepper, arriving in June, took for himself as bedroom and office the middle room, separated only by a door from the Wetherills. This made an intimate arrangement unplanned for. Perhaps Marietta occasionally longed for the comparative privacy of a tent. The room at the west end was the largest. Richard outfitted it as a trading post and over its counter Marietta presided a good share of each day with sagacity, good humor, and a growing understanding of the Navajos who came to trade.

"Our new building," Pepper wrote Talbot Hyde soon after his arrival, was a great improvement over the accommodations of the previous two years. In his own room, for example, "one is free from the wind and heat that make life in a tent unbearable, and plans may be spread out for inspection without having to be weighted down to keep them from blowing away."

The comfort of Marietta and their baby son had been Richard's major concern but only a part of his problem, as he made apparent to Hyde:

> I had to get into something to make a living, and had decided on this point for a store. I had a good stock of goods amounting to a little over $1200.00 . . . The new building will be so arranged that my wife can do most of the trading giving me time to carry on the expedition work. Mr. Swanton [a young Eastern archaeologist and former student of Putnam's who came out that summer with Pepper but wilted under the hardships] has done what he could but is not strong enough to continue in the way he has begun.
>
> Mr. Pepper told me the work would continue right along. Such being the case I turned the Store over to him or rather to you leaving my money in the business and getting 10% for it if agreeable to you — and will put in my wages as a large stock will pay the best — The trade has been from 20 to 60 dollars per day up to the present — We

buy everything offered of marketable value — Sheep, Goats, Mules, wool — Pelts etc. — All the Blankets in the region come to us — The store and sheep will make the work [in Pueblo Bonito] almost self supporting. The [nearest] Post office will be Cabezon and supplies will be drawn from Albuquerque —

I expect this week to be in regular work — and hope to push it so that a good showing will be made.

Although he had no personal interest in the store and no part in running it, Pepper believed it would operate to the advantage of the Hyde Expedition. "In the first place," he told Talbot, "most of the money paid out to the men, finds its way back into your coffers, and then the general trade brings in a good revenue; this is, of course, greater in the winter season but even now we have a brisk business when all the other stores that we know of have either closed or are thinking of doing so."

At the same time, apparently, some thought was given to protecting the Hyde Expedition against interference by others who might wish to excavate in Pueblo Bonito or by the Territorial or Federal governments. As early as the previous October Richard had warned Hyde that "All work in Arizona in ruins is prohibited. New Mexico is waking up to that point also." He meant that unauthorized digging was being prevented; indiscriminate looting and destruction of ancient ruins had resulted in Arizona's ban on further vandalism and already some officials in Washington were beginning to show interest. Something of this sort probably was in Pepper's mind when he wrote Hyde on July 30:

Richard will make this his home, and can therefore carry on the work next winter, at a very small outlay; then by his staying here, we can claim squatters' rights and, in time, have a government surveyor survey the cañon and by that means probably acquire a tract of land embracing Pueblo Del Aroza [Del Arroyo], Bonito and Chettro Kettle. As it stands at present, Richard can prevent anyone from digging on the grounds.

The accuracy of Pepper's concluding remark is doubtful, since Richard had not yet filed a homestead entry and for one reason or another delayed doing so for another two years.

Admittedly, Richard was thinking of himself and his family as well as

ANASAZI   177

of the Hydes' interests when he built the trading post at Pueblo Bonito, since the $110 a month he received while working for the Hyde Expedition was scarcely enough to meet his needs. Nevertheless, the store was opened with Talbot's approval and with Fred Hyde's enthusiastic support. To the $1,200 worth of stock which Richard put in at the start, Fred in the summer of 1898 contributed $1,000 in cash, and the arrangement jointly agreed upon was that Richard would be responsible for running the store and entitled to ten per cent of its profits. Thereafter, both brothers contributed heavily to the development and expansion of the trading business, which was operated under Richard's management until a few months before its collapse.

Just as they had approved his plan for the store, the Hydes favored Richard's homesteading in the Chaco. The work of the previous two summers had attracted some notice in the East and at least a few visitors wanted to join in the excavation of Bonito. In 1897, Warren K. Moorehead, editor of The *Archaeologist* magazine and curator of the Department of Archaeology at Ohio State University, had brought a small party out to the Chaco and for a few weeks worked side by side with Richard and Pepper in the ruin. (A photograph of one of the rooms excavated by Moorehead, taken at the time, shows it was left an archaeological shambles.) Moorehead had been received cordially enough but the men of the Hyde Expedition were fearful that others might follow his example unless they could establish some legal title to prevent what they regarded as poaching.

It was to the Hydes' benefit, therefore, equally as much as it was to Richard's, that he should apply to the General Land Office for the 160 acres embracing the three large ruins: Pueblo Bonito, Del Arroyo and Chetro Ketl. Richard filed the homestead papers with this mutual understanding, under his own name, but at no time afterward did he suggest by any word or action that his claim altered the Hydes' interest in the slightest degree.

WINDS of early winter were blowing through Chaco Canyon when Richard received word of his father's death. The news was late in reaching Pueblo Bonito and by the time it arrived the funeral already had been held. John and young Win also were away and unable to reach the Alamo Ranch in time, and their sister Anna was with her husband, Charlie Mason, at Creede. Only Al and Clate, of all the large family, stood beside the grave with their grieving mother.

Benjamin Wetherill's illness had become acute in the spring of 1898.

After receiving treatment in Mancos from a Dr. Taylor, he was taken to a hospital in Durango to be operated on there early in August. His wife Marion was at his bedside to comfort and reassure him as best she could. The operation, to remove one of his kidneys, was a shock to the frail old man's system. He never recovered his strength but finally his doctor allowed him to go home to the Alamo Ranch in October, when the leaves on the cottonwoods were yellowing and falling from the branches. His time now was very short, just long enough to see autumn pass into winter.

On November 18, 1898, Muldoon Kelley entered a brief notice in The Mancos Times just before the the last form was locked up to go to press.

"Benjamin K. Wetherill, an old residenter, an excellent citizen and a good friend went to the realms of mystery at 4:30 this morning. He was entirely conscious up to the last, and notwithstanding extreme suffering, smiles of hope and faith greeted the loved ones who hovered around him. . ."

Two days later a small coffin of plain pine was lowered into a grave at Cedar Grove cemetery, which occupies a rise of land on a bend of the Weber Canyon road overlooking Mancos Valley and the Alamo Ranch. In the distance looms the great dark shape of Mesa Verde. There being no Quaker church in this vicinity, the services were entrusted to an Episcopal minister.

In the next issue of his paper, the following week, Mr. Kelley printed a longer story, and paid his respects to Benjamin Wetherill, in part, in these words:

"On Sunday last, Cedar Hill cemetery received the remains of one who has ever been an enthusiast in the possibilities of Mancos, and one who had a kindly smile and cheering word for all of God's creatures. According to his lights, he lived a good life and passed into the future without a tremor of fear, or repining for deeds unaccomplished on this earth . . . [His] family of five sons and one daughter are honored and respected by all, while bright people from all parts of the civilized world — those who have visited the Cliff Dwellings — will bow in sorrow for the grand, good woman who has so long been the companion and helpmate of our departed friend."

In his will, Benjamin had named Richard his heir-at-law, but since Richard had made his home at Pueblo Bonito and was fully occupied there, the father left everything connected with the ranch to his widow and to Al. The ranch was divided equally between them, Benjamin also bequeathing to Marion "all household and kitchen furniture, one span of gentle horses, together with harness and buggy; also her choice of two milk cows and calves . . ." As an afterthought, Benjamin added that he also wished Marion to have "the garden and fruit patch — also, exclusive use of the ranchhouse during her natural life."

The other sons and Anna Mason were not mentioned in the will and evidently received no share in the small estate. The best explanation, perhaps, is that the ranch, with its depleted assets and its large debts, was all that Benjamin possessed and the others would be unable to take an active interest in maintaining it. For Al the task of managing the ranch without help was a hopeless one.

It was a bad time for all of the ranchers of the valley, apparently. Hardly a month after Benjamin's passing The *Mancos Times* commented that "During the year now almost ended, Montezuma County has shown many evidences of prosperity, but it is show only. The truth is, there is greater scarcity of money now than a year ago, and certainly farmers are not obtaining near as good prices for their products as they did then."

For the next three years life at the ranch outwardly appeared to go on much as before. Richard and Marietta occasionally arrived for a visit from Chaco Canyon, sometimes John and Clate and Win would be there, the crops were planted and harvested and parties of tourists continued to turn up unexpectedly as in the older days — but not in such great numbers — to be guided by one of the Wetherills to the cliff dwellings. Barns lacked paint, fences needed repairing, harness wore out, and Al did what he could. For three years the Alamo Ranch coasted quietly downhill.

In 1901 there was a month when Al was unable to meet a mortgage payment of over $3,000. The holders of the mortgage, a Henry LeB. Wills and Luce Henry, obtained a judgment against the ranch in the sum of $3,404.30. Al was given another few months to raise the money and when he could not, the Alamo Ranch was sold at public auction, to satisfy the debt, on February 24, 1902.

The loss must have caused mingled sorrow and relief. Marion Wetherill moved to Creede where she spent the rest of her days with her son-in-law and daughter, the Charlie Masons. Al and his wife went to Pueblo Bonito where Richard, who had lacked the money needed to save the ranch, arranged to establish Al in a partnership in a trading post at nearby Thoreau. For a year Al did his best but the store was not a success. He sold out his share in the business and moved on to Gallup where shortly afterward he was appointed postmaster, a position he held for the next fourteen years.

THIRTEEN

FROM Seven Lakes to the Lukachu-
kais and from the Shiprock agency to Gallup, word spread among the Navajo:
at a new trading post called Bonito, on the Chaco Wash below the Escavada,
a man named Wetherill and known as Anasazi would buy all of the blankets
their women could weave. And he would pay an unheard-of price. From all
parts of this region the Indians turned their horses toward Chaco Canyon,
many of them traveling by wagon but none arriving without blankets to trade.
It was spring, 1899 — the beginning of the fourth year of excavation in
Pueblo Bonito.

The rumors, of course, were exaggerated. Still they were true enough
that the Indians did not turn away disappointed. During the winter just past,
when all work in Pueblo Bonito had been suspended until the spring thaws,
Richard had found outlets for certain types of Navajo weaving and had determined to extend his blanket trade far beyond the needs or limits of the
Hyde Expedition's Chaco store. To accomplish his purpose, he would pay
as fair a price as given by Lorenzo Hubbell at Ganado, or any of the other
major Indian traders; at the same time he would not be cheated nor would he
accept just any blanket that was offered to him. Certain standards in the weaving, the design and the dyes were demanded. Blankets were traded at so much
per pound.

Watching closely and listening as her husband quietly bargained in
Navajo with the shy, brown-skinned women, Marietta Wetherill learned how
deceiving appearances can be, and how sometimes the shyest manner and
softest tone can conceal a most knowing trader. Not one of these Navajo
women but knew exactly the fair price for a blanket, and was bound she would
get it. And there were a few at first who, not knowing Richard Wetherill,
tried to get more than a blanket was worth.

A night or two before arriving at the Bonito post, a maiden of the most
retiring demeanor and downcast eye might — almost accidentally — spill
water on the blankets and the sheepskins or goat hides which she was bringing to trade. The maiden might then bury the wet blankets and skins in the

sand, recovering them early the next morning, not wet or even damp but just faintly moist. And then, having brushed off the sand, or at least as much as showed, she would hasten on to the trading post before worse happened.

As Richard lifted the blankets and dropped them before him upon the counter, Marietta sometimes would hear him whistle with astonishment.

Smiling, he would remark: "This — and this — and this, I will take. But will you first leave them all day in the sun? Then shake them good. Bring them back tomorrow when they are dry and we will trade."

There were rare cases of Navajos who would try to take advantage of Richard not once but several times, or who might, with sometimes childlike innocence, expect him to extend limitless credit and never ask for payment. One of the latter was a young man named Chis-chilling-begay who lived not far from Pueblo Bonito and went about with a perpetual air of injury because Anasazi wanted Chis-chilling-begay to settle his debts. With such types Richard could be brusque.

These were exceptional instances, however, and on the whole Richard and the Navajos understood each other and got along together on excellent terms. Mutual trust and friendship was firmly established and it was not one Navajo in a hundred who did not have Anasazi's fullest confidence.

With his own money Richard began to buy blankets in large quantities. Probably on the advice of George Pepper, who had been studying native dyes and was becoming something of an expert on the subject, he would not buy blankets in which aniline dyes had been used. He turned down blankets woven with cotton warp or Germantown yarn. No blanket with the color green or purple was acceptable. Instead, he asked the Navajo women to use vegetable dyes which their grandmothers had used.

"When we started our store at Pueblo Bonito hardly anyone bought Navajo blankets," Marietta once recalled. "Except for museum people and the like, and of course the Indians, practically no one had seen or heard of them, unless it was the cowboys who favored them as saddle blankets.

"Mr. Wetherill wrote to H. H. Tammen and to a Mr. Hurd, who both had curio stores in Denver, asking if they would care to take any of our Navajo blankets. They weren't interested. But then Mr. Wetherill wrote to the owner of a store in Dallas, Texas, who wrote back that if we would send him such and such a saddle blanket at such and such a price, he might consider it. We sent six saddle blankets of black and white design and heavy weave. The man in Dallas was pleased and asked us to send more. We got thirty cents a pound, usually, the bigger saddle blankets weighing five to six pounds. We also sent blankets to Waco and Austin, Texas, and to St. Louis and New York." The New York outlet was a small store opened by the Hyde company that fall.

Richard discovered that people were willing to buy larger and better examples of Navajo weaving. As this trade increased, he encouraged the wives of some of the Indians working with him in the ruin to set up their looms close by. The place the women chose was in a shallow branch of the Chaco arroyo where a brush shelter and a few tarpaulins provided shade.

"They used their own designs, always," Marietta said, "but being great imitators, occasionally put in a brand or a letter and then Mr. Wetherill made them ravel it out. Except for this they were allowed to create anything in their own minds; we never supplied the designs. At the same time, Lorenzo Hubbell was doing the same thing" — though Hubbell did supply his weavers with a choice of excellent designs. "Our weavers used their own hand spindles, and they used few colors — blue, red, black, white and gray. Many of the Bonito blankets were thick and heavy, about three and a half by six feet. Our best weavers were the wives of such men as Joe Yazzie, Thomas Padilla and Hostine Chee."

Although thickness of weave was not essential to quality, the grade of wool used always was most important; for this reason Richard sought to improve the strain of Chaco sheep. The Indians of the region at first had precious few sheep, good or bad, but some which they owned had a long-staple wool, unlike the greasy short staple of the French merino strain. These, Marietta believed, at one time had been crossed with mountain sheep. They were long-legged, hardy grazers in a poor land, and tough enough to stand the rigors of the Chaco climate. To improve this promising strain, Richard first crossbred them with black-faced Shropshires and then with twelve Lincolnshires which he imported from Canada. The Lincolnshires also were tall and long in the leg, with wool measuring six to eight inches and shearing about twelve pounds to the ewe. In time, as the Navajos' sheep improved, the quality of Bonito blankets improved.

During the early stages of this experiment in the blanket trade, Richard supplied the Chaco weavers with a large part of their wool. Then, as their production slipped off and he depended more upon blankets brought in from distant points of the reservation, he divided his own sheep among the Chaco Indians on a shares basis. In a letter he once wrote to the Commissioner of Indian Affairs, Richard explained how this worked:

The Indian takes care of the Ewes or Nannies for one half of the Wool & Lambs. We furnish improved Rams & herd same at our own expense. We stand all losses, we pay for all dipping expenses for their Sheep as well as our own. We furnish sufficient Rams for the Indian Sheep. We have dug Wells and made Reservoirs for the use of the Indian without any expense to them. The Indian gets all the supplies that he wants and pays for the same out of his share of the increase.

At about this time Richard also helped the Navajos to increase and improve their silverwork. Four or five years before he had found the Chaco Indians so poor that there was little silver for them to work with and then only with the crudest of tools which they had been able to fashion from pieces of scrap iron. Now he supplied them with the tools they needed — punches, hammers, tongs, pliers and anvils. Also, Marietta said, he furnished the Mexican silver which they preferred to American silver.

"We ordered the Mexican dollars from banks in Albuquerque and Gallup, getting about 2,000 a month and paying fifty cents apiece for them. The Indians used these to make bracelets, rings, squash blossom necklaces — all of the things they never had before. I remember when we first came to Pueblo Bonito they had limited their silverwork mostly to bridles and conchas for belts."

Richard's motives were not entirely altruistic. Since his fortunes to some extent would parallel the Indians', it was as much to his advantage as theirs to see them prosper. As the years passed it pleased him tremendously to notice the improvement in their way of living. In one year of unusually severe drouth many of his and the Navajos' horses died, but out of this disaster Richard managed to salvage something. He installed a tannery in the big corrugated iron warehouse which had been built to accommodate the increasing trade of the Bonito store, asking the Indians to bring in the hides of their dead animals. Big vats were constructed of two-inch staves and the native canaigre plant was utilized in the tanning process. This was not intended as a permanent addition to the trading post, but was an emergency measure only. Even so, Marietta recalled that "We produced some wonderful leather, shipping most of it to hide markets in St. Louis."

George Pepper did not arrive until the end of July for his last season in the Chaco. Richard, meanwhile, was directing operations in Pueblo Bonito and at the same time looking out for the store. It was a summer also when

RICHARD WETHERILL

many visitors came, overtaxing Marietta's ingenuity in providing them shelter.

A bedroom was added to the northeast corner of the house, and space was cleared in back for two or three tents which could be used when the house no longer would hold guests. At about the same time, a small one-room dwelling of stone and adobe was built between the Wetherill home and Pueblo del Arroyo, and was used by Pepper for the remainder of the summer.

Even this was not enough. Work was started on a larger building of nine rooms, close to the southeast corner of the Del Arroyo ruin. Stones for this structure were brought from the rubble surrounding nearby Kin Kletso, a small ruin lying about a quarter of a mile to the west. When finished late that summer or fall it was put into service as a boarding house for staff members of the Hyde Expedition, their guests and chance visitors.

Each week brought larger numbers of Navajos into the Chaco, many coming from far away to trade at the Wetherill store. As the season wore on Richard conceived the idea of an Indian fiesta or rodeo, to be held in the early part of September on completion of the work in Bonito. Word spread across the reservation and when the day approached the canyon began to swarm with more people than had been seen there since the departure of the Anasazi.

Two hundred Navajos on horseback and in wagons converged on the Chaco from all directions until the area surrounding Bonito became a hive of movement and flashing color. At night the glow of fires on the dark canyon floor sparkled back at the cold stars, and the voices of singing Navajos carried far over the mesas.

On the big day of feasting and games a long trestle table was set up on sawhorses behind the Wetherill house. Beginning in the morning, the Navajo women prepared food which Richard had furnished for the celebration — two beeves and a score of fat sheep, along with plenty of flour for bread and several boxes of coffee. A long log was suspended over the fires on heavy forked stakes driven deep into the ground, and food kettles were hung on iron chains.

While cooking odors flavored the dry canyon air, the men were putting an edge to their appetites. They had a choice of contests. Those with the fleetest horses ran races across the level sand on the south side of the Chaco Wash; for others there were foot-races and a chicken-pull — with a bag of silver instead of a live rooster buried in the ground. The games lasted well into the afternoon, finally breaking up so that the feasting could begin. For the winners there had been small prizes of money and trade goods.

Unmindful for once of the blazing sun, George Pepper was out in the

canyon all day as official starter and scorer of the races; now in the early evening he relaxed on the Wetherills' porch, which was shaded with a roof of
brush and sections of tarpaulin. Dr. Prudden and Clate Wetherill had come
in a few days before from another exploring trip through the San Juan country, and these three started a game of cards. At the other end of the porch
Richard sat reading near a hammock where Marietta, snatching a few moments of rest, reclined gratefully and let the cool evening air fan her flushed
face. She had been trotting between the house and the store and the camp-
fires in the back yard all day, seeing that the Navajo squaws had everything
they needed. Behind the house a great hubbub continued around the fires.

There was a considerable coming and going of Indian horsemen as
evening approached, but finally a hush fell over even this large gathering.
Appetites were sated; all had a sense of well-being. The sun washed the canyon walls with golden light. Overhead, the sky deepened from a green turquoise into fathomless blue. Millions of stars came out with flashing white
fire, a broad glowing band spanning the canyon like a celestial bridge between
the two mesas.

It was the sort of evening Dr. Prudden might remember during long
winter months in the laboratory and classrooms back in New York — the
sounds of his friends' voices and the Indians' laughter echoing dimly in his
ear. And running faintly as a thread through this memory was the far-off
sound of Marietta's music played on a guitar.

A few days afterward the canyon appeared deserted. Dr. Prudden and
Clayton once more had left, the doctor to meet his train at Gallup. George
Pepper had packed bags and boxes with the accumulations of four seasons,
and left Chaco Canyon for the last time. The Navajo workmen had been
paid off. A melancholy stillness settled over Pueblo Bonito.

But riding in from Mancos in a mud-splashed surrey came John Wetherill and two friends: Professor Frederic Ward Putnam, now in the Chaco
for the first time, and his second wife, Esther Orne. The anthropologist and
his wife had been guests at the Alamo Ranch for a week or two, and had inspected the cliff dwellings.

Richard and Marietta both were drawn by Putnam's open, bluff manner, the keenness of his mind, his perception, and his utter lack of pretension.
"He was a short little man," Marietta remembered, "stout, with a big white
beard, who right away got along beautifully with everyone at Pueblo Bonito.
Mrs. Putnam used to dress for dinner every afternoon. She wore little dinner

dresses, very lovely and ruffly" but, to Marietta, it seemed they were "maybe just a little low in the neck."

Richard was delighted to satisfy Professor Putnam's wish to see everything. This man was a tireless dynamo despite his sixty years. First they explored the canyon, on horseback, from one end to the other. Then with bedrolls, some food, and two Navajos for companions, they rode through the Gap and across dry, sandy country to the large ruin of Kin Biniola, the House of the Winds, some fifteen miles southwest of Bonito.

In the day or so they spent there they uncovered several burials accompanied by fine specimens of pottery of the Classic Chaco period. And in the broad valley stretching south and eastward they discovered an irrigation ditch built by the Anasazi perhaps a thousand years in the past, and running about two miles from a natural depression, or reservoir, to fields once planted with corn.

During their discussions, Richard and Professor Putnam reviewed the cost and the accomplishments of the past four years. The cost to Talbot and Fred Hyde had been approximately twenty-five thousand dollars, possibly a trifle less. And the results? One hundred and ninety rooms, or about half of those still remaining in Pueblo Bonito, had been excavated. All of the material recovered amounted to a staggering, unparalleled total when compared with the results of any previous similar effort in this country. It had been crated and shipped to the American Museum of Natural History, where only a small fraction of the collection had been unpacked and put on display. The vast bulk of the material, for lack of exhibition space, was to be buried in the museum as thoroughly as it ever had been buried at Bonito.

More important than the number of artifacts found and shipped off to a museum, was the archaeological significance of the Hyde Expedition's work. The excavation of Pueblo Bonito — until then — was the major effort of its kind in the Southwest. Whatever the shortcomings, it shed an entirely new light on the archaeology of the region, provided a starting point for other scientists, caused a dawning realization that this area, like Greece and Egypt, was rich with the primitive remains of prehistoric civilizations.

JOURNALS OF SCIENCE had published notices of the work being done by the Hyde Exploring Expedition, but it had passed virtually unnoticed by the public. Even in Albuquerque and Santa Fe scarcely anyone knew that a great excavation was in progress in the Chaco, and had they known they probably could not have told where Chaco Canyon was. To mention the names of Talbot and Frederick Hyde, Jr., in either of those cities would have drawn only blank, inquiring stares. This situation prevailed until the early spring of 1900, when Edgar L. Hewett, then president of the New Mexico Normal University, complained to the Surveyor General of the General Land Office that professional pot-hunters were vandalizing the ruins of the Chaco. The *Santa Fe New Mexican,* in its issues of April 30 and May 1, published stories to the same effect. These protests marked not only the general public's first awareness that Chaco Canyon existed, but the opening of a relentless campaign to make the Hyde Exploring Expedition cease its operations.

Whether Professor Hewett had been to the Chaco in person before he communicated with the Surveyor General or whether his complaints were based on hearsay is not certain. In any case, he called upon the Government for an immediate investigation and at the same time summoned the support of his fellow members of the Santa Fe Archaeological Society.

As a consequence, Special Agent Max Pracht proceeded from Santa Fe to Durango on the first stage of a trip to inspect the reported depredations of "cliff dwellings" in the Chaco. Arriving at Durango, Pracht inquired among individuals who were acquainted with the Hyde Expedition's work and on May 10 sent a night wire to Binger Hermann, the Commissioner of the General Land Office (punctuation added):

> Referring to your telegram eighth and tenth excavations being made Pueblo Bonito in Chaco Cañon, crescent shaped four story terraced stone building, not cliff dwelling. Purely scientific undertaking, relics and entire rooms being removed to American Museum of Natural History, Central Park, New York. Prof. Putnam of museum due here with scientific party about May twentieth to superintend. Richard Wetherill and band of Navajo Indians reported already digging. Work of unearthing this building, the first of a series extending for miles, has been progressing two years. Well informed parties here say it will require six to seven years more to fully uncover and explore this building of over seven hundred rooms alone. Mr. Hyde, New York, furnished money for the scientific work but has stocked a trading store for Richard Wetherill on the side, a commercial necessity perhaps. Entire matter can best and most economically be handled by Secretary direct with Prof. Put-

nam. Distance from Durango, the nearest available point to Pueblo Bonito one hundred and ten miles. Will require three days hard driving each way plus one, say seven days, at heavy expense. Don't think trip necessary. Answer if I must make it anyhow.

Commissioner Hermann wired back that the Department of the Interior wanted an immediate report. He asked Pracht if he could submit a report without a personal investigation at the scene and, if he could, to do so at once. Pracht replied that he could comply without traveling to Bonito, and on May 16 sent his report. He gave a detailed, and for the most part accurate, description of Pueblo Bonito and the nature of the work being done there by the Hyde Expedition.

Pracht said he had obtained his information from several members and officers of Durango's Historical and Archaeological Society, and the Register and the Receiver of the Land Office, "as well as Judge Richard McCloud, the ex-Register, a man well versed in all that pertains to the ruins . . . The work, so far as it has progressed, is undoubtedly a great help to archaeological research."

From a purely objective view, Pracht said there was no present law to prevent the exploration of ruins situated on the public lands. He cited Nordenskiold's experience at Mesa Verde as an example. If, however, his superiors in Washington thought it necessary to halt the work of the Hyde Expedition, it might be done either by Presidential order or through a system of permits and licenses issued at the discretion of the Interior Department.

"By this means," Max Pracht said, "hunters of relics for revenue only and irresponsible despoilers can easily be prevented from committing vandal acts, while the direct results of the investigation of such responsible scientific bodies as may secure permits . . . will be universally beneficial."

Commissioner Hermann apparently accepted Max Pracht's findings, because in the weeks following, Richard and his Navajos continued to work unmolested. Professor Putnam was informed by the Commissioner that a complaint had been lodged against the Hyde Expedition, and possibly may have made an answer for his museum that was satisfying; in any case, Putnam delayed his second visit to the Chaco until September of that year.

Perceiving that the excavation of Pueblo Bonito continued, the Santa Fe Archaeological Society took up the matter in earnest. A resolution was drafted on November 16, calling upon the Secretary of the Interior and the Commissioner of the General Land Office to

. . . make an investigation of the location, historical value and condition of the ruins existing in the northwest of New Mexico, and especially in the Chaco Cañon and its vicinity, with a view to their preservation and the prevention of the system of spoliation and destruction that now prevails.

Chaco Canyon was being despoiled "by parties in search of relics for commercial purposes," the Society declared with more dudgeon than accuracy. At no time was it stated, but the probable grievance of Hewett and his friends in Santa Fe was the fact that relics of great value were being taken from New Mexico and transported to New York.

A political tinge was lent to the affair when former Governor J. Bradford Prince, still a potent figure in territorial matters, wrote to Commissioner Hermann adding his voice to demands for an investigation. He had conferred with Professor Hewett and others, Prince said, and had been shocked to learn of the "depredations" being carried on among the antiquities of Chaco Canyon.

Prince had been annoyed by a sharp answer he had received from Special Agent Max Pracht, in reply to an inquiry.

"It may interest you to know," Prince advised Commissioner Hermann, "that the answer of Mr. Pracht to my letter of inquiry consisted of the following important suggestion! 'The only people capable of giving you correct information as to Chaco Cañon are those excavating under the auspices of the N. Y. Museum of Natural History. Write to the President in New York.' " Of course Pracht was right, but his ruffling of official plumage was unnecessary.

Commissioner Hermann could hardly ignore the various accusations. He ordered another investigation, the assignment being given on December 8, 1900, to an agent in Phoenix, Arizona, named S. J. Holsinger. The latter acknowledged his orders on the twenty-first, and would have started for Chaco Canyon at once had not several members of the Santa Fe Archaeological Society (well informed, at least, on the climate of the Chaco), counseled against such a trip during the dead of winter. With the Commissioner's assent, Holsinger postponed his investigation until the following spring.

Meanwhile, along the lines suggested previously by Max Pracht, Hermann secured an order, transmitted to Professor Putnam, forbidding any further excavation at Pueblo Bonito pending the outcome of Holsinger's inquiry.

FOURTEEN

ORDERS from Washington to cease their work in Pueblo Bonito caught the Hyde brothers and Richard entirely by surprise. Their good intentions and the valuable work already accomplished in the past five years had been falsely represented. In the spring, after Agent Holsinger had made his investigation, they believed they would surely be vindicated and the work allowed to continue. But in the meantime, what of the establishment and their investment in Chaco Canyon?

Richard proposed an answer. The blanket trade which he had started at the Bonito store showed great promise for much larger development. While waiting to resume their major effort, why not use the Hyde Expedition's wide connections in the Indian country to build up a trading business? The suggestion appealed to both of the Hyde brothers, Fred particularly.

In that one year — 1901 — the stores and retail outlets of the Hyde Expedition, under Richard's management, mushroomed through New Mexico, crossed into Arizona, and jumped two thousand miles eastward to New York, Philadelphia, Boston, and then into resort communities in the Adirondacks and elsewhere on the Eastern seaboard.

An accurate count of the number of places where the Hyde name appeared and the HEE Navajo blankets were sold probably has never been made. The John Wanamaker stores of New York and Philadelphia and other outlets did much to familiarize Easterners with Navajo weaving. Three company stores bearing the Hyde name, one succeeding the other, had been opened in New York, the first in the fall of 1899 on Twenty-third Street. A second store a year later replaced the first, at Fortieth Street and Sixth Avenue; that one was closed in 1901 for a more advantageous location at the city's crossroads, later called Times Square.

Back in New Mexico, headquarters were established at Pueblo Bonito (named Putnam on the letterheads, in honor of Professor Putnam). Retail stores or trading posts were opened at Ojo Alamo, a few miles to the north; at Farmington on the San Juan, at Thoreau, a whistle stop on the Atlantic and

Pacific (now the Santa Fe) Railroad, on the Escavada Wash; at Largo; and at Raton Springs. Just west of Gallup, near the Arizona line, another store was opened at Manuelito.

At Albuquerque there was a wholesale store. Farmington also had a wholesale store, a harness shop and a fruit evaporator plant that for a few years provided income for a number of inhabitants of that town and its adjoining valley.

Richard kept the books for this astonishing, far-flung enterprise in a rolltop desk at Pueblo Bonito. His duties took him frequently away from home but only rarely out of the Southwest. Fred Hyde, so far as his access to the Babbitt fortunes permitted, spent recklessly in developing the company beyond any dream of income, plunging into the affairs of the business with erratic zest.

Always unpredictable, Talbot Hyde's younger brother was never more so than now. Today Fred might be at Pueblo Bonito, tomorrow night at a squaw dance fifty miles across the mesas — and next week or next month, without having dropped a hint to anyone, show up in New York or London. Richard and Marietta learned to overcome their surprise when Fred walked off in the morning after breakfast with nothing but the suit of old clothes and moccasins he was wearing, not to return for two months.

Fred Hyde is said to have once boasted that while dining in a Paris restaurant, he was served fruit that had been processed through the Hyde company evaporator in Farmington. The story might be true, since dried fruit from this narrow green valley on the San Juan was shipped to many cities in Europe. The unfortunate fact was that the fruit was literally worth its weight in gold, since the income from the evaporator plant never amounted to more than a fraction of the cost.

The Hyde company's evaporator plant not only filled the settlement's greatest need, but of more lasting value, opened up new markets throughout the country for the valley's fruit growers. Within a few weeks after it went into operation, freighters multiplied on the wagon road to Durango, carrying crated boxes of dried fruit for rail shipment to Chicago, Philadelphia and New York.

There were minor and unforeseen drawbacks, however, as Marietta Wetherill recalled.

The drinking faction of the valley was tickled to death with the applejack press. The "low wines" or drippings were nearly all alcohol. And strong! Nobody in those days thought much about fancy improvements, or even sanitation — the pulp was tossed out in the back yard of the press and the drippings flowed out over the floor. I am sorry to say it, but it's true: cows and pigs, yes and even some of the town boys came around to nuzzle the pile and, well — my goodness!

Agnes Furman, the first white child born in Farmington, daughter of the A. F. Millers who went there in 1876 to open the first store and post office, recalled the time "practically everybody in town worked in the evaporator." She also remembered when the Hyde company store, a two-story brick building with an adjoining one-story annex, was the most imposing business establishment between Durango and Gallup.

Young Clyde Colville was a bookkeeper at the Farmington store. (A few years later he formed a partnership with John Wetherill, opening a trading post at Kayenta.) An occasional caller at the home where Colville boarded with Agnes Furman's mother, was a huge young fellow with a booming voice and gay manners — Jim Jarvis, a Colorado boy who had worked for a short time with the Wetherills at Mesa Verde and now was the Hyde company manager in Farmington.

Farmington was incorporated as a town in this same year, 1901, its chief business interests being fruit growing and cattle raising. The quarter century since Agnes Furman's parents arrived as early settlers, had smoothed off some of the town's rough corners but barroom fights and shootings were still frequent. One victim of this lawlessness was Scott Morris — stocky, powerfully built, peace-abiding and afraid of no man alive. The circumstances of his death, not unusual in Richard's day, have been related by Earl H. Morris, his son:

My father was shot in the Griffin and Jackson saloon on December 4, 1903. The murderer was J. W. Reagan, Locating Engineer for the Harriman interests, on the survey of a proposed railway line from the Rio Grande valley into the San Juan country. In preceding years, he and my father had been close friends during their association in railroad construction on the Katy Line [the Missouri, Kansas & Texas Railroad] in what was then Osage country of Indian Territory.

When Reagan showed up in Farmington, he willingly gave my

father the job of providing a string of freight teams to haul supplies to the survey camps strung out across the uninhabited (except by Navajo) country between the San Juan and the Santa Fe railway. It was a lucrative job and there was much local jealousy because my father had gotten it.

I never did know how or over what the first friction arose between my father and Reagan. But once there was a hint of it, busybodies carried tales back and forth between the two, embodying threats which I am sure neither man ever uttered. Finally father decided to have a heart to heart talk with Reagan with the hope of getting to the bottom of the matter and clearing up the tension for which there was no basic justification whatever.

When father stepped up to him to broach the discussion, Reagan, who had been drinking, fired through the pocket of his coat with fatal effect. At the trial he was cleared by as clever a distortion of the evidence as money and ingenuity could devise.

This was a part of the atmosphere of the town that saw much of Richard Wetherill during these years. To some townspeople whom he knew, the spring of 1883 still seemed almost as yesterday — when they locked their doors against several hundred Navajo who encircled the town and sought revenge for the shooting of one of their people by a drunken cowboy. That incident ended without further bloodshed when the war chief of these Indians arrived and wisely persuaded them to disperse.

John Wetherill and Louisa Wade of Mancos, married in John's home one evening in March of 1896, left the Alamo Ranch in 1900 to run the Ojo Alamo trading post, near Bonito, which Richard had opened for the Hyde Expedition. It was lonely country and a hard life, as John's courageous young wife learned and later described in *Traders to the Navajos*. They remained at Ojo Alamo two years and during that time John helped to build a wagon road over the sixty rough miles between Pueblo Bonito and the railroad at Thoreau. Louisa's young brother, also named John and then a husky lad of sixteen or seventeen, spent a few months with them one winter and had good reason to remember it for the rest of his life.

John Wade was there at about the time the wagon road was completed. He saw it when even in the harsh, stormy month of December it was in

RICHARD WETHERILL

almost constant use by the heavy four-team freighters of the Hyde Exploring Expedition. Southbound, the wagons were loaded with Navajo blankets, hides and wool; northbound from Thoreau the teams hauled crates of trade goods and supplies from Albuquerque or Gallup, to replenish the shelves of the Pueblo Bonito, the Escavada and the Ojo Alamo stores.

If the weather was favorable — which is to say, if there was a minimum of ice, boggy mud or wind-driven snow — the drivers made the trip in two days; otherwise it could take a week. One "normal" journey of two days, returning to Bonito, John Wade would never forget:

John Wetherill and I had two freight teams which we loaded in Thoreau with produce at Christmastime. Coming back we were so awfully cold we had to alternate, riding and walking. When it seemed we were about to freeze, we got down and walked at the head of the lead teams; then, when we got too tired to walk any more, we would ride again.

It was one of the rawest winter days I ever saw. Darkness came on early, of course, all but blotting out the road. John said we couldn't stop — it was just too cold — so we kept on going and finally came to the trading post at Seven Lakes. I don't know what time it was then, but it was late. I was so tired and cold I fell right down on a bed and went to sleep just as I was, with all my clothes on. John was much smarter. His feet were so numb he got some Japanese oil from the trader, before turning in, and rubbed it on good. Next morning I wished I had done the same thing.

He and Richard had to cut my boots off, when we at last got to Pueblo Bonito. Both feet and both ankles were frozen. Clyde Colville was down visiting at the time and they sent him back to Farmington to get a doctor. Several days later Clyde showed up again, alone. The doctor had said he was too busy, or something, to come and see me. But he had told Clyde to bring me in to town because the only thing to do was to amputate my feet, and he would do it right there.

In the meantime, however, while Colville was riding to Farmington, Richard brought a Navajo medicine man to look at the boy. And the Indian had gone right to work. Wade later felt he owed his life to that Navajo.

ANASAZI

He got a bowl of white clay from the arroyo and mixed it with pure vinegar, making a mud of it which he spread on my feet and ankles. When he had my legs thoroughly plastered, right up to the knee, he wrapped them up with cloth bandages. The mud and the bandages stayed on for a month or six weeks. When the old Navajo took them off I was able to hobble around with the help of some sticks. And then pretty soon I didn't need the sticks. I was all right, and could walk again as good as before.

AMONG Richard's last letters to Talbot Hyde was one in which he described the uncertain affairs of the Hyde Expedition. It was written from Farmington on April 17, 1901. He had spent the previous ten days looking into various problems of the Farmington stores and now wrote with a curious mixture of optimism and concern. Business was good and promised to be better. But Fred Hyde had been buying heavily on credit, and could not raise the money to make payment. Richard felt at once pulled and driven by forces beyond his control.

We purchased largely during February — the Goods are now arriving — Fred may have overreached himself in this but I do not know — more than this that the purchases were over $40000 which he said he could raise he made a trip back to do it and returned without it — Business houses will not stand such treatment and neither will I.

We have requested the Bank to make a sight draft on him for the amount —

You need have no fears but that it is all right so far — as we have a fine Manager here and good assistants — We are reaching out for the whole trade of the San Juan Country and will get it

I am mightily pleased to see it coming our way

We are buying all of this wool offered We will probably get 400000 [pounds] at an average cost of 10 cents per pound. This means it takes a lot of cash We are now getting all of the Blankets. . .

Richard then went on to say that a man named Clarke, an employee of the Farmington store, had quit without a word to anyone and returned East.

Now Richard was getting reports that Clarke was talking indiscreetly about the Hyde mercantile operations, and it troubled him.

> . . . from the outside I hear that he [Clarke] talks publicly that the Hyde Exploring Expedition will not last very long as he says Mr Hyde['s] Father objects to his investment here and the probabilities are that he will close them out — Whether this is true or not he should keep his mouth shut.
>
> All now that is required is that Fred be encouraged in this as it is the Thing — but not to speculate.

Two days later Richard was back at Pueblo Bonito. He arrived just in time to greet a stranger who for the next few weeks would give him something more to think about than Fred Hyde's erratic business ventures. The stranger was quiet, level-eyed, coolly purposeful. He introduced himself as S. J. Holsinger, special agent for the General Land Office, acting on orders of his Commissioner and the Secretary of the Interior. His orders were to investigate the alleged plundering of valuable antiquities from Pueblo Bonito by the Hyde Exploring Expedition.

FIFTEEN

AFTER a good night's rest in the Chaco's dry, clean air, especially in April, it takes a person of really prickly disposition to awaken in the morning with a sour outlook upon life. Such is the magic of the Chaco's atmosphere that one is more apt to awaken at peace with himself and with a more reasonable attitude toward other miserable mortals.

This much at least was favorable when Agent Holsinger arrived at Pueblo Bonito on the evening of April 23, 1901. His attitude toward the business at hand, however, as Richard showed him to his quarters in the Del Arroyo house, cannot be suggested with certainty. Perhaps he still had an open mind.

Holsinger was not a job-holding hack. A Westerner, a man experienced in this work, he was thorough if a trifle careless in matters of detail; he was humorless, literal-minded but honest; possibly he was too easily swayed by the person with whom he talked last.

Fred Hyde either was present at Pueblo Bonito with Richard when Holsinger arrived or he appeared on the scene before Holsinger departed on or just after May 20.

Within a month's time, the special agent visited every major ruin in the Chaco, took scores of photographs, and filled the three volumes of his report with measurements and archaeological and other data that students of the Chaco still find valuable as reference material today. When he mailed his report to Washington the following December it was an impressive show of effort. It would have been far less impressive had Richard not served agreeably as his guide and informant.

Holsinger's first obligation was to investigate the charges made by the Santa Fe Archaeological Society and Gov. J. Bradford Prince — that the Hyde Exploring Expedition had been engaged in the "spoliation and destruction" of the Chaco ruins; also, that those in charge of the HEE "are accustomed to say that all the relics excavated go to a public museum in New York, but as a matter of fact they are believed to be sold wherever they will bring the most."

If Holsinger found evidence to support these accusations, it does not appear in his report. On the point of alleged destruction, he said the Navajo workmen had used great care in the excavation of Pueblo Bonito's rooms. As for selling relics for profit, he remarked:

"All of these articles were, it is said, donated to the Museum of Natural History of Central Park, New York City. Mr. Hyde declares that every effort has been made to make the collection entire, not a single specimen of any character having been retained, not even a souvenir by any member of the company or their families."

Aside from the large sums of money he and his brother had invested in the trading business, Fred Hyde told Holsinger, they had spent $25,000 in excavating Pueblo Bonito, "and all of the collection was donated to the Museum, with many other valuable additions purchased from Wetherill, who secured them in Colorado and Utah."

Holsinger then added these observations:

After making an investigation of the Chaco Ruins, the Hyde Bros. concluded to undertake the excavation of Pueblo Bonito, and in 1897 [1896] operations were commenced; Wetherill turning over to them all the material discovered by his work. There being no trading stores nearer than 50 miles, and as about 100 Navajo Indians were employed, it became necessary to carry a considerable stock of provisions and this suggested the idea of a trading post at Bonito.

The Indian men were paid good wages and the squaws high prices for their blankets, and the Navajos of the region were soon making long pilgrimages to the Bonito store, with their produces. A private company was formed known as the Hyde Exploration Expedition and soon other stores were established, until at the present time, the Expedition has twelve stores, aggregating a stock of merchandise, invoicing over $100,000. The Hyde Exploration Expedition's wagons are now encountered on every road in the Chaco region, hauling merchandise from the railroad to the interior and returning laden with blankets, woven by the Navajos, wool and hides. Indians are employed wherever they can do the work.

The company are, unquestionably, doing a great work for the

Navajos. Blankets, for which the Indians never in the history of the country, obtained more than 50 cents per pound, now sell at from $1.10 to $1.25 per pound. This manner of dealing with the Indians promises to revolutionize the Navajo rug and blanket trade, and make this ingenious product as valuable and as much in demand as the famous rugs of Smyrna.

The Hyde stores, Richard and Fred Hyde told Holsinger, did sell modern curios as well as blankets, but "in no instance has a single specimen of pre-historic origin been made an article of merchandise." Turning to the HEE's work in Bonito, Holsinger reported that Richard and Fred "declined to furnish an itemized list of the relics obtained from the Chaco Canyon Ruins." This statement is misleading since the only "list" of Bonito relics that existed was then in the possession of George Pepper, and Richard therefore could not furnish the room-by-room tabulations of artifacts found.

Richard complied as well as he could from memory, however, swearing in an affidavit that "The material excavated from the ruins consisted approximately of 50,000 pieces of turquoise, 10,000 pieces of pottery, 5,000 stone implements, 1,000 bone & wood implements, a few fabrics, 14 skeletons and a few copper bells."

Holsinger summarized the work involved in Pueblo Bonito's excavation, allowing a few careless errors to slip into the report: for one, the correct name of the Hyde Exploring Expedition eluded him. At one point he said the Hyde Expedition had excavated 185 rooms — and in the same paragraph gave the number again as 500. Actually, 190 rooms and kivas were uncovered. He confused the areas where work was done, tripped up over Richard's business relationship with the Hydes, and overestimated the brothers' financial resources as being "practically unlimited."

He noted that several rooms found in a state of perfect preservation had been dismantled stone by stone, marked, crated, and shipped to the museum in New York. It was the Hyde brothers' intention that the Bonito rooms would be restored there and exhibited in their original form, but this has never been done and the stones and timbers presumably remain in unopened crates.

Perhaps Holsinger felt, because his findings so closely paralleled those of his predecessor, Agent Max Pracht — which had not satisfied the Santa Fe Archaeological Society at all — that it was necessary to ferret out something really derogatory. In any case, he did. His attention focused upon the homestead entry of Richard Wetherill.

Holsinger's investigation revealed that Richard had filed his first homestead entry May 14, 1900, on two lots of Section 30 within Chaco Canyon — or supposedly so. Then, for reasons Holsinger regarded as highly suspicious, Richard had changed his entry only a few months later to include nine lots of Section 12, at the same time relinquishing claim on Section 30. What did this indicate? Holsinger believed he knew. On Section 30 (now Section 25 by re-survey) there was only one ruin — Kin Klizhin — which is relatively small. On Section 12 there were three major ruins: Pueblo Bonito, Chetro Ketl and Pueblo del Arroyo.

> It is difficult to understand . . . It is a curious coincidence that upon the land first applied for there is located a valuable ruin and that it is of much more value for agricultural purposes than that in Section 12. The land now claimed by Mr. Wetherill is of strictly desert character and of no value whatsoever for agricultural purposes until reclaimed by some artificial system of irrigation. It is occupied and used for purposes of trade and not as a homestead.

There Holsinger left it, implications dangling. According to Holsinger, Richard had switched his claim from fertile land to barren land to acquire title to three of the Chaco's greatest ruins. To suggest there was something irregular about all this, Holsinger stretched the truth until it snapped: the land of Section 30, lying several miles outside of the canyon proper, was more barren than the land of Section 12, and he knew it.

Aside from this, Holsinger was right: Richard did want to file on Bonito and the other two large ruins, and never intended to claim Kin Klizhin. The error had been made by the surveyor who originally confused the two sections. Richard discovered the surveyor's mistake, and when he got around to it, he had it corrected. Deception never entered his mind, as shown by Pepper's letter of July 30, 1898, to Talbot Hyde saying that Richard would file on Bonito, Del Arroyo and Chetro Ketl in order to keep off interlopers.

Holsinger also observed that Fred Hyde had filed a homestead entry on land at the mouth of South Gap. Examining it, Holsinger found the land was used only as a horse pasture and the only building on it was a large Navajo hogan. There were no ruins. Whim or passing fancy had impelled Fred to

ANASAZI   201

file his claim. He raised no objection when Holsinger pointed out his claim was invalid under terms of the Homestead Act, or afterward, when his entry was cancelled by the General Land Office.

Richard told Holsinger that if he were requested to do so by the proper Government authority, he would be perfectly willing to relinquish his claim to the three ruins. He explained his position in two affidavits, saying in the first that his principal interest was to preserve the ruins from damage. He added:

"Having spent many years of [my] life in exploring ruins of the South-West [I have] only a desire to see the work carried on in a scientific manner and it is entirely proper that it should be under Government supervision."

Richard said he was aware he was the target of criticism because of the nature of his work and his methods, "but such criticisms have been made by persons who have never been in Chaco Canyon, know nothing of the ruins and who have reached conclusions from rumors and idle talk."

In his second affidavit, Richard said he believed Chaco's ruins "should be owned and protected by the Government of the United States under some appropriate reservation or park." To accomplish this, he would be willing to retain for himself only the part of Section 12 not occupied by ruins. Marietta, Richard continued, had acquired Sections 11, 13 and 15 from the Santa Fe Railroad, those lands including three more large ruins and many small ones. He said that she, too, was willing to grant title to the ruins to the Government should Chaco Canyon be included in a national park or reservation.

On one question the agent had raised Richard was silent. This was his failure to plant the required number of acres with crops to qualify his homestead entry under the existing statutes. This omission was noticed when officials of the Interior Department studied Holsinger's report and reached a decision that had stunning effect.

The Hyde Exploring Expedition was forbidden to continue its work in Pueblo Bonito. The order was permanent.

And in March, 1902, Richard was notified that his homestead entry in Chaco Canyon had been suspended.

It had been "clearly established," Commissioner Binger Hermann said, that Richard's claim "was not within the contemplation of the Homestead Act, this land being desert in character and having been applied for clearly with the sole purpose of gaining possession of the valuable ruins thereon."

Nothing at all was said of Richard's offer to relinquish title to the ruins and cooperate with the Government in their preservation. Perhaps the Commissioner regarded it as an issue already settled.

ADVERSITY had a sharp, familiar taste to Richard. He had lived with it intimately from the days of his boyhood. It had taught him not to accept defeat easily.

His immediate reaction to Commissioner Hermann's letter is not known, but one may imagine his sense of shock as he realized how, by dictating a short and quite impersonal letter, a stranger in Washington could wipe out the efforts and hopes of five hard years, and at the same time take away a man's home and his career.

The question now was whether he would accept defeat without a fight. He decided he would not. The Commissioner had not advised him of it, but Richard found he was entitled to an appeal. In the normal course of such things it would be months, perhaps a year or more, before his homestead entry could be cancelled. This would permit him time, he thought, to establish the mercantile operations of the Hyde Expedition on a sound basis, and develop his land at Pueblo Bonito so it would qualify under the Homestead Act. Of the two, he was to find cultivating the arid, alkaline soil of Chaco Canyon easier by far.

Early in 1902 or shortly before, Talbot Hyde had withdrawn from active participation in the affairs of the Hyde Expedition, and Fred Hyde was technically in command.

Technically, but not actually. For in the preceding December the Hyde family had made its first move toward persuading Fred to abandon this wild adventure. One of Talbot's final acts was to pay his brother's debts, which amounted to some forty or fifty thousand dollars. The next step was to bring in a former Arizona cattleman named J. W. Benham as New York manager. Quite possibly Benham had the tacit approval of the Hyde family in his stratagem to take over control of the company and break every connection the Hyde brothers had with Richard Wetherill.

The first indication of Richard's awareness of Benham's role appears in a letter to Fred Hyde dated from Pueblo Bonito on March 21, 1902.

"Have needed your help here very much," Richard began. "I have telegraphed you to come to Farmington — needing some one to hold Brown [a creditor] down — also to see that Collections were made — Will go there myself at once after leaving here — We had money enough to have paid the first $10,000. . ."

With a touch of irony, he commented upon Benham's activities in New York.

> You seem to have plenty of advisors these days. I hope they are good ones . . . it seems to me that I am to stand alone against all the New York end — that is all right. You will find me here at the Old stand, trying to do business. Of course I know that we have made mistakes — and things are not in the shape they ought to be. But in places where our interests have been large you will find that you have the goods, or something to show for them. — Now it seems that Benham has taken the business from you in N. Y. in that all his papers have J. W. B., Manager — and that the Bank account is carried in his name instead of yours. He evidently thinks you are not a fit Custodian of the Funds — How would you like me to do the same thing here — You would not like it.

Benham regarded himself as "the whole push," Richard thought, recognizing in him a real adversary but underestimating his ability. His last paragraph accurately foretold Benham's intentions but miscalculated the outcome.

"I might just as well say now that here is one place where he isnt in it — But he can depend upon us as long as he is honest in his work for the Expedition. But under no circumstances will he ever get to run the whole business unless you and I arrange for it."

A man about the same age as Richard, William Benham had worked in the cattle business from 1885 to 1895, later owning a large curio store in Phoenix, Arizona. He had a bluff, imposing manner which inspired confidence. Soon after the Hyde family brought him into the business in New York, he gleaned from Talbot and Fred the important details of their relationship with Richard Wetherill. He was particularly interested in the circumstances surrounding the investigation of the HEE's excavation of Pueblo Bonito, to the extent that he was presently writing to Commissioner Binger Hermann expressing the fondest hopes that Chaco Canyon might be speedily proclaimed a national park.

An element of mystery is attached to Benham's concern since he had been to the Chaco only once, on a short business trip in 1902. Benham took no more interest in the Anasazi and their prehistoric towns than Richard would have taken in the latest acquisitions of New York's Battery Park Aquarium. There is circumstantial evidence, also, that Benham corresponded at the same time with Holsinger to report continuing "depredations" by Richard Wetherill in the Chaco. Proof is lacking but it would appear that Benham was far less interested in a national park than he was in eliminating Richard from the Hyde horizon. As long as Richard remained at Pueblo Bonito Richard would be in possession of, if not in command of, the heart of the Hyde enterprise. If Benham could separate Richard from Chaco Canyon, through the good offices of others, he could all but end Richard's effectiveness and eliminate the latter's influence with the Hyde brothers.

In April, 1902, Commissioner Hermann recommended to the Secretary of the Interior that 746 square miles of the Chaco region be set aside as "Chaco Canyon National Park"; thus began an undertaking which ended successfully five years later when President Theodore Roosevelt established the Chaco as a national monument.

During that same April Richard hurried to New York to see the Hyde brothers and to learn what could be done to straighten out the tangled affairs of the company. There is nothing to show what, if anything, his trip accomplished. In all of the remaining correspondence there is only a sentence in a letter from Dr. Prudden to Clayton Wetherill with any reference to it.

"I had a pleasant call from Richard," Dr. Prudden wrote. "He, however, was in such a mighty hurry to get away that I did not see much of him."

If Richard had unburdened his mind to his friend there is every reason to believe that Dr. Prudden would not have referred to the visit as a pleasant one. It was characteristic of Richard to keep his troubles to himself. His business was with Talbot and Fred Hyde — possibly also with Benham — and if he had regarded the outcome as favorable he might then have communicated some information which Dr. Prudden could have mentioned in writing to Clayton.

Next in this gathering web of events was a message from Holsinger to Commissioner Hermann, reporting he had learned that Richard and one of his brothers were violating the Government's order and were digging again in a ruin a few miles west of Pueblo Bonito.

"I receive this information indirectly," Holsinger wrote, on May 15, "from the [Hyde] Co. itself through an employee who does not desire that his name be used."

The evidence points to Benham, who, two years later in a letter to Hermann's successor remarked, "Of course it is needless to say that all of the correspondence in this matter is confidential." That Holsinger's informant regarded himself as a spokesman for the company, rather than a mere employee, is indicated in the next paragraph of the agent's message:

> My information is that the Hyde Exploration Co. does not approve of this work and has protested against it, or at least the Hyde Bros. have protested to Richard Wetherill. Wetherill, however claims to them that he has nothing to do with the matter and that his brother is acting upon his own responsibility, while at the same time Richard Wetherill is assisting in the disposal of the pottery and other relics found.

These accusations were made to the same office in Washington which ultimately would decide on Richard's homestead claim; yet Holsinger offered them without proof, basing his own construction of the situation on information supplied by an unnamed person.

"To persons casually passing through the country and the uninitiated generally," Holsinger continued, "Richard Wetherill states that the excavations are being carried on by the Hyde Exploration Expedition. This is not true and the work is the purest vandalism. The more I know of Richard Wetherill the more I am convinced he is a man without principle. He boasted to me that he was known as the 'Vandal of the Southwest', which, at the time I did not accept seriously but have since learned was a matter of some pride with this man."

Holsinger ended on a stern note, and by a strange coincidence his words would re-echo in the cry of others in the future, under more fateful circumstances:

"This matter should be early investigated and if possible Wetherill brought to justice."

Spring passed into hot summer and then came fall, with Richard seldom at home but traveling by horseback or wagon through the Indian country trying to make collections to satisfy the Hyde company's many creditors. Nothing had been heard on his appeal from the order suspending his homestead entry. He had heard nothing more from Washington, either, about his offer to relinquish his claim to the ruins, or about the plan to make Chaco Canyon a national park. Unknown to him, however, an anonymous informant was continuing to give Agent Holsinger "reliable" information about Richard, as in this letter that Holsinger wrote to Commissioner Hermann on December 18:

" . . . I am satisfied that Wetherill is and has been engaged in unlawful excavating in the ruins and that he will continue to do so. I have understood upon reliable information that he has openly boasted that he would pay no attention to the warning notices given by me in the name of the Interior Department G. L. O., and that he defies anyone to prevent his despoiling said ruins."

Holsinger recommended that secret operatives be put on Richard's trail, that he be exposed and "be made an object lesson for others who would follow his example."

Early in January, 1903, Commissioner Hermann met Benham in New York. They talked about plans for Chaco Canyon and then Hermann returned to Washington where he was preparing to retire from office. Benham saw need for haste. The day following, Benham sent the Commissioner an urgent reminder, saying he had talked with someone named McVane about the proposed Chaco Canyon National Park — "which is no other than the Wetherill homestead entry, which is being held for cancellation." McVane had mentioned there might be delays in getting the proposal before the Secretary of the Interior.

"I suppose the terrible press of business preliminary to your resignation is the reason that this has not been taken up," Benham wrote. "Would it be asking too much of you if you could find the time to look over these papers, which I understand are now on your desk, and if they meet with your approval, sign and get started on their long journey."

He was sorry to trouble the Commissioner when he was so preoccupied with his last-minute official affairs, Benham said, "but my extreme interest in seeing this tract of land made a National Park is my only excuse in taking this liberty."

There were others who had a sincere — if not extreme — interest in the same proposal, among them Professor Edgar L. Hewett of Santa Fe, who actually had initiated the idea and done more than anyone else to bring it to the attention of authorities in Washington. Largely because of his efforts the plan for creating Chaco Canyon National Monument was kept alive and slowly moved forward to approval.

Benham's devious maneuverings brought results in the same month of

January: he was made manager of the Hyde Exploring Expedition and Richard Wetherill was relieved of all connection with the company.

A few days after notifying Richard that the end of their partnership had come, Talbot Hyde wrote again wondering if Richard would come East and join him in attending meetings of the American Association for the Advancement of Science. Richard had to reply he could not, adding, "I certainly regret my inability to be a part of and listen to the talks . . . However, I may be able to . . . in the future." And then an allusion to his plans for the uncertain months ahead: "Being out of the mercantile business except as an onlooker, I will have time to dig up more earth and see what other people are doing. As soon as the ground is thawed sufficiently I will commence operations to the south of us. I understand a great deal of rare material is found there."

Would this bear out Holsinger's information that Richard was defying the Government order? Hardly, since that order referred specifically to Chaco Canyon. The location Richard had in mind is unclear, since all of the country south of the Chaco is rich with prehistoric ruins. His next sentence continued with the sincerity which was familiar to those who knew him:

"I hope in that time to learn a little about this region that may be of value to some one who will know how to use it. I want to get some of the best publications on what others are doing and their methods. I may or may not derive benefit from them; a good deal depends upon who is associated with me."

This is the last letter found in the correspondence between the two men. The project which Richard had hoped would occupy him for the next four years came to nothing. Those persons so bent on stopping the man who had discovered the great cliff dwellings of Mesa Verde, the Basket Makers of Grand Gulch, the painted kiva of Montezuma Valley, the Long House on the Chinle, the ruins of Marsh Pass and Kiet Siel in Tsegi Canyon — the man who directly was responsible for the first scientific work in Chaco Canyon — those who were determined to stop him could now relax and congratulate themselves.

Richard Wetherill's exploring days were over. Others now could come in, work over what he had discovered or initiated, and win recognition never accorded to him.

Benham, meanwhile, had not been idle. A syndicate was formed, with himself at the head, which bought the name and remaining assets of the Hyde

Exploring Expedition in the early spring of 1903. Fred Hyde was in Farmington, his brother Talbot in New York when the story appeared. The *Farmington Hustler*, then owned and published by Richard's good friend, Col. D. K. B. Sellers, picked up the item as first printed in The *Albuquerque Journal-Democrat* and reprinted it on May 28:

> A deal has just been consummated whereby the Hyde Exploring Expedition's stores in Albuquerque and in New York City have been sold to a New York City syndicate headed by J. W. Benham. The Hydes also have disposed of their store at Farmington and the reason given for the sales is that they want to be relieved of the care and responsibility attached to the business. . .
> The action on the part of the Hyde Exploring Expedition, of which Mr. B. T. B. Hyde of New York is the head, does not mean that the expedition will no longer be identified with the territory of New Mexico. The Hydes in the future will devote an increased amount of money and more time to archaeological and ethnological research in the southwest, unhampered by the necessity of attending to a large mercantile trade. Scientific work is hereafter to be the object of the expedition.

This, unfortunately, was not to be. It was the end. Talbot remained for a while in the East, his attention now centered on the Boy Scouts and other youth movements. Fred Hyde, like a wandering ghost, spent his time drifting about the Indian country he had come to love, making the Wetherill home at Pueblo Bonito his headquarters before taking off on his lonely, unannounced excursions.

Bits and pieces from the picture of the Hyde Expedition's final days dropped into small one-paragraph items printed by Colonel Sellers in The *Hustler*. Thus in early February this happy irrelevancy:

> Albert Wetherill, of the firm of Wetherill & Horabin [at Thoreau, where Richard had made a place for him when the Alamo Ranch was sold] is the proud daddy of a big baby girl.

The parents named her Martha and she would grow to womanhood with bright, flashing mind, an abiding love for her father and an inerasable memory of her Uncle Richard. In the same issue of The *Hustler* were advertisements for the trading post at Pueblo Bonito, now owned by Richard; for John Wetherill's store at Ojo Alamo, and for Win Wetherill's Two Gray Hills trading post, between Shiprock and Gallup. Clayton Wetherill's name did not appear in this family roster since he was at Creede, Colorado, employed with Charlie Mason raising mountain trout in a hatchery and occasionally guiding tourists through the San Juan region.

On April 2 there was this item:

> Clyde Colville, formerly connected with the Hyde store, is now in charge of John Wetherill's trading post at Ojo Alamo, Mr. Wetherill having gone to the railroad and his family to Mancos.

John's employment with the railroad was for a brief time only, and preceded his moving his family to Kayenta where he and Colville founded a trading post that was to become one of the best-known in the Southwest.

And in the week following, this epitaph to Al Wetherill's days as explorer and Indian trader:

> The firm of Wetherill & Horabin, Thoreau, has been dissolved, Albert Wetherill retiring. At last account Mr. Wetherill had not decided what he would do.

Soon Al would decide — and become fenced-in for the best of his remaining years, as postmaster at Gallup. And in the same *Hustler*, this item about the deposed founder and manager of the Hyde Exploring Expedition:

> Richard Wetherill passed through town Sunday on his way to Pueblo Bonito, to which point he was driving a bunch of horses and beef cattle which he had been wintering in the valley. While here he purchased several tons of hay of Foster Blacklock, to help tide over until the grass is suitable for grazing. He says owing to shortage of feed, he was compelled to abandon his ditch work for this year and will devote much time to archaeological research.

Richard had been building a reservoir at Pueblo Bonito, a large but shallow-walled affair just south and east of the ruin, to water his stock and irrigate fields now planted with corn to satisfy the officials in Washington. But he still talked archaeology.

Having no further business to attend to, Fred Hyde had turned over the Farmington stores to the Benham interests. His departure was noticed by The *Hustler* on June 25: "F. E. Hyde Jr. passed through last week on his way to Pueblo Bonito, crossing the river at Bloomfield."

There were other rivers to be crossed.

For the next year or two the good name of the Hyde Exploring Expedition was retained by the new owners. Then it was dropped and the name on the letterheads and store fronts was changed to the Benham Trading Co., dealers in curios, leathergoods and knicknacks. For a time there was a store in New York. Then it was closed and the stock removed to Los Angeles. It foundered there, quietly and unnoticed.

Charles Avery Amsden, growing up in boyhood in Farmington during the skyrocket-and-Roman-candle days of the Hyde Expedition, appraised its best remembered contribution in his *Navaho Weaving, Its Technic and History*. Confining his comment to one aspect of the HEE's mercantile ventures, Amsden told how the company helped to revive the fine art of Navajo weaving at a time when it was rapidly degenerating. He concluded with this summation:

> The Hyde Exploring Expedition was short-lived, and its influence on the nascent rug industry is hard to appraise. It did much ardent propaganda in the East at a time when the market for Navaho rugs was still in the making, for good or ill; and for that reason if no other its name should be immortal in this small corner of history.

In his struggles to save the Hyde Expedition, Richard had as adversary a man who operated at a distance of 2,000 miles from Pueblo Bonito, disguising his moves with anonymous false tales and protestations of extreme interest in something truly vital, but which interested him not at all. The outcome was inevitable. It left also a black mark against Richard in his fight to save his homestead.

When Holsinger came to the Chaco in the spring of 1901 he found that the improvements of the Wetherill homestead included some five buildings and sheds, two windmills and only 5 of the 160 acres under cultivation — not enough to qualify under the Homestead Act if one cared to make an issue of it, as a number of persons evidently did. Holsinger valued the property at $10,000, which was $7,000 more than Richard thought it was worth.

Richard's homestead entry was suspended, as already noted, on March 22, 1902. Shortly afterward he entered an appeal and a hearing was ordered the following June, at which time it was decided to make a new survey of the land. It was November 30, 1906, before the new survey was made and approved. In the meantime Richard applied himself so diligently that when another agent of the General Land Office appeared to look things over in July of 1905, the Wetherill homestead was a fairly impressive oasis in the midst of the semi-arid desert.

The agent, a Spanish American gentleman named Frank Grygla, submitted a report strongly inclined in Richard's favor. Holsinger's earlier report, Grygla said indignantly, was "erroneous" and not "substantiated by facts." This, wrote Grygla, "I can account to his entire ignorance in regard practical farming, or value of building material and the cost labor in construction of buildings." Perhaps Grygla was too partisan and went too far. In any case, he reported that he found five more buildings than listed by Holsinger, 60 acres planted to corn, 5 to wheat and another 2 acres set apart as a family vegetable garden. And whereas in 1901 Richard had owned scarcely any livestock aside from sheep, he now had 200 horses, 50 head of cattle, 5,000 sheep, 400 chickens and several hundred rabbits.

On April 16, 1907, the action to suspend Richard's homestead entry was dropped and he was notified he might proceed to file final proof on his claim. This he did the following August, but it was promptly protested in Santa Fe because it had been found that his land in Section 12 contained deposits of coal.

Half a mile west of Bonito, and on the south side of the canyon, Richard at one time or another had built a road and mined for coal forty feet into the cliff face, but the small deposits of coal in Section 12 interested him not at all. Nevertheless, the discovery that coal was there delayed action on his claim for another five years. On November 4, 1912, the Government finally concluded that Richard had no ulterior designs on rich mineral deposits, and granted a patent.

This document, earned with patient labor and untold anxiety, eventually found its way into the hands of Marietta Wetherill, then living in a remote little valley of the Jemez Mountains, high above the village of Cuba. Richard had been dead nearly two and a half years.

One other question raised by Holsinger's investigation was still unresolved: Richard's title to the three great ruins, Pueblo Bonito, Chetro Ketl and Pueblo del Arroyo — an important matter indeed as the Government moved toward acquiring Chaco Canyon as a national monument. Would Richard cause trouble over this? Or had he meant it when, in his affidavit of 1901, he said that he would cooperate with the Government and relinquish title when the proper authorities requested him to do so?

Richard had meant exactly what he said. The Antiquities Act to preserve the country's prehistoric ruins from vandalism or unauthorized search had been passed by Congress on June 8, 1906. A few months later, and for the first time, it occurred to someone in the Interior Department to ask Richard if he would sign over his title to the three ruins. He replied that he would, and promptly. His relinquishment of title, signed January 14, 1907, removed any claim he had held previously and reduced his homestead entry in size from 160 to 113 acres. No recompense was received, but none had been expected or desired.

SIXTEEN

It WAS 1904. Once a jumping-off place of civilization, St. Louis now was a booming metropolis, a major trade center for the entire West. To celebrate its supremacy (which Kansas City would not acknowledge), but officially to commemorate the Louisiana Purchase, St. Louis chose this year for staging its giant World's Fair.

Remembering his success at the World's Columbian Exposition of 1893, Richard had started more than a year ahead of time to plan a Hyde Exploring Expedition display in St. Louis. Then suddenly his connection with the Hyde company ended. He still had his trading post at Pueblo Bonito, drawing upon the Navajo of the San Juan for blankets, silver, wool, hides and pelts; in addition he had established a firm in Denver, the Navajo Indian Blanket Company.

The Denver store occupied space at 1712-16 Broadway in the heart of the city. It carried a large, impressively authentic stock of Navajo weaving, but Denver folk cared little about such things and the store soon failed. It was decided that Win Wetherill, who owned some shares in the enterprise, should take nearly everything in the store to the St. Louis Fair. Richard would join him later, as soon as he could leave Bonito, and bring ten or twelve Chaco Navajos with him.

Win arrived in St. Louis in April, rented store space temporarily in a downtown building and later found exhibition space in the Manufacturers Building at the fairgrounds. Richard, and the Navajos who would make moccasins and demonstrate weaving and silverwork, followed in early August. They soon discovered they had as neighbor and fellow exhibitor the man who had forced Richard out of the Hyde company. Although their somewhat similar interests now brought them accidentally together, the Wetherills and Benham avoided each other when possible. When they did meet, the atmosphere would have chilled a polar bear.

Meanwhile, Marietta Wetherill had taken the three children, Richard, Elizabeth and her youngest son Robert, to her parents' home in Burdett, Kansas, leaving them there after a few weeks to go alone to St. Louis. August downpours had caused rivers to flood and made her train hours late. She had brought only enough money for the normal length of the trip, expecting to be met by Richard. A telegram sent to him en route, explaining the train's delay, was lost and never reached him. She arrived at night in the strange city without money. No one was there to meet her.

Her first thought was to go to the downtown store Win had rented, the only address Richard had given her. She found it dark and the door locked, but worse, the empty windows and the deserted interior showed that the building had been vacated. Wavering with indecision, fighting back alarm, she was standing at the locked door when a policeman approached.

When Marietta had told her story the policeman offered assurances that everything would turn out right; he took her to a hotel nearby and saw to it that a desk clerk gave her a room. At the fairgrounds next morning she found her husband, now in something like a panic himself. He had not received her telegram, knew only that she had left Burdett two or three days before and, until this moment, apparently had vanished.

Richard left Win in charge of the Wetherill exhibit while he and Marietta combed the city for a house where they could rent rooms. Finally they found a place, furnished, about two miles from the fairgrounds.

Fred Hyde, who had been wandering about in the Navajo country collecting debts owed to the shattered Hyde company, arrived about the same time and, with Win, they all moved into the house together.

The August heat was terrible, Marietta thought, and it was still oppressive a month later when she returned briefly to Burdett to collect her three children and bring them back with her. Elizabeth immediately became colicky and Marietta herself took sick in the heat. A doctor advised them not to stay longer than they had to. As far as Richard was concerned, his exhibit at the Fair was a disappointment, but he felt he and his homesick Navajos had to remain as long as his family could stand it. Clearly, the great things of the Chicago Fair were not to be repeated here.

Through Talbot Hyde, Benham had met George Pepper in New York; the two had become friends, and now Benham relayed gossip he believed would interest Pepper.

"Win Wetherill is here with a very good stock, closed their Denver store and he has opened here downtown," Benham wrote in April. "Has also an exhibit under the Colorado State Board in the Mfg. Bld. But no selling Concession with this except what they sell on the quiet — which I am thinking will be quite a lot. They may make some money here and of course Fred Hyde has no interest. He is only let in on the losing deals."

Benham himself was planning to make as much money as possible. Fairgoers were being attracted to his Indian Hill exhibit in great numbers. One Eastern buyer gave him a $1,000 order for "Indian" sofa pillow covers worked in leather, and like the Wetherills, Benham had an Indian making moccasins. The sale of these moccasins to tourists brought in more than $3,000. But Benham was hungry for more customers and more business and sought ways to attract them. He asked Pepper: "By the way, do you know where I can get a mummy from any of these cliff caves? You haven't got one you can loan me have you?"

Benham had a moment of bubbling affection. His wife, he said, wished to send her love to the Peppers, "and I'll join in that." He added that he looked forward to seeing the young archaeologist and his wife at the Fair.

"Write us in advance and possibly we can take care of you at our own home. We have one or two rooms that we intend keeping for the use of friends . . . If you have no better place let us know when you are coming and we will take care of yourself and wife for $25.00 a week and make you feel as much at home as possible."

The Peppers came out to St. Louis late in August, but other loved ones had leased all of the Benham hospitality: by then Benham had rented everything in his house but the broom closet. The young couple found quarters in a house next door for their week's stay.

During the last months of the Hyde Expedition, before its liquidation and sale to the syndicate headed by Benham, George Pepper had watched with interest the struggle between Benham and Richard Wetherill. All of his sympathies were with Benham and he had made no effort to conceal the fact. Since finding Richard's letters to Talbot Hyde, Pepper carried a grievance. He was embarrassed, therefore, by a sudden encounter with Richard and Marietta at the fairgrounds. But it had turned out smoothly enough, as Pepper informed Talbot Hyde in a letter written from Chicago:

We had lunch with them and I learned that Fred was in town. I waited nearly two hours in the hopes of seeing him but he did not put in an appearance. I then decided to stay over until Tuesday morning which was the last day of my ticket limit.

Monday morning I went to the Wetherill Booth determined to

keep it in sight until F. E. [Fred Hyde] put in an appearance. When I reached the booth he was behind the counter. I had but a few minutes with him before Richard put in an appearance. He kept pretty close to us throughout our conversation which lasted until noon.

Fred spoke of the work that he was doing in the West and said that Lummis [Charles F. Lummis, the author] had written him to the effect that he, Lummis, would send out a phonograph outfit if Fred would make a study of Navajo songs. It seems that Lummis is working on the Spanish 'love songs' and folk songs in general and he intends to extend the work and take up the Indian music as well.

I endeavored to interest him in the work of Northeastern New Mexico but he said that he felt that he ought to keep at the collections that he had been working on for some little time. He said that he had adopted the Indians method of doing business: that is, to visit a family and then stay with them until they settle their bill. He claims to have been very successful . . . and wishes to keep at it.

There was some truth in what Fred Hyde told Pepper — he had been able to collect some debts, but this actually was an excuse to remain in the Navajo country, which he preferred, and at Pueblo Bonito with the Wetherills, for whom he retained a deep affection. Pepper, interested in extricating Fred from what he considered the hypnotic clutches of the Wetherills, probably was not deceived.

Pepper told Talbot of a little scheme Benham had tried to rid himself of the Wetherills' competition.

It seems that a Denver man named Dockarty, who had nothing in particular to exhibit, with some foresight had obtained a lease from the Fair's Concessions Department for a display area well located in the Manufacturers Building. Win Wetherill had come along with some fine things to exhibit, but on arriving in St. Louis found all of the space in the Manufacturers Building rented or promised. It was a pretty fix. Win rented temporary quarters downtown while he studied the problem.

Presently, he met Dockarty, who had only a few items of burnt leather work to show — and they made an agreement: the Wetherills would move their stock into Dockarty's location at the fairgrounds and share in his selling concession. All would have been well, but for one reason or another, Pepper said, Dockarty "did not get along well with the Wetherills, at least with Win, and had had a number of talks with Benham.

"Benham had told me of the state of affairs and he thought of helping Dockarty out of the fix and joining stocks for the balance of the time." Presumably, if Benham could separate Dockarty and his burnt leather goods from the Wetherills, the Wetherills would lose their selling concession and be forced out. Pepper continued:

> As soon as I saw Richard behind the counter I knew that it was all off. He had been there but a few days but he was running the whole outfit. Nothing was done without consulting him and he was taking charge of all of the cash.
>
> I told Benham that he had better keep clear of the crowd for the present at least. Dockarty is a man who would be but a plaything to Richard and I can see where he comes out the little end of the horn. The Wetherills are sure to make a good thing out of the Fair. I wish there was some way of turning the stream of coin into your pockets, where it belongs.

IN THE FALL of 1904, as the Richard Wetherills were returning home to Pueblo Bonito, the new Hotel Astor was opening with great fanfare at Broadway and 44th Street in New York. The Muschenheim brothers, who were the managers, had advertised this as one of the city's largest and most sumptuously appointed hostelries. But instead of an ordinary bar or rathskellar the Muschenheims had decided to use an Indian theme to decorate the hotel's large grillroom, and called upon George Pepper for counsel. Pepper undertook the assignment and had photo enlargements made from negatives in the collection of the Hyde Exploring Expedition. These were used as wall decorations.

In this way the image of Chaco Canyon appeared in Times Square. Guests in evening clothes coming to the new Astor for refreshments after the theater could tilt their glasses and over the rims see Chaco Navajos swirling on horseback, or a group of them lined up in haughty pose beneath the high broken walls of Pueblo Bonito.

If the New Yorkers were to look closely enough, in one of the photo murals they could make out the bearded face of Richard and the long-skirted figure of Marietta Wetherill at ease near their tent among evening shadows cast by ten Navajo horsemen.

218

III

In short, sir, Mr. Shelton has always constituted himself a kind of czar on the reservation, not even exceeding, as in this case, the limits of his authority as agent; approaching on territory not under his jurisdiction; permitting, in the case of other Indian officials, missionaries, traders and others, no rival near the throne. Though the Indians themselves do not like him, he has them thoroughly cowed, and no white man doing business with the Indians can call his soul his own, unless willing to put his neck under Shelton's foot.

> — Indian Trader ALBERT BLAKE, in a letter
> to Commissioner of Indian Affairs Robert
> G. Valentine, 1910.

SEVENTEEN

MEN who saw him on the streets of Albuquerque or Farmington or on any of the trails or wagon roads within two hundred miles of Pueblo Bonito, now recognized him as Richard Wetherill, Indian trader and owner of the Triangle Bar Triangle Ranch. He was as restless as ever, never content to stay at home for more than a month or two. But his exploring days were over. He was forty-six years old. He had many friends, few of them close. There were others who disliked him because they envied him or had heard he was difficult to deal with.

Almost everyone believed that Richard Wetherill was a rich man — or, comfortably fixed. And because Richard always was tight-mouthed about his affairs, the belief persisted. A story was told by the envious that he had emerged from the wreckage of the Hyde company "with a barrel of money" — having "done" the brothers Hyde, who of course were millionaires and, in this instance, innocent lambs. The truth is nearly the opposite.

Richard's appearance in the six years following the St. Louis Fair depended very much on where he was and what he was doing. On horseback, riding into the Navajo country, he was heavily bearded, wore leather chaps unadorned with fancywork or silver. He could easily be mistaken for a hard old cowhand.

When in Gallup or Albuquerque on business, he drove a buckboard and pair of horses handsome and spirited enough to make folks turn and stare. Except for a moustache he was clean shaven. A low crowned hat with a four-inch brim, pulled down tight or pushed way back but never tilted sideways, covered a thinning spot on the back of his head. His clothes were neat, dark and conservative. He wore galluses.

For one so deep-chested, Richard's voice was higher than strangers expected; he was thought of as a quiet-spoken man, even when his eyes were snapping. He was forbearing in his judgments of people but two things about another man could inspire his dislike: what he called "talking too much" or talking in loud bluster. Unexcitable as a rule, he could get excited;

at such times, one of his cowboys noticed, he remained cool "but moved like lightning."

The one who would be most observing and perhaps most critical was his wife Marietta. She remembered that

"Mr. Wetherill never wore overall jeans, he hated them. He liked California corduroys, a heavy material with a pebble design in brown and tan. He wore flannel or light wool shirts. He never wore boots, but a high black shoe that laced. Sometimes he would wear chaps when he knew he had to ride through brush, but the chaps were always very plain. One time I had an Indian make six big silver conchas for his chaps, as a birthday present, but he thought they were too fancy and wouldn't wear them. I gave up after I had some silver and turquoise buckles made for a pair of spurs. And wouldn't you believe it? — he wouldn't wear them. He didn't use spurs anyway, unless he had to."

Richard never used a map; he depended on an Indian guide if he were in a hurry but preferred to find his own way. "Maps were for people who didn't know how to get around," Marietta said. "If Mr. Wetherill went one hundred miles out of his way it didn't matter to him. He would just see something new of interest."

Marietta found Richard slow in forming a bad opinion of a man. "I would say, 'Now that fellow is a crook.' And he would say, 'Oh, how are you going to tell?' "

Hardly ever did Richard discuss a man's religion or politics. Those were private subjects and no affair of his. "Mr. Wetherill was a Republican, but took no part in politics and never talked about it. My father also was a Republican and I guess I first knew that Mr. Wetherill was too when they just mentioned it one day on that trip back in 1895."

Richard disliked show-offs, but once Marietta thought she caught him brazenly guilty himself.

"We had a visitor from Albuquerque, a man who prided himself on the way he could handle a rifle. The three of us were riding in a buckboard on the north mesa, when Mr. Wetherill noticed a hawk sitting on a fence post some distance off. There happened to be a rifle in the buckboard and Mr. Wetherill asked our friend if he would like to take a shot at the hawk — he'd heard our friend was a dead shot. Why, sure, the man said, and fired. But he missed and the hawk didn't even stir a feather, just sat on the post.

" 'Maybe you would like to see what you could do,' this fellow said to Mr. Wetherill. He was sort of mad.

"My husband gave what I thought was a pretty smart-alecky answer. 'Aww,' he said, 'I'd never think of shooting at a sitting bird. I'll wait 'till he takes wing.'

"So he waited. Then after a time the hawk spread his wings and flapped away, and as he rose in the air Mr. Wetherill lifted the rifle and fired, and that bird dropped to the ground. Nobody said anything but when Mr. Wetherill laid the gun down he had a smile on his face from ear to ear, and I thought it was pretty darned smug."

Richard's Quakerism made him seem more reserved than he was. That his young wife should address him as "Mr. Wetherill" did not strike him as unusual, and yet she remembered him as a warm, kind, and gentle husband. He was undemonstrative. If others were around, and many times when they were alone, his show of affection was to pat her hand. Marietta was sure that had she kissed her husband in the presence of others, "he would have sweated right down to a little puddle."

But in little ways he gave her assurances that a wife needs. It didn't matter if sometimes these ways made her smile to herself. "He loved flowers and he always brought me some from wherever it was he had been — wildflowers. If he had been up on the San Juan he would come home with a large bunch of flowers which he had tied in a wet rag when he picked them. But you know how hot the sun is out there, they were always wilted when I got them."

She would never forget a "letter" she received from him soon after their marriage. It came following the work in Grand Gulch, in 1897, when she was staying with the Allen family in Bluff City while he and the others went on to Marsh Pass and Kiet Siel. A week and more had passed beyond the time he told her he would be gone and she had begun to worry. Then one day a Navajo appeared at the Allen home and handed her an odd bundle tied in a rag. Opening it she found a large, curved fragment of pottery, the concave surface protected by sticks from the outer wrapping. On it, scrawled in charcoal, was a message:

"Dear Wife — Have been delayed ten days by windstorms. Will be with you soon — Your husband. Richard Wetherill."

For years she kept the potsherd on a shelf but it fell one day and shattered.

SOMEONE besides Marietta observed Richard Wetherill with a perceptive eye during these days at Pueblo Bonito

— a cowboy named Joseph Schmedding. Joe was seventeen years old when he hired on with the Triangle Bar Triangle. He was six feet two inches tall, and he towered over the man he called the Boss. He stayed at Pueblo Bonito for three years and seven or eight months. Schmedding has told his own story and related many of his experiences at Pueblo Bonito in a book that is a colorful chapter of Western history: *Cowboy and Indian Trader*.

Soon after Joe came to Chaco Canyon he was in Richard's office when his eye lighted on a rifle standing in a corner.

"As any young fellow might do, I picked it up by the barrel and said, 'Is it loaded?' The Boss looked at me for a second with those piercing eyes of his, and answered quietly: 'What good would it be if it weren't loaded?' "

Joe Schmedding, who lived the last years of his life in California and died in 1956, retained a clear, sharp memory.

"Mr. Wetherill usually carried a rifle or shotgun in the buggy with him. He knew about guns and he was a good shot. Mrs. Wetherill had a flock of chickens on the ranch, so of course hawks would swoop down on them once in a while and try to carry one off. She also had several guinea hens. They could see twice as far and quick as those dim-witted chickens and they would bust out with a warning every time a hawk circled above. Usually Mr. Wetherill was in his office when this happened. When he heard those guinea hens cut loose he would grab up a shotgun and dust through the door. He'd hardly have got to the corner of the building before up the muzzle'd go and — bang! He usually got the hawk."

Richard impressed his cowboys as being a good horseman. But now he used his buckboard more often, although he had several horses of his own which were a cross between two strains: Steel Dust and Hambletonian. The resulting breed was rather tall but short-coupled with good shoulders and good haunches.

"He bought a pair of matched pintos up in Denver for his buckboard," Schmedding once recalled. "The buggy was made for rough prairie travel, not the sort of buggy or carriage you would see in town with delicate lines and light spokes. His buckboard had extra heavy springs, the tires were a little wider than usual. He knew how to drive it, too. He could drive the 125 miles into Albuquerque in two days and do it without putting a big strain on the horses."

There was no road from Pueblo Bonito to Albuquerque, just a meandering stretch of wagon ruts that would fan out or come together haphazardly, depending on conditions or the whim of the driver. The route was by way of Pintado, the little town of Cabezon — where the conspicuously unfriendly Mexican inhabitants didn't make a lone gringo feel it would be safe to stay overnight — and a crossing of the Rio Grande at Alameda, a few miles below Bernalillo. Marietta Wetherill accompanied her husband on these fast journeys only infrequently, but Joe Schmedding made the trip many times with the lumbering freight wagon, usually as a side rider. And while the Boss could cover the distance with his buckboard in two days, it might take a week or longer for the freighter — much longer if the Rio Grande was in flood.

There were qualities about Richard Wetherill which Joe Schmedding considered out of the ordinary.

"I never heard him swear. This was unusual for this time and this part of the country, where just everyone cussed as naturally as he breathed. Also, he didn't drink and he didn't smoke and he didn't play cards, and I suppose that is because he was a Quaker. Now and then he would lapse into the Thee and Thou when speaking to someone. If he was a particularly religious man there wasn't any outward demonstration of it although he may have been, inside himself."

Richard seldom gave orders to his men, after telling them what must be done when they hired on. He may have carried this to a fault. Once in a while a reminder was needed, and he could make it sharp.

"He would get provoked if anything was neglected. One time he sent me out to find and bring back Old Joe, which was the name of a big Durham bull we had. Padilla — one of the Navajos living in the canyon — had come in to report this bull had wandered away, looking for a new harem probably. The Boss told me to go out and find him. Old Joe wasn't hard to trail because one leg had a deformed hoof. But after a while it got quite dark. And because I was twelve or fourteen miles from the ranch by that time, and getting hungry, I thought I would come on back and start out again next morning.

"The family was sitting out in front of the house when I rode in. 'Did you find Old Joe?' the Boss asked. 'No,' I said, 'but I picked up his trail and I don't guess he's very far away.'

"The Boss gave me a hard look and said: 'Didn't I send you out to get Old Joe? You go back out there and get him.'

"Everyone else at the ranch had had their supper, but I got something to eat at the cook shack and then went out and camped on the trail. The next morning I found the bull and sure enough, he was with six young heifers.

It was afternoon by the time I had him back where he belonged and when I stopped by the office the Boss said, 'All right. And remember when I send you out to do something, you do it.' "

Joe Schmedding took this in good spirit, as "just one of those things that is part of the education of a cowboy," and was seldom rebuked again during his days at Pueblo Bonito. There were other characteristics of Richard Wetherill which he remembered, both as a man and as an Indian trader.

"Mr. Wetherill was fair. He was as honest as any other man of his time — and he was kind. No matter who came to Pueblo Bonito, he never turned them away or sent them on hungry. White people or Indians, it didn't make any difference. There were many times for some little reason or other, when he gave food or presents to Navajos who came to his post.

"He was a good trader, conforming to the rules and customs of his time. And it could be a pretty hard or uncertain business.

"A trader has to sell to the Navajos at just about the market price, and that means the price fixed by other traders in the vicinity, not just what the Government may say the price of wool should be. Supposing the Government sets the price at thirty cents a pound. The Navajo doesn't care anything about that. All he's interested in is what the traders will give him for his wool. When Navajos clip sheep they don't take the wool to just one trader. They will take a sack of maybe ten pounds to one trading post and get the very best they can for it. The next day they will take another ten pounds of wool to a second trader and see what he will give them. Some may even go to a third trader. The one who gives them the most for their wool will get the bulk of the shearing."

BEYOND the 113 acres which now comprised his homestead, the grazing boundaries of Richard's stock extended for miles. Depending on the season or grazing conditions the area may have reached eastward to the Divide, north to the San Juan and south to Thoreau. The country west of the Chaco was sandy desert. It was primarily a horse ranch in the later years, there usually being twelve hundred to sixteen hundred head of horses and eighty to one hundred head of cattle; besides this stock he owned perhaps as many as five thousand sheep, nearly all of them let out to the Indians on shares. The horses pastured on the north mesa along a strip some eight miles long by three miles wide. Part of this was fenced where the land sloped down to the Escavada Wash on the north.

226   RICHARD WETHERILL

The Navajos who took Wetherill sheep on shares grazed them for miles in nearly all directions. To a lesser extent the cattle had free range but were under the watchful eye of Thomas Padilla. Usually, however, the cattle grazed north of the Escavada and from time to time one of the cowboys rode out to make sure Padilla was keeping the herd together and the water holes clean. Joe Schmedding's job, for the most part, was looking out for the horses.

"Mr. Wetherill would buy his horses from the Indians," Schmedding once said. "He had two preferences — young mares used for breeding, and good-looking horses he thought might make all-around saddle horses, especially ponies. These Indian ponies were short-coupled, very quick, and they had a lot of stamina which made them good as polo ponies although not worth a darn in a four-mile race or steeplechase. Officers from Fort Wingate used to come out to pick up some of our ponies and horse buyers would come from Oklahoma, from Texas and back in Missouri."

Often, after these visits by buyers, there would be long drives of as many as several hundred head of horses into other states, or occasionally, if bound for Kansas City or St. Louis, they would be transported by rail and one of the cowboys would go along.

Schmedding once led a drive for the Boss, to Goodnight, Oklahoma. "Mr. Wetherill wouldn't go on these trips, but would give the cowboy in charge a bill of sale which made him, for the time being, the legal owner of the stock. When he reached his destination, if the horses hadn't already found a buyer but were going into the open market, the cowboy would sell at any price he thought was right and report what he had done when he got back to the home ranch. From the money he received the cowboy would deduct his expenses during the drive, for corral fees, the auctioneer, feed and his own food and lodging and so forth."

Over a period of years Richard bought other ranchers' stock, but the only brands he used in the Chaco were the Triangle Bar Triangle ⟨Ⱶ⟩ and the ⱵE of the Hyde Exploring Expedition.

Every year Richard sold small numbers of his cattle to buyers who always came to Bonito, since the herd was never large enough for a drive to Albuquerque. The buyers, Schmedding said, "would arrive in a buckboard, followed by two or three cowpunchers. They would look over what we had, then take what they wanted and drive them to Thoreau or to Grants, or maybe to Bluewater."

Richard's office was at the western end of the ranchhouse. During the day, when he was working there, he sat at a rolltop desk placed against a wall nearly opposite the doorway. Visitors to Pueblo Bonito were entertained in this room, and at night it was the gathering place not only of the family but of the ranch hands as well. There were books or magazines to read, couches to sprawl out on and a big potbellied iron stove to keep the room warm on cold nights. During long winter evenings the stove glowed red while the room filled with tobacco smoke and the men's lazy conversation.

Four bronze lamps, each holding a gallon of coal oil, were suspended from the ceiling. The ceiling itself was an oddity in an altogether unusual room: the exposed beams, as solid as when cut nearly a thousand years before, had been salvaged during the excavation of Pueblo Bonito's deep, dry rooms.

Navajo blankets in designs of red, white and black, were piled three deep on the floor and Richard had a bearskin spread out near his armchair. Somewhere he had found several buffalo robes and these covered the two couches and another big chair. Trophies from all parts of the Indian country were hung on the walls, dangled from the ceiling beams, or stood in the corners or on the window sills. Among the wall trophies were mounted heads of wild game, samples of Ute beadwork, Apache baskets, Navajo war weapons and woven sashes, kachinas and pottery from the Hopi villages. The place of honor was reserved for a Navajo chief's blanket, traded years before to a Plains warrior of the Ponca tribe, its design in bayeta red, indigo blue and white.

In this room, all of the usual barriers between employer and employees ceased to exist during these evening hours. While Marietta sewed the men would talk, or, tiring of that, pick up something to read. Richard subscribed to a number of periodicals, including *Scientific American* and *Scribner's* — and there were books, perhaps as many as three or four hundred.

Richard was not a literary man, but he was a hungry reader in a region where books were seldom read and more rarely bought. Some with covers loose, others with spines cracked, all of Richard's books showed the wear of use. They could be divided into three groups: books of a scientific or semi-scientific nature related to his work, classical novels and poetry by nineteenth-century authors, and books Richard used as a schoolboy in Leavenworth.

Among the titles in the first group were the *Annual Reports of the Bureau of American Ethnology*, from 1879 through 1890, and Francis Parkman's *Complete Works;* in the second group Mark Twain was represented by *Tom Sawyer* and *The Connecticut Yankee*, A. Conan Doyle by *Sherlock Holmes*, and Victor Hugo with *Les Miserables*. There were complete sets of the works of Charles Dickens, Rudyard Kipling, Robert Burns, Tennyson and Whittier. All had been read, some many times.

As interesting, if less revealing, are the books Richard used as a schoolboy. The earliest, not really a textbook, was *Nuts for Boys to Crack,* by the Rev. John Todd, D.D. It was given to the boy in 1868 and inscribed by one Sere Lecaf, who may have been Richard's Sunday-school teacher. There were textbooks of German grammar, ancient and modern history, algebra — Olney's Elements of *Geometry and Trigonometry,* which Richard studied and presumably absorbed at the age of thirteen. On the flyleaf of a *Dialogues to Teach German Conversation,* in a boy's firm hand, this inscription:

> R. *Wetherill, Leavenworth, Kansas*
> *Don't steal this book for fear of your life*
> *for the owner carries a butcher knife.*

Perhaps a hundred of the books had traveled a thousand miles in a wagon bed, when space was precious and every ounce of weight counted. From Leavenworth to Rico, from Rico to Bluff City and then to Mancos; from Mancos to Pueblo Bonito — and each time under pressure of hardship — there was a winnowing out of possessions. The books were never left behind.

A TALL, cold-eyed cowboy rode through the Gap one day and applied to the owner of the Triangle Bar Triangle Ranch for a job. It was in 1904 or 1905 and his name, he said, was Bill Finn.

The first person to notice Finn's arrival was Joe Schmedding, who was at work in a corral near the arroyo crossing. As they confronted each other Finn coolly stated his name as though the big, broad-shouldered youth before him could go to the devil if the sound of it didn't please him. Then he asked Joe where he could find "the boss of this outfit" and Schmedding pointed to Richard's office. After an hour the stranger emerged, turned his horse into a corral, and with scarcely a look around stalked off to the bunkhouse. He had been hired.

His first meeting with Finn told Joe Schmedding almost as much as he ever knew of the tight-lipped cowpuncher although for the next two years their work for Richard Wetherill made them daily companions. All that Schmedding ever really learned of the new hand was his name. Where Finn came from and the events that had colored or stained his past would remain a complete mystery to everyone except Richard and Marietta Wetherill. Even his age, which then may have been twenty-two or twenty-three, Finn concealed. Naturally this led to speculation.

"I think that Bill Finn had gotten into some sort of mess before he came to Pueblo Bonito, either a shooting or a bank robbery," Schmedding said years afterward. This idea was shared by others. "Bill never said a word about his past and while we hinted a question once or twice we never asked him, of course. Bill never told us where he had come from, didn't even talk about where he had worked before he came to Bonito. But it was clear right away that he was a good cowpuncher. He could ride and rope with the best of them.

"He was a slim-hipped fellow, not what you would call handsome, and there was nothing special about his face worth remembering — except his eyes. Those eyes were pale blue — icy — and looked as though they never could smile. He talked in a soft drawl, still drawling and soft when he got angry and swore. I had the idea he was a pretty hard-bitten character and perhaps he was, or perhaps he had convinced himself he was a bad man and had to act like one. He always went around with a sort of unspoken warning about him that seemed to say: 'Don't get in my way.' "

Schmedding noticed that Finn wore a single-action .45 caliber pistol slung low and with the barrel end of the holster tied with a leather thong to the right leg of his chaps. This could be a fancy affectation, or it might mean the cowboy had reason to think of himself as a gunfighter. There was another clue nearly unmistakable: Finn tied the end of his lariat to his saddlehorn, a practice common in Texas.

Bill Finn hadn't been in the Chaco long before his bunkhouse companions discovered something else. He was sitting on his bed one night in the smoky light of an oil lamp when Schmedding and one or two others saw him reach over to his discarded chaps and draw an ugly little derringer from a concealed inside pocket on the left flap. Whistling a soft little tune, Finn oiled the weapon and reloaded it, ignoring the surprised glances at his hands. The derringer added to the legend that Finn would be a tough customer in a fight.

"He always carried that little weapon with him," Schmedding said, "and often at night he would bring it out and sometimes reload it and then shove it back in that hidden pocket. But I never saw him fire it."

If Finn ever made any friends there is no record of it. Stories were told in the towns of Farmington and Aztec and at the Navajo agency at Shiprock, that Finn was rough in his treatment of the Indians and more than once stole stock from them. That he could be rough there is no doubt; also it is likely that he made free use of his running iron. As Finn's unpopularity in the San Juan region grew, more and more people transferred some of their dislike for him to his employer and attributed the same characteristics to both. It is hard to explain why Richard Wetherill hired him in the first place and kept him on, although there is evidence that his patience with the cowboy began to wear.

Marietta Wetherill once said that during the first hour-long talk with the cowpuncher, her husband learned all about Finn's background, Finn pouring out a story he would tell no one else but her. It is hard to say, but most men in Richard's place probably would have given Finn no more than a night's lodging.

Bill Finn was not a bank robber and he had not been mixed in a shooting scrape, as Joe Schmedding and others half suspected. He had grown up in Texas, Finn confided to Richard and then later to Marietta, as an ornery kid. To discipline him, his family sent him to a military school in New Mexico, hoping the school might file off his edges and that eventually he would take up a respectable career. His people hoped that he might study law. But while in military school he met an older man named McFarland, a cowboy who was becoming known in the territory as a rustler. The two became friendly, formed a partnership, and Finn dropped out of school. The pair found a remote hideaway in the Capitan Mountains and set up a camp.

From here they raided cattle herds in all directions and for a time did well at it. Finally, however, someone caught up with McFarland and he was put in jail. Finn managed to escape and headed north. Exactly what had brought him to Chaco Canyon is uncertain, accident perhaps, but at least two things were in his favor. At this particular time it was known that Richard Wetherill was looking for an extra hand — and the Chaco was about as far from anywhere as a cowpoke could get and still make a living.

His uncle, he boasted, was the well-known evangelist, Dwight Moody. And his own name was not Bill Finn — but Joe Moody.

The fact that Finn, or Moody, was a good range rider, a man whom he could depend on when he needed such a man, possibly made Richard overlook faults which he would not have otherwise; possibly Finn convinced him he would reform, and deserved another chance.

In character with his silent, ominous demeanor, Finn could handle a revolver with fine accuracy. Next to Fred Palmer, he was one of the best marksmen in a region where nearly every man knew how to use a gun well.

Fred Palmer, Marietta's uncle, worked for several years as the blacksmith at Pueblo Bonito. He was the only man around who sometimes could beat Finn in a shooting match. Finn usually began each new contest with Palmer by having Joe Schmedding or one of the other men toss a two-pound tomato can into the air while he bounced it about with his six-shooter.

When all of the available tin cans had been sieved, the contest sometimes continued with a different sort of target. A dozen empty bottles would be placed at random on the ground and then Finn and Uncle Fred would stand side by side about fifty paces away with their backs turned. At a shout from Joe Schmedding or Gus Thompson they would spin around and start firing. A good many bottles were broken this way without determining which of the two was the better shot.

Gus Thompson was a middle-aged man, crippled in one foot. He had been hired as a driver for the heavy freight wagon on its frequent trips to Albuquerque. When he was at the ranch he kept the wagons and carriages in repair and looked after the horses.

Others employed at the ranch at this time included a slow-witted boy named Lee Ivy, who did odd chores, and a quick-tempered young cowboy known as "Black" Phillips because of his thick thatch of unruly black hair. And finally, though not a ranchhand but a permanent guest, there was old Uncle Clayton Tompkins, the brother of Richard's mother.

Years before, Uncle Clayton had lost both of his legs at the knee when they became frozen during a season of winter trapping in Canada. After that he had been forced to rely on his own folks for support. Soon after Richard and Marietta moved to the Chaco from Mancos, they invited Uncle Clayton to make his home with them. The old man, then in his eighties, accepted gratefully. With a handful of possessions and female collie dog called Fannie, he settled down to spend his last years in one of the rooms of the bunkhouse.

"Fannie always slept on the bed with him," Marietta once said, "and he had six hens which he insisted on having in the room with him, too. Mr. Wetherill was terribly disgusted but he never said anything. Uncle Clayton spread papers out on the floor for the hens but they avoided them if they could. At night Uncle Clayton, Fannie and the hens all shared the same bed — the hens roosting at the foot."

Marietta humored the old man in his small crotchets. His favorite tobacco was Mail Pouch, so she ordered it for him in five-pound tins from St. Louis; he refused to eat bread but had a great fondness for pancakes made with hand ground graham flour, so Marietta ordered the flour in hundred-pound sacks from a mill at Bernalillo and made the pancakes herself. Once Richard bought a pair of wooden legs for him in Albuquerque but no good came of it — Uncle Clayton looked at the wooden limbs suspiciously and grumbled that he was too old to learn to walk again. But these quirks were little things and Marietta remembered him as a welcome addition to their family life at Pueblo Bonito.

"He was all my responsibility, but it wasn't hard because I always had enough help with Indian and Mexican girls. He loved our children and used to regale them with his stories of hunting and trapping up in Canada. Sometimes, when I would bring him a tub of hot water which he didn't intend to use, he would pat my hand and say: 'Thee's been such a good daughter.' "

Richard and Marietta were at the St. Louis Fair when they received word that Uncle Clayton had caught a cold and died a few days afterward of pneumonia.

EIGHTEEN

PROBABLY the strangest, and one of the most likeable persons who frequented the Triangle Bar Triangle Ranch was Fred Hyde. The failure of the Hyde Expedition had cemented the friendship between young Hyde and Richard. They discussed that failure sometimes, Marietta remembering that "Mr. Wetherill used to say that in another five years the Hyde company could have been successfully established, if they had only been able to keep going. Giving it up broke Fred's heart and it hurt Mr. Wetherill terribly.

"Fred Hyde was generous to a fault. One Christmas he gave each of the cowboys working for us a fine saddle and a splendid rifle with boxes of ammunition."

Joe Schmedding recalled him as a man about thirty years old, tall, husky, a bit aloof, but with a storehouse of conversation about strange, far places of the world.

"One time in 1905, or maybe it was 1906, we had freighted some wool and hides into Albuquerque and soon after arriving in town we found Fred Hyde was there too. He was all aglow with pride over an expensive new car he had just bought, one of those big high brutes and about twice as long as a wagon. Well, he started off ahead of us in the car, saying he was going to drive it across the prairie to Pueblo Bonito. Just like that, no 'ifs' or 'buts' — just as a man would say he was going to ride down the canyon a piece and be back in half an hour. How he ever expected to accomplish a thing like that I don't know.

"Anyway, he got as far as the crossing of the Rio Grande at Alameda [about twelve miles] and there he got this big monster stuck in the sand. After a while we came along in the wagons, each of them with a trailer hitched on behind, and he told us to tie his automobile on behind one of the trailers and pull him out. It took both teams but we finally managed it and then made a raft and ferried him across the river. On the other side he got the engine started again, but something or other happened and it just quit. So we hitched

RICHARD WETHERILL

him on behind the trailer again and managed to snake that thing all the way to Pueblo Bonito.

"When we got it there he jacked it up in the blacksmith shop and took the engine down, part by part. He had parts spread out everywhere on the floor until you could hardly step around between them to shoe a horse. Well, he never could put it back together again. The chassis and all those engine parts just lay there, shoved to one side of course, until the blacksmith shop was torn down and everything in it was sold.

"He had the most peculiar habit of walking off without a word to anyone, disappearing without so much as a toothbrush in his pocket. He would just go away quietly in the moccasins and clothes he happened to be wearing at the time, walking down the canyon or through the Gap as though he would be back in an hour or two. He did this several times and for days we wouldn't hear from him until he turned up in Thoreau, or Grants or Albuquerque. Once when he disappeared like this there wasn't a trace of him until we learned he was in London. He could ride and he knew how to pack a horse or mule as well as any man, and so you would think when he went off he would at least take a horse. But he never did. He always walked."

Even with those closest to him Fred never discussed these disappearances. Perhaps he was trying to prove to himself that he could exist in a dry, barren land with nothing but his own resources to rely upon; a Spartan way of proving to himself that his grandfather's fortune which he could dissipate so easily was not essential to his survival. Possibly, in light of the deep melancholia that darkened his last years, these wanderings were in search of peace he couldn't find.

In Farmington, Agnes Furman observed that "Fred Hyde used to roll up in his blankets by fires and sleep in the Navajo camps. He liked their singing. He was very quiet. He just liked to wander off alone and do as he pleased."

Other events at the isolated ranch could cause concern. Late one winter day ten or twelve sheepherders, riding through the canyon, asked for lodging against what promised to be a bitterly cold night. Richard had Gus Thompson see that they had something to eat and then put them up in a large, unused room in the bunkhouse. Smiling and nodding their thanks, the sheepherders moved off with Gus and presently settled down in their room with their saddles and blanket rolls. The evening wore on peacefully and finally, one by one the lights went out in the windows of the ranchhouse, in the house over at Pueblo del Arroyo and in the quarters shared by the ranchhands. At last only the one window in the bunkhouse where the guests were gathered glowed like a bright yellow eye in the canyon's darkness. And now from behind that window and the crack of light escaping around the closed door came the sounds of excited voices, laughter and then bursts of song.

Stored in the room given to the visitors, but forgotten by Richard and Gus Thompson, was a barrel of cider brought down from Farmington some weeks or months before. Time and the natural processes of fermentation had worked well. Richard's guests found the contents of the cask frozen at the bottom, thereby rendering the spigot at the bunghole unresponsive. But when they knocked off the head of the barrel they were beautifully rewarded — several gallons of ice cold apple brandy floated free at the top. Such liberal hospitality could not be disdained, and the appreciative guests set to work. Somewhere on the long side of midnight the singing in the bunkhouse rose to a crescendo that threatened to crack the adobe plaster and splinter the ancient ceiling beams. It aroused everyone else who until then had been sleeping. Suddenly there was a shout louder than all others, a splintering crash of glass and then pandemonium.

Richard was still pulling on his trousers as he stumbled out of the house and collided with Gus Thompson, who was running to the scene from another direction. Just then the bunkhouse door exploded outward and with its shaft of light came the flying figures of two sheepherders, a chair or two and a barrage of cooking utensils. From within came the noises of murderous riot. To Marietta, still in her bed, "It sounded like the massacre of a whole village of women and children."

The screaming brawl ended as quickly as it had begun when every man at the ranch converged on the open doorway. The drunken celebrants were lugged off by Gus Thompson and locked up separately for the remainder of the night. About noon of the next day it was possible to liberate them. Tattered and aching, the guests mounted their horses and trooped off.

Another time, in the heat of late August, an incident of another sort upset the usually even life of the ranch. On the day the Navajo girl Mocking Bird was to be married, her young sister, Des-pah was in a field of the canyon picking corn. Moving carelessly, the child stepped on the back of a rattlesnake and it coiled around her thin little leg, drew back its head and struck at her three times.

Des-pah was unconscious when, a few hours later, she was carried to the hogan of her family. Thinking she would soon die, they left her on the ground outside but someone rode to the Wetherill home to ask for help. Dr. Prudden was visiting the ranch and offered to go to the girl with Marietta.

Marietta Wetherill recalled that "When we got to the hogan Des-pah was lying on the ground outside, apparently dead. Dr. Prudden gave her an injection in the arm of strychnine, a new drug then, but there was no blood circulation and it seemed to do no good. Then he forced some whisky down her throat by pulling out her tongue and then rubbing her throat. In about half an hour Des-pah's eyelids began to quiver and we knew she was alive.

"I asked her mother if she minded if we took Des-pah home with us to care for her and the mother said, 'No, you may take her because my daughter is dead.' She just wouldn't believe that Des-pah could still be living.

"During the next three or four days I wished we had let Des-pah die, her pain was so great. Her leg swelled up to three times its normal size, the skin tightening until it split — and then her knee drew up under her chin. There was nothing we could do for her. She screamed and screamed until we couldn't hear her because she had finally lost her voice. Of course, Dr. Prudden gave her morphine but after a time even that didn't help her.

"A week went by and Dr. Prudden had to leave, so I took care of Des-pah myself and in a few weeks the swelling went down. But her mother and her own people wouldn't look at her or come near her because they said she was dead — a chindee. Always after it was that way. Des-pah lived far up the canyon with an old, old Navajo — Shema-o-sonni [Old Woman] — and until her death she was a cripple, one leg shorter than the other. I have always thought I should have let Des-pah die."

Dr. Prudden had given Marietta advice about medical first aid, left a few instruments and bottles of drugs and antiseptics, and to this she added other medicines from Albuquerque and bought a popular book on home doctoring. The experience of Des-pah, which might have befallen one of her own children, together with the knowledge that the nearest doctor was more than sixty miles from Pueblo Bonito, convinced her that she must know how to handle emergencies herself.

There was the time when a Navajo named Solde got into a fight with Rosita, a raven-haired woman of some beauty, numerous children, but no one in the vicinity whom she called husband. The fight occurred one night when the two, after enjoying each other's company, gradually fell to arguing and then to shouting at each other. Rosita took up a knife sharp and big enough to fell a heifer and with one slashing stroke opened Solde's stomach cleanly, from one side to the other. In the excitement someone thought to call Marietta.

"Another Navajo," she said, "came riding to our house and called for me to come quick — 'because Rosita had cut Solde.' I didn't stop to find out more about it, as I should have done, but got on one of the horses and went back there with him. I took one look at Solde, and sent an Indian back for a bottle of peroxide of hydrogen and another of turpentine, and told him to bring along my book on home physiology. Because Solde was sitting on the edge of a chair, holding his insides in with his hands, and I had to try to put him back together again — right.

"Well, I studied my book and after washing everything with the peroxide of hydrogen I put this fellow back together, sewed him up with silk thread, and washed the wound with turpentine. In a few weeks Solde was up walking around again, almost as good as new. Oh, turpentine is a great thing for healing cuts — I don't know what I would have done without it.

"After he was well enough to get about, he and Rosita made up their quarrel and were friends again."

It was almost a miracle, Joe Schmedding thought, that the Wetherill youngsters escaped disaster. "The children were always climbing on horses — broncs, even," Schmedding said. "If a grown person had fooled around a horse the way they did, he would have been kicked clear across the canyon.

"When a Navajo rode in and tied his pony at the hitching rack by the store, the children would just swarm over it. Maybe it was a pony they had never seen before. All the better. Young Richard would pull himself up by the mane, the other two by grabbing the pony's tail and going up the back way. And there all three would sit on the pony and for some reason, darned if I know, the pony wouldn't mind a bit.

"Out in the corral I used to see them race and frisk around just as though they and the horses had some special understanding between them, and they probably did. Playing tag under the horses' bellies. Mounting them from the right side as often as from the left. It didn't matter to them and it didn't seem to matter to the horses.

"Young Richard was a good rider and even as a little fellow of eight or nine he was a regular hand. One day when he had been out alone on a horse he rode back, white as a sheet. We could see from the streaks on his cheeks that he had been crying. He couldn't use his right arm at all. Then he told us his pony had stumbled and thrown him. He had fallen on a rock and broken his collarbone and maybe he had also broken his arm or wrist, I'm not sure. Anyway, he was pretty plucky and tried to show it didn't hurt. His father looked him over carefully and then took him in to Albuquerque to have a doctor set the broken bone."

Richard Wetherill was devoted to his children, loved to have them with him on his various duties around the ranch, and taught them how to be self reliant. Whenever he returned from a trip to Gallup or Albuquerque he brought them toys. But even when they were very small he had no pet names for them, calling them by their given names, Richard, Elizabeth and Robert.

There was a difference of two years between the three children. Elizabeth Ann had been born early in 1900 and Clate Wetherill, still a bachelor and staying with his brother at Pueblo Bonito at the time, had written Dr. Prudden on February 14 that "Rich's family has increased by a small female. It's a queer little critter that has nothing to say for itself."

Expecting her third baby in the summer of 1902, Marietta escaped from the heat of the canyon by taking young Richard and Elizabeth with her to Creede to stay in the cool mountain air at the home of Anna and Charlie Mason. There Robert had been born, on August 6. Two months later Richard Wetherill came for his family to bring them back to the Chaco. On the first night out they were caught in a heavy snowstorm. Marietta remembered that "Mr. Wetherill set up the tent and opened the flaps after building a big fire in front to keep me and the children and little Robert warm. We were driving a number of horses and sheep on this trip, but the next morning the snow was so deep we couldn't go on and we stayed right there. But the day after that we were able to start again, Mr. Wetherill driving the horses on ahead to break trail in the snow for the sheep."

Four more children were born to Richard and Marietta: two boys, who died at birth; and two daughters, Marion Jane, who was born August 27, 1907, and Ruth, who was born June 5, 1910, both in Albuquerque.

Impressions of early childhood can sometimes be perceptive and uncompromising. Martha Wetherill Stewart, Al Wetherill's daughter, grew up retaining a vivid memory of her Uncle Richard on the occasions when he came to Gallup.

"One of my first memories," she wrote, "is standing on the cross-piece of the gate of our white picket fence watching for Uncle Richard and his pinto ponies to come up the hill and 'round Aldrich's corner. He would stop at the post office first and Papa would phone Mother, and I'd take my stand to wait for him.

"He was a quiet man — all of the Wetherill brothers were — with that common gift of all gentle people of making children feel that they are loved and understood. He'd reach down and swing me up on the seat beside him, and the ponies would trot around the block to the stable and vacant lot across the alley from our yard. It couldn't have been more exciting had he been a knight in shining armor on a white charger with silver trappings."

Al Wetherill's duties as postmaster kept him busy for long hours each day, so after Richard had taken care of the errands that brought him to town, he usually came back to the post office where his younger brother was working.

"At that time, the Federal government did not believe in spending money it didn't have. So my father was allowed $25 a month clerk hire. Since the local clerical jobs paid $50, he made up the other $25 out of his own pocket, and because of the amount of work in the Gallup post office my mother went down almost every afternoon and evening and worked 'for free' for eight of the nine years he was there.

"So, most visiting among the family was done in the post office as the work of the day was from 6:00 A.M. to 8:00 P.M. excepting Sunday, which was just when the mail trains came in. I had a drygoods box for a playhouse in the back of the office and Mother's desk where she worked on the ledgers was right beside it.

"Uncle Richard would go down with us at noon and sit, reading the paper when the folks didn't have any time to visit, or he'd play games with me — my choice. That way, I picked up the trading post news and especially the current adventures of the cousins whom I'd never seen. It just gets too complicated to transport a flock of small fry by buckboard to town on a merchandise buying trip."

There was one visit of her Uncle Richard's that above all others clings in her memory. It was during an epidemic of smallpox that swept through the town. "I was a skinny, frail little mutt that caught everything that came down the pike. All smallpox cases were being put out on the edge of town in the 'pest-house,' irrespective of age or family.

"Our family doctor was Dr. Coudert, a misplaced genius, who was a graduate of some European university — Heidelburg, I think. His word was practically law in Gallup, so when I broke out with spots and ran a high fever and was completely delirious, he told Mother that I had chickenpox and to keep me isolated in the back bedroom. He said Papa was not to come into the room and it would be better for her not to see anyone as long as I was sick — but that it was only chickenpox.

"Uncle Richard came to town. I was miserable, but not too miserable to demand that he come in to see me. I remember that much. Mother says he sniffed and said, 'Smallpox.'

" 'No, Richard, really it isn't. Dr. Coudert says it's just a bad case of chickenpox.'

" 'All right, Mary, then we'll call it chickenpox, but I know the smell.'

"So my Uncle Richard stayed at the house and helped keep a sick, petulant little girl as quiet as possible so she wouldn't scratch and be scarred, until the worst of it was over.

"Then, before he went back to his own small flock, he had Papa get him new clothes, and seeking refuge in the 'wash-house' in the back yard pitched the clothes that he had worn in the sickroom onto a bonfire. He waved at me through the window, threw me a kiss and was gone."

During the years of the excavation of Pueblo Bonito, and for some time afterward, a number of scientists stayed with the Wetherills, often for a few weeks or even for several months. Among them were Prof. Richard E. Dodge of New York, a geologist, who made numerous tests at Bonito and elsewhere in the canyon, seeking a clue to the great pueblo's age by studying the rock formations. Another was the Bohemian anthropologist, Ales Hrdlicka — crusty, hot-tempered, completely dedicated to his work: in this case, the measurement of Anasazi bones, particularly skulls.

Professor Dodge spent two summers in the Chaco, in 1899 and 1901, and Hrdlicka was there frequently between 1899 and 1903 when he was director of the physical anthropology section of the Hyde Expedition. Hrdlicka worked in a brush-thatched second-floor room at Bonito's southwest corner and frequently called upon Marietta for assistance in recording his measurements of skeletons.

"He spoke little English, but he had very positive ideas," Marietta remembered. "He came to Pueblo Bonito to make measurements of the skeletons and while there he also measured the heads of some of our Navajos, at that time strongly believing the Navajo came to this country from some place to the south. He wore a scraggly Van Dyck beard and just didn't seem to care how he looked.

"His tent was just outside my back bedroom door. One time he and Mr. Wetherill went to the Lukachukai Mountains where there had been a terrible fight between the Navajos and Mexicans. They found a great many skulls, which Dr. Hrdlicka brought back with him and lined up in a row in his tent.

"Elizabeth, who was not walking yet, crawled into the tent a few days afterward. Suddenly Dr. Hrdlicka happened along, saw what Elizabeth was doing — and screamed. Oh, how angry he was! Something just terrible had happened, I thought. I came running out to see what the matter was and found them both in the tent. Elizabeth had pulled a fistful of teeth out of the skulls and put them into her own mouth. He was absolutely speechless when I found them, standing there, gasping and pounding his chest with his fists and then pointing at Elizabeth. She, poor thing, probably knew she had done something awful but didn't have the faintest idea what. She just sat there among all those grinning skulls, her mouth filled with old teeth, looking up at him with big innocent round eyes.

"He couldn't stand for this, he screamed at me finally. He couldn't stand for it! He was going straight home. Well, of course, he didn't. But he was a temperamental, high-strung man, no mistake."

The visitors usually came to Pueblo Bonito during the spring or summer but occasionally a few hardy souls found their way to the Chaco in the wintertime, when the skies were often dark with snow and the temperatures near zero. It was during one such frigid spell when Richard and Fred Hyde went to Thoreau, riding over the frozen wagon road in Richard's buckboard, to meet a small party of Eastern scientists. The train's late arrival at the little station kept them waiting in the cold and delayed their return. It was after midnight of the second day when the six or seven men, stiff with cold, finally came in sight of the Triangle Bar Triangle Ranch.

Much earlier, Marietta had prepared an elaborate supper for the expected guests but when the hours had dragged by and they still hadn't come, she went to bed. The sound of the men's voices and stamping feet awakened her and she was rubbing her eyes, starting to get out of bed when Richard came to the door. He asked if she could just put some coffee on and maybe heat up a little something — just anything.

Then while Richard took the men into his office and built a roaring fire in the iron stove Marietta went out to the kitchen. A short time later she called them to the table, and it was their turn to rub their eyes. The lavish dinner she had put aside was now spread out before them. They fell to, attacking a big roast of meat, bowls of cottage cheese, potatoes, steaming greens, and finally a bowl filled with baked apples. When that was gone there were two or three apple pies with cheese and cream, and a chocolate cake for those who preferred it.

"They ate and they ate," Marietta said. "It was almost morning before they got to bed. And then afterward, Mr. Wetherill said to me he just couldn't get over it, just couldn't. He said: 'Asthanne, thee are a good wife to me.'"

The Wetherill ranch became known for its hospitality, Marietta noticing one summer that a day hadn't passed when there were fewer than twenty people seated around the table for each meal — this number including the ranch hands, guests from the East, Clayton who came quite often, Dr. Prudden who stayed for several days or a week at a time, Indian agents, horse and cattle buyers, and chance wayfarers.

A wagon pulled into the ranch one day, driven by a woman and loaded with her seven or eight children and a pathetic array of household belongings. The woman said they had come from Texas, were on their way to the green farmlands on the San Juan — she'd heard it was good country there with a chance for a widow to make a living. Her husband, she said, had died leaving her the children and only the few broken objects she could put into a wagon.

Richard listened quietly, noticed how worn-out she and the youngsters looked, how grimy and tattered from their long trip. Then he spoke a few encouraging words, saying he was sure she had done the right thing and at Farmington or beyond, toward Shiprock, could find something to do. But before they started on again, he said, they ought to rest a little. He invited the tired woman and her children to come into the house and meet his wife. They stayed for three days.

On some nights there was music and dancing at the ranch. Richard, who didn't dance and couldn't sing or even carry a tune, liked to see others having fun. Marietta enjoyed playing the guitar at such times — as she did, too, on quieter evenings — and also she liked to dance. In sympathy with this, Richard always managed to have someone at the ranch who could play the fiddle or some other instrument.

"In the summer or spring we always used to dance in Mr. Wetherill's office, moving the big stove outside to give more space," Marietta remembered. "Then later we added a room at the rear of the house and since it had a good solid floor it was even better, but otherwise it was used as the children's room." Marietta preferred the waltzes, but also there were fast Spanish tunes and such lively popular things as "The Roan Horse" and "The Devil's Dream."

While Marietta and most of the others were dancing, Richard would read or look on, although in later years he became fond of duplicate whist and would cajole others into a game with him in another room. "I remember

ANASAZI   243

how he would come to the doorway and stand there smiling, his hands raised out bracing the door frame. He would watch us dancing for a few minutes, and then would ask me if I was having a good time."

On quiet summer evenings, when they were alone and sitting outside under the brush and timber roof of the porch, Marietta often fingered the strings of her guitar while Richard read or just sat and listened.

An epidemic of diphtheria moved through the San Juan country late one fall, bringing death to nearly every hogan in the Chaco. In some cases whole families were wiped out. The disease was no respecter of color or station, whites and Navajo alike falling sick.

Marietta quarantined her children against exposure, while Richard appealed for medical assistance from Superintendent William T. Shelton, in charge of the Navajo agency at Shiprock. Days went by without response from the agency. Shelton preferred to abide by a technicality: Chaco Canyon was just outside the limits of the Navajo reservation. He would do nothing. When Richard saw that his appeal was ignored, he talked the situation over with Fred Hyde and then grimly took matters into his own hands.

It was possible, he thought, that the disease was being spread by starving Indian dogs as they left the death-stilled hogans to wander at large, often in small packs, looking for food. With Clate Wetherill and Gus Thompson in charge, he sent several men out to shoot every stray dog they encountered, and to leave poisoned bait for the coyotes which lurked wherever there was the stench of death. Richard's orders also were to burn the hogans where the dead were found, and to bury the bodies. The task was heart-breaking, as the victims of the epidemic now numbered in the scores. Several weeks passed before there was any sign of the sickness abating and the men could rest.

During this time they learned that few families had suffered greater loss than that of Hostine George. This Indian was one of the wealthiest Navajos between the Lukachukais and Nacimientos. He and his family lived near the Chacra Mesa, five miles above Fahada.

Shortly before the outbreak of the disease, Hostine George's wife and married daughter Carrie had come to the trading post at Pueblo Bonito driving seven cows and a small flock of sheep. These animals, the property of Mrs. George, they had traded for four or five Buel robes, coffee, sugar, flour, several bolts of calico and manta cloth. Good cows then brought from ten to fifteen dollars a head and sheep anywhere from fifty cents to a dollar and a half. The Buel robes, fringed on four sides and brilliantly colored, were valued at about the same price as a good heifer and were coveted by all of the Indians.

The negotiations over this trade of stock for goods, therefore, had dragged on through the afternoon and into early evening. Carrie and her mother were invited to have supper with the Wetherills, stay at the ranch overnight, and complete their trading in the morning. This they did. The next day the bartering was completed. Mrs. George took eleven silver dollars in change. Also she agreed to winter the animals she had just sold with her own herd, returning them the following spring to Anasazi "when the corn was a foot high."

As another part of the bargain, Richard said he would give her one dollar more for each of the seven cows when they were brought in. Mrs. George and her daughter Carrie then left the post with their trade goods and the livestock. A record of the trade was made in the Pueblo Bonito ledger but it was forgotten when the epidemic of diphtheria broke out.

Old Hostine George brought the news one cold day as a pale sun hung low over the Gap. He came on foot, leading a small child by the hand and with the other arm holding an infant laced in a board-and-buckskin baby-carrier. Thinking of his own children, Richard went out to meet the Navajo. From the doorway Marietta looked on.

"He sat on the ground as Mr. Wetherill approached, and began to cry. He said the little girl and the baby were Carrie's, that his wife and all of his family had died with the sickness, while he stayed at his hogan watching them go. Then he had left — he said, still crying — to see his daughter Carrie. He found her in the hogan, dead, and her husband nowhere about.

"Near Carrie's body was her baby, in its baby-carrier and sucking on an ear of corn. He hadn't found the other child until, half a mile from the hogan, he discovered many coyote tracks near a large clump of greasewood. There he had heard crying and saw the little girl hidden deep in the bushes. She told him that the dogs (meaning coyotes) had barked at her all night, and she was cold and had had nothing to eat for a long time.

"That was the story Hostine George told, as he sat on the ground with the little girl and the baby, crying. Mr. Wetherill put them in one of the hogans we had for the Indians, and sent out two tubs of hot water with an antiseptic in it. He told Hostine George to bathe the children and himself and to throw out all of their clothing, which he burned. We gave the old man clothes and bottles of baby milk and food and bedding for a quarantine period. Then I took the little girls and cared for them several months. Near the end of that time I learned that Carrie George's husband was one of the survivors. He came for the children finally and took them away."

As long as the epidemic lasted there had been no word from Superintendent Shelton. He had sent no one from the agency to help the Chaco Indians. Months later, when he did get around to visit Pueblo Bonito, Shelton encountered Hostine George. The old Navajo said he had a complaint: Anasazi had sent a cowboy one day who had taken away seven cows from his herd of cattle. Shelton came to Richard's office, saying an Indian had accused Richard of stealing his stock — would Richard explain what had happened? Hostine George was called in. Richard asked the old man if Mrs. George had not told him about the trading of the Buel blankets and other things the previous fall, the agreement for wintering the seven cows until the spring corn was standing a foot high?

He had heard nothing at all about this, Hostine George said. Then Richard brought out his ledger so that Shelton and Hostine George could see where the entry for the trade had been made. The old Navajo shook his head doubtfully and drew marks on the floor with the toe of his moccasin. No, he knew nothing about it, or about those marks on paper, and his woman had said nothing to him about such a trade. There the matter rested.

Shelton returned to his agency at Shiprock. A few years later, when Richard was dead and Shelton was doing everything possible to protect the murderer, the agent made it a part of the official record that Richard Wetherill had stolen seven cows from Hostine George.

Richard was called upon many times to settle disputes arising among the Chaco Navajos, his fairness and success as an arbitrator having won him the Indians' confidence. Marietta occasionally doctored a sick or injured Navajo when the powers of a medicine man apparently failed. Shelton was made uncomfortable by the knowledge that hundreds of the Navajos just outside his limits of authority looked to the Wetherills of Pueblo Bonito, not to Shelton, for guidance or help. It displeased him when he heard the Wetherills, although not legally, had adopted a ten-year-old orphan boy.

Richard and Marietta had an instant liking for the boy. He was somewhat older than their own children but they took him and made him a part of the family, Marietta giving him the name of Jack Edway. When the lad was about fourteen, Fred Hyde offered to pay for educating him in the East. Since Jack himself was eager to go, the Wetherills consented and did not see him for six years. Then he showed up at Pueblo Bonito one day, saying his education was completed but he was unsure about the future; he had missed his own people and wanted to see them again. Richard gave him a horse and an outfit and for a month there was no word from him except that he had stayed at the hogan of Joe Hostine Yazzie, and then with Thomacito.

Then Jack Edway came back to Pueblo Bonito and talked again with Richard and Marietta. He was a sad, very confused young Indian. His Navajo boyhood he couldn't recapture; nor did life in a white man's city promise much future. And yet, he thought, it might be better if he could go back East. Possibly there was some niche there he could fit into. He had a sympathetic audience. Richard gave him the money for his fare to New York and Jack Edway left almost at once, saying he would board a train at Gallup. That was the last the Wetherills saw of him. He did not write and for all they knew he had been swallowed up by the big city.

Many years afterward Marietta learned that Jack Edway had been seen in Farmington. He had decided the East held no more for him than the reservation. So for three years he had stayed at Fort Lewis in Colorado, then had moved to Shiprock and had become an agency policeman.

NINETEEN

ENEMIES of Richard Wetherill pictured him as a cattle rustler and "bad man," engaged constantly in a running fight with the law. The record, open to all, proves only that he had life's full share of troubles.

Richard was involved four times in court proceedings for nonpayment of debts. One case might almost be called fantastic: originally involving a simple loan of $263, it grew like Jack's beanstalk into litigation enmeshing the sheriffs of three counties and two states, a battery of lawyers, Fred Hyde and Marietta Wetherill as co-plaintiffs in a weird counter suit, the Territorial Supreme Court, and a Navajo blanket of possibly historic interest.

The case dragged on nearly fifteen years before it was settled, cost Richard and Fred Hyde together $1,204 in court assessments alone — and left Richard with exactly $10 to his credit at the First National Bank of Albuquerque.

Richard's entanglement began when he borrowed $263.41 from a Mancos man, Harrison Hill, on November 26, 1892. Probably the money was needed to settle a note on the Alamo Ranch. In any case, he signed a promise to repay Hill, with interest of one and one-half percent, on or before February 1, 1893. Two months passed, still more time went by, and Richard still owed Hill the full amount. Hill apparently was a reasonable man because he waited until July of the following year and then filed a claim against Richard in the District Court at Cortez. When Richard failed to answer a summons, the court awarded Hill a judgment of $340.90, including costs and interest. An execution of the order was issued on August 29 to Sheriff S. P. Thomas with instructions to collect the money or place a lien on any property of Richard's which he believed would satisfy the judgment.

Sheriff Thomas presently reported back that "After diligent search I could not find any property belonging to the within named Richard Wetherill" — which causes some doubt over the sheriff's diligence. Whether Richard held any animosity against Hill after the latter's first resort to law is not

RICHARD WETHERILL

known, but subsequent events show clearly that Richard was determined icicles should form in hell before he repaid the debt and one cent of interest.

Six years went by and then Hill brought suit against Richard a second time — in San Juan County District Court at Aztec, New Mexico. Richard was summoned to appear but the order was ignored. Since Richard refused to respond, Hill was granted a judgment of $608.60 including costs. From Pueblo Bonito there was nothing but stony silence. Then, after nearly seven months more, the case took a new turn when Sheriff James E. Elmer, who had succeeded Brown in the job, was instructed to ride down to Pueblo Bonito and attach anything in sight belonging to Richard Wetherill.

Carrying out the full spirit of these instructions, if not obeying them to the letter, Sheriff Elmer placed attachments on the following property which, probably, he supposed was owned by Richard: one pinto team and one heavy surrey, a Navajo blanket of striking design and presumably of considerable value, a Stevenson buggy and its team of horses (a gray and a bay), and six other horses. Since it would have been awkward for one man to drive two buggies and ten horses back to Aztec, the sheriff told Richard he was impounding the seized property where it was.

Three days later Fred Hyde signed an affidavit in replevin, his statement charging that Sheriff Elmer had wrongfully attached certain things belonging to Marietta Wetherill and to himself. Soon thereafter, on February 5, 1903, Marietta also swore out a complaint against the sheriff, and from that point on the efforts of Harrison Hill to recover the money due him were all but lost in a court battle of magnificent proportions. Confronted with the accusations of Fred Hyde and Marietta, Sheriff Elmer filed counter charges against them, alleging they had illegally dis-impounded the pinto team and the surrey.

Behind all of this was a quiet little story of a birthday gift and a trade. It seems that Win Wetherill, then the proprietor of the Two Gray Hills trading post, had secured from a Navajo medicine man what may have been the first Yei-bi-chai blanket ever woven — this a reproduction of a sacred Navajo sand painting incorporating in its design, contrary to all tribal rules, the figures of Navajo Yei, or gods. The blanket had come from the loom of the medicine man's wife and in its detail and workmanship, from various accounts, it was superb. At that time the making of this blanket was regarded by the Navajo as a serious breach of unwritten tribal law. It has been said, although the actual circumstances are unclear, that the woman who made it and her husband who sold it to Win Wetherill were ostracized by every Navajo in the region.

The blanket, nevertheless, had come to Marietta as a birthday present from Win. Although she realized the unique blanket was valuable, Marietta attached no other significance to it and Fred Hyde persuaded her to give it to him in exchange for his pinto team and surrey. It was this blanket, this pinto team and this surrey which Sheriff Elmer had attached, among other things, on his visit to Pueblo Bonito, assuming them to be the property of Richard Wetherill. In her suit against the sheriff, Marietta claimed that the value of the team and surrey was $400.

During the legal scuffling that ensued, everyone apparently (except Fred Hyde), forgot all about the *Yei* blanket, which rightfully was his but which technically, had it not been forgotten, was claimed by authorities for Harrison Hill. While the case was still in litigation, Fred Hyde, possibly short of ready money as quite often he was, offered to sell the blanket, writing to George Pepper from Pueblo Bonito on January 27, 1904, that

> I want to drop you a line about an extraordinary Navajo blanket that I expect to bring on with me in a few days and that I have rescued from the open market. It is an exact reproduction of a medicine man's sand-painting and as you can appreciate, is properly a museum specimen.
>
> I have the full data respecting the blanket: — the name of the Medicine Man, now dead whose exclusive property the painting was — the name of his wife, who made the blanket also dead, by the vengeance of the gods as the Navajos think: — and the complete significance of all the figures and symbols.
>
> The blanket itself is very fine weave about 5 x 8 feet, and is held at $500.00, not an excessive price when it is understood that no Navajo woman will make another. [Many more were made. In 1956, a Navajo woman living near Shiprock undertook a *Yei* blanket depicting the sand painting of the Whirling Logs ceremony, from a drawing in color supplied by the author's daughter. According to trader Russell Foutz, who had commissioned the blanket, the woman was warned that if she finished it she would lose her sight.]
> I cannot give the blanket myself to the Museum [the American Museum of Natural History] but perhaps you know of someone who would like to donate it. If no one cares to donate it to the New York Museum it will probably go to the Chicago Field Museum as Win Wetherill has been asked by them to interest himself in curios

and ethnological material for their display of South Western Ethnology.

What Pepper did about this, if anything, is not known. Amsden, in his *Navaho Weaving,* made a thorough study of the whole subject of Navajo blankets and apparently was unaware of the circumstances mentioned here. In a very brief discussion of so-called ceremonial or *Yei* blankets, now standardized for the tourist trade in gaudy colors and intentionally added symbols of no meaning, he made this reference to an episode related by George Wharton James:

> James has an interesting account of the furore which greeted the first appearance of the *Yei* blanket, about the beginning of the present century. The Navaho were shocked and outraged, he says, by the sacrilege of one of their weavers in reproducing sacred symbols and figures in a blanket which was put on display in a trader's store. "Councils were held over the reservation to discuss the matter, and the trader was finally commanded to remove the blanket containing the offending emblems from the wall of his office."

Neither James, whom Amsden here quoted, nor Amsden himself identified the trader, but evidently it was Win Wetherill. Also, it is almost certain that this is the same blanket Win gave to Marietta Wetherill as a birthday gift.

Harrison Hill must have regarded the squabble over the team and surrey a digression. On October 11, 1905, he appeared as a joint complainant with Sheriff Elmer against Fred Hyde and Marietta Wetherill. And on that date, in Aztec District Court, Judge John R. McFie ruled that the pinto team and surrey had been unlawfully disengaged (by Marietta and Hyde) from the sheriff's absentee custody. Acting more on principle than anything else, Marietta and Fred Hyde appealed to the Territorial Supreme Court at Santa Fe.

When the case was heard in 1907, the ruling of Judge McFie was upheld. Fred Hyde, now for some obscure reason the principal figure in this action, was ordered to pay $699 in court costs quite apart from the large sum he was obliged to pay to his attorneys. He declared that he would ask for a re-hearing, but evidently he changed his mind.

Meanwhile, these diversions and the passage of years had done nothing to shake Hill's resolve to bring Richard to account for his debt. Naturally, however, nothing would occur with breath-taking speed. On March 8, 1909,

Judge McFie, striking off on a new tangent, ordered the sheriff of Bernalillo County to attach funds in Richard's checking account at the First National Bank in Albuquerque. The amount to be garnisheed was $599.35 damages, and $7.75 costs: a total of $607.10.

On March 17 officers of the bank forwarded information to Judge McFie at Aztec that the account of Richard Wetherill, on that date, showed a total balance of no more than $515.38.

Judge McFie was a merciful man. His instructions to the bank, modified to meet Richard's circumstances, were delivered March 29. He requested the bank to pay to Harrison Hill the sum of $495.38; he further stipulated the bank was to withdraw $10 more from Richard's account for the bank's own trouble and expense in the matter. This left Richard just $10 to draw upon in conducting the affairs of the Triangle Bar Triangle Ranch. But the case was closed.

Another occasion when Richard found himself badgered by a creditor was late in 1902. In August he had ordered merchandise valued at $693 from the Tootle, Wheeler & Motter Co. of St. Joseph, Missouri. The order was for overalls, pants, bolts of cloth and so forth, for the Pueblo Bonito trading post, and to the purchase price was added a freight charge of $42. When, after three months, Richard had failed to make payment, Tootle, Wheeler & Motter filed complaint with the court at Aztec. Again the underlying circumstances are unclear, but in this case Richard possibly became stubborn when he thought his creditors were pressing him. When served with a summons, Richard ignored the order to appear, and a judgment was entered against him for the full costs plus interest. Two years went by with no further development. Then in November, 1905, Sheriff Elmer paid another visit to Pueblo Bonito with the same instructions as before: attach any property belonging to Richard Wetherill sufficient to settle the claim.

This time Sheriff Elmer was as wary as a man who has backed into a red-hot stove. Upon his return to Aztec he reported: "After diligent enquiry [I certify] that I have been unable to find any property belonging to Richard Wetherill to satisfy this judgment or any part thereof."

Another year and a half went by in stalemate and then the sheriff came again. On this trip he was either more determined or the fires had been lit behind him, because Richard capitulated and soon came to a settlement with the firm in St. Joseph.

Old court ledgers help to reconstruct the past, but sometimes careless omission on the part of a court clerk long since gone leaves a story dangling.

The record of the civil court at Durango tells part of the story of a small claims suit filed against Richard by the attorney, Charles A. Johnson, alleging that Richard, on October 17, 1894 — a year and a half after the trial — still owed him a balance of $22 for defending him in the Hamilton cattle case. The record here shows that Richard failed to answer the complaint although a subpoena had been served, and a judgment for the amount plus costs and interest was awarded to the attorney. At this point, entries in the ledger under this heading cease. There is no way of knowing if Richard ever paid the judgment. Perhaps he did not.

Also in doubt is the outcome of a fourth action brought against Richard. On August 5, 1895, when he was living in Mancos, Richard signed two notes, both for $150, agreeing to pay Thomas Thornell ten per cent interest; one note was to be paid off in three months, the other in a year. Thornell transferred the notes to a woman living in Kansas named Eliza Bowman. The records of Aztec court show that as a result of a suit by Eliza Bowman, Sheriff John Brown served a summons and complaint against Richard on January 30, 1901. Richard again failed to answer and a month later Judge McFie issued a judgment ordering Richard to pay the plaintiff $457.45. There is no further entry to indicate the outcome.

This is the complete record of Richard's difficulties with the law — a record not spotless, nor very unusual.

TWENTY

WILLIAM T. SHELTON was the most controversial figure in the San Juan country just after the turn of the century. Appointed as superintendent of the Navajo agency at Shiprock in the summer of 1903, Shelton was a big, aggressive man who inspired either respect or intense dislike. He was a native of North Carolina, a member of a once prosperous slave-holding family; those who knew him said he had somewhat the same paternalistic attitude toward Indians his father and grandfather had held toward their Negro slaves.

There was a positive forcefulness about everything Shelton did, an uncompromising air that his wish was naturally right, his word was law. This made it nearly impossible for anyone who knew him to remain impartial. And that is the way Shelton liked it: he wanted people to understand they were either his friends and sycophants or his implacable enemies. There must be a sharp dividing line with nothing in the middle for him to bother about.

Shelton had been at his new post only a short time when he concluded that Richard Wetherill was the man in the whole Four Corners country whom he detested most. Wetherill, he decided, must go.

For months Richard remained unaware of this, scarcely mindful, even, of Shelton himself. It is doubtful if he ever had any conception of the extent of Shelton's enmity. He was too preoccupied with his own affairs at Pueblo Bonito.

Until the latter part of 1907, Chaco Canyon lay just beyond the limits of Shelton's jurisdiction, the eastern boundary of the Navajo reservation falling eighteen miles short of Bonito. This did not lessen Shelton's determination to drive Richard out of the Chaco, but his hand was strengthened when, by Presidential order, Chaco Canyon became a part of the reservation on November 9, 1907. (Since then the order has been amended, but the region surrounding the Chaco Monument is still largely restricted to Navajo use.)

Shelton visited Pueblo Bonito not more than two or three times, on each occasion staying as a guest at the Wetherill home. Outwardly, everything

between the two men was pleasant, Marietta recalling only that on the evenings of his visits Shelton drank heavily. She did not remember her husband
then or later saying anything about Shelton that would indicate there was a
strain or unfriendliness. The jealousy he was beginning to feel for Richard's
obvious hold upon the Chaco Navajos, Shelton masked carefully.

At the time of his arrival at the Shiprock agency, the Navajo reservation
was comparable in size to Massachusetts and within its boundaries there were
approximately twenty-five thousand Indians. Shelton was in charge of the
northern half of the reservation; affairs of the southern section were directed
by Jacob C. Levingood, from Fort Defiance.

There are those who, for various reasons, believed that Shelton was a
good and conscientious agent. Among these was John Wade, brother-in-law of
John Wetherill, who generally thought well of Shelton. Charles Avery
Amsden, who lived in Farmington during Shelton's regime, said that "Much
credit is due Mr. W. T. Shelton, who as agent at Shiprock in 1909 started
the annual Shiprock Fair, an event which has been a potent force for excel-
lence in weaving. Mr. Shelton also was active in improving the quality of
Navaho sheep, being one of the pioneers in this neglected field of reform."

George Wharton James, in *Our American Wonderlands*, wrote that "the
most intelligent work I am familiar with in the education of Indians is being
done [at Shiprock] by the superintendent, W. T. Shelton." Others of equally
dependable judgment have said that in many respects Shelton was capable,
enlightened, and sincerely concerned with the welfare of the Navajo.

Agnes Furman knew him as "a big man, very positive in his ways and
ideas. He could get things done." Most people respected him, she thought,
although in manner he was "fairly loud and in some things arbitrary."

Jim Jarvis, managing one of the Hyde Expedition stores in Farmington
at the time of Shelton's arrival at the agency, was among the first to meet
him. "When Shelton came to Shiprock," Jarvis said, "there was law and
order at Pueblo Bonito. The relations with the Indians there were good and
everything was peaceable. So far as I knew, Richard Wetherill was very much
liked by the Indians. But Shelton told us not to 'interfere' with the Navajos
any more. By that I suppose he meant they were his responsibility. Shelton
didn't like Wetherill because Richard could handle the Indians and he
couldn't, and so there was that cause for jealousy."

Other people at Farmington, including Earl H. Morris, did not count
themselves among Shelton's admirers. John Arrington said: "He did have a
lot of friends who claimed he was one of the best agents we ever had. He was

a big man with an important air. He was domineering — what he said went."
Richard, on the other hand, impressed Arrington as a different sort. "Richard
Wetherill was a typical Quaker gentleman. I never heard him say anything
bad about anybody." And as for Shelton's hostility towards Richard:

"It was simply because Wetherill had been among the Indians for years
and they would come in to him for advice. When Shelton came here it was
plain to see this didn't set well — Shelton was the king snipe and he wanted
the Indians to come to him if they needed anything. Besides, Richard Wetherill had forgotten more about Navajos than Shelton would ever know."

Earl Morris recalled:

> I knew [Richard Wetherill] by sight when he was a mature man
> and I just a youngster, but never did I hold a conversation with
> him. My impression is that he was a strong man, fearless and per-
> haps a bit ruthless, but no more so than those of his kind in the
> place and time in which he lived.

In later years Morris came to know John Wetherill well and,

> . . . bit by bit [I] pried out of him a good deal of information
> about the Wetherill family. They were, in my opinion, an upright
> and honest tribe, as might be expected from their Quaker back-
> ground. This would seem to be borne out by the fact that they got
> along so well for so long with the Indians, first with the Utes in the
> Mancos vicinity and then with the Navajo.
>
> I believe my judgment that [Shelton] was an evil character is
> not far from the truth. Certainly he was a despot in the little realm
> over which he had command. His high-handedness in general and
> the pretty clear evidence of his immorality with Indian girls in the
> Shiprock school stirred up a real tempest in the San Juan valley
> . . . Shelton's enmity for Richard would have been inevitable, be-
> cause a man who had been so long a law unto himself would have
> paid no more attention to Shelton's orders or wishes than he would
> to the blowing of the wind.
>
> My father regarded Shelton as a good administrator, but a hard
> and self-seeking man. In the autumn of 1903, father [Scott N.
> Morris] superintended for Shelton improvement of the wagon road
> from the Hogback to Shiprock. Shelton wanted to have a trading
> post opened near the Agency and promised should father apply for

a permit, he would see that it was granted. The next time father got up to Farmington, he talked the prospect over in detail with mother and the following was his conclusion, I think verbatim: "Beyond question, the post would be a big money maker, but I have been too long my own boss to stand a situation in which every move I made would be under the thumb of a man like Shelton."

A story told in the San Juan Valley relates to an encounter between Shelton and Henry (Chee) Dodge.

The son of a Navajo woman and Mexican father, Chee Dodge was respected in the Shiprock area as an interpreter and as one of the most influential men of his tribe — since he proudly chose his mother's side of the family and regarded himself as an Indian. Others besides Chee Dodge were present when Shelton made some coarse reference to Chee's parentage. Normally a gentle, peaceable individual, Chee's eyes gleamed for a moment with fire as he replied: "Some of what you say is true, but at least my father was honorable enough to take my mother for his wife!"

In his travels about the reservation Shelton informed the Indian Service personnel, confidentially, that Richard Wetherill was mistreating the Navajos of Chaco Canyon and cheating all who went there to trade. Shelton was watching him, though, and until the time came when Wetherill could be driven out he would appreciate any information given to him that would help toward that end. Without his realizing it, Richard was put under surveillance and Shelton's ablest, or at least most prolific, informant turned out to be a sturdy little man from Ohio named Samuel F. Stacher.

Stacher had entered the Indian Service the same year Shelton was appointed superintendent at Shiprock, first as farmer at the Sac and Fox School in eastern Oklahoma. In 1905 he served as a ranger on the Santa Clara Indian reservation in New Mexico and the following year was appointed financial clerk and teacher for the Ute sub-agency at Navajo Springs, Colorado. Three years later he was chosen to fill the superintendency of the newly created Eastern Navajo Jurisdiction, making his headquarters — with approval of both Shelton and Wetherill — at Chaco Canyon. Then in his early thirties, he brought with him his wife Flossie who was dark haired, pretty and full of life. The young couple had four children, three daughters and a son. Richard and Marietta welcomed them to Pueblo Bonito and arranged that they occupy the stone and adobe house near the southeast corner of Pueblo del Arroyo. Their rent, fifteen dollars a month, was paid by the government. The newcomers were friendly at first, often visiting the Wetherills in the evening, and the children of the two families had interests in common.

At the time of his transfer to Pueblo Bonito, Stacher knew some words of Navajo, but employed a Navajo interpreter as well as several Navajo policemen. Short and stocky, he was a sincerely earnest, plodding, and hard-working man. All might have been well except for the domineering influence of Stacher's equal at Shiprock — Superintendent Shelton. Fate brought them together at an unpropitious moment. Stacher did not know it, however, and until too late never gauged the human elements involved.

From Shiprock, Shelton controlled the northern part of the old reservation while the southern half was under the authority of Peter Paquette at Fort Defiance. Stacher's new jurisdiction was the largest, extending from the San Juan to the Zuñi reservation and below Zuñi, from Arizona to Canoncito, west of Albuquerque. These boundary lines, on paper only, did not contain Shelton's exercise of power.

After he had been at Pueblo Bonito only a short time Stacher learned of Shelton's bitter animosity toward Richard Wetherill. During their later meetings at Shiprock and elsewhere the new agent was advised of Shelton's determination to get the Wetherills out of Chaco Canyon. Stacher increasingly reflected the hostile attitude of Shelton in his own relations with Richard until, near the end and just before a domestic crisis in Stacher's family precipitated a break, the atmosphere at Pueblo Bonito became uncomfortably tense.

Stacher did not appear in the picture officially or otherwise, but he may have been aware of a report Shelton sent, on July 18, 1908, to Robert G. Valentine, the Commissioner of Indian Affairs. Studded with grotesque misrepresentations, the report told of a visit Shelton made to Pueblo Bonito and of what he characterized as Richard's brutal treatment of the Chaco Navajos.

At the end of the report Shelton asked Commissioner Valentine to authorize an investigation by someone with "a knack for looking into criminal matters" and made apparent his own desire to get rid of Richard Wetherill.

He had just returned from a ten days' trip, Shelton wrote, and with one exception — Richard Wetherill — found there were good relations between the Indians and the Anglo and Mexican settlers of the region. He came quickly to the point:

> There is located at Pueblo Bonito a man named Richard Wetherill, who has done more in the past few years to retard the progress of the Indians in this section than all other causes combined. If all

reports are true, he has robbed them of thousands of dollars worth of property. He has not hesitated to assault and abuse them when they displeased him. He has had, for some time, some thirty families of Indians herding sheep for him on the shares, and the Indians claim that when the time comes to divide the wool and the increases in the sheep, that Mr. Wetherill gets all, always claiming that they are indebted to him. If they remonstrate with him he curses them and threatens to send them to jail. It is reported that in times past a dark room in one of the old ruins . . . was used as a jail. Mr. Wetherill and others associated with him employed a police force and furnished them with badges, and if an Indian incurred the displeasure of Mr. Wetherill and his associates by not paying his bills, or otherwise, he was arrested and put in this jail. However, I have not known of this being done since I came here.

I found, while at Pueblo Bonito, that Mr. Wetherill had from one to two sections of Indian lands under fence together with some railroad lands that he claimed to have a lease on. The Indians claim that Mr. Wetherill will not permit them to run stock on this land, even where some of them have allotments. He has a homestead where he is residing, and has leased several thousand acres of railroad land located near him and undertaken to control the range and water for miles around him. I was informed by what appears to be reliable information, that early this spring Mr. Wetherill took one of his hired white men and an Indian man and went to the home of an Indian named George, who lives seven or eight miles away, and selected seven of the best cattle, four or five years old, out of this man's herd while he was absent from home, drove them away and sold them. When the Indian returned and found what had been done, he went to see Mr. Wetherill, who told him that he had bought the cattle from his wife before she died four years ago, paying her ten dollars each for them, with the understanding that he was to get them whenever he got ready. The Indian claims and can prove that the cattle did not belong to his wife, and says that if his wife had been paid seventy dollars in money he would have known of it. Mr. Wetherill admitted to me that he had taken the cattle but claimed to have bought them from the man's wife as stated above. In my opinion, this man Wetherill stole these cattle and should be prosecuted for it.

ANASAZI   259

The incident is the same as related in a previous chapter, when the wife of Hostine George and their daughter Carrie brought the stock to Bonito to trade for Buel blankets and other goods just before the fatal diphtheria epidemic. Shelton's report continues:

Sometime during the spring Mr. Wetherill passed by where an Indian was herding sheep in his own corn field, he got out of his buggy and went to where the Indian, an old man, was, first cursed him and then knocked him down. The Indian was laid up for several days from his injuries. Mr. Wetherill admitted this to me, saying he had told the Indian to keep his sheep higher up on the mesa and not to come down near his range. This same Indian had a wire fence around his field, Mr. Wetherill's horses got out of the barn one night and attempting to get into the man's field were cut by the wire; Mr. Wetherill went down, cursed the Indian again, and cut down the wire fence.

When I was leaving Mr. Wetherill's place and was some five miles away, an Indian named Joe was waiting for me and said that Mr. Wetherill had told him the night before that if he made any complaint to me of any kind that he would put him in jail. After I assured the Indian that Mr. Wetherill would not harm him for anything he told me, he proceeded to tell me that last year when he and Mr. Wetherill had settled up he was indebted to Mr. Wetherill, and the night after the settlement Mr. Wetherill with one of his hired men came to his camp and drove away fifty-two of his sheep.

I only mention a few instances of Wetherill's rascality among these Indians to give an idea of what is going on at that place. It is reported that a short time ago Wetherill stole twenty odd burros and a number of horses and sold them to white people, when the Indians found out their stock had been stolen they kicked up such a row that Wetherill turned them loose, then the white people made him buy others to make good. I did not mention the burro and horse stealing to Mr. Wetherill for fear he would get alarmed and buy the Indians off.

Or possibly the superintendent remained silent because he knew that even a Quaker, accused of horse stealing, might react firmly and with unpleasant consequences. Shelton then went on to say that Wetherill had been

RICHARD WETHERILL

stealing lumber from the Navajo reservation, hiring Indians to cut timber for telephone poles. Richard in fact had sent Navajos out to cut poles, but not to "steal" them. He learned later that the Indians had cut some of the logs on their reservation, some on ungranted public lands. Technically, the Indians had no right to sell, or Richard to buy, lumber from the reservation.

A large number of Indians [Shelton continued] were at Wetherill's place wanting to make a complaint of his treatment toward them. My time being limited, and thinking it not the proper time to go into a full investigation, I advised them to wait until I or someone else would come and hear all they had to say.

"With reference to the necessities of these Indians," Shelton recommended that a "suitable person" be sent as soon as possible to investigate the abuses he himself was too busy to verify, and then prosecute Wetherill in the criminal courts.

"This nest should be cleaned out and the situation left clear for some one to take charge and look after these Indians," Shelton concluded. "It will require someone with nerve as well as honor. . ." A separate superintendency for the Navajo of this area should be formed, Shelton said, under a man "who has ability as well as physical courage to protect the interests of the Indians. He should be located as near as practicable to Pueblo Bonito on account of this place being the center of the Indian population and near the worst element within the territory."

For the job he had in mind Shelton recommended a special officer in the Indian Service, A. G. Pollock. "I have but slight acquaintance with him having met him only once, but I have received information which leads me to believe that he would be a suitable man for a task of this kind."

A willing Commissioner granted Shelton's wish. Pollock came to Pueblo Bonito five months later, in December, presumably well-advised by Shelton of what was desired and primed to hang Richard Wetherill from the nearest viga. No doubt he did his best, but his findings were oddly at variance with those in Shelton's report to Valentine.

He had found, Pollock wrote Shelton at the conclusion of his inquiry, that "Richard Wetherill has certainly run things in a very high-handed way among the Indians." Of cursings and beatings Pollock could report none. But to the best of his knowledge it was true that Richard had illegally fenced a strip of grazing land on the north mesa (land which had been allotted Jack

Edway, the Navajo boy raised by the Wetherills, who by choice did not remain at Pueblo Bonito). This was a clear-cut violation of an 1885 statute, Pollock said, entitled "An act to protect unlawful occupancy of public lands." Pollock confused "protect" with "forbid" — but his meaning is clear.

The best Pollock could produce as evidence that Richard Wetherill had been stealing Indian stock was the old story of Hostine George. "I am convinced," he told Shelton, "that Wetherill did steal those cattle, but . . . his system of keeping his accounts . . . would make it practically impossible to get a conviction in this case." This was not very helpful.

With nothing more criminal to offer than the 1885 land statute violation, if it was a violation, Pollock suggested there would be "a nuisance value" in bringing Richard to court anyway. He withdrew from the affair with the final recommendation that Shelton should "push these cases against Wetherill and try to get him out of there."

Before his high hopes in Pollock were dashed, Shelton had sought elsewhere and found support for his cause. A person named S. M. Brosius, employed as agent for the Indian Rights Association, called upon Shelton that summer, took copious notes as Shelton related the crimes of Richard Wetherill, and sent in the gist of what he had been told as a report to Commissioner Valentine. The brief interview was disguised to appear as a report of firsthand information — certain to impress the Indian Rights Association with their man's zeal in behalf of the downtrodden Indian — but actually Brosius had not gone near Chaco Canyon.

Shelton's cause appeared to gain force when one of Sam Stacher's assistants, a man named B. P. Six, volunteered testimony to prove that Richard was involved in illegal liquor traffic with the Navajos. After considerable sleuthing, B. P. Six reported to Commissioner Valentine on the activities of one Pablo Wiggins and one Santiago Gomez, residing either at or near the Triangle Bar Triangle Ranch.

Pablo, Six gravely informed the Commissioner, was known to have given a Navajo woman named Jessie three drinks from a bottle of whisky. This had happened right at Pueblo Bonito and under Richard Wetherill's nose, practically. Wetherill wasn't there at the time of course, but . . . well, it had happened at a house near Pueblo Bonito — and Six had a witness who would swear to it.

Santiago's case, equally well supported, was even more serious. Taking a weaving course homeward from the town of Cuba, literally loaded and toting not less than forty bottles of whisky (so Six said), Santiago had fallen to brawling with two Navajos met along the way. One of the Indians had been hurt.

"We have been unable to secure conclusive evidence that Richard Wetherill himself has actually sold liquor to Indians," Six admitted to the Commissioner. "But there is an abundance of evidence showing that liquor traffic has been conducted on his homestead . . . It is our opinion that if the liquor case against Pablo Wiggins can be properly conducted, Richard Wetherill will most probably be implicated." The abundance of evidence, Six confessed, all concerned the three drinks given by Pablo to Jessie, and the forty bottles of Santiago Gomez. Six, like Pollock, had tried hard. His report was filed.

EARLY IN 1910 there was an open break between Richard and the agent. It involved the conduct of a young temporary clerk employed by Stacher, T. H. Jones, who had recently married a nurse. The time finally came when Richard told Stacher that at the end of the next quarter Stacher and his family would have to move out of the Del Arroyo house and out of the canyon. Jones, meanwhile, had been fired by Stacher and departed with his wife for Farmington where later he would say he was "very friendly disposed toward Mr. Wetherill" but counted himself a "bitter enemy" of Stacher.

The agent's son, Herbert C. Stacher of Gallup, has recalled that in traveling over the jurisdiction his father had "selected several sites much more desirable than Chaco Canyon for his agency and school. His favorite place, which he named Crownpoint, had already been approved by the Indian office construction supervisor. It was only twenty-five miles from the railroad, while Pueblo Bonito in Chaco Canyon was about sixty-five miles from Thoreau."

There is an irreconcilable disagreement between the Wetherill and Stacher families over the issue, at that time, of the location of the proposed school. Nevertheless, on the testimony of Herbert Stacher, it appears certain that his father was not at all dismayed at the prospect of leaving the Chaco.

All of these events became a part of the Indian Service's growing file on Chaco Canyon, once a peaceful place but now only a source of trouble. An unhappy observer of this growing hostility was a maiden lady named Eleanor Quick. An Eastern girl, she was vacationing with relatives in Mancos when Richard employed her as a teacher for young Richard, Elizabeth and Robert.

ANASAZI   **263**

The Stachers' children also were to attend her lessons. Miss Quick arrived at Pueblo Bonito on September 6, 1909.

For the first few weeks she roomed and boarded with the Stachers. It was agreed they would pay part of her salary and accept her thus as their guest in exchange for her teaching their children — for two weeks out of five. During the other three weeks she would be a guest of the Wetherills. This plan, which also included her returning one quarter of her salary to Richard for her room and board, was not followed.

"I continued to room at the Stacher home," she wrote later, "until the end of the ninth week, then because of lameness from a sprained ankle and the unkindness of Mrs. Stacher my room was moved to the Wetherill house. At the beginning of the eleventh week relations had become so strained between Mr. Stacher and myself that I refused to go there to board and Mr. Stacher withdrew his children from the school. My quarrel, however, did not interrupt friendly feeling or kindly offices between the two families."

"Miss Quick liked her set-up at our house," Herbert Stacher recently recalled, "so did not move when the time came, as agreed, to the Wetherill home. She liked to talk about people and would tell us tales of the Wetherills, and, we learned, she talked about us to them. Mother lost her temper and said: 'Shut up — I don't want to hear any more gossip about the Wetherills or anyone else.' My father scolded mother for being so rude. The next day Miss Quick walked with a limp. She said she had sprained her ankle and requested to have her things moved to the Wetherill home in order to have less walking to the school room."

Miss Quick, who had been devoting part of her time to helping Richard with his business affairs, was dismayed to learn that while Stacher and his wife were enjoying the Wetherills' hospitality in their home, the agent was plotting against Richard and behind his back calling him a scoundrel.

"By the end of the first week," she said, "Mr. Stacher had begun to ask me impudent questions about Mr. Wetherill's private business, such as his postal accounts and his books on which I was working. About the same time he began to insinuate that Mr. Wetherill stole and had stolen for years the Indians' horses, cattle and sheep. He told of an incident when Richard, Mr. Wetherill's twelve-year-old son, had been allowed to steal a Navajo calf, bringing it home on his saddle. In his accusations he mentioned others."

Caught in a harsh, strange environment, confronted by a situation involving people who were still strangers to her, Miss Quick's practical mind wrestled with her feminine intuition. Why, she asked Stacher several times, if her employer were guilty of such offenses, had he not been brought to court? Stacher's replies were windy but vague, leaving her dissatisfied.

"By the end of the second week," Miss Quick said, Stacher "was talking very unguardedly. He told me that the Government was trying to buy Mr. Wetherill's holdings at Pueblo Bonito as a location for the projected school, and that Mr. Wetherill wanted thirty thousand dollars for them. 'Thirty thousand fiddle sticks,' he continued, 'I will get them and I won't pay any thirty thousand dollars, either.'"

Near the end of her stay in the Del Arroyo house, Miss Quick heard Stacher boast one morning at breakfast that he would have Richard Wetherill sent to the penitentiary, adding that before he got through "the population of Pueblo Bonito would be much lessened."

"During the time that Mr. Stacher was manifesting these unfriendly feelings towards the Wetherills," Miss Quick continued, "Mrs. Wetherill was inviting the Stachers to the house, Mr. Wetherill was renting him a house at a nominal charge, carrying him on the books and furnishing him a cow free of charge that the Stacher baby might have good milk. Nor did I hear Mr. Wetherill say anything spiteful of Mr. Stacher although he was cognizant of what was going on. He did laugh at some of the agent's egregious blunders and when I spoke bitterly of the Ojo Alamo incident, he laughingly said, 'You must excuse him, Miss Quick, for he is not grown up yet.'"

Of trifling importance, the "incident" shows the sort of thing Stacher was seizing upon to help Shelton prove that Richard was mistreating and stealing from the Indians. The Ojo Alamo store, built during the early years of the Hyde Expedition, was maintained by Richard after the Hydes sold out in 1903 but the amount of business it did under a succession of hired traders steadily declined. By 1909 Richard was ready to abandon it. Because lumber was scarce, he sent Bill Finn and "Black" Phillips to Ojo Alamo in a wagon to salvage whatever they considered worth taking away.

Stacher learned of this and pompously ordered his clerk, Julius Jerome, to carry a note several hundred yards to Richard's office. The note was an ultimatum, instructing Richard he must not take so much as a nail from the Ojo Alamo building. To justify this, Stacher later explained that the trading post occupied part of a Navajo land allotment and therefore — in his opinion — lawfully was Indian property. Richard quietly ignored Stacher's note. He had erected the building for the Hyde brothers on what was then public land.

Hyde money had paid for the lumber and hardware. Once abandoned, the Indians had not come near and had no interest in it. He was more amused than concerned when Stacher sent off a report to Shelton, promptly forwarded to Washington, accusing him of "stealing" building materials from the Navajos.

Eleanor Quick was no longer living in the Del Arroyo house, she said, when "Sometime in February or March there was a very scandalous happening . . . Mr. Wetherill then notified Mr. Stacher that he must vacate the house . . . About the same time Mr. Wetherill sold his trading store [at Pueblo Bonito] to a Mexican. He told me at the time that Mr. Stacher had made it so hard to collect from the Indians that the store was no longer profitable."

The schoolteacher had arrived in the Chaco with no previous knowledge of Richard Wetherill other than he was widely known for his work in ancient ruins, and as an explorer and Indian trader. The accusations made against her employer by Stacher dismayed her, in the beginning, since she had no idea of the true circumstances; later, they angered her. After living for nine weeks with the Stachers she had moved to the Wetherills' home, and then to a room in the bunkhouse. Her liking and respect for Richard increased with the chance to know him better.

"During the winter I used to sit in the office for hours at a time watching Mr. Wetherill talking and dealing with the Indians," she said. "He would often tell me what they were saying, or what transaction was going on when he thought it might be of interest. They used to bring their disputes among themselves for him to settle and always went away apparently satisfied with his adjustment of the matter. They often appealed to him when they did not like the Nataani's [Stacher's] orders and sometimes got him to go to Mrs. Stacher and interpret for them instead of their official interpreter."

This situation, Marietta Wetherill observed, irritated Stacher and he issued an order scarcely heeded: the Navajos should bring all of their problems to him. When the Indians still brought their squabbles to the man they called Anasazi, Eleanor Quick could not fail but notice. She remarked that "In all the conversations that I watched, I never saw an ugly gesture or heard an angry tone either from Mr. Wetherill or the Navajos."

So far as she could tell, not speaking or understanding Navajo, "there was friendly feeling and confidence on both sides." She noticed also how frequently Richard gave the Indians medicine and otherwise helped them in distress.

"On one occasion a girl called Jessie was doctored at the house. She said that the agent [Stacher] had refused her medicine though she was plainly very ill. A few nights before his death Mr. Wetherill spent the whole evening hunting medicines and doctoring a little Navajo boy who had been hurt in the corral.

"On two or three occasions after he sold the store, I saw him go to the kitchen to get food for the Indians whom the Mexican storekeeper would not trust. A day or two before he died he said that he had ordered fireworks for the Fourth of July because the Indians would expect something. . ."

It was late June, 1910. The Stachers had moved away from Chaco Canyon leaving behind them an atmosphere tainted with resentment. Among a few of the Navajos, who had traded heavily on credit at Richard's Bonito store, a seed had been planted. The seed germinated on hostility and childish avarice. If the man called Anasazi were to be driven out of the canyon, the money owed to the store would be forgotten. Debts would be rubbed into the sand . . . forgotten.

In such an atmosphere, Marietta returned from an Albuquerque hospital with her baby daughter Ruth. She had been away too long, was too glad to be home again and too happy with this new baby, to pay serious attention to the somber face and warning words of the Navajo girl who had been housekeeper while she was gone.

Des-glena-spah was the daughter of Hostine Joe Yazzie, who lived on the Escavada. She had been with the Wetherills for many months, a quiet girl, capable and loyal. Now she spoke out forcefully as she could, haltingly, but from a troubled mind.

"There is trouble here, Asthanne. Let us go away quickly with the children. Mr. Stacher is saying bad things." Joe Yazzie, the father, came to the Wetherill house one bright, hot noon-time on the twenty-second of June. While Des-glena-spah went to the kitchen to fix something for lunch he sat with Marietta and held baby Ruth in his lap, gently. Then he put out one hand and touched Marietta lightly on her shoulder, saying, "I love you and your children." A shadow flickered across his face and almost in the same sentence he added, "But in my heart I am no friend of Blue Eyes."

Blue Eyes? Marietta wondered. Joe Yazzie could mean Bill Finn, of the pale, cold blue eyes. Or he could mean he was the foe of all white people, the term sometimes used thus and all-embracingly by the Navajo. Marietta was startled.

At two o'clock, later than customary for him and in a hurry, Richard appeared. With him was Sheriff Tom Talle, up that morning from Gallup with a herd of cattle the sheriff had bought in Texas and which Richard had agreed to graze over the north mesa. The men ate their lunch quickly since a part of the herd still milled about on the canyon bottom, waiting to be driven up a steep trail to where some grass grew in parched, scattered cover.

Richard, upon entering and seeing Joe Yazzie there, asked the Indian if he would help the others with the sheriff's cattle. Hostine Joe nodded his head silently and walked out. Now the two men rose from the table to leave and at the door Marietta asked Richard when he would want his supper.

"Oh, the usual time — about six," he said.

A little later, standing at a window and looking out into the shimmering afternoon heat, Marietta gradually became conscious of a feeling that something was wrong. In the sunlight the canyon framed by the window appeared bleached to near-whiteness. Marietta squinted her eyes. There was something more. An absence of something. In the roof and wall shadows of the Bonito store there usually were a score or so of Indians of both sexes and all ages, lounging at ease. Now, strangely, the cool shadow area around the store was as deserted of life as the rest of the canyon hotly enclosing it. There was not an Indian in sight.

TWENTY-ONE

SOMETIME in the dust and heat of that afternoon Bill Finn went to Richard Wetherill's office, found it empty, and sat down to wait. When Wetherill arrived later he stopped just inside the doorway, his eyes fastened on the cowboy. An hour before he had been told that Finn had gotten into a fight with an Indian and had been killed.

"What's this all about?" Richard said.

There had been a scrap, Finn admitted in his usual terse way. Not he but the Indian had been hurt. Nez-begay. How badly hurt? Finn shrugged. He didn't know. The fight was over a horse stolen the day before and goaded into running so hard it had foundered. Others had seen Nez-begay mistreating the animal cruelly, beating it with a whiplash on the flanks, striking its head with the whipbutt until blood came on the glossy black coat. Now the horse was dead. It belonged to Richard's daughter Elizabeth.

Hardly more than a colt, the horse was a thoroughbred given by Richard to his daughter and prized by her. She would cry when she heard what had happened. We will attend to it, Richard said grimly, attend to it later. Now there is work to do.

All but a few stray drags from Sheriff Talle's herd of cattle had been driven onto the mesa. These last had been rounded up and were waiting. Talle was on the mesa. If Finn would help him they would get it done and be back in time for supper.

They went out, mounted their horses, and rode to the nearby place where the strays were bunched and grazing. At Pueblo del Arroyo a small group of Navajo men were gathered, watching as Richard and Finn approached behind the cattle, and at the same time listening to the excited jabber of one man who stood out from the others.

A few of them were armed, one old man on horseback holding an ancient rifle across his saddle. When they came abreast of this group, Richard reined in and stopped. The short, thickset man who had been doing the talking came forward. Richard recognized him. He was Chis-chilling-begay, a Navajo of such little account his own people rarely listened long to what he had to say. He had traded heavily on credit at Richard's Bonito store, before the store was sold, and still owed Richard much money.

The two men faced each other across the necks of their horses. Neither carried a weapon. Speaking in Navajo, angrily and loud, Chis-chilling-begay demanded:

"Are you on the warpath, Anasazi?"

Richard's gaze was stony. "If you want trouble it will start here and right now."

The old man with the old rifle edged his horse forward. There was trouble already, he said, bad trouble. A young man had been beaten — to death, perhaps — by that Blue Eyes, that man over there in the pay of Anasazi . . . As he spoke, the old fellow's voice rose to a shout, and he waved his rifle in Richard's face.

Richard leaned across his saddle and seized the gun out of the Navajo's hand. From the chamber he shook out the ammunition. Then angrily he grasped the rifle by the barrel and beat the stock to splinters against a fence post.

The sheriff's cattle were trailing down the canyon, a hundred yards or so now between them and where Finn had halted on the road, and twice that distance between Finn and Wetherill. For the moment, Chis-chilling-begay was silent.

This will wait, Richard told the Indians, just as he had told Finn when he received the information about Elizabeth's colt. This will have to wait until later. He turned his back on them, rejoined Finn, and together their horses broke into a trot to catch up with the cattle. In his left hand, unmindingly, Richard still grasped the old Navajo's gun barrel. A few minutes later, over the tops of the low sagebrush and in the roiling dust, his figure and Finn's became indistinct and then disappeared. The group of Indians broke up, the Navajos moving off quickly in several directions.

The distance by road between Pueblo del Arroyo and Rincon del Camino is about half a mile. It was, and is now, a dirt road that winds and turns as the canyon's north face of yellow sandstone projects or retreats. At one place the road runs straight as it skirts the standing walls, to the right, of Yellow House. From the rubble of this ruin Richard once brought wagonloads of faced stone to build the Del Arroyo guest house.

Shortly beyond, the dirt road swerves closer to meet the advancing rock of the cliff, and then canyon wall and road, now wedded, move downstream together. A slide of fallen rock — blocks of jumbo size — bend the dirt road outward into a tight curve. Pecked low into the cliff face, in some places visible from the road when the light is right and there is not too much dust, are strange whorls, snake shapes and man-figures — petroglyphs left by the Chacoans eight centuries ago. Canyon swallows nest higher up, in clay-and-stick nest clusters built under protective ridges of cliff overhang.

To the left of the road, still winding downstream, the bed of the Chaco River cuts dry and deep in its arroyo, its course traceable by a green line of cottonwoods and willows that grow roots into the sand of the arroyo bottom.

Except for its turnings the road runs almost due west and therefore, a few minutes before six o'clock on a June evening, a rider's eyes are nearly level with a setting sun. The light is so blinding that only the nearest clumps of brush dotting the canyon floor are made out with any clarity (the natural dusty green color turned almost to black), objects distant thirty or forty yards blurring into shapes of unrecognizable form and reddish color.

At the big turn of Rincon del Camino, several head of Sheriff Talle's cattle — sun-blinded — wandered off the road to plod straight ahead into sagebrush. Bill Finn followed the main bunch of cows keeping to the road while Richard circled out into brush to head-in the strays.

Ahead and nearly between Richard and Finn a rifle was raised and sighted.

Richard heard the echoing blast of the first shot but not the whistling lead that missed Finn. Still unseen, the rifle barrel swung in an arc of nearly sixty degrees. The second shot tore through Richard's raised right hand, the hand holding the reins, and smashed into his chest.

He fell from his horse, not knowing who had killed him. Or why.

TWENTY-TWO

RICHARD WETHERILL'S body
lay crumpled in the greasewood when Sheriff Tom Talle passed it on his return to the ranchhouse from the north mesa. Breathless in his haste, the
sheriff asked Marietta for her best, her fastest horse. The Chaco Navajos were
on the warpath, Talle was convinced. Probably they would attack the ranch
the following morning. Pueblo Bonito had no telephone lines or other communication with the outside world. The sheriff saw it as his duty to leave at
once to secure help. At Thoreau he could telegraph for troops from Fort Wingate to put down this uprising. His impatience was hard to control, as a strong,
fresh horse was saddled for him. The sun already was sinking behind the
Lukachukais.

Eleanor Quick felt Sheriff Talle only "did his duty" but those he left
behind at the ranch, she said, "were very anxious . . . for five Indians had
ridden out of the Gap just ahead of him." She noticed with scorn that Talle's
hired cowhand, Tom O'Fallon, was agitated because he was left behind to
help protect the women and children. "Mr. O'Fallon," she said, "was so
frightened that he would have gone that night but his horse was played out."

Darkness fell, bringing deeper silence to the canyon. It was a night of
wakeful terror for the women, and of one question burning in the minds of
the men: Where were the Navajos — when would they attack? Besides Marietta and her five children, gathered in the ranchhouse were Miss Quick, Bill
Finn, a handyman named Lee Ivy (who was only seventeen or eighteen years
old and "not quite right in the head"), Marietta's house girl Des-glena-spah,
six Mexicans, and O'Fallon. Doors were barred, only one dim light was left
burning in the room where they all waited. Five or six rifles, all that could
be found at the ranch, were held loaded in readiness.

Before his departure, Miss Quick recalled later, Sheriff Talle "stopped
in the office where most of us were gathered. He told us where the body
could be found, then stated quite firmly that someone must be sent at once

to bring the body in. He thought that the Navajos would come back after Finn and probably attack us the next morning."

O'Fallon's feeling of panic was not entirely shared by the other men present, but there was no disposition on the part of any of them to venture out to do Talle's bidding. Angered by their silence, Miss Quick stalked from the office and into the yard in front of the store where she found several of the Mexican ranchhands huddled in a group. "I asked two of them to hitch a team to the Wetherill surrey and fetch the body," Miss Quick said, "but they put up a barrage of excuses. . . . Finally, after pleading with them and shaming them, they agreed to go if I would go with them. I lost no time — went into the house, got two sheets and stepped into the surrey as the last trace was hooked. We had less than half a mile to go. The Mexicans wrapped the body in the sheets and set it into the surrey beside me. I steadied the body and kept it from falling out until we reached the back porch. With the help of the Mexicans, I prepared a cot and they placed the body on it.

"All the rest that I can remember about that night is that we all stayed together in the office until daylight the next morning, much too scared to sleep." While the children dozed fitfully, their elders shifted about in their chairs, the few firearms close at their sides.

The following night Marietta was deep in sleep, exhausted from shock and the first night's vigil. The attack feared and predicted by Finn and Sheriff Talle for dawn had not taken place and not a single Indian had been seen during the day.

It had been a day of quiet, nightmarish unreality. O'Fallon slipped off before daybreak with no word of good-luck spoken. The sun was still low over Fahada when Marietta stepped outside to breathe the cool morning air. Then she turned loose a string of Indian ponies left tied since the previous afternoon at a rail in front of the store. The bridles and saddles she hung on the porch of her house. (Days later she noticed they were still there, unclaimed.)

At four o'clock in the afternoon, the trader George Blake arrived to find how things were at Pueblo Bonito and to suggest that a Mexican be sent to Farmington to summon the coroner. (The Mexican got a late start and then drove his horse so hard the animal foundered and died before reaching Dick Simpson's store.) Still later in the afternoon, Stacher's former clerk, T. H. Jones, who now was established hopefully at Farmington in a law practice, came unexpectedly with his wife. They had not heard the news of Richard

Wetherill's murder and so their first cheery words of greeting seemed to echo in the silence that followed, when they were told. The presence of these three was some comfort. Marietta went to bed early.

Sheriff Talle reached Thoreau without difficulty. Distance and the refreshing night air failed to cool his fears of an Indian uprising. When he reached that outpost on the railroad he had not altered his plan to call for troops. When B. P. Six and Charles Pinkney offered to go to Pueblo Bonito immediately with twelve Indian policemen, the sheriff approved but still thought the soldiers would be needed. Stacher himself returned from a vacation in Oklahoma and arrived later the same day (June 23). Talle proceeded to Gallup with the news of Richard Wetherill's death, evidently riding the next train through.

The effect of the sheriff's alarms was to start riders toward Chaco Canyon from three directions: Pinkney and Six with the Indian policemen from Thoreau; George Ransome, a friend of the Wetherill brothers, from Gallup; and a combined posse and coroner's jury from Farmington. Although he had the greatest distance to cover, George Ransome was the first to arrive at the ranch, reaching Bonito at midnight of the twenty-third. He brought word that Al Wetherill and Sheriff Talle would follow the next morning. Stacher's men and the Indian police arrived during the night, but waited for daybreak before going to the ranchhouse.

From Farmington, Justice of the Peace James T. Fay started out in his buggy at sunset twenty-four hours after Richard's death, accompanied by the Arrington brothers, John and Paul, who had been sworn in as deputies. At Simpson's store in Gallegos Canyon, twenty-five miles from town, they were joined by Sheriff William F. Dufur of Aztec and continued on through the night until, with the first pale light of day, they came to Joe Yazzie's hogan on the Escavada. Here they were startled to find in sober and very subdued gathering seven of the Navajos who had participated in the shooting. This was no war party, they perceived at once, but an assemblage of the most dejected, frightened Indians they had ever seen.

The Navajos told Judge Fay and his party that Anasazi had been killed by a Navajo named Chis-chilling-begay, adding also that another Indian had shot Bill Finn — which at that time they all believed was true. They were waiting now at Joe Yazzie's hogan for the inevitable reprisals. When, they asked, would the soldiers be sent to shoot them?

If there was an element of grim humor in this situation, wherein both sides concerned in the shooting were in mortal fear of each other, it was not apparent to the Farmington men until they reached Pueblo Bonito shortly before noon. There they found Al Wetherill and Sheriff Talle, who had just come in from Gallup, the latter talking loudly of three railroad cars of militia from Fort Wingate who were expected momentarily. The Indian police from Thoreau had been deployed protectively around the house and it was apparent that Talle still expected the Navajos to come whooping up the canyon, hungry for blood.

Any alarm felt by others on this score was promptly relieved by Judge Fay's men, who told of the frightened gathering on the Escavada, and then turned to the business which had brought them here. (By some means never made clear, Sheriff Talle's call for troops was countermanded. Therefore an already bad situation was not made worse.)

Judge Fay's first act was to ask Sheriff Dufur to summon and swear in a coroner's jury. Witnesses at the inquiry were those who had been at the ranch on the afternoon and evening of June 22, principally Marietta Wetherill, Bill Finn, Sheriff Talle, and Eleanor Quick; the testimony was given hurriedly and presented only the sketchiest outline of the shooting and its underlying causes. Attorney Jones had been selected jury foreman, the other members being George Ransome, John and Paul Arrington, Sheriff Talle and young Lee Ivy. When all had been heard (excepting the Indian participants who were not present), the six men returned a verdict:

> We, the Coroner's Jury . . . being first duly sworn and having listened to the testimony adduced, find that the said Richard Wetherill came to his death by gun shot wounds on June 22nd, 1910, from a gun or rifle in the hands of a Navajo Indian by the name of Chis-chill-ing-begay, being aided and abetted by Juan-at-cetty, Billy Williams, Tomacito, Thomas Padilla and Pesch-la-ki, also Navajo Indians.

During this simple, awkward and yet necessary little inquiry, Richard's body lay for the second day on a cot on the back porch of the house. Once during the time it reposed there, and defying her mother's admonition, young Elizabeth stole around to the back porch, lifted an edge of the blanket covering her father's mutilated form, and then shrank back in horror. The cot was sheltered from the direct glare of the sun but there was no protection from the canyon's unusually intense heat.

Eleanor Quick, who had taken over all of Marietta's household cares, ordered that a grave be dug in a sandy slope close under the north cliff some three hundred yards west of the house, where Richard several years before had said he wished to be buried someday.

His coffin was carried from the house to this grave at three o'clock in the afternoon and rested on the ground for a moment while the small group of men stood about, ill-at-ease, wondering how to proceed. John Arrington, who was one of the group, said Al Wetherill finally asked: "Isn't there somebody who could say something?" The men shifted their feet, exchanged glances, and then, according to Arrington, "Jim Fay quoted a few words of scripture as the coffin was lowered and then threw a pinch of dust into the grave. After that we all sang 'Nearer My God to Thee.' My brother Paul carved a stone and put it on the grave a short time later."

Marietta had come from the seclusion of her room only once, and then briefly, to tell the coroner's jury what little she knew of the shooting. She was not present to observe the final scene as Judge Fay and his party prepared to leave Pueblo Bonito. Six and Charles Pinkney, claiming they represented Agent Stacher with all of the agent's authority in his absence, vigorously opposed the implication of any Indians in Richard Wetherill's death, other than Chis-chilling-begay. They demanded that the five Navajos accused as accomplices should not be arrested.

When Judge Fay waved this protest aside, Pinkney and Six insisted that Bill Finn should be arrested also. On the morning of Wetherill's death, they said, Finn had brutally assaulted a Navajo named Hostine Nez-begay. Some evidence to this effect already had been heard at the inquest although the details were unclear. Judge Fay and Sheriff Dufur asked Stacher's men if they were entering a formal complaint against the cowboy. They were, they said, and their charge was assault with intent to commit murder. Finn, who had been listening silently, was told he was under arrest; he would have to return to Farmington with Judge Fay to make a formal answer.

After thirty-six sleepless hours, Fay and his men departed on a return trip of some sixty miles and a second night without rest. Their intention was to stop at Joe Yazzie's hogan and arrest the five Navajos named as accomplices. John Arrington recounted the incident:

276 RICHARD WETHERILL

I was in a buckboard with Sheriff Dufur. Finn's gun had been taken away from him and he was riding along right behind us on Marietta Wetherill's black mare. One of the Navajos with us at this time was a fellow named Yoddle-chol-thee, who lived near Ojo Alamo and had no connection at all with the shooting of Wetherill, but was a friend of the Chaco Indians. This fellow was riding in the rear, behind Finn, and one way or another was letting us know he thought Finn was a so-and-so. Several times Finn came up alongside the buckboard and said, "For God's sake, watch him — he's going to start something."

For a while I watched but nothing happened and so I thought Finn was just imagining things. Then about the time we were coming in sight of Joe's hogan something made me turn around — what it was I don't know — and I saw this Navajo starting to go for his gun. Quick as I could I pulled a six-shooter out of my belt and levelled it, ready to shoot. There was still a big bunch of Indians waiting for us around Joe's hogan and I'm sure this Navajo had been biding his time, intending to plug Finn when we got to where his friends were. But as soon as he saw I had a bead on him he let his gun slide back in its holster, and that, thank heaven, was the end of that.

At Joe Yazzie's hogan Sheriff Dufur arrested the Indians accused as accomplices in Richard Wetherill's murder. After they had been searched for arms they were told to saddle their ponies and follow along. Maintaining a brisk pace through the night, Judge Fay's party arrived in Farmington with the prisoners early in the morning of Saturday, June 25.

A Navajo horseman carried word of Richard's death to the canyons of Marsh Pass, two hundred miles west of Pueblo Bonito. In the foothills of Navajo Mountain, on June 27, he found Clayton and John Wetherill with Dr. Prudden, who had arrived only two weeks before to continue research on small ruin sites. The three men dropped their work at once and started for the Chaco. In a letter to Dr. Prudden's sister afterward, John said, "We drove night and day until we reached Bonito where with his [Dr. Prudden's] help we were able to stop some of the injustice that was being done."

To this Miss Lillian Prudden added: "It was a thrilling ride . . . and revealed how closely [Dr. Prudden] identified himself with these friends . . . He immediately abandoned that summer's expedition, and, by a succession of fresh horses and mules, the trip through the desert country in the hot season was accomplished in a few days. It was too late to help much, save as a defender of the good name of Richard Wetherill . . ."

Prudden and the Wetherill brothers learned in Farmington that Shelton was spreading slanderous stories about Richard and telling a fantastic version of his death. They hurried on to Bonito, where they found that Al Wetherill and Sheriff Talle had returned to Gallup, and that Marietta, Miss Quick and the children were carrying on the ranch affairs alone, with Pinkney and Six harassing their every move. The slow-witted Lee Ivy was there, as well as another youth named Ralph McJunkin who had offered to help out for a few days.

The object of Pinkney and Six, it appears, was to put a decisive end to any communication or cooperation between the Chaco Navajos and Richard Wetherill's widow. If this also brought ruin upon the ranch, Shelton's desire that "this nest should be cleaned out" would be realized. The Navajos were ordered to stay away from the ranch. They were not to dig waterholes for Wetherill stock. Those who had been paid to look after Wetherill sheep, horses and cattle — spread out over many miles of the surrounding highlands — were told to stop herding any but their own animals.

Dr. Prudden found Marietta grief-stricken and frantic with worry. Lacking attention, the Wetherill stock had wandered off. Half of her sheep were gone. The situation was so desperate that young Richard, Elizabeth and even Robert, then only eight years old, were out riding the mesas every day trying to round up and bring back any strays they could find.

So quickly and so thoroughly had the damage been done that the Wetherill brothers and Dr. Prudden were unable to offer much assistance. Remaining at the ranch would accomplish little. It was important to be in Farmington.

AND MEANWHILE, what of the Navajo who had shot Richard Wetherill?

Until he killed a man, Chis-chilling-begay had done nothing to attract notice or distinguish himself from the poorer, quiet-living Navajos whose homes were in the vicinity of Chaco Canyon. He was married, had one or two children and a small amount of stock, and lived near George Blake's Tsaya trading post on the Charlie Bidoga draw, about fifteen miles west of Pueblo

Bonito. He was neither ambitious nor entirely shiftless. In common with most of the other Navajos of the region he had done most of his trading with Richard and on a number of occasions was carried for many months on the Wetherill ledgers for the debts he owed. He had little turquoise or silver for pawn, so he was carried on the books anyway. This alone was not unusual but, unlike most of the other Indians, Chis-chilling-begay perversely looked upon his debts as grievances caused by Anasazi.

The more he borrowed for the coffee and flour and many other things his family wanted, the more injured and indignant he became. These feelings Chis-chilling-begay concealed when at Bonito, and Richard found nothing exceptional in the situation. The same credit allowed to others was extended and occasionally payment was asked, in part at least. It was all quite routine, or would have been if, when asked to pay, the Indian had not nursed a strong sense of outrage.

This single characteristic, and one tragic circumstance of his childhood are about all that make the personality of Chis-chilling-begay, before June 22, 1910, add up to more than a cipher. When he was a boy a band of cowboys shot and killed his father in what is understood to have been a cold-blooded, unprovoked murder. This happened at the mouth of the Gallegos, six miles east of Farmington; the boy had seen his father die before his eyes, and it had filled him with profound bitterness against anyone who was white.

His physical appearance was not out of the ordinary. For a Navajo he was relatively short and stocky, being five feet eight inches tall and weighing a trifle under 150 pounds. His face and features were chunky rather than sharply cut, usually impassive though not sullen, and his complexion was somewhat darker than usual. He bore a one-inch scar under the left eye. His age was a mystery: he didn't know it himself and the closest guess placed it at about forty, or a few years younger. He had had no education whatever in a white school, which also was not unusual for that time and region.

This is about all that is known of the Indian who, after his first fatal shot and before his next bullet tore away the right side of Richard Wetherill's head, bent over to ask, "Are you sick, Anasazi?"

Chis-chilling-begay's curiosity was soon satisfied. He did not take part in the chase of Bill Finn, back to Pueblo Bonito, but whipped his pony in the opposite direction. At George Blake's Tsaya store he dismounted and entered, trembling.

Seven hours earlier he had swaggered through the same door. On his first visit that day, with a show of arrogance, he had tossed his silver belt on the counter and told George Blake to give him, in return, two boxes of cart-ridges for his rifle — and credit for the remaining value.

"I am going to kill Wetherill," Blake later remembered the Indian as saying. The trader had regarded it as a senseless joke, and paid no attention. Chis-chilling-begay had shouldered his way out, cocky and mean. (A little later he had met Juan-et-citty who asked where he was going with a rifle. "To kill Anasazi," Chis-chilling-begay repeated. He refused to listen when Juan tried to make him drop this crazy plan and go back home. He had urged his pony on, and in the arroyo near Rincon del Camino had left the rifle, hiding it in some bushes.)

Now the cockiness and swagger were gone. He asked Blake for advice, after telling what he had done. Should he turn himself over to the soldiers at Fort Wingate, or go to Superintendent Shelton at the Shiprock agency? The trader advised him to go to Shelton at once. And so that his own part in the affair would not be misconstrued, Blake gave the Navajo a letter to take with him. It was written in ink on two small sheets of ruled paper torn from a pad:

Tsaya N.M. 6/22 1910

Mr. Shelton,

Dear Sir—- An indian named Niz Begay had a fight with Finn over a horse this morning and I think he hit him over the head with a gun. Then this fellow with this note got mad and folled up Finn. He told me they had a fight up there this evening and he killed Wetherill he wanted me to rite this note to you

He said he shore killed

You had better send some body out wright away because it looks like troble. The indian thot that Finn had killed the other indian but he come to this evening and I think he will get well if he has a doctor wright away. I don't look for any troble my self because they are not mad at me. but there is lots of indians around the Wetherills so they say.

Yours Truely Geo. Blake

Chis-chilling-begay drove his pony hard through the night. By early morning he was in Shiprock, more than seventy miles away, relating his story to Shelton, first in the presence of others and then privately. Several of Shel-ton's assistants were present when the Navajo arrived at the agency and they listened to the conversation — one of the men later telling it around (until stopped) that Shelton had complimented Chis-chilling-begay, saying he had "done a good job." As word of this spread like a grass fire through the San Juan Valley, stirring the wrath of many who had been Richard Wetherill's friends, Shelton and the loose-lipped employee both denied hotly that Shelton had said anything of the sort.

A day or so later Shelton turned the Navajo over to Sheriff Dufur to be locked up in Farmington. No one living knows what Chis-chilling-begay and Shelton said to each other in private. It is doubtful, however, if the Indian would have had the wit or the guile to frame the account of Richard's death that Shelton telephoned to The *Farmington Times-Hustler:*

> Last night Richard Wetherill, well known Indian trader and stockman who resides at Pueblo Bonito was shot and killed by a Navajo Indian. The Indian went at once to Shiprock and gave himself up to Indian Superintendent Shelton.
>
> The Indian claimed that Wetherill and another white man drew their guns and fired on him first and that he returned the fire with deadly effect.
>
> There has been feeling existing between Wetherill and the Navajos for sometime. The latter declaring that Wetherill had not treated them fairly, and had taken their stock without paying for them.

Shelton's next move was to wire Commissioner Valentine in Washington, asking that the defense of Chis-chilling-begay be transferred from Agent Stacher's jurisdiction to his own. This was no time for bungling.

TWENTY-THREE

ONLY two of the principals involved — Chis-chilling-begay and Bill Finn — appeared for the former's arraignment, before Judge Fay on the morning of June 27. Others in the little court room were Superintendent Shelton, the attorneys for Finn, a reporter for The *Farmington Enterprise*, and a few witnesses.

The solid bulk of William T. Shelton was a commanding presence. The set of jaw, the challenging flash of eyes, the firmness with which the big arms were folded across his shirt-front, all bespoke a man who was confident that Right was on his side, and was fully determined to see Justice done. Next to him, in odd contrast, sat Chis-chilling-begay. The Navajo's dark face was blank, his downcast glance fixed as though researching every bone, muscle and crease of the hands folded in his lap. Posture and attitude spelled resignation, not hope. Bill Finn sat a little apart with the Farmington lawyers, Edwards and Martin. His face, too, was blankly glum. Charges against the other Indians were to be heard later and they were not present.

Shelton had reason to be satisfied. After wiring twice to the Commissioner of Indian Affairs, the first time saying it might be impossible for Agent Stacher to reach Farmington in time for these proceedings, he had been authorized to take charge of the Navajos' defense. Jurisdiction in the case clearly was Stacher's, he had returned from his vacation in ample time to handle the problem, but now, with Shelton's intervention, Stacher allowed the older man to move into the region for which he alone was responsible, and take command.

To defend the Navajos in court Shelton engaged Charles A. Johnson, the Durango lawyer who had represented Richard Wetherill seventeen years before in the D. V. Hamilton cattle case and then sued Richard for non-payment of fee. Johnson was to remain in the background for several weeks more, however, while Shelton assumed the preliminary responsibilities of shaping the defense.

The report of the coroner's jury on its findings at Pueblo Bonito was read and then Bill Finn was called as the only witness for the prosecution. He began by recounting incidents of the day before Richard Wetherill's death. And as he stumbled through his story it may have occurred to Shelton that this cowboy would make the best witness the defense had.

Finn's responses to Judge Fay's questions were halting, grudging or evasive; to those listening it must have sounded as though the cowboy was hiding something. He was: the past of cattle rustler Joe Moody. His manner, then, struck no sparks of sympathy, but fogged with suspicion nearly everything he said.

On the night before the shooting, Finn related, several Indians came to Mr. Wetherill's office. Earlier that evening Wetherill had asked them to bring in to the corrals a bunch of horses that would be used the next day in helping Sheriff Talle drive his cattle onto north mesa. The Navajos, on returning, said the horses had been brought in. They added that while out on the range they had seen young Nez-begay riding the thoroughbred black colt recently given to Elizabeth by her father. Nez-begay was riding the colt so furiously and maltreating it so brutally, the Indians said gravely, the animal almost certainly would die.

Wetherill thanked them for telling him, and they left. Early the next morning — the morning of the day he was murdered — he called Bill Finn to the office and told him to take Lee Ivy with him, go to Nez-begay's hogan, and bring back Elizabeth's colt, presuming they found it alive.

Finn and Ivy started out at once. Nez-begay's hogan was twelve miles or more down the Chaco Wash, not far from George Blake's Tsaya store. On arriving there the first thing they saw, after the snarling dogs that advanced to greet them, was the black colt. It was tied to a stake out in the blazing sun, its head hanging, and one look was enough to tell it was done for. In response to Finn's call, Nez-begay came out of the hogan. He was a tall, slender Indian, of approximately the same build and weight as the cowboy. Finn sat his horse, jerked a thumb toward the colt, and demanded:

"What have you been doing to Elizabeth's colt?"

Nez-begay blandly denied the colt was Elizabeth's. It was owned by a friend of his who had let him borrow it, he said. This was a lie and they both knew it since the colt was recognized everywhere in the canyon as Elizabeth's. Also the Wetherill triangle bar triangle brand was plainly visible on one glistening flank.

Finn was turning his horse toward the stake where the colt was tied when Nez-begay suddenly reached out and grabbed Finn's bridle, jerking on it with both hands.

The cowboy was angry enough to shoot the Navajo. Instead, rising in the stirrups, he brought his six-shooter down in a whistling arc on Nez-begay's head, and then struck again, the blows stretching the Indian senseless and bleeding on the ground.

Finn left him where he fell and with Lee Ivy started back for Bonito, leading the colt on a halter. Even though they held their horses to a slow walk, the colt was unable to keep up. They had to abandon it before reaching the ranch and the colt died. By this time the sun had circled over the Gap and it was late afternoon.

Finn's testimony, then as later, was not challenged by anyone. It was truth he told, as the Indians knew, but his manner gave his words a doubtful ring. As his recital continued the cowboy could feel a hardening of sentiment against him.

Judge Fay proceeded with his questioning. What had happened then? He went to Wetherill's office, Finn said, and found it deserted, but a short time later Wetherill came in from the mesa, gave him a queer, searching look, and asked bluntly:

"What's this all about? Pesh-la-ki just told me a Navajo had killed you."

The cowboy answered he hadn't seen Pesh-la-ki that day; what the Indian had said was as much a mystery to him as to Wetherill. Then he related the affair of the morning, Richard wincing when he heard Finn and Lee Ivy could do nothing but leave Elizabeth's black pet alone to die. Not long after he had finished his report of the happening, Finn said, he and Wetherill left the office to drive a bunch of drags from Talle's herd onto the mesa. It was late afternoon, maybe half an hour before six o'clock.

Ten or twelve Navajos were gathered near Pueblo del Arroyo, listening to a harangue by Chis-chilling-begay. It was obvious that the Indians were angry. A few of them were wearing pistols and old Welo, ordinarily a mild fellow, had an ancient rifle slung across the saddle horn. Chis-chilling-begay prodded his horse away from the group and advanced to meet them, making angry gestures and demanding to know "if they were on the warpath." There was a flurry of hot tempered words between Chis-chilling-begay and Wetherill, Finn said. Then old Welo butted into the fracas, waved his decrepit firearm in Wetherill's face, and shouted angry words Finn could scarcely hear — or make out. Richard had snatched the rifle away from Welo and battered it against a fence post. After that, he and Wetherill had continued driving Talle's cattle down canyon.

Finn's manner became even more guarded as Judge Fay questioned him about the precise circumstances of Wetherill's death. On the streets and in the saloons of Farmington a rumor had spread that it was Finn, not Chischilling-begay, who really shot Richard Wetherill. That Finn for some time had been "sweet on" Wetherill's wife and in the ambush he had seen a perfect chance to kill the man who kept him apart from Marietta. Finn knew this lie was being told around town, knew the power of its source, and he was dry-tongued and sweating as he answered the judge's questions.

JUDGE FAY: What took place at this time, if anything that you know, that resulted in the death of Wetherill? Where were you?

FINN: Well, we were one-half mile below Putnam, Wetherill and I.

Q.: What then took place?

A.: At this point a man passed us and went into an arroyo and we continued driving cattle and then at this arroyo I saw this man, Chis-chilling-begay, come out of the arroyo on a horse and fired two shots at Wetherill. It seems that the first one missed and the second took effect.

Q.: Where was this Navajo?

A.: He was on the left side of his horse between the horse and us.

Q.: What then took place?

A.: He [Wetherill] felled off his horse and did not move a muscle any more while I was there. I looked at Wetherill and saw that he was dead.

Q.: Was there any more shots?

A.: They continued shooting.

Q.: At who?

A.: At me, I suppose.

Q.: What occurred next?

A.: I left.

Q.: How many shots did they fire?

A.: I don't know.

Q.: Were any other Navajos there?

A.: Yes, sir, six I know.

Q.: Where were they at?

A.: They were scattered around, probably fifty yards away.

Bill Finn then told how he broke out of the ambush, making a run for it back to Pueblo Bonito. Thomas Padilla had followed him, he said, and just before reaching the ranch Hostine Joe Yazzie (the one who had admitted a hatred for "Blue Eyes") and Hostine Tso-bakis raced out from the shadows of the north cliff. The questioning continued.

JUDGE FAY: What did they do?
FINN: They shot to head me off.
Q.: What kind of gun did you have at this time?
A.: .38 caliber Colt's automatic.
Q.: Did Richard Wetherill have a gun?
A.: A piece of a gun, the butt was broken.
Q.: Did you see him shoot at this Navajo [Chis-chilling-begay]?
A.: I did not.
Q.: Do you know what kind of a gun [it was] that killed Wetherill?
A.: I do not, I just know that he was shot.
Q.: Was it a revolver or a gun?
A.: Some kind of a Winchester or a rifle of some kind.
Q.: Did you find any cartridge shells at this point?
A.: No sir, I did not.
Q.: After this trouble, when did you next see Wetherill?
A.: At the house, probably an hour later.
Q.: Was he dead?
A.: He was dead.
Q.: Where was he shot?
A.: Through the breast, through the right hand and on one side of his head.
Q.: How much of his head was shot off?
A.: There was a big piece of his head gone.
Q.: Was there any quarrel between Wetherill and this Indian prior to this trouble?
A.: No sir.
Q.: Did you see any other Navajo shoot at Wetherill?
A.: No sir.
Q.: How many Navajos shot at you?
A.: I don't know.
Q.: We will now hear what the defending side has to say.

Shelton had entered a plea of not guilty for Chis-chilling-begay; he now stepped forward to say he would waive examination of the defendant prior to his trial in the District Court at Aztec. Chis-chilling-begay, charged with murder, was held under $10,000 bond for the next Grand Jury term.

Finn's performance had been singularly unimpressive. Judge Fay fined him the maximum penalty of $100 and costs for committing assault and battery against Nez-begay; charged with assault with a deadly weapon against Tso-bakis, Finn was held in $1,500 bond and the case was continued until July 11.

From Shelton's point of view the proceedings were favorable indeed. One slip, however, threatened his plan to show that Chis-chilling-begay had killed in self-defense. This happened when Shelton was interviewed by H. R. Elliott, the assistant editor of The *Farmington Enterprise*. Some of his remarks, Shelton said, were to be considered confidential, but he failed to make clear to Elliott which they were. The *Enterprise,* therefore, printed virtually everything Shelton said — and in particular this:

> When interviewed by an *Enterprise* representative Superintendent Shelton stated that while he believed the killing was premeditated to a certain extent, he thought there were some extenuating circumstances.

A murder premeditated even by a little bit is different from killing in self-defense. When the story appeared in print Shelton perhaps felt it would do more harm than good to emphasize the point by denying he had said "the killing was premeditated to a certain extent." In any case, he reverted to his first position when he wrote to Commissioner Valentine on July 6, five days later. Again he had the Navajo the object of assault, firing in self-defense.

Shelton wrote that Wetherill had cursed and threatened to kill Chis-chilling-begay in their first encounter at Pueblo del Arroyo, and added that Chis-chilling-begay thereupon had ridden off down the canyon to get his rifle, which he had hidden previously in the arroyo at Rincon del Camino. Then, said Shelton:

> He got the gun and started down the road towards Pueblo Bonito and saw Wetherill and Finn near the road with a bunch of cattle. When he was within about 150 yards of them they saw him and started towards him, loping their horses. Both of them had guns and

were cursing and threatening him. He said that when they got within 25 yards of him, he jumped off his horse, and they began shooting at each other. He said that he shot at Wetherill six times knocking him off his horse.

This was substantially the same story that Shelton and Chis-chilling-begay told thereafter until the Navajo finally heard his sentence pronounced two years later. In his letters to the Commissioner Shelton portrayed Finn as being nearly as criminal as Richard Wetherill. He avoided mentioning that the trouble on the day of Wetherill's death started after Nez-begay stole a Wetherill colt and rode it to death; his only reference to this was a comment that Finn had all but killed Nez-begay because Finn claimed a colt which the Indian said belonged to a friend of his. Shelton revealed his position in these sentences:

> The friends of Richard Wetherill and Finn will make every effort to have these Indians punished, just because Wetherill was killed by an Indian. . .
> Wetherill and Finn have done just about as they pleased with the Indians and it has been predicted for a long time that one or both of them would be killed. Now that Wetherill is out of the way, Finn should be put where he belongs. . .

Commissioner Valentine may have been puzzled by Shelton's version of the shooting since Agent Stacher had written to him on June 27, more than a week before, that

> As Wetherill and Finn were about to drive their cattle across the aroya, Chis-chilin-begay came out of it amidst the dust and was upon Wetherill and Finn before they saw him. He fired a shot at Finn but missed. The second shot was fired at Wetherill who fell from his horse mortally wounded, the bullet having struck him in the breast. Chis-chilin-begay then rushed up to him and fired again, this time tearing a large hole in the side of his head.

Stacher told the Commissioner that these were the facts of the case as reported to him by B. P. Six, who had made a personal investigation at the scene two days after the murder.

Meanwhile, a view opposite to Shelton's was expressed in The *Farmington Enterprise*:

"The case, when it comes up for trial in the district court, will undoubtedly attract a great deal of attention throughout the territory, as Richard Wetherill undoubtedly has a great many warm friends who will do all they can to avenge his death. Notable among them is Colonel D. B. Sellers of Albuquerque [former publisher of The *Hustler* and two years later Albuquerque's mayor], who formerly resided here and was a personal friend of the dead man. He scouts the idea that Wetherill was engaged in any crooked dealings with the Navajos, claiming that he was held in high esteem among them, often acting as an arbitrator in their petty disputes."

Two weeks after the arraignment of Chis-chilling-begay, Bill Finn appeared before Judge Fay again on the charge of assaulting Tso-bakis. Such a large crowd gathered to see Finn and hear what he would say, the judge moved the proceedings from his tiny courtroom to Allen's Hall, where public dances usually were held, and still there was difficulty in finding seats for all who jammed through the doors. In all of his experience Judge Fay could not remember a hearing that aroused such avid curiosity.

For his defense, Finn had called Marietta Wetherill, still pale and wearing black; Miss Eleanor Quick, the schoolteacher, and Salvador Hernandez, who had been employed at Pueblo Bonito for the past several months. Sitting with them were Dr. Prudden and Al, John and Clayton Wetherill.

On another side of the hall a score of seats were occupied by sober-faced, blanketed Indians, among them six of the Navajos who would be arraigned the following day charged with attempting to kill Finn. Seated with them were Superintendent Shelton, Agent Sam Stacher, and Stacher's two aides, Pinkney and Six.

Finn was scarcely less nervous than he had been while testifying earlier. This time called as the defendant, he answered the charge of assault with a plea of not guilty, asserting he had fired at Tso-bakis in self-defense. There were a few angry snorts and sounds of muttering from the side of the hall where Shelton was sitting, and Judge Fay rapped for order. Then the cowboy repeated in substance his previous testimony, relating it now in more detail. Before he took the stand, Tso-bakis and Joe Yazzie had been called as witnesses.

The two Navajos swore they had intended Finn no harm. Tso-bakis, showing no serious effects from the wound in his side, was the first to testify.

He said that he and Joe Yazzie were near the Bonito trading post on the evening of June 22 when they heard shooting, and had started down the canyon to find out what it was about when they saw Finn's horse galloping in their direction. They realized there had been trouble, thought Finn was returning to the ranch for more ammunition, and so turned their ponies into his path in an effort to stop him.

Tso-bakis said he was not armed, that when his pony brought him alongside Finn's racing horse the cowboy yelled at him: "God damn you, I'll kill you." Even then, said Tso-bakis, he was not "mad" at Finn, but Finn turned and fired, wounding him with the fourth shot.

Joe Yazzie substantiated all of this, adding that when Wetherill had taken old Welo's rifle and broken the stock, he had first pointed the gun at the Indians gathered near and cursed them and shouted he was going to kill them all. Yazzie admitted he was carrying a pistol at the time but swore it was not loaded.

A reporter for The *Enterprise* then caught this part of the testimony: "Yazzi[e] said he told Tso-ba-kis to keep Finn from going on to the house, but witness himself played Willie Wise and stayed in the background . . . He caused a laugh when he said that Tso-ba-kis had nothing in his hands but his fingernails, but he admitted that he might have had a quirt."

Marietta and Salvador Hernandez said they had seen the two Indians trying to head Finn off and stop him, but only the schoolteacher, Miss Quick, could testify in support of the cowboy's statement that Tso-bakis had a club and had used it. She was sitting in the doorway of her room, Miss Quick said, had a clear view of the approaching riders, and had seen Tso-bakis swinging a club down on Finn's shoulders before Finn finally fired.

Earl H. Morris, then only a boy, was among the spectators that morning and found it hard to draw his fascinated attention away from Finn. "I watched him closely," he recalled years afterward, ". . . he was shifty, inarticulate enough to seem sub-normal — a sorry comparison to some of the fine old Navajo patriarchs who were present at the hearing."

When all of the testimony had been heard there was a pause, a rustle of whispering through the hall, and then Judge Fay announced in a dry voice that he found no cause to hold the defendant Will Finn — the case was dismissed.

"Finn was discharged as we expected he would be," Shelton wrote to

Commissioner Valentine. "It was plain to see that the Justice of the Peace was in sympathy with Finn and the Wetherill forces from the start."

But Shelton would not let the matter drop. He hurried to Aztec, the county seat fifteen miles away, and filed a complaint charging the cowboy with assault with a deadly weapon against Nez-begay. And for good measure, he swore to a second complaint accusing Finn of stealing and unlawfully branding Indian stock. He said he was anxious that there should be no delay and was successful in having the cases scheduled for the District Court in Aztec, before Justice Curren on July 12, two days later.

In the meantime, the townspeople of Farmington again crowded into Allen's Hall to hear the arraignment of seven Indians, including Chis-chilling-begay, accused of assault against Finn. The clerk had no sooner announced that court was in session than Shelton, now firmly convinced that Judge Fay was prejudiced, demanded a change of venue. His request was denied, and Edwards and Martin, attorneys for the prosecution, called their witnesses, including Finn, Marietta Wetherill and Miss Quick. Agent Stacher reported to Commissioner Valentine that "The most important evidence submitted was that of Will Finn, the only white person who was an eye witness to Wetherill's death." He summarized Finn's testimony of how Finn saw Wetherill snatch away the old rifle from Welo, break the stock over a fence post, and then carry the barrel in his hand as they rode together down the canyon. Stacher continued:

> He denied that Wetherill pointed the gun in a threatening manner towards old Welo or towards Chis-chilin-begay. He stated that Chis-chilin-begay was present when Wetherill broke the gun . . . As Finn and Wetherill arrived at the place where the latter was killed, they met Billy Williams and Thomicito . . . and saw Thomas Padilla and Pesh-la-ki coming down the road at a considerable distance behind them. Wetherill had a conversation with Thomicito and had just started on when they saw Chis-chilin-begay get off his horse and commence firing.
>
> The Indian fired more than 4 shots. Wetherill fell at the second shot. Finn stopped when the first shot was fired and after the third shot was fired he commenced shooting at the Indian. He then turned his horse and rode as fast as he could towards Wetherill's house. . .

Stacher said he firmly believed all of the Indians except the murderer were innocent, and added that

> . . . statements have been made to the effect that the Indian Agents have been indirectly responsible for inciting the Indians to commit this deed. We believe, however, that the better class of white people in this community understand the circumstances, and are in sympathy with the Indians in this trouble.

As dryly as he had dismissed the similar charge against Finn, Judge Fay dismissed charges against Tso-bakis, Joe Yazzie, Thomacito [or Thomicito] and Billy Williams — all accused of assault against Finn. Thus "The Indians who were required to await the action of the Grand Jury," Stacher wrote, "were Chis-chilin-begay, who was already in jail charged with the murder of Richard Wetherill, Thomas Padilla, and Pesh-la-ki."

Navajo friends of the latter two furnished $500 bond for each and they were allowed to go to their homes on assurances from Shelton and Stacher that the agents would be responsible for their appearance in court at the required time.

A complaint entered during these proceedings — but belatedly — by Bill Finn, charged Nez-begay with the theft and death of Elizabeth's colt. It was heard at the conclusion of arraignment of the seven Navajos. Judge Fay found sufficient evidence to hold Nez-begay for trial and bound him over to the next term of District Court. As in the cases of Pesh-la-ki and Thomas Padilla, Nez-begay was released in the custody of Shelton and Stacher.

When the charges against these Indians finally came to trial, in December, 1912, all were found not guilty. For assaulting Nez-begay, Finn was sentenced to the penitentiary for one year to eighteen months, sentence suspended, and was ordered to pay costs of nearly three hundred dollars. The charge of stealing Indian cattle was dismissed.

Dr. Prudden and members of the Wetherill family were present at Finn's arraignment before Judge Curren, in Aztec, for assaulting Nez-begay and for branding Indian stock. For more than two weeks the doctor had watched and listened with growing indignation, since, in his opinion, the conduct of Shelton, Stacher, and their assistants had been "outrageous."

Now, as they waited for the judge to appear, he overheard one of Stacher's men talking in a corner to the slow-witted, thoroughly frightened

RICHARD WETHERILL

Lee Ivy. In a few minutes the boy expected to be called to the stand to tell what had happened when he and Finn went to Nez-begay's hogan to get Elizabeth's colt. Charles Pinkney was holding the red-faced youth firmly by the lapel and, as Dr. Prudden heard it, was advising him to be careful of anything he said "lest his — Ivy's parents — should be made to suffer." To the doctor, this sounded very much like the intimidation of a witness. On the stand later, Lee Ivy was all but tongue-tied.

Boiling inwardly as he watched, Dr. Prudden wondered if there was not something that could be done.

TWENTY-FOUR

DR. PRUDDEN spent the last three wearying weeks of his vacation giving such help as he could to the young widow of his long-time friend. Now, for the last time as a guest in the Wetherill home, once so noisily alive with ambitious plans, ideas and good fellowship, Dr. Prudden was saying goodbye.

Al Wetherill, tallest and most gentle-mannered of the brothers, stooping slightly and now quite bald, had gone back to his Gallup post office. John Wetherill, graying, grizzled, given to long silences, was returning to his trading post at Kayenta. Knowing, perhaps, they would not meet again, Dr. Prudden said goodbye to Marietta Wetherill, whom in other times he had referred to as "the Chatelaine of the Chaco." With Clate Wetherill, who had the most affable grin and readiest laughter but now was unsmiling, Dr. Prudden was preparing to ride north through the Animas Valley to Durango to board a train for the East.

Richard's death, more than once in these past weeks had started hot tears of anger in the doctor's eyes. Violence, he felt, had been done to more than a good man's life and to his family. Shelton had done equal violence to the good name of his friend, and there seemed to be no stopping the agent from painting Richard as a brute and a thief who had been crooked in his dealings with the Navajos.

Rankling in the back of the doctor's mind was a statement of Shelton's quoted in the same *Farmington Enterprise* interview of July 1 when Shelton said the murder of Richard was premeditated to a certain extent. A few lines below, Shelton was quoted as saying that he had "been expecting something of this kind for some time, as Wetherill and Finn [had] repeatedly 'done' the Indians in numerous deals for cattle, sheep and horses."

Thinking back on it, the doctor found it peculiar that Shelton — alone of all in the region who knew Richard Wetherill — had been expecting some violent occurrence, some decisive stroke that would remove the man now safely dead and safely silent.

In Durango, Dr. Prudden called upon the editor of The *Herald*, a cer-

RICHARD WETHERILL

tain briskness or sharpness replacing his usual air of quiet good humor. In his hand was a statement, a rather long statement, which he had prepared and now gave to the editor. Would the newspaper consider printing it? It would indeed. On July 21 The *Herald* published Dr. Prudden's remarks almost in full and, at the end, the editor added his own comment:

> He [Prudden] blames the reservation officials for most of the trouble, and believes the Indians were led to think it would be a benefit to get rid of Wetherill and that falsehoods were told to stir them up . . . The *Herald* will add that Mr. Wetherill was always understood to stand well among the Indians and people with whom he had dealings.

Dr. Prudden rode on to Denver and while waiting for a train connection there, did some more brooding over the death of his friend. Then, on the spur of the moment, he wrote to the Commissioner of Indian Affairs demanding an investigation of Richard's murder. It was an angry expression from a man noted for moderation:

> I have just returned from the scene of the murder of Richard Wetherill on June 22nd, 1910 by a Navajo Indian at Pueblo Bonito in New Mexico.
>
> This affair, obviously a part of a plot of several Navajos to murder not only Wetherill but his confidential stock man Finn, has, I am informed, been placed by your office in charge of Mr. Shelton at the Ship Rock Agency.
>
> I know most of the Navajo Indians concerned in this matter; I have known Richard Wetherill for many years; I have made most exhaustive personal inquiries of those upon the scene for months before, at the time of, and after the murder; I was present at most of the preliminary trials at Farmington and at Aztec.
>
> I am convinced that I am doing a public service and presumably also a service to yourself as Indian Commissioner, in informing you that I have learned from the most reliable sources that the Agent or Superintendent Stracher [S. F. Stacher, whose name Dr. Prudden misspelled throughout] has been for a long time slandering and threatening Wetherill before the Navajos as well as before white men.
>
> The unbridled talk of Stracher has been such that the Navajos

could not help believing that he, Stracher, would be well pleased if Wetherill were removed.

I charge Mr. Shelton with public slander and villification of Wetherill shortly after his murder and before even the preliminary trials were begun; see *Farmington Enterprise*, July 1st, 1910, in which he publicly accuses him of crooked dealings with the Indians and falsifying his books.

I charge the Farmer of Stracher, Pinckney [Charles C. Pinkney], with attempting to intimidate a witness for the Wetherill interest at one of the trials at Aztec . . .

I call your attention to the fact that the Clerk of Stracher, — Six [B. P. Six], for unwarrantable interference with a witness of the attempted murder of Finn, was arrested by authorities of Farmington, N. M. and is bound over for trial.

The personal conduct of the representatives of your office, Shelton, Pinckney and Six, at the preliminary trials at Farmington was undignified and outrageous in ways which I am ready to specify at any time. . .

Dr. Prudden concluded by saying that if he had been misinformed in any of these particulars he would appreciate being told so by Commissioner Valentine before bringing "the facts and conditions to the attention of the general public." As for his own personal reliability, he referred the Commissioner to Columbia University, where he had been a professor of medicine for many years, and to the National Academy of Sciences in Washington, of which he was a member.

Commissioner Valentine never replied to Dr. Prudden, but turned the correspondence over to E. P. Holcombe, Chief Supervisor of the Office of Indian Affairs branch office in Denver. The Commissioner did, however, authorize an investigation. While Holcombe was exchanging letters with Prudden on a pretense of obtaining specific charges, Valentine quietly sent three investigators into the field to gather information. He named for the task Maj. James McLaughlin, to be in charge; H. B. Peairs, a supervisor of Indian education; and W. M. Peterson, a supervisor of Indian schools. It developed that the last two were supernumeraries; the work was done by the Major.

MAJOR McLAUGHLIN was a tall, white-haired veteran of many years with the Indian Service, first as agent for the Sioux at Devils Lake and then at Standing Rock reservation. In this same year, 1910, a Boston firm published his book *My Friend the Indian,* one of the first factual accounts of the battle of the Little Big Horn and which showed George Custer as something less than a military hero.

The Major called first on Superintendent Shelton at Shiprock, during the last week of August. One of the first matters raised was Shelton's unfortunate interview with Elliott, the assistant editor of The *Enterprise.* Just how they agreed to handle this prickly issue, and then approach Elliott, is not known, but it is clear that either one or both of them did, and Elliott was asked to print some sort of retraction or explanation. Elliott printed no retraction, but a stiff, formal statement. He admitted misunderstanding which of his remarks Shelton wanted to make public — he did not admit misquoting the man:

> This is to certify that the undersigned, assistant editor of the *Farmington Enterprise* . . . on or about the 28th day of June, A.D. 1910, had a conversation with Mr. W. T. Shelton . . . relative to matters connected with the murder of Richard Wetherill. . . .
>
> Mr. Shelton, during the course of that conversation, related to the undersigned a number of facts pertaining to said Richard Wetherill, as published in the *Farmington Enterprise* of the date of July 1st, with the request that they be withheld from publication. The undersigned, in preparing the article for publication, was confused as to which parts of said remarks Mr. Shelton had asked to be withheld, with the result that they appeared in the issue of July 1st, as stated above. Mr. Shelton was in no way responsible for their appearance, and told the undersigned these things merely to show why the Indians were incensed against Mr. Wetherill and how he proposed to protect their interests, not expecting them to appear in public print.

Elliott's statement absolved Shelton of blame for using the newspaper to influence the outcome of the trials or to prejudice the public's mind against Wetherill and Finn. But it also confirmed Dr. Prudden's accusation that Shelton had been accusing the two men in street-corner discussions, so freely, in fact, the doctor considered his statements to be slander and villification.

Having secured this clarification at least, Major McLaughlin next obtained Sam Stacher's affidavit that he had not "at any time or place slandered or threatened Richard Wetherill before white persons, Navajo Indians or any person whomsoever." He had not, Stacher swore, even "talked in an unbridled manner before Indians or whites."

Pinkney raised his right hand and swore that on July 13, at Aztec courthouse, he had engaged the youth Lee Ivy in a little friendly talk. He had known both the boy and his parents for years, Pinkney declared, and he spoke to Ivy "with the intention of giving the boy some good advice, and told him he should be careful and not get into trouble." He denied emphatically that his conduct was undignified or improper.

When Dr. Prudden accused B. P. Six with interfering with a witness, he had specific reference to Salvador Hernandez, who had appeared at Pueblo Bonito several months before Richard's death and asked for a job. Richard had not known it, and Dr. Prudden did not know it now, but a short time before Hernandez had escaped from jail in Santa Fe with a Chaco Navajo named Zah-he. Rewards of $25 each had been posted for their capture. For two weeks Hernandez lived in the Navajo's hogan, hiding, and then came to Bonito and was hired as a minor ranch hand. His present eminence was due to the fact he had been a witness to the attack upon Bill Finn by Tso-bakis.

All went well with Hernandez until the morning of Finn's arraignment in Aztec, when he was recognized by an Indian policeman while driving Marietta Wetherill's surrey through town. There had been a flurry of excitement, observed by Dr. Prudden, when Six and the Indian policeman rushed into the street, pulled the horses to a stop, and dragged Hernandez off the driver's seat. All of this Six explained in his affidavit for Major McLaughlin, the substance of it being confirmed long afterward by Mrs. Wetherill, who also at the time knew nothing of Hernandez' jail break and shared Dr. Prudden's mistaken belief that Six's part in arresting the Mexican was unjustifiably outrageous.

Hernandez subsequently had caused Six to be arrested, on complaints of false arrest and impersonating an officer, but when Six came into court no one appeared against him and the case was dismissed. It should be added that Hernandez was locked up in Farmington, but not for long. A man of one real talent, he broke out of jail again, disappeared, and was never seen in the Four Corners region again.

Major McLaughlin then went to Pueblo Bonito and Gallup, where he secured affidavits from Marietta Wetherill and Eleanor Quick. He neglected to obtain statements from Bill Finn and Lee Ivy, which is curious in view of the parts both played in events leading directly to Richard Wetherill's death.

It is curious also that after talking with Marietta and Miss Quick, the Major confined his attention to securing as many sworn statements, letters, telegrams and various other memoranda as possible from individuals who would say Richard Wetherill was a thief and brutal tyrant. Shelton provided the bulk of this material, including a sworn statement regarding the shooting from Chis-chilling-begay, as well as some two hundred letters and depositions he and Stacher solicited from Indian Service employees. Many of the writers were personal friends of Shelton's, all of them were loyal to the Indian Service, and few had known Richard Wetherill more than slightly.

The picture they drew of him was a fascinating composite of Jesse James, Billy the Kid and Jack the Ripper — a swearing scoundrel who threatened with knives and guns and even his bare fists to kill any Indian who crossed him; who handcuffed helpless Navajos, cursed them, and threw them in dark dungeon rooms of Pueblo Bonito with only candle-lit skulls for company; who cheated Indian women of pennies, beat up old men and shot or poisoned such Navajo stock as he didn't steal; who was a notorious rustler, indicted many times in several counties for running off cattle and horses.

David F. Day, the fire and brimstone publisher of The *Durango Democrat*, responded to an inquiry from Shelton, saying: "From what I can find out Wetherill *has* been *stealing* stock from the Indians *for years* . . ." (The italics are Day's.) And in a second letter to Shelton, on July 12: "Was talking Saturday with Sheriff Gawith of Montezuma County and he said he had known Wetherill for twenty-four years and never knew of him doing other than stealing cattle . . ."

Day's motive for aiding Shelton's cause is a mystery since nothing has been found to indicate that Day and Richard had ever met. Among his fellow townspeople, however, Day had a reputation for lurid writing, his free resort to abuse making him the target of numerous libel actions. Court Clerk Herbert McGregor recalls hearing his parents speak of Day as a man who "would write anything for his paper that came into his head."

In answering a letter from Stacher asking for information about Richard Wetherill, Alfred Hardy, who was then retired in California after two years with the Indian Service at Canyon Blanco, wrote that Wetherill had committed various outrages against Navajos living near Pueblo Bonito "including the rounding up of Indian stock & selling it to a white man, etc. - etc."

An Aztec rancher named Price Walters was more specific. He wrote Shelton on August 23: "Yours of the 16th inst. received this A.M. Will say that I did not know Richard Wetherill personally. In the fall of 1895 I was a member of the Grand Jury for San Juan Co. and Wetherill was indicted for cattle stealing in this county. You will find a record of this in the office of the Clerk of the District Court at Santa Fe."

An Indian Service agent named Joe O. Smith, who claimed he had known Richard Wetherill in the Mancos days, wrote Shelton that "I will gladly give you any information of the late Richard Wetherill. I am surprised that there should be any question as to his dishonesty . . ."

Sheriff James Gawith of Montezuma County, Colorado, wrote on August 8 that "I have known Mr. Wetherill for 24 years and from what I know of him can truthfully say that his reputation has not been the best, he having been arrested two or three times that I know of and accused of stealing cattle in this county."

These letters and dozens more in the same vein Shelton turned over to Major McLaughlin to be included in the Major's report to Commissioner Valentine. McLaughlin, no fool, may have wondered if Shelton and company had not over-reached themselves. It was necessary, of course, to protect the spotless record of the Indian Service and its personnel. But some of these charges against Wetherill, McLaughlin already had found, were ludicrous. What if the New York doctor who had stirred up this hornet's nest — Prudden — belted on his armor and demanded proof? There is reason to believe the Major was not happy with the role he was forced to play.

On September 3 the Major reached Gallup. The *McKinley County Republican* six days later reported the purpose of his visit and added:

"Mr. McLaughlin secured sufficient testimony to forever set aside even the semblance of the charge of 'cattle stealing' which was so unjustly brought against the deceased [Richard Wetherill]. The character of the evidence in this connection was so direct and conclusive that the inspector practically dismissed the matter from his mind."

If the Major dismissed from his mind the idea that Richard was a cattle thief, he did not dismiss the spurious accusations from his report: they all went in, and nowhere in his summary of findings did he even suggest he had found them to be false. Strange, too, was his decision to include in the report a copy of the true bill of November, 1893, indicting Richard Wetherill and Henry Mitchell on a charge of stealing a cow from Daniel Hamilton. Although the file containing this document also included other papers showing the outcome of the trial and exoneration of the two men accused, the Major for reasons of his own reported only that Richard had been accused and then indicted.

As found in the letters solicited by Shelton, there was, of course, the categorical statement by rancher Price Walters of Aztec saying that in the fall of 1895 he had served on a Grand Jury which indicted Wetherill for cattle stealing in San Juan County, with records at Santa Fe to prove it. In following this lead the Major had gone to Santa Fe, examined the ledgers in the District Court, and then in pencil made this notation across the bottom of Walters' letter to Shelton:

"Nothing in records of Clerk of Court at Santa Fe, N. Mex from 1894 to 1901 inclusive showing an indictment against Richard Wetherill."

Could the Major have been mistaken? Because this seemed possible, all of the court records in Santa Fe were checked during the preparation of this book, both in the District Court and the State Supreme Court. No entry could be found against Richard's name for any year, from the time he moved to Mancos through the month of the year he died. Possibly Price Walters had confused his courts? A similar search was made in the court records at Aztec — with the same result. Price Walters had been confused — or he had lied.

When the McLaughlin report finally was submitted to Commissioner Valentine it contained approximately one thousand pages of numbered documents and a four-page summary of findings, dated September 16, 1910. In an accompanying letter, Major McLaughlin and the two who had been named to assist him, H. B. Peairs and W. M. Peterson, declared that all of the charges made by Dr. Prudden were entirely unfounded. They offered no conclusions of their own as to the cause of Richard Wetherill's murder or of the guilt or innocence of anyone concerned.

Forming a minute part of the bulky whole, amounting to fewer than twenty pages, the material favorable to Wetherill's side of the case was contained in four or five affidavits and letters. Of these, one was a letter written to Commissioner Valentine on July 11, 1910, by a man named John Charles, a supervisor of construction for the Interior Department, with headquarters in Denver. Charles apparently was somewhere in the vicinity at the time of Richard's death and either of his own accord or under instructions had made inquiries and then reported to the Commissioner. He gave an account of the shooting, as told to him by B. P. Six, and then added that

I visited Pueblo Bonito Agency on June 29th after spending a day at Gallup, N. Mex. The unfortunate affair which resulted in the killing of Richard Wetherill by a Navajo Indian a few days previous was the general subject of discussion at Gallup, where a brother of the dead man is Post Master.

The general expression at Gallup, is that the Indian had taken the life of a man who had been a good friend to his people. Unpleasant remarks were being made on the streets suggesting that the Indians had been influenced to rash acts by white people. . .

In discussing the matter with Superintendent Stacher, I learned that some ill feeling had existed between Stacher and Wetherill and each had known how the other felt. I thought the subject was being discussed rather freely at the Agency and advised Superintendent Stacher to avoid expressing his personal opinions regarding the matter as there was great danger of his being misquoted. . .

Dr. Prudden was unaware that the McLaughlin investigation had been authorized. Even while it was under way he corresponded frequently with Supervisor Holcombe regarding specific charges against Shelton and Stacher, Holcombe permitting Prudden to think a decision on his demand for an investigation was still to be made. Their correspondence continued until a few days after the inquiry was concluded and Major McLaughlin's report was submitted to Commissioner Valentine. By ending the investigation before Dr. Prudden knew it had begun, the Indian Service saved itself the possible embarrassment of taking any evidence the doctor was prepared to offer.

Even this was not enough. Dr. Prudden's original letter to Commissioner Valentine outlining his charges and asking for an investigation, and all of his correspondence with Holcombe were conveniently "lost" before they could be made a part of the Indian Service file. Fortunately, however, Dr. Prudden had made copies of his letters and with them saved the curious letters he received from Holcombe. These documents are now preserved in the Yale University Library.

THE EVENTS immediately following her husband's death had all but brought ruin to Marietta Wetherill. Her courageous efforts to maintain a home for herself and her children at Pueblo Bonito were doomed. Fearful of arousing the displeasure of Shelton and Stacher, the Navajos carefully avoided the Wetherill ranch.

Marietta found it impossible to collect anything from the Indians on their old debts to the Bonito store. Late in July, desperate, she filed suit against Stacher asking $8,000 in damages for loss of her stock; also she asked for an injunction to restrain the agent from further interfering with her operation of the ranch. Her action charged that Stacher had "conspired with the Indians to claim and drive away large numbers of horses, sheep and cattle" and was even now conspiring to defraud the estate and prevent her from collecting debts owed by the Navajos.

Her appeal for an injunction was granted while Stacher's attorneys were preparing an answer. His response, when finally submitted to the court, denied all of Marietta's charges. Further, it denied Marietta's assertion that Richard had been murdered. Now on the defensive, Stacher in effect denied everything he had written to Commissioner Valentine regarding the circumstances of Richard's death. He found it expedient to adopt Shelton's version.

Wetherill's death, he said, had resulted from "a fight or melee." True — Richard Wetherill had been shot by a Navajo named Chis-chilling-begay, but the fatal shot was fired "at a time when the said Richard Wetherill was committing a violent and unlawful assault upon the said Chis-chilin-bega."

For days after the shooting, Indian police and white deputies from Crownpoint and Shiprock had ringed the Wetherill home at Bonito. All normal trade or contact with the surrounding Navajos had been cut off. Weeks later, when trader George Blake was attempting to collect debts owed to the estate, it was found that Shelton had moved again into Stacher's jurisdiction, interfering with Blake's efforts and advising the Navajos not to pay.

Stacher, meanwhile, claimed that Marietta "swore falsely to the charges and was unable to prove that a single head of stock had been stolen, or that I had conspired in any way or manner whatever to hinder or harass her. . ." Her accusations, he said, were "simply for sympathetic effect, but I believe the effect will be reactionary."

When her suit against Stacher finally was called for trial on November 17, she appeared before Judge John R. McFie of Santa Fe without witnesses or friends to speak for her. Stacher came surrounded by individuals prepared to swear to his innocence — Sheriff Dufur, James Bryant, B. P. Six and Charles Pinkney, James C. Clifford, and Harry McDonald, Stacher's interpreter at Crownpoint. All except Sheriff Dufur, who was a good friend of Shelton, were employed by the Indian Service.

Judge McFie gravely weighed the testimony, instructed the jury; the verdict came back: Stacher was innocent on all counts.

TWENTY-FIVE

Chis-chilling-begay was indicted for murder in the first degree by a Grand Jury that was impaneled during the November, 1910, term of the District Court at Aztec.

The indictment charged the Navajo with having slain Richard Wetherill "willfully, of his deliberate and premeditated express malice aforethought." Judge Edmund C. Abbott continued the defendant under $10,000 bond, a legal formality. The preceding July, after two weeks in jail, Chis-chilling-begay had been released in Shelton's custody and ever since had lived with his family at the agency. Now, over the objections of the prosecuting attorneys, Judge Abbott ordered that the same comfortable arrangement should be continued. This led The *Denver Post* to comment critically that "For months he [Chis-chilling-begay] has roamed about the agency grounds at at Shiprock, with nothing to prevent his escape to the distant mountains."

With rare prescience Shelton wrote Commissioner Valentine that, "I am satisfied that all of the Indians, except the man who killed Wetherill, will come clear, and that he will be tried for a lesser offense than murder in the first degree, with a very good show of a light sentence . . . If we are not hampered for want of assistance . . . we will make a cleaning in the Pueblo Bonita section that will put that reservation on a clean business basis."

Part of the strategy in Chis-chilling-begay's defense had been to delay his trial for as long as possible, meanwhile preventing him from talking to anyone about the shooting. So far the plan had worked well and under Shelton's watchful eye the Navajo had maintained, for the most part, a sphinx-like silence. The trial, to be held in the courtroom at Aztec, had been postponed until the first week of June, 1912 — or for almost two years.

Except for a few new faces, a few absences, the participants in this final scene were cast in familiar roles: there were the same Indians who in one way or another had been involved in the shooting appearing for the defense; Marietta Wetherill and Finn and Lee Ivy were back as chief witnesses for the prosecution; the strongly partisan Eleanor Quick was not present. To tell bluntly such facts as he knew, and for the first time, there was the trader George Blake. To help Charles Johnson, the Durango lawyer, to present the strongest possible case for the defendant, Shelton had secured the services of another attorney, William A. Palmer, and also U. S. District Attorney H. W. Clark of Las Vegas, New Mexico. Appearing as counsel for the prosecution were Attorneys Edwards and Martin of Farmington, District Attorney Alexander Reed of Santa Fe and Assistant District Attorney E. P. Davies.

By now the story of Richard Wetherill's death was so well known to everyone in the San Juan region that the only uncertainty was what Chischilling-begay would say about the shooting. While witnesses for the prosecution were on the stand, these questions remained unanswered. To hurry the proceedings along, Judge Abbott extended the trial into night sessions.

It was ten o'clock on the night of June 6, the small courtroom hot and crowded with spectators. Marietta Wetherill was testifying under cross-examination, wilting after hours on the stand. Did she know any motive the Navajo may have had for shooting her husband? None, she replied. There was no motive — except the Navajo had owed Mr. Wetherill for purchases from the Bonito store.

"When did you see your husband last?"

White, her expression numb, Marietta stared at District Attorney Clark for a moment and then bent forward covering her face with her hands, her shoulders shaken by sobs.

At this point Judge Abbott intervened and recessed court until the following morning. Early the next day the prosecution rested, having finished with Mrs. Wetherill and having heard the testimony of Finn and Ivy and also of George Blake, who related how Chis-chilling-begay had come to his store twice on the day of the shooting, and what he had said and done.

The defendant was the next witness. Had he killed Richard Wetherill? In a low voice the Navajo answered: "I had to shoot Mr. Wetherill in self-defense."

This was the moment everyone in the courtroom had awaited, for two years. A correspondent for The *Albuquerque Journal* covered sheafs of paper with notes, late that day telephoned his office giving the substance of the Navajo's testimony in direct quotations:

The day . . . Wetherill was killed by me I was at my hogan when the wife of Nes-en-be-gay [Nez-begay] came and told me that Finn had killed her husband. I went over to Nes-en-be-gay's hogan and found him lying on the ground outside. I raised his arm but it fell to the ground. I thought he was dead. I got a quilt and put him on it and dragged him into the hogan.

Then I went to the Blake store, and bought a box of cartridges, went home, got my gun and went up to the Wetherill store, where a lot of Indians were gathered. I saw Finn and Mr. Wetherill ride up to a Mexican's house [near Pueblo del Arroyo] where the Indians were. Mr. Wetherill cursed all the Navajos and called them thieves and said he would kill them all with a gun.

He rode up to an Indian's pony that had a gun on the saddle, took the gun and broke it over a post. I then saw him turn and ride toward me, pointing the gun at me. I went down into the arroyo, where my gun was hidden, got it and came back into the road just as Wetherill and Finn came along, driving cattle. Wetherill asked me if Nes-en-be-gay was all right, and I told him he was dead. Wetherill said, "Good, all Navajoes are thieves and ought to be killed."

Then Finn and Wetherill rode toward me on a run, and Finn pulled a revolver and shot twice at me, and Wetherill had the broken gun pointed at me. The gun would shoot.

I got off my horse and shot, and Wetherill fell from his horse. Then I began shooting at Finn, who shot at me again and then ran. Then I got my pony and rode to Blake's store. . .

Twice Chis-chilling-begay slipped badly. The first time, when he said that when he looked at Nez-begay, bent over him and raised his arm, he thought his friend was dead; that he had then dragged Nez-begay into his hogan. This was the sort of thing a white man would do. Chis-chilling-begay or his advisers should have realized that the white men on this jury knew a Navajo would touch a dead person only in extreme necessity — but never, for any reason, drag the body of a dead Indian into his hogan. Chis-chilling-begay's second mistake was to insist the broken rifle barrel Wetherill carried could still be fired, and that Wetherill actually had raised it to shoot him. The other Navajos already had testified that Anasazi had emptied the cartridge chamber before smashing the rifle stock. Chis-chilling-begay was even closer and better able to see it done.

The jury returned its verdict at one P.M. on Saturday, June 8, finding the Navajo guilty of voluntary manslaughter. Judge Abbott four days later sentenced the Indian to serve from five to ten years in the State Penitentiary at Santa Fe, and ordered Chis-chilling-begay to work out and pay $500 for costs of prosecution.

His attorneys immediately filed notice that they would appeal and the Navajo again was turned over into Shelton's care under reduced bond of $1,000. On July 8 Sheriff Dufur and Chis-chilling-begay boarded a train at Durango, arriving the next day in Santa Fe, where, presumably, the Indian was to remain in jail until called for his appeal. There was a change of mind at the last minute, however, and The Santa Fe *New Mexican* reported on July 10 that

> Chis-chilling-begay, the Navajo Indian convicted of having shot and killed Richard Wetherill . . . yesterday dismissed his appeal from the district court and threw himself upon the mercy of the court. He was given from five to ten years in prison. Late last night he went to the State Penitentiary near the city and turned over his commitment papers to John B. McManus, the warden. He was then locked up and today will be assigned to light work . . .

Months before Chis-chilling-begay was sentenced, and for years afterward, there were many who believed that the Navajo — in spite of what he had told George Blake — actually intended to kill Bill Finn and only by accident shot Richard Wetherill. While he was at Shiprock awaiting trial, Chis-chilling-begay broke his silence to tell Jim Jarvis, "I didn't mean to kill Mr. Wetherill." In the few days when they were together in the courtroom at Aztec, Marietta Wetherill had spoken with the Indian during a recess and he had told her, "When I killed Anasazi I killed my best friend." Mrs. Martha Stewart, Al Wetherill's daughter, said her father talked with Chis-chilling-begay just before he was taken to Santa Fe. As her father related it many times later, "He broke down, and putting his face in his hands moaned, 'Oh, Ail, Ail, I have killed my best friend.' "

To John Arrington it was conceivable that the Indian had learned to regret what he had done — but Richard Wetherill's murder had been no accident. Two days after the shooting Bill Finn had taken Arrington over the ground, relating what had happened in the space of a few seconds before Richard's death.

"Finn was positive that the Navajo's first shot was intended for him, because it missed him only by a few inches. He said he could not possibly have been mistaken about this because he was with the main bunch of drags in a bend of the road where it turns right, or north, before turning again to cross the draw. Before reaching the bend Richard had turned off to the left, heading after one or two strays that had taken to the greasewood. And then, through the dust, Finn said he saw Chis-chilling-begay standing about fifty yards out in front and just about between them."

After the first shot missed him, Finn told Arrington, the Navajo turned deliberately, slowly — though it did not seem slow — and aimed again.

"Anyone who knew him well," said Arrington, "knew that Richard had a habit of riding with his right hand up. The second bullet went through his right hand and into his chest, going through that hand as though it had been cut by a hot wagon rod. It killed him instantly."

EPILOGUE

$\mathbf{F}$OR five years after Richard's death Dr. Prudden returned each summer to the Southwest, its inner recesses less remote now with the coming of the automobile and the web of dirt roads spreading everywhere across the Navajo country. Clayton or John Wetherill, or both, were his companions on these trips, which each year became shorter and ended always with the doctor resting at a camp he owned on the rim of the Grand Canyon.

After 1915 an illness prevented his returning again. But in letters to his friends it was apparent his thoughts frequently took him back in memory over the old trails. He died in 1925. John Wetherill spoke for the family when he wrote Miss Lillian Prudden, "I feel that there is nothing I can do that will begin to pay him for what he has done for my brothers and myself . . . I cannot tell you the grief we felt on hearing of his death."

The passage of time has served only to associate more closely the names of Richard Wetherill and the Hyde brothers, the generous philanthropy of Talbot and Fred Hyde nearly always linked now with the exploring and pioneering archaeological work of Wetherill. During their years together the Hydes invested more than $100,000 in the Hyde Exploring Expedition, a sum that went four or five times as far then, in that field of effort, as it would now. Some of the money had been wasted in chimerical business schemes, but most of it had been spent frugally and well. The Hyde brothers and Richard were the leaders, though they lacked recognition, in a rich, almost totally unexplored field. Scientific refinements were introduced later as greater knowledge and new techniques were developed — but in a true sense they were trailblazers in Southwestern archaeology. After more than half a century the Hyde-Wetherill collections are still the finest to have come from the San Juan region, scene of the highest development of prehistoric civilization north of Mexico.

A sharp conflict of personalities made it impossible for George H. Pepper and Richard Wetherill to get along, although both managed a pretense of harmony as long as they were working at Pueblo Bonito. After learning of Richard's murder, Pepper, then assistant curator of archaeology at the University of Pennsylvania Museum, wrote to Commissioner Valentine to say, "A certain piece of news has drifted in from the West; it is in the form of a newspaper clipping and it states that Richard Wetherill of Pueblo Bonito . . . has been murdered and mutilated by the Navajos. If this is true I hope you may care to give me the particulars." Pepper was curious, but hardly more. Later he became associated with the Heye Museum of the American Indian in New York where he did valuable work. Although he wrote a number of scientific papers, the one for which he is best remembered is his report on Pueblo Bonito.

SAMUEL F. STACHER emerged from the difficulties attending Richard's murder unscathed. Essentially an honest, well-intentioned man, he had allowed himself, at the age of thirty-four, to be guided by Shelton's ruthless will, and so became a participant in an affair that unintentionally ended in tragedy. There is reason to believe that Stacher was shocked by Richard's death ("we deeply deplore the fact that such a crime has been committed," he wrote Valentine five days later), but continued in the conviction that Wetherill was a man of bad character. In the years following, Stacher won the firm respect and friendship of the Navajos and has been called by them one of the best superintendents they ever had. He was instrumental in helping to organize the inter-tribal Indian ceremonial held annually at Gallup since the 1920's, but his establishment of a school and agency at Crownpoint, in the face of discouraging obstacles, was his major achievement. For more than twenty-six years he remained in charge before his retirement from the Indian Service. His last years were spent in Albuquerque, where he died at the age of seventy-seven on August 28, 1952.

AND CHIS-CHILLING-BEGAY? Perhaps it is to Shelton's credit that once the Navajo disappeared behind the brick walls of the State Penitentiary, Shelton did not forget him. While the Indian was serving his term, rumor got about that he was tubercular, that he probably had only a few more years to live, and therefore it was argued he should be given an early parole. The story was common gossip, the source of it never clear. Possibly the Parole Board had the rumor in mind when it queried Chis-chilling-begay on May 25, 1915. The transcript indicates the proceedings were perfunctory:

Q.: Age?
A.: 40.
Q.: Crime?
A.: Killed a man.
Q.: Minimum sentence?
A.: Don't know.
Q.: Minimum term expires?
A.: Don't know.
Q.: Where was the crime committed?
A.: Pueblo Bonito.

Thus the testimony opened. It appears that the stenographer or clerk took down only such words as his ear and pencil caught. Chis-chilling-begay said he was living at Pueblo Bonito at the time he shot Richard Wetherill, that no one else had participated in the crime "either as principal or accessory." This was not challenged and the questioning continued:

Q.: Tell your story of the crime in as few words as possible.
A.: Man was stealing my stock and I just killed him.
Q.: Are you guilty of the crime?
A.: Yes.

Shelton previously had assured the Parole Board he would be responsible for the Indian's compliance with all conditions of his parole. Should it be granted, Shelton also promised to see that Chis-chilling-begay was gainfully employed. Warden John B. McManus thereupon wrote to the man who had sentenced the Navajo and Judge Abbott replied: "I should recommend that he be released at the expiration of his minimum sentence providing his conduct warrants such action."

In response to a similar inquiry, District Attorney Alexander Reed, who had directed the prosecution, said: "Dear Sir: I do not care to make any recommendation in the above case, the murder for which this man was convicted was a cold blooded one. Yours very truly. . ."

Although neither Judge Abbott nor the District Attorney favored it, Chis-chilling-begay was released June 11, 1915, after serving just short of three years. Nothing in the parole record suggests that the prisoner was in bad health. Chis-chilling-begay returned to his home near Chaco Canyon and died there in 1950 in about his eightieth year, of old age.

WILLIAM T. SHELTON is remembered in the San Juan country for various reasons. Among others, he is remembered in connection with a Methodist missionary couple named Antes.

In a harmless, negative sort of way, Howard R. Antes first aroused Shelton's antagonism in 1905, when the missionary and his wife were living in something just better than poverty at a place called Aneth, in southeastern Utah. Shelton's anger flared when he found the missionary selling trade goods to the Navajos without a license, having taken over the post and remaining stock of a trader who was moving away. A feud started which continued unremittingly until 1913, when Antes and his wife finally left the country.

On the pretext that Antes had acquired 116 sheep by unlicensed and therefore illegal trade with the Indians, Shelton sent Navajo policemen across the reservation boundary line in Utah to seize the sheep and drive them to the Shiprock agency. When this and other devices failed to overwhelm the missionary, Shelton ordered his police to bring in a Navajo orphan boy whom Antes and his wife had taken under their protection. He forced the lad to remain at Shiprock, never to see his adopted parents again. The Navajo boy who was four years old when an old Indian woman left him at the Antes home, now was twelve. His foster parents, feeling that Shelton's act was no less than kidnaping, appealed to the White House in Washington. They enclosed a letter from the boy, in an awkward pencil scrawl, that added poignant emphasis:

THE PRESIDENT:
I have a good home with Papa and Mama, and I love them. They are good to me. Please let me stay with them. My Grandma gave me to Mama Antes when I was a little boy.
(Signed) SAMUEL S. ANTES

Preoccupied with more pressing affairs, Woodrow Wilson made no reply. Shelton won this victory, the Antes boy remained a ward of the Government at the agency, and the missionary couple moved to Texas.

Shelton's career with the Indian Service ended in 1916 after employees of the Shiprock agency, as well as large numbers of the Navajos, rebelled against his conduct. Charges of moral turpitude were filed against him, the Indians joining the agency personnel in the complaints. An investigation was conducted by the Indian Service while the people of the San Juan Valley divided into sharply partisan camps. The results of the investigation were guarded by the Indian Service in secrecy, but Commissioner of Indian Affairs Cato Sells allowed Shelton to offer his resignation. It was accepted effective March 15 — but not before the superintendent became embroiled in further trouble.

During the untidy proceedings that accompanied the investigation, Shelton became incensed over things that were being said about him by the editor of The *Farmington Enterprise,* a man named Brame, and by a Farmington minister named Wells. Characteristically, he filed suit against them and threatened to do the same in the case of any employee of the Shiprock agency who uttered a word against him. Nothing came of this, but later it was found expedient to transfer four or five of the agency employees who had been most hostile to Shelton to posts in other parts of the country.

Shelton was replaced on the date his resignation took effect by H. F. Coggeshall, a man of more tractable disposition and habits. Instead of departing, however, Shelton embarrassingly lingered for a number of weeks more. He gave as excuse his wife's illness. As soon as Mrs. Shelton was sufficiently recovered the couple packed their belongings and departed for Waynesville, in his native state of North Carolina, where he dropped into total obscurity as far as the Wetherill case was concerned.

MARIETTA WETHERILL was thirty-three when her husband died. For the first few months she struggled fiercely to hold things together, thinking she might save the ranch. But each day brought fuller realization that for a widowed mother of five small children the home at Pueblo Bonito soon could be no more than a place in their past. They could not stay and survive.

Many in the San Juan region who had not known him well thought of her husband as a prosperous if not wealthy man. Richard Wetherill was fifty-two years old at the time of his death; beyond the assets of the ranch property and uncollected debts, all he had in the world lay in his account with an Albuquerque bank. The balance sheet, on the day he was murdered, showed a total of $74.23.

She had been appointed administratrix of the estate, a responsibility which required candid examination of how ominous her situation was. The trader George Blake was appointed appraiser of the ranch property July 19, 1910, and soon after reported to Probate Court these findings:

The ranch, its buildings and the physical equipment, itemized by Blake and reading like the inventory of a country general store, all were valued at $5,000. Ledgers from the Bonito trading post showed that at the time he died Richard had outstanding extended credit of about $8,000 owed by Navajos and $3,000 more owed by various Anglos and Mexicans. In addition, Marietta Wetherill personally held notes from Indians amounting to $1,519, thus fixing her total assets, virtually all on paper, at $17,500. The debts, as she knew well, covered a period of about ten years and the whereabouts of the scores of debtors, scattered all over the country, was largely unknown.

She saw little hope of settling these accounts, but made a stab at it and the results were disheartening. From Juan-et-citty she collected $90, from Julio Lopez, $3.50. And that was all.

George Blake then suggested that his younger brother Albert be named as agent to take over the collections. It is well he did because claims amounting to over four thousand dollars for sheep Richard had bought before his death were being pressed by the Hatcher Mercantile Co., and her lawyers were inquiring about their fees.

All of this, a matter of open record, gives final answer to the spurious stories so frequently told by Richard Wetherill's enemies, that he had cheated the Indians with whom he traded and lined his pockets richly at the expense of all who were gullible. The Navajos, who would have traded elsewhere if they had been cheated, on the contrary had received unusually generous credit and if anyone had suffered it was Richard who died with over ten thousand dollars owed to him and only seventy-four dollars in the bank.

Late in his life, while living on the outskirts of Farmington, Albert Blake recalled those weeks in the saddle, riding hundreds of miles through the Navajo country seeking families who for so long had owed debts to the Wetherills. Stacher, he said, sent with him an agent of his own, a man named James Bryant, as an observer who would see that all interests of the Indians were protected. This precaution Blake took in good spirit and had no trouble; he remembered all of his relations with Stacher as friendly and mutually cooperative. With Shelton it was different. Blake hardly knew the man but it was immediately clear that Shelton regarded him with suspicion and sought by every means possible to interfere with him.

Besides Stacher's man Bryant, Blake was accompanied on his trips by two Navajos, one of them an interpreter and the other assisting by virtue of his wide acquaintance among the Navajo families and his knowledge of the country. Shelton learned the Indians were helping Blake and ordered them to report to him forthwith at Shiprock; when they failed to do so, Shelton sent out Indian police who arrested the pair and hauled them back to the agency. In the meantime, Blake was advised that if he, too, didn't report to Shelton for instructions, the superintendent would issue blanket orders to all Navajos not to pay any debts claimed by the heirs of Richard Wetherill.

For Blake, who was easy-going and until now had merely been performing a job as well as he could, this was too much. He explained the whole situation in a long letter to Commissioner Valentine. Obviously the letter, part of which is quoted at the heading of Part III and refers to Shelton as constituting himself "a kind of czar on the reservation," was prepared with the assistance of someone who could put Blake's indignant thoughts into well-measured prose. At the end, Blake said:

> These accounts were all made off the reservation. They should be paid. To encourage the Indians not to pay them is to cause trouble for the Indians, and trouble for the white men with whom they have lived in neighborly peace for years before Mr. Shelton appeared in the region.

For the first time, Commissioner Valentine gave evidence that Shelton's behavior disturbed him. He instructed Shelton by letter, tersely, to cease his interference.

With a free hand once more, Blake collected $785 in money from the Indians, as well as cattle, sheep, blankets, rope, horses, jewelry and buckskins which he reported had a trade value of $2,695. This might have been better, as Marietta Wetherill observed in her report as administratrix, telling the court she had been "unable to make a better showing in the collection of Indian accounts owing to the interference of Indian Agent W. T. Shelton . . . but desires to state that Indian Agent Stacher rendered every possible assistance."

ANASAZI   315

Barely enough was salvaged to enable Marietta to pay off her debts and make a fresh start. Less than a year after Richard's death she closed the windows and doors of the house at Pueblo Bonito, took one lingering last look around at her home — the yard bare and the out-buildings silent and empty — and then with her children beside her in the wagon, rode eastward out of Chaco Canyon. As she passed them and named them to herself one by one, the massive ruins of Bonito, Chetro Ketl, Hungo Pavie, Una Vida, Wijiji, and then finally Pueblo Pintado, they all stood as sad, lifeless sentinels of the centuries when there had been others departing in sorrow and defeat.

A prosperous rancher of the little town of Cuba, named Miera, who had known and liked her husband and herself in the happier days, helped her to acquire a few sheep and cattle. With these she moved high into the mountains far above the town, heartsick and almost as though fleeing from the world and what it had done to her. In a grassy clearing among the tall pines a cabin was built and here she settled down with the children in a new home. Bill Finn and Lee Ivy came with her, running the stock, buying new brands as they could, gradually increasing the numbers of her sheep and cattle. Without Finn, she remembered long after, it would have been a story of different ending.

"He always was a mystery to me," she admitted, "a hard, cruel man in some ways, but he was loyal. He looked after my interests and was wonderful to my children until he died. He was one of the best cowboys in our part of the country and if it had not been for him I would have lost everything."

After a few years in the mountains above Cuba — where she buried her youngest daughter one year to the day after her husband's death — she moved again, to a small ranch and trading post at Sanders, Arizona. Finn and Ivy remained with her and for an extra hand she hired a man named Jamie McCoy. A time came in 1918 when, with a neighboring rancher, she had enough cattle to send to the stockyards in Kansas City. The cows were loaded on the cars from a siding and Finn rode along in the caboose to handle their sale at the end of the line. But for the cowboy as well as the cattle it was a journey of no return. On arriving in Kansas City, Bill Finn — or Joe Moody — fell victim to the influenza epidemic which that year gripped the country. In a few days he was dead.

During the next years Marietta moved restlessly from one Southwestern town to another, settling down, when her sons and daughters were grown, in a little white house shaded by cottonwoods on the outskirts of Albuquerque. Navajo rugs of some antiquity, the better ones hung on the walls, together with a few pieces of old basketry, were reminders of those long-gone years in the Chaco, years of struggle and of pain, but of happiness too. In this house, while sitting alone in a rocking chair after company had left her, cheerful as always, she died of failure of the heart, on July 11, 1954.

Her most often-expressed wish was granted. After cremation, her ashes were taken to Pueblo Bonito and there were placed in the same grave with her husband.

MULDOON KELLEY had slipped off his eyeshade and was gone from the office of The *Mancos Times*, and from Mancos too. Where, no one seems to remember. It therefore fell to another, a man named I. S. Freeman, to write the obituary of a one-time Mancos man killed in a shooting affray down in New Mexico. Had he been there still, Muldoon Kelley might have stopped a while in the Buckhorn Saloon before settling down to it. Then he might have quoted a passage from Shakespeare, because it was like him, and because it was a passage the Wetherill boys, Richard and Al, sometimes quoted — from Act III of Julius Caesar, Mark Antony speaking

> The evil that men do lives after them:
> The good is oft interred with their bones.

But Muldoon Kelley was gone and the task was left to Mr. Freeman. The new editor followed an old tradition of misspelling names. The obituary of Richard Wetherill, read by the folks of his home town, occupied one short paragraph at the bottom of an inside page under a small heading:

A telegraph message was received yesterday from Allen Witherill at Gallup conveying intelligence of the death of Richard Witherill at Pueblo Bonito he having been killed by the Indians. From the information that can be obtained thru Supt. Shelton at Shiprock it appears that a quarrel arose with Mr. Witherill, and a hired hand on one side and the Indians on the other, the hired man struck one of the Indians, whereupon the Indians began firing and in the affray Mr. Witherill was killed. Mr. Witherill is the oldest of the Witherill Bros. and is known to nearly all the people of Mancos. He has been running a trading post at Pueblo Bonito for several years and owns large interests in sheep in those parts. He leaves a wife and five children to mourn his loss. The body will likely be brought here for burial. Information of his death has been conveyed to all relatives that can be reached by wire.

In the same issue, The *Mancos Times* carried a long story on the front page telling how Congress had appropriated $20,000 for completing a road from Mancos to the great cliff dwellings of the new Mesa Verde National Park. This augured well for the town, the new editor wrote, since it could result only in a booming tourist trade — thousands of visitors each year.

Richard Wetherill's name in this story was not misspelled. It was **not** mentioned.

RICHARD WETHERILL

SOURCES & ACKNOWLEDGMENTS

WHEN THE FIRST EDITION of this book was published in 1957 I was aware that Richard Wetherill, and others involved in the late years of his life, were controversial. This certainty has only been confirmed in the eight years since, and on some occasions I have been reminded that the biography itself is regarded as controversial. To illustrate the point: one evening last month when I was visiting friends in Chaco Canyon, the young archaeologist who was my host turned to me and a bit hesitantly said, "May I ask you a very personal question?" Wondering if I had run over anything important on the road in, I replied that he could, of course. "Why," he asked then, "did you whitewash Richard Wetherill?"

He spoke with such a gentle candor that there was no sting to his words, but I was puzzled by the implication. If a person has been whitewashed, obviously it follows that the person has been guilty of some fairly serious offense. What offense, I asked my friend, was Wetherill guilty of, that I had neglected to mention or had whitewashed? The archaeologist replied that he had in mind no specific wrongdoing on Wetherill's part, nor did he know of any not mentioned in the book, "but you have made him appear just too good. No man is that perfect."

Possibly the criticism is fair, and possibly others will feel that in trying to show that Richard Wetherill was not the pothunting, Indian-beating ogre that some have made him out to be, I went too far in the other direction. I don't know. But if the book is read in its proper context — not as the defense, but the advocacy of a grievously maligned man — it may be found his failings have not been entirely omitted.

I was surprised, too, to learn while in New Mexico last month, that the late Earl H. Morris was under attack by a National Park Service ranger for his alleged "vandalizing" of the ruins of Canyon de Chelly. What sort of weed, I wondered, are the custodians of our national parks and monuments putting in their pipes now? I have wondered also why so many Southwestern archaeologists today speak and write with such contempt of the groping efforts of the men who pioneered their field. Surely the men who came early

ANASAZI 319

to uncharted fields were aware of their limitations, as Richard Wetherill most certainly was of his. I would claim no more for them than they deserve, which is a great deal, but to deny them even that is about as silly as saying, in our jet and space age, that the pioneering of Louis Bleriot, Wilbur and Orville Wright, and Glenn Martin, is undeserving of serious consideration.

Some errors that appeared inadvertently in the first edition of this book have been corrected in the revised second printing, and new material has been added to the appendices. Superintendent Samuel F. Stacher, who appears frequently in the final pages, died in Albuquerque before I had an opportunity to call on him. I am indebted, however, to the assistance of his son, Herbert C. Stacher, in helping to set the record straight on a number of points concerning his father. Superintendent Stacher is well spoken of in the Southwest today by all who knew him. Not so well remembered, but clearly evidenced by his own letters and those of others in the Indian Office files, is the fact his early friendship with Richard Wetherill turned to bitterness. In the last months of Wetherill's life Stacher came to share Superintendent Shelton's opinion that Wetherill was not a fit person to deal with the Navajos and should be made to move from Chaco Canyon. The controversy is too well documented to leave any of the essential circumstances in doubt.

I regret now that I did not provide footnotes, giving my sources of information. It might be helpful, for example, to know that the dialogue between Marietta Wetherill and B. P. Six, in the Prologue, is not imaginary but is quoted exactly from Supervisor Charles' report of July 11, 1910, to Commissioner Valentine, found at the National Archives, Office of Indian Affairs, File 51520-1910-175 Pueblo Bonito. Also, that the remarks of Eleanor Quick, on the same page, are quoted from a letter she wrote on June 27, 1910, to Mrs. D. K. B. Sellers, a friend of the Wetherills in Albuquerque.

In a longer passage (pp. 264-66) Miss Quick is quoted again, but not — as one reader has assumed — from a letter written in recent years to me. The passage is quoted directly from a deposition taken by Major McLaughlin at Gallup on September 5, 1910, included in the Indian Office file mentioned above. This file contains approximately one thousand documents. It is divided into two parts, comprising the report by Major McLaughlin on the murder of Richard Wetherill.

Too late, I have learned that the omission of footnotes can be construed as meaning that a writer either draws from sources too unreliable to mention, or from his own imagination. At this late date I can only summarize some of this book's major sources.

At the American Museum of Natural History in New York, I found and made copies of the following materials used in this book: Richard's original field notes for the Grand Gulch expeditions of 1893-94 and 1897; thirty-five letters written by Richard to B. T. B. and Fred Hyde, 1893-1902; eleven letters from George H. Pepper to B. T. B. Hyde, 1896-98; several letters, and a report on Richard's work written for Clark Wissler by B. T. B. Hyde; a letter from W. H. French to Jesse Nusbaum relating to Richard's work at Grand Gulch; a letter relating to Tsegi Canyon exploration written by John Wetherill to B. T. B. Hyde; field notes and photographs by Nels C. Nelson on a post-Wetherill exploration of Grand Gulch. I had prints made from some two hundred glass-plate negatives in the museum's collection — most of them I believe made by Richard Wetherill on the basis of his and Pepper's correspondence — taken in connection with their work at Pueblo Bonito. These prints, in three volumes, I have since given to the National Park Service library at Chaco Canyon.

Indian Office files at the National Archives in Washington offered the largest part of the material quoted directly or otherwise used in relation to Richard's difficulties with government Land Office and Indian Office agents. In addition to the McLaughlin material mentioned previously, and alone a major source, these files included: 52817-1908-126 (Liquor Traffic); TO.35, Parts I-II-III (Holsinger report); 91845-1911-308.2, Parts I-II (Antes case: some thousand documents); 44676-16-FW; 91295-13-FW; 58000-13; 72294-13; 43444-11-253 San Juan; 51251-16-154 San Juan; 20696-10-126 Pueblo Bonito; 90893-10-313 General Services; 62925-10-175; and 6067-08-916 Navajo. Other sources found at the National Archives, or at the Library of Congress, are listed in the bibliography.

During several visits to her home in New Rochelle, New York, Mrs. James Cameron, the daughter of George Pepper, allowed me to make copies from her father's collection of photographs, letters and time book, all relating to Pueblo Bonito, and letters written to her father by William Benham.

Old newspaper files contributed a large amount of information, those of the Mancos *Times,* the Farmington *Enterprise,* and the Farmington *Times-Hustler* being the most helpful. Others included the Aztec *San Juan Democrat,* Denver *Post,* Albuquerque *Morning Journal,* and Durango *Weekly Herald.*

Numerous conversations with the late Herbert Cowing of Hamden,

Connecticut, are reflected in the early passages of the book, and material also was drawn from his journal of a horseback trip with Richard to see the Snake Dance at Oraibi. He arranged for us to spend a day at the Yale University Library and there helped me to make copies from the collection of papers of Dr. T. Mitchell Prudden, used in passages relating to the Wetherill family, Chaco Canyon, and Richard's murder.

Information bearing on the Wetherills' work at Mesa Verde was obtained from the University of Pennsylvania Museum and the State Historical Society of Colorado. At the Peabody Museum in Cambridge, a search of a dusty closet resurrected Richard's letter inviting Frederic Ward Putnam to visit Mesa Verde.

Accusations that Richard Wetherill was arrested many times for cattle stealing and other crimes, as well as court testimony bearing on his murder, were investigated in a thorough check of records I made at the District Courts in Albuquerque, Gallup, Aztec, Durango, Cortez, and Santa Fe, and the New Mexico Supreme Court at Santa Fe. At the State Penitentiary in Santa Fe I was permitted to make a copy of the jail and parole record of Chischiling-begay — whose name more accurately might be spelled Chis-chili-begay.

Information that aided materially throughout the book was gained in interviews with more than a score of individuals who either had known Richard Wetherill, or his brothers and associates. Because their names were mentioned here in the first edition of the book, and my other sources were scarcely noted, I would only again like to express my indebtedness to all of them for their generous assistance.

Frank McNitt

North Woodstock, Connecticut
June 25, 1965

RICHARD WETHERILL

APPENDIX A

THE STORY OF THE DISCOVERY AND EARLY EXPLORATION
OF THE CLIFF HOUSES AT THE MESA VERDE

[Written by Charles C. Mason, with the approval of the Wetherill brothers. Original owned by the State Historical Society, Denver, Colorado.]

About the year 1885, the Wetherill boys began to winter their cattle in the Mancos Cañon and its numerous branches. The Mancos River cuts through Mesa Verde from Northeast to Southwest. On the Southeast side three large branches enter the main cañon, known as Ft. Lewis, Johnson and Grass Cañons. Those coming in from the Northwest are Moccasin, Cliff, Navajo and Ute Cañons. Nearly all of the Cliff Houses, those ruined dwellings of an extinct race, that have made Mesa Verde famous are in three of these side cañons, Johnson, Cliff and Navajo.

One of the favorite camping places of the boys was in Johnson Cañon, a short distance from the river. Previous to this time only a few of the smaller buildings had been seen by white men. The Indians occupying this part of the Ute Reservation were not friendly and made it unpleasant for all who came into their country, so no one thought it worth while to explore the side cañons.

Richard and Al Wetherill and a few other cowboys were in this Camp a greater part of each winter, Al spending more time there than anyone else.

It was soon learned that up the cañon were several Cliff Houses much larger than any yet discovered, and Al more than anyone else explored them.

Through conversation I had with him and Richard, I became interested in their explorations, so as soon as I was able to do so I spent a few days in their Camp. This was during the winter of 1887-88. Al went with me and we visited the larger houses, and by scratching around in the rubbish we found several pieces of pottery and other articles used by the inhabitants. I also climbed around the cliffs alone and reached several small houses that had not been entered by white men.

On our return to the home ranch with the stuff we found, B. K. Wetherill, father of the boys, sent it to Mrs. Chain, wife of Mr. Chain, of Chain-Hardy & Co., Stationers & Booksellers, of Denver, Colo. Mrs. Chain had taken a short trip down the cañon and visited some of the Cliff Dwellings, and she was much interested in them.

In December 1888, Richard and I started out to explore. We followed the Indian trail down Chapin Mesa, between Cliff and Navajo Cañons, and camped at the head of

ANASAZI   323

a small branch of the Cliff Palace fork of Cliff Cañon. There is a spring of good water in this cañon just under the rim rock. On the smooth rock near our camp we found a series of concentric circles cut, which we supposed were meant to represent the sun, and we called it the Sun Rock, and the spring the Sun Rock Spring. We rode out to the point of the mesa in the angle between the Cliff Palace Cañon and the small fork on which was our camp, and saw the ruins that Prof. Fewkes excavated in 1915 and called the Sun Temple. From the rim of the cañon we had our first view of Cliff Palace just across the cañon from us. To me this is the grandest view of all among the ancient ruins of the Southwest. We rode around the head of the cañon and found a way down over the cliffs to the level of the building, where we spent several hours going from room to room and picked up several articles of interest, among them a stone axe with the handle still on it. There were several skeletons scattered about. A year or more before this Al had seen Cliff Palace, but did not enter it; he was on his way to camp after a long tramp on foot and was very tired. He was following the bottom of the cañon and only got a partial view so did not climb up, and so it remained for Richard and I to be the first to explore the building.

On this trip we also discovered the Spruce Tree House and what we called the Square Tower House, from a square structure, the tallest building we found standing. This has since been named the Peabody House in honor of Mrs. Peabody, who was instrumental in having Mesa Verde made a National Park. We also discovered several small houses. On our way home we came across the camp of some old friends, Charles McLoyd, Howard Graham and L. C. Patrick. They were much interested in what we had discovered and decided to go to the big house and try and make a collection of relics; John Wetherill went with them. As it was a long way around to get there with horses, they took what camp outfit they could carry and made their way up the cañon the best way they could. They only had provisions for three or four days, but before this was gone they had found as much stuff as they could carry out. Many of the rooms had only a few inches of rubbish in them, and it appeared as though the inhabitants had left everything they possessed right where they had used it last.

McLoyd and party camped with us for some time. We did some work in Johnson Cañon, also examined Spruce Tree and Peabody Houses but did not find much; we had not yet learned that much hard work was needed to get results.

Early in the spring the collection was taken to Durango and exhibited there; we had not expected that other people would be as much interested in the collection as we were; of course we learned our mistake.

Clayton Wetherill and I, having two or three weeks at our disposal, we went back to the cañon and made some good finds. Among these was the first mummy ever found in Cliff Houses. The mummy was that of a child a few months old. These mummies were not embalmed but they simply dried, from the corpse having been buried in ground so dry that complete decomposition did not take place. This was added to the other collection and taken to Denver, McLloyd being in charge; it was soon sold to the State Historical Society.

In December 1889 we started out to make another collection. This time we went at it in a more businesslike manner, as our previous work had been carried out [more] to satisfy our own curiosity than for any other purpose, but this time it was a business proposition. In no work I ever did were one's expectations so stimulated, something new and strange being uncovered every little while.

We left the Wetherill ranch, five of us consisting of Richard, Al, John and Clate Wetherill and myself. Win Wetherill, the youngest of the boys, was still at school and did not take part in the work until later.

We began work in the first Cliff House in Mancos Cañon. This house has only ten or twelve rooms in it, but it panned out well. A considerable portion of the cave is not occupied by buildings, and as is usual in such cases this space was used as a dump ground; all kinds of rubbish thrown out here — ashes, corncobs, husks, squash necks and rinds, worn out sandals and sweepings from the house; also much broken pottery and implements of bone and stone.

These rubbish heaps were found in the caves with all Cliff Houses and were used as hiding places for various articles apparently put there for safe keeping. This one proved to be a rich one and in a few days we were able to send a pack horse load of stuff back to the ranch. We found an unusual number of sandals and named it Sandal House. The sandals were made of yucca leaves torn into narrow strips and plaited into a mat the size and shape of the foot, and were held in place by a string over the foot. In cold weather corn husks and cedar bark were placed under these strings to keep the feet warm.

When Sandal House was worked out we moved farther down the cañon, and later up on the mesa north of Johnson Cañon near the head of a branch which we named Acowitz Cañon, after a Ute Indian who lived in Mancos Cañon.

Just under the rimrock at the head of this side cañon is a building to which we gave the name of Fortified House; some walls along the ledge on which the house is built were undoubtedly put there for defensive purposes. This house did not yield much until one day John found by measurement that there was space near the center of the building for a small room to which no entrance could be found, so he made one through the top. The room was small, not over five or six feet square, but in it were five skeletons, about a dozen pieces of pottery, several baskets, the finest we had ever seen, also a bow and a dozen arrows, all nearly perfect except the bow which was broken. The bow was the heaviest one we ever found and it was well wrapped with sinews. Part of the string remained; it was made of twisted sinews and was larger than a slate pencil and he who could draw one of those arrows to the head with such a bow must have been a powerful man. One of the skeletons was that of a large man [who] had been clothed in a suit of buckskin including a cap which was nearly perfect; the balance of the clothing had been badly damaged by rats. It was to him the bow probably belonged and he may have been a great warrior chief.

In the left hand fork of Johnson Cañon are several houses; the largest has about forty rooms. In a [kiva] in one of these houses were the skeletons of four people, a man and a woman; one was that of a child about twelve years old, and the other a child a few months old. The skulls of each of the three older people had been crushed in and between them was a stone axe, the blade of which just fitted the dent in the skulls. The bones of the skull of the child were scattered all over the room, so we could not tell in what manner it had been killed.

Beneath the floor of an open passageway is a small pit formed by a semi-circular wall, the arms of which were against the cliff which formed the other side of the pit, we found our second mummy, that of a woman. The face was not handsome but we called her "She"; we had been reading Rider Haggard's story "She," [so] we called the house She House.

After this we moved across the river and did some work at Cliff Palace, Spruce Tree House and Square Tower House. All of these houses had been named the year before. When these houses had been worked out to our satisfaction we were at the end as far as known houses were concerned, so we started out to explore and found several more buildings the first day. We worked these out and again found more houses which we worked out also. We continued in this way until all the branches of Navajo Cañon had been explored.

Beyond a certain point there is a change in the rock, a different stratum of sandstone comes to the surface and forms the cap of the mesa, which does not break into caves or cliffs that overhang, so there are no large Cliff Houses in that region. To the larger houses discovered by us that winter we gave the names of Spring House, Long House, Mug House, High House and the Step House. Of all these houses the one most remarkable for what we found in it was the Mug House, so named because of the four or five mugs found tied together with strings through their handles.

It appeared that the people had been frightened away with no opportunity to carry anything with them. All seemed to have been left just where it had been used last. No house on Mesa Verde yielded so much in proportion to size.

Spring came before we were able to excavate all of these buildings. We all had other work to do, and having made a splendid collection we decided to quit.

During the winter of 1890-91 no work was done in the Cliff Houses, but the following winter we were again on the job, enlarging our collection of two years previous, that had not yet been disposed of. Early in the spring of 1892 H. Jay Smith and C. D. Hazzard, of Minneapolis, bought the entire collection and placed it on exhibition at the World's Columbian Exhibition at Chicago. Mr. Smith and an artist from Minneapolis made extended trips with us through Mesa Verde and McElmo Cañon, the artist making colored sketches of the Cliff Houses and their surroundings.

On the Midway at the Chicago Fair a building was erected in imitation of the Battle Rock of McElmo Cañon. In this was shown a Cliff House all painted in true colors, and the collection was exhibited within. After the exposition closed the collection was taken to the University of Pennsylvania.

During the summer of 1891 the Wetherill boys made a collection for Gustav, son of Baron Nordenskjold, of Sweden; this collection is in the National Museum of Stockholm.

Nordenskjold also gave the world, in book form, one of the best descriptions of the Cliff Dwellings ever issued, with colored plates showing pottery, baskets and other articles.

During the year 1892 we made a collection for the State of Colorado to be used as part of the State exhibit at Chicago. This was done under the supervision of A. F. Wilmarth, of Denver, with D. W. Ayers of Durango and Richard Wetherill successively in charge of the field work.

In spite of the fact that all of the Cliff Dwellings had been worked over two or three times we succeeded in making a very good showing.

In our earlier work we seldom cleaned out a room that was filled deeply with rubbish; often the walls of one or more of the upper stories had fallen into the rooms below, filling them several feet deep with rock and mortar. This was almost invariably the case with the "estufas" or kivas. These are circular rooms below the surface of the ground, the roof being on the same level as the floor of the buildings around them, and were often nearly full of debris of fallen walls. At first we did not excavate any of these rooms as we could always find something easier, but they were well worth the labor required to clean them out. The "kiva" was the living room of the Cliff Dweller; there is always a fireplace in the center of the room, mats of rush and willows were on the floors, also tools of bone and stone were nearly always found, and the walls were always smoked.

The square rooms seldom have fireplaces in them. The State collection was the last we made in Mesa Verde; after the Fair it was brought back to Colorado and is now in the State Museum at Denver.

In making these collections we learned much of the Cliff Dwellers' life. They were agriculturists and raised crops of corn, beans and squashes, and kept tame turkeys. Their corn is a yellow dent with some red ears, not at all like the corn grown by the Navajos. Their beans are similar to the beans of the Mexicans; the squashes were of good size.

It is not certain where they did their farming, except in a few places. Almost every house has its turkey pen in which the birds were probably fastened at night. They also used the seed of lambs quarter and other wild plants for food, as the Navajos do today. Their clothing seems to have been limited to the feathered blanket and sandal, often with short skirt and breechcloth of cedar bark, and these probably were not worn in warm weather. They were no doubt successful hunters as most of their bone implements were made of deer bones; beads and many of their awls were made of turkey bones. Not much buckskin was found.

As to the antiquity of the Cliff Dwellings nothing definite can be said. The earliest Spanish explorers did not mention them, no scrap of writing, no article of metal or other material that would indicate the presence of white men were ever found in Mesa Verde. On a wall in Inscription House, in Northern Arizona, is what appears to have been a name and [the date] 1661, no doubt the year in which the inscription was made, and the building was a ruin at the time.

Only a few letters of the name are legible now. There can be but little doubt that none of the inhabitants remained at that time. This carries us back at least four hundred years. The buildings themselves where protected by the overhanging cliffs, do not show age; this is easily accounted for by a dry atmosphere and absolute protection from rain. Some front walls that are partly exposed are complete ruins. On these ruins trees as large as any in the vicinity are growing in a perfectly normal way, showing that but little change has taken place during their life. The spruce tree at Spruce Tree House was growing in the ruins of an outer wall. Nordenskjold counted 162 annual growth rings, showing that these walls were in ruins 200 years ago, so that there can be no doubt that the Cliff Dwellings have been unoccupied at least four hundred years and probably for a much longer time. Considerable as this period seems it was very short compared to the time the caves of Mesa Verde have been inhabited by human beings. The cave in which Spruce Tree House stands has probably been as long and continuously inhabited as any in this region. It is dry, well protected from wind, and near plenty of good water.

On the wall of one kiva sixteen coats of clay, which has been used as a white wash, with as many layers of black smoke, were counted; near this a hole six feet deep did not reach the bottom of ground made up almost entirely from the clay mortar of walls that had been torn down and the rock used for rejoists on which floors and roofs were laid had been wrenched out. These timbers are built into the walls and are difficult to remove; even the little willows on which the mud roofs and upper floors are laid, were carefully taken out. No plausible reason for this has been advanced except that it may have been used for fuel. Another strange circumstance is that so many of their valuable possessions were left in the rooms and covered with the clay of which the roofs and upper floors were made, not to mention many of the walls that were broken down in tearing out the timbers. It would seem that their intention was to conceal their valuables so that their enemies might not secure them; or perhaps the people were in such despair that property was not considered. There were many human bones scattered about as though several people had been killed and left unburied. Had Cliff Palace

328   RICHARD WETHERILL

been abandoned as has been suggested, and the timbers used in other buildings, all movable articles of value would have been taken away instead of being covered, and much of it broken and destroyed unnecessarily.

It seems to me that there can be no doubt that the Cliff Dwellers were exterminated by their more savage and warlike neighbors, the men being killed and the women perhaps adopted into the tribe of the conquerors, though in some instances migrations may have become necessary as a result of drouth or pressure from outside tribes.

(Signed)

JOHN WETHERILL
Kayenta, Arizona

CLAYTON WETHERILL
Creede, Colo.

B. A. WETHERILL
Manuelito, N. Mex.

W. WETHERILL
Ganado, Arizona

C. C. MASON
Hermit, Colo.

[The foregoing was written after the death of Richard Wetherill.]

APPENDIX B

[Two years after he and Charlie Mason found Cliff Palace, Richard Wetherill wrote to Prof. Frederic Ward Putnam, director of the Peabody Museum, Harvard University, seeking to interest him in the cliff dwellings of Mesa Verde, and inviting him to visit Mancos. The original copy of this letter is in the files of the Peabody Museum.]

Mancos, Montezuma Co. Col.
April 7th 1890

PROF. F. W. PUTNAM
Cambridge   Conn
DEAR SIR —

Through the kindness of Frederick W. Chapin, of the Hartford Archaeological Society, I received your address [but evidently Richard lost it before writing], and the request that I send you a short description of one of the Cliff houses, and a list of the relics found there. I also received a number of pamphlets from you, which I have not yet had time to study.

We recognize the fact, the principal scientific value of collections existed in the circumstances of their original position, or reference to the implements or objects with which they were associated, and we worked accordingly, with a view to throw as much light upon this subject as possible, we explored a great number of cliff houses in the Mancos Cañon and its tributaries.

We found in the first cliff house explored by us in the Mancos Cañon, where visitors and tourists have been going for the past fifteen years, that nearly everything of value had been overlooked, and during all this time a great amount of dirt and rock had been handled, back & forth.

This house is situated upon the West side of the Mancos River on the side of the mountain 150 feet above the river bottom. It has twelve rooms on the ground floor, was originally three stories high, a portion of the walls still standing above the first story, the walls of which are in a good state of preservation.

The rooms range in size from 3 x 6 to 10 x 12 feet. There is a circular room 21 feet in diameter, at the n.e. corner of the house which is plastered on the inside with mud mixed with cedar bark, and corn husks.

We found in this house a great number of sandals, bone implements, skeletons, feather cloth, matting, pottery, baskets, bands &c.

I think a visit to the Mancos Cañon would amply repay any one interested in prehistoric man.

In a single letter it is impossible to give even a faint outline of the extent of the ruins. We explored 182 houses and 250 miles of cliffs, and have secured the largest and most interesting collection of Cliff dweller relics in the world.

Hoping to see you in our beautiful valley during the present season I am

Very truly yours

Richard Wetherill

APPENDIX C

[With experience, Richard Wetherill gained in knowledge. The following description of Basket Maker remains found in the Grand Gulch region, appeared in the Collectors' Department of The Archaeologist magazine, May issue, 1894. The article is unsigned but most probably was written by Richard after his winter 1893-94 expedition.]

In the region of Southern Utah, famed for its cliff houses, and valley and Mesa ruins, we have recently made interesting discoveries, which would tend to prove the existence of an earlier tribe of Indians than those formerly occupying the cliff houses.

One special cliff house, beneath which we found these evidences of early occupation, consists of two rooms on the ground floor, and two more on the ledge above. The walls are only a few inches in thickness, and the construction is inferior to those found in the Mancos Cañon. We found nothing in the rooms. The relics uncovered in the loose debris on the outside, were readily distinguished from the relics of the earlier tribe.

Two feet below the lowest remains of the Cliff Dwellers, we have found remains of quite a different tribe.

This difference is determined by the shape of the head, which is natural, long-headed or dolichocephalous. The Cliff Dwellers, as we find them, have a perpendicular flattening at the back of the head, making it artificially brachycephalous. We have taken ninety-two skeletons from the cave at depths varying from four and a half to seven feet, including three cliff dwellers lying at a depth of from two to three feet. In the central portion of the cave the skeletons were lying close enough to touch each other.

The first excavation penetrated three feet of loose debris and waste from the still existing cliff houses. Their foundation walls are not less than three feet above many of the skeletons. The lower four feet in which we have worked is clean, yellow sand, except where discolored by burials. There are a few indications that the bodies found were buried in wrappings of feather, rabbit fur and buckskin; near them are baskets, spear points, bone awls and ornaments, but no pottery.

The number of skeletons found at one level and in one place would suggest a sudden and violent destruction of a community by battle or massacre. Many of the skulls are broken, as well as the ribs, and the bones of the arms and legs. In the backbones of two different skeletons we found the ends of spear points imbedded; in one case the break in the bone was partially healed, showing that the person must have lived for some time after the wound was inflicted.

This is, by far, one of the most interesting collection[s] of human remains of a single tribe yet found in America. Each skeleton, carefully studied, reveals the manner of death. We found one interesting group, a mother with an infant on each arm, and another lying on her breast with its head under her chin. There are warriors, "mighty men of valor," with ten or twelve spear points lying near; younger men with bone tools near them, and the unwarlike counsellors or priests, with decaying baskets originally filled with food, or possibly tools of trade. These latter have left little trace save a dark stain in the sand.

A careful record has been made of the work, and photographs taken of the better preserved groups and skeletons. Negatives have been developed on the spot, so that there should be a certainty of success.

Later there will be more to tell of this important discovery.

APPENDIX D

[Richard Wetherill wrote a series of articles for The Mancos Times *during his long trip with the Palmer family in 1895-96. The following, printed March 20, 1896, is one of them, and describes Montezuma's Castle in Arizona.]*

To-day I visited the old Cliff Dwelling, known as "Montezuma Castle." It is on the north side of Beaver Creek and nearly three miles from the old fort, and is the one so graphically described by Charles Lumis. [Charles F. Lummis, the author. The error in spelling may have been Muldoon Kelley's.]

The cave in which the ruin is found is a small one, being not more than 70 feet long, 50 feet high and 20 or 30 feet deep. The house is a tier of rooms five stories high, and reached at the present time by ladders placed at convenient points on the face of the cliff by some enquiring investigator.

The lower tier of rooms are small and unconnected, dug out of the solid cliff, with the fronts walled up, as are the cave dwellings of the lower Mancos.

The second tier consists of but two small rooms, side by side, through which we have to ascend to reach the next, or third, floor.

This one has six small, rectangular rooms, except the west one, which was used as an estufa. In this room is a fireplace, in which the household baking was done. This is at the west side of the room and not in the center, as we usually find them. The smoke escaped through a small hole in the wall next to the cliff. At the east end of this tier of rooms is a small ledge 25 feet long and 4 or 5 feet wide. It adjoins the row of rooms, and over it all have to pass to ascend to the rooms above. In this small space I found, after a few minutes' work, the remains of at least half a dozen children, one of which is a very fair mummy. All of these, except the mummy, were in a promiscuous mass and nothing with them. The mummy was the lower burial, and it rested in a very small excavation next to the rock on the floor of the cave. It was laid straight out; head to the east; face up; hands at its sides.

A bowl was found at the left of the head, and a small bow and arrows were lying lengthwise at the right side. The body is wrapped in cotton cloth, which is still in a state of good preservation. The grave was covered with small, round sticks placed three or four inches apart, and parallel with each other, supporting a rush mat which had been spread over the grave. Over all this was about 2 feet of debris, among which was found so many other remains.

The fourth floor contained eight rooms similar to those below. The roofs of these rooms are in good condition. The longer floor joists are supported by timbers or posts set in the middle of the rooms. The doors are all of an irregular shape, being nearly a foot wider at the top than at the bottom.

The fifth floor contains four small rooms, connected by doorways. The roofs and floors of these rooms are in good condition. There are no loopholes from these rooms looking out, and but one outside opening.

The sixth, or upper, floor is a cave 60 feet long, the front of which has a parapet three and a half feet high, extending almost the entire length of it. There are two large rooms in the rear of this part, one of which contains a great amount of debris, which cannot be moved unless something could be contrived to settle the dust.

In the front of these rooms is a space about 6 feet wide in which there is about a foot of debris, containing all such things as the Cliff Dwellers used in their work, but covered by sweepings from these rooms. Many loopholes are in these upper walls, covering all approaches to the river below.

I am highly elated at my success in finding relics here where so many have visited, and in a ruin that has always had especial mention made of it in works upon this deeply interesting subject.

I have finished the work of to-day, and if I meet with further success tomorrow, the report will be sent in.

APPENDIX E

[In the May, 1897, issue of The Antiquarian, *editor J. F. Snyder wrote that two friends who some years previously had visited Mesa Verde with Richard Wetherill as guide, had given him a collection of objects taken from one of the cliff dwellings. Among these objects was a flat implement of sandstone shaped carefully in the form of a sandal. At first, Snyder wrote, he could not determine what it was, later discovered it was a sandal last. This brought the following letter from Richard, printed in the September issue.]*

The Sandal Last, the subject of your article in the May number of *The Antiquarian,* is still to me the same mysterious thing it was when the one in your possession was found some years ago.

A great many have been found since that time, and the most careful student has been unable to find any use for them other than you mention in your article. Baron Nordenskiold had a fine specimen, which is now in the Academy of Science at Stockholm. The Hyde Collection in the American Museum of [Natural] History in New York contains several fine specimens. The state collection of Colorado, in the Capitol building at Denver, contains several, one of which is of very fine white stone.

Those in the collection at the University of Pennsylvania vary in size considerably, one of them being 16 inches long and 8 or 9 inches wide, if I remember correctly; and one just found here, made from a piece of pottery, is two inches long by one and a quarter wide, and five-sixteenths of an inch thick.

It was found on the floor of one of the excavated rooms among broken pottery, but not in connection with anything to determine its use. Many of them have been found here (Chaco Cañon, N. M.); also in Marsh Pass, Arizona; Grand Gulch and Allen Cañon, Utah, and in many of the Cliff Houses of Montezuma county, Colorado, both in the Cliff Dwelling and Valley Ruins, and in no case have we found the sandal and this stone in connection in any way. And yet that is the only probable use we can find for them.

Sandals have been found in great numbers partially completed, from fine threads of yucca to the whole leaf, and all seemed to be worked off-hand. Those made of fine thread and unfinished have been found with the loose ends tied in a bunch to keep from tangling until time could be had to complete them. The coarser kinds merely had the ends sticking out at all angles. In all cases the toe was made first.

I refer here only to the sandal of the Cliff and Mesa Dwellers, as the Basket-Maker made a round and a square-toed sandal with the same material, but without the offset at the little toe, specimens of which can be seen in great variety in the University of Pennsylvania collection and in the American Museum at New York City. We have in our Museum at the Ranch hundreds of specimens of the sandals, and several of the sandal-shaped stones from Arizona and from no particular place about the various ruins in which they were found. We hope to establish beyond a doubt the use of these queer implements, and when it is done we shall be glad to make it known.

RICHARD WETHERILL

MANCOS, COLORADO.

APPENDIX F

CHACO BURIALS

The 302 burials found in Chaco Canyon are too few to provide all-reaching answers to the question of funerary customs in that region — and yet enough to permit certain conclusions.

The oldest burials found in the Chaco (at Frank H. H. Roberts' Shabik'eshchee Village and Gordon Vivian's Three-C site) may be representative of the canyon for the respective occupation periods of those sites: Basketmaker III and Pueblo I. Between the two are some similarities; both indicate funerary customs different from later periods in the Chaco.

At Shabik'eshchee (14 burials), Roberts found 12 skeletons lying partially on the left side, head to the west and facing north, with knees drawn up in flexed position. The other two burials also were flexed, one with the head to the north facing west, the other with head to the east. Choice of grave sites apparently was haphazard. According to Roberts (1929, p. 149), "The village had no definite cemetery. The dead were interred wherever it was found convenient to scoop out a shallow grave." Seven were found near outdoor firepits. All had undeformed skulls characteristic of the Basketmaker, and funerary offerings (which once may have included baskets or other perishable objects) amounted to only a few pieces of pottery found in three of the village's latest graves.

Skeletons of 11 adults and 5 children were found by Vivian at the Three-C site. One of the adult skeletons was found fully extended on its back, arms extended at the sides, covered with a stone slab and interred below the floor of a room. All of the other burials were found in the small village's refuse mound, 9 in flexed position, the remainder in such "extremely poor" condition as to make identification doubtful. The poor state of preservation may have been due to the fact the burials were within a few inches to two feet below ground surface.

Excavation in or near four large dwelling sites north of the Chaco Wash (Pueblo Bonito, Pueblo del Arroyo, Chetro Ketl and Kin Kletso) has resulted in the finding of 127 burials. All but one or two of these were found either in abandoned rooms or beneath the floor of rooms that for some time after continued in use. The majority of undisturbed (see below) burials were in extended position, on back or side, and usually accompanied by comparatively rich offerings of pottery, baskets or jewelry.

On the south side of the wash opposite Pueblo Bonito, two dissimilar methods of interment were discovered: placing the graves within the limits of the small village sites (in rooms or refuse mounds), or dissociating them from the villages in what may be referred to as small cemeteries. Again, most of the village burials were found in rooms, but usually in flexed position on back or side, with the knees partially or fully drawn back to the chest. The second type, which as yet has not been reported on the north side of the canyon, was discovered by Richard Wetherill in 1895 and more fully explored by him and George H. Pepper the next year, when 30 such burials were found. These graves were shallow, all were within a few inches to not more than four feet from the ground surface, and extended in groups from the level area north of Casa Rinconada to the west slope of the Gap. Here, as elsewhere on the south side of the canyon, the majority of burials were in flexed position and usually accompanied by not more than one or two pieces of pottery, most often placed near the head. In only a few cases was jewelry found with the dead.

During the 1936 excavation at Bc-50 and Bc-51, two small house sites on the south

ANASAZI 335

side of the canyon, 16 burials were found by the University of New Mexico. Five were flexed, 2 extended, 9 disturbed, and all but 1 were found in rooms. Commenting upon these, Donovan Senter (1937, p. 144), said: "On the basis of what is known concerning Chaco burials at present, we can conclude that adult bodies were usually flexed but frequently extended for inhumation in open cemeteries or in room fills, and that occasionally they were placed along the talus slopes or in a refuse mound. Infants were frequently buried extended, although the number observed is too small to indicate what the general custom may have been."

These conclusions may be modified in light of more recent data. Present evidence indicates that flexed burials were most common to the early periods of Chaco history (Basketmaker III through Pueblo II), that extended burials are of a later period, perhaps beginning some time in Pueblo II and extending through the classic period of Pueblo III. There is very little evidence to support the conclusion that position of burial — flexed or extended — was determined, ever, by the age of the deceased; evidence instead indicates that adults and children alike, of both sexes, were buried in the prescribed or accepted position of the time — and regardless, too, of whether burial was in room fill, refuse mound, or small group cemetery.

Differences in burial customs between the villages north and south of the Chaco Wash are only emphasized by the fact both sides of the canyon were inhabited during the same period of time. Pueblo Bonito, which may or may not serve as an example for the other great communal dwellings on the north side, was developing from a pithouse village and then as a unit-type pueblo of some 20 or 30 rooms about the time neighbors across the river were building the Bc villages in the vicinity of Casa Rinconada. Bonito continued to expand greatly, but the Bc villages — for reasons not yet determined — reached 20 or 25 rooms and then ceased to be enlarged.

Most of the burials found in Pueblo Bonito (65 out of a total of 91) were so badly molested and scattered about that identification of the original burial position was impossible. Of the 18 found by the Hyde Expedition, 15 had been molested, 2 were buried in extended position, and 1 in flexed position. The National Geographic Society expedition found 72 burials, Neil M. Judd reporting (1954, p. 335) that "the prescribed burial position . . . appears to have been on the back, full length and head east. Of the 22 undisturbed skeletons in the Society's four burial rooms, at least 15 occupied this position. . . . Only 3 of the 22 were flexed and then but partially."

Judd believed the graves were made at a very late period of Bonito's occupation and the molestation of burials was "the work of plunderers" who dug up the graves for loot soon after the bodies were interred — in two instances "while flesh and ligaments still held joints together." (Ibid., pp. 325-342.)

This supposition, with inference that Pueblo Bonito harbored grave robbers on the eve of its abandonment, is discounted by Vivian. "It seems to me," he wrote the author in May, 1956, "that there are a lot of disturbed burials around the Southwest but I can't recall anyone else ascribing this condition to prehistoric grave robbers. . . . I expect [the Bonitoans] were too busy trying to catch a rabbit or two to do any digging . . . I cannot agree with Judd that the room burials at Bonito represent the last hastily interred defenders of the place. I think they had been there a long time. (They may or may not have been important individuals.) There are several reasons for this line of thought.

"One is the pottery. While Judd recovered a lot of pottery with the burials he does not . . . say which pots came from which burials. (Thus 17 bowls with 23 burials in room 330 and 62 bowls with 11 burials in room 326 and so forth.) As far as I can tell from just pictures this pottery with the burials was not all late pottery. Some of it could well have been made 200 years before the last defenders were out there on the ramparts dearly selling their lives . . . No — those pots were put in there with burials shortly after the pots were made and the burials represent almost the entire range of Pueblo Bonito history.

"Another item is burial habits of Pueblo Indians. In very many instances in areas where there are a lot of burials, earlier burials were often disturbed in making later interments. These disturbed burials were either just pushed aside or were gathered up and reburied somewhere else and you have then secondary burials. . . . Bonito was occupied for around 300 years. Burials were made in some open [abandoned] rooms. . . . Time went by. The individuals were forgotten, fifty or seventy-five years after a burial was made another burial or group of burials were made in the same room. The earlier one was disturbed in making these later burials. . . ."

Frank Roberts added another comment on funerary pottery found with burials at Pueblo Bonito, in a letter to the author in January, 1957: "There is a possibility that in a few of the burials the accompanying pots may have been heirlooms which had been kept by the family and actually were not made shortly before the death of the individual. Elsewhere in the Southwest I found burials accompanied by several types of pots which definitely represented different periods and in my mind there is no question that the older ones represented vessels which had been in the family for a long time, perhaps had even been handed down through several generations. Such a thing could easily have happened in a few instances in the Chaco Canyon."

One comparison of burial customs at Pueblo Bonito and the neighboring small sites on the south side of the canyon shows a surprising numerical difference. At four small villages on the south side (Bc-50-51-53-59), which combined had about one-sixth the number of rooms as Pueblo Bonito (and by the same measure, one-sixth of the population), 105 burials have been found — 6 more than found in Bonito.

Vivian, in the same letter quoted above, said that where intramural burials do show up in the Bc sites, there is a "trend" — but to a lesser extent — to intramural burial customs in Pueblo Bonito: i.e., burials extended rather than flexed, and also disturbed. "A large part of the Bc-50-51 burials were in rooms. Almost all of the Bc-59 burials [46] were out in the refuse. But — these burials in the refuse were comparatively early. Is it possible that the later inhabitants of Bc-59 were buried in abandoned rooms in Bc-50-51? . . . There is just no way to tell how many burials were made in the refuse of Bc-50-51 and from this what percentage of the total [37], most of them in rooms, represent. However it is certain that of all the burials that must have been made somewhere, those that have been found represent but a very small proportion. Is it possible that these few room burials represent important or otherwise divergent individuals?"

Probing the drifted sand for every square yard of a canyon 18 miles long obviously would be an impossible task. Yet attempts have been made to find in the Chaco cemeteries of the unfound thousands of Chaco dead. Judd once dug three trenches near the cliff between Bonito and Chetro Ketl in hope of finding such a cemetery. His efforts, as Richard Wetherill's in the excavation of Bonito's two vast refuse mounds, produced nothing in the way of human remains. In August, 1936, Edgar L. Hewett of the University of New Mexico had Navajos dig a trench on the south side of Chetro Ketl — 50 feet long and 18 feet deep for most of its length. Again: nothing.

Roberts, in a letter to the author on the subject, said: "What was done with all of the people from the large houses in the canyon who undoubtedly died during their occupation is indeed a puzzling question. Somewhere in the area there must be extensive cemeteries." He added this comment on his own research in the Chaco, hitherto unpublished, that merely heightens the mystery:

"While I was working with the Pueblo Bonito expedition [National Geographic Society] in the summer of 1926, I dug a small house ruin nine miles east of Pueblo Bonito on the south side of the arroyo. It was located at the mouth of a tributary canyon which so far as I know did not have a name. Beneath the paved floor of one of the rooms in the structure we found the remains of five individuals ranging from about 10 to 18 years of age. The bones were in a jumbled mass and many of them showed the effects of fire. Most of the long bones had been split and the marrow removed while the skulls were broken into several pieces and were cupped. Whether they represented the remains of ceremonial cannibalism or of human sacrifice is a question. Your explanation would be as good as mine."

One other instance of cannibalism or sacrificial cremation in the Chaco has been reported. Pepper (1920, p. 378) told of this discovery of the Hyde Exploring Expedition: "During the period of our work in Pueblo Bonito some of our Navajo workmen cleaned out a number of rooms in Penasco Blanco and in one of these a great many human bones were found. Some of these, including portions of the skull, were charred, and the majority of the long bones had been cracked open and presented the same appearance as do the animal bones that have been treated in a similar way for the extraction of the marrow. It would therefore seem that these Pueblo Indians, either through stress of hunger or for religious reasons, had occasionally resorted to the eating of human flesh."

Very little excavation is being done in Chaco Canyon at the present time, and no major research is contemplated for the future. For this reason it is entirely possible that the absorbing mystery of where the great numbers of Chaco dead lie buried may always remain a mystery.

In the table following, which does not take into consideration some few fragmentary discoveries, or the unknown and unreported efforts of early pothunters, the location of known burials in the Chaco to date is given — with some analysis by the discoverers.

BURIALS FOUND IN CHACO CANYON, NEW MEXICO

From 1895 to 1956, and as reported by those who discovered them

Discoverer and Date	Site	Age & Sex	Total Found	Position Flexed	Position Extended	Disturbed	Room Burial	Other Location	Not Described
Col. D. K. B. Sellers "late 1890's"	Pueblo Bonito	Adult Female	1	-	-	Part of "mummified" body	1	-	-
Hyde Exploring Expedition 1896-1900	Pueblo Bonito	2 Ad. Males	18	1	2	15	18	-	3
Natl. Geog. Society 1921-27 Judd et al.	Pueblo Bonito	38 Ad. Fem., 15 Ad. Males, 19 Ch.	72	3	"at least 15"	50	72	-	3
Natl. Geog. Society 1921-27	Pueblo del Arroyo	-	15	-	-	-	-	-	15
Ripley P. Bullen 1941	Bc-54 (in rincon e. of Chetro Ketl)	1 Ch. Bet. 6 & 10	1	1	-	-	-	in refuse	-
Natl. Park Service Gordon Vivian 1949	New Head-quarters Site	1 Ad.	1	1	-	-	1	-	-
Natl. Park Service Gordon Vivian 1949	Pueblo del Arroyo	1 Ad. Male	1	-	-	1	1	-	-
Natl. Park Service Gordon Vivian 1951-52	Kin Kletso	-	7	-	-	-	-	-	7
E. L. Hewett & UNM students "before 1936"	Nr. Una Vida & Chetro Ketl	-	12	2	"a few"	-	10	1, refuse mound, C.K.; 1 under boulder nr. Una Vida	12
Totals		39 Ad. Fem., 18 Ad. Males, 20 Ch.	128	8	17+	66	103	2	

RICHARD WETHERILL

BURIALS FOUND IN CHACO CANYON, NEW MEXICO
From 1895 to 1956, and as reported by those who discovered them

Discoverer and Date	Site	Age & Sex	Total Found	Position Flexed	Position Extended	Disturbed	Room Burial	Other Location	Not Described
Richard Wetherill 1895	West side of the Gap	-	1	-	-	-	-	Small "group" cemetery	1
Hyde Exploring Expedition 1896-1900	Vic. Casa Rinconada & the Gap	14 Ch. (?) 6 Ad.	30	15	7	7	-	Small "group" cemetery	1
Frank H. H. Roberts, Jr. 1926	Knoll west of Shabik'-eshchee	-	1	-	-	-	-	-	1
Frank H. H. Roberts, Jr. 1926	Sm. house site 9 mi. east of Bonito	Bet. 10 & 18 Yrs.	5	-	-	5 (bones burned & broken)	5	-	-
Frank H. H. Roberts, Jr. 1927	Shabik'-eshchee Village	-	14	14	-	-	2 (?)	12 (?)	-
Frank H. H. Roberts, Jr. 1940	Bc-53	5 Ch. 5 Ad.	10	7	-	3	9	1, in refuse mound	-
Univ. of N.M. Senter et al. 1936	Bc-50	8 Ch. 4 Ad.	12	3	2	7	11	1, in trench	-
Univ. of N.M. Senter et al. 1936	Bc-51	1 Ch. 3 Ad.	4	2	-	2	4	-	-
Univ. of N.M. Senter, Kluckhohn. 1937	Bc-51	4 Ch. 2 Ad.	20	8	6	6	19	1, in trench	-
Natl. Park Service Gordon Vivian 1939	Three-C site	11 Ad. 5 Ch.	16	9	1	3	1	15, in refuse	-
Natl. Park Service Gordon Vivian 1950	Bc-59	10 Ad. F., 6 Ad. M., 16 Ch., 2 (?)	34	18	-	8	2	31, in refuse 1, in kiva	-

ANASAZI

BURIALS FOUND IN CHACO CANYON, NEW MEXICO
From 1895 to 1956, and as reported by those who discovered them

SOUTH SIDE OF CANYON

Discoverer and Date	Site	Age & Sex	Total Found	Position Flexed	Position Extended	Disturbed	Room Burial	Other Location	Not Described
Natl. Park Service Gordon Vivian 1950	Bc-51	Young Adult (?)	1	1	-	-	1	-	-
Univ. of N.M. Bertha Dutton 1934 & 1936	Leyit Kin	1 Ch.	1	-	1	-	1	-	-
Univ. of N.M. Tom Mathews 1947	Bc-59	-	12	-	-	-	-	-	-
Paul Reiter & UNM students. 1941	Bc-53	7 Ad. F., 1 Ad. M. 3 Ch.	12	6	2	3	10	2 (?), in refuse	1
E. L. Hewett & UNM students, "before 1936"	Nr. Casa Rinconada	-	1 (?)	-	-	-	-	-	1 (?)
TOTALS		62 Ch. 56 Ad.	174	83	19	44	65	95	

RICHARD WETHERILL

APPENDIX G

[Richard Wetherill's sincere affection for Julia Cowing followed closely and perhaps as a reaction to a one-sided, frustrating attachment he formed for Marcia Lorraine Billings, a Denver girl whose brother Wirt later joined Richard in the first Grand Gulch expedition. This I learned in 1963 from Mrs. William M. Tanner, of Cambridge, Massachusetts, who described Marcia, her aunt, as "a vivacious person, with gold-red hair and very blue eyes – a flirt."

Marcia and a younger sister, Anna Elizabeth (Mrs. Tanner's mother), had gone from Denver to see relatives in Durango in the summer of 1890, and there were persuaded, because the town "was buzzing with talk about the old cliff dwellings that Dick Wetherill had discovered in Mesa Verde," to visit the Wetherill ranch at Mancos. Mrs. Tanner has allowed me to use four letters Richard subsequently wrote to Marcia, and also gave her permission to quote from an unpublished manuscript relating the experiences of that summer as later told to her by her mother. From the latter, the following excerpts are taken.]

Nothing would do but for Marcia and me to go to the Wetherill ranch and find out what all the excitement was about.

We had a long, hot, dusty ride — awful long. Thirty miles or more. . . . The Wetherill ranch looked mighty good to us, I can tell you . . . the Wetherills were Pennsylvania Quakers, and their ranch looked the sort of ranch that Pennsylvania Quakers would fix for themselves ... large barns and corrals, all well-built and well-kept.

I can't remember how long Marcia and I stayed ... but it was weeks. It was just about the high spot of my life.

There wasn't anything I wouldn't try in those days. At first Dick and Al Wetherill brought around their gentle horses for us to ride.... Before we left, I was riding everything they had ...

Mrs. Wetherill took Marcia and me aside and told us that going to the cliff dwellings would be a two-day trip on horseback. She told us that if we were possessed to go, we would be going alone with Dick and Al. "If I didn't know my boys so well," she said, "I never would permit this, but you'll be perfectly safe. My boys are good boys."

Marcia and I were not quite the first white women ever to visit Mesa Verde. There had been at least one other, a school teacher. I know, because I was given her dress to wear. It was made of mattress ticking. It had to be tough to go where I was going.

As we rode along, I couldn't see any trail, but the boys knew the way. They did the cooking. We had bacon, hot bread, and coffee ...

We slept on the ground, all four together, each wrapped up in a blanket. Dick and Al were on the outside to sort of guard us from snakes and such. We slept with our heads under a sort of little tent — just a piece of stretched canvas like. There was one for each couple. Dick was on Marcia's side. He must have been right pleased having her head so close to his for that one time. He would have liked to have had Marcia stay down on the Mancos, but Marcia wasn't cut out for a rancher's wife. For a long time after we left the Mancos, Dick used to write her. When my brother Wirt went to live with the Wetherills, Dick talked to Wirt quite a bit about Marcia.

Al was on my side. You might almost say that I slept with a man before I married your father.

The cliff dwellings looked like something in a dream, but it was more like a nightmare getting into them ... we had no ladders, only ropes. I went down with a rope under my arms. The boys lowered me. I was pulled up the same way. It seems to me that the boys just climbed up and down those ropes, bracing their feet against the cliff when they could. ... The rooms had a good many things in them in those days. They weren't really empty, but they *felt* empty.

[The publication of love letters, no matter how humble or how ardent or how long-deceased the writer, always to me has seemed an invasion of privacy — excusable only if, by being so exposed to public curiosity, they provide some deeper understanding or appreciation of the person who wrote them. Marcia Billings was twenty-four years old when she met Richard Wetherill and he was thirty-two. If the poetry and fire of a Cyrano tormented his being, they certainly found no release from his pen; his phrases came awkwardly, haltingly, stumbling with classic entreaty of the lover liked but not favored. Doomed he was and knew it. Five years more and the vivacious Marcia would marry Benjamin Prosser Thomas, a man of successful mercantile and mining interests. Read alone, these letters should reveal much about Richard Wetherill; if compared with his other letters relating to his work, they might reveal more. They follow here, just as they were written, found long afterward in a Massachusetts attic.]

RICHARD WETHERILL

My Dearest Marcia

What I told you was the truth, but I aimed to tell it in such a way that it could be taken either as a joke or the truth. At the same time I did not dare to hope that my hopes could ever be realized. So I have been trying to quelch all feelings in this matter, as my position and circumstances are such at the present time, that to engage myself to one in your position, would only be dragging you down instead of being on an equal footing and perhaps be a continual mortification to yourself as well as freinds. At the same time I see no wrong to either You or myself in having a kindlier feeling for you than mere freindship provided I do not air it before the world. Although love is nothing to be ashamed of, if it is the proper kind It is rather something to be proud of.

I don't see how I can see you at Your freinds. As at the present time I havn't a presentable suit and to go among Your freinds as I now am would certainly put a veto on the whole thing

I want you to be sure of one thing and that is, that when I am with you I do not want you to have any cause to blush for me on account of appearance or manners. Stage is coming —

I am sincerely Yours

Richard Wetherill

My Dear Marcia:

I received Your kind, but cold hearted letter last evening, and it has taken me all this time to get its full import. Tis' kind in allowing me to write to you at all, and cruel in dropping me so hard and suddenly. You forgive and excuse me in words but not in actions. Now my dear girl I will not take a dismissal in any such haste For I know that you are not so fickle minded as that. For if you ever had any regard for me at all it will be all the stronger for just such a test as the Durango Episode as you name it. As for myself I am unchangable in respect to my regard for you. And as for writing to G. S. never did so except what you had seen. She is a notorious [here an expressive row of circles, twice underscored] Any one is my kind that can be a Lady or a Gentleman at any and all times let their station be what it will high or low. I recognize no caste or set as a matter of Policy almost every one has a set the higher the better: but that is merely from the greater amount of favors that can be confered upon each other by the higher and richer class. Yet to be anything one needs a certain

ANASAZI   **345**

amount of respectability. As you say Clothes do not make the man But a man without clothes had better stay at home. Of course I feel nothing but regret at not seeing you in Durango. that can't be helped now.

You need have no fear of the Boys in regard to happenings here — even if you were my worst enemy and I had given my word as I have to you to keep mum that is what I would do tis' my nature I am sorry we made the trip on your account in the manner that we did, But we have the knowledge of doing right at any rate. [He refers to their trip that summer to the ruins.] I have never heard a word and have been in D[urango] since you left.

I will tell you now that if my finances were in proper shape I would be right there with You and I would show you what kind of stuff I am made of. Of course I had made up my mind a long time ago never to buy a girl but I would in Your case, what I mean is this by giving her full time and attention, bouquets Parties theaters &c — I wanted to save all that until later, because if I went in so heavily in the start I could not keep it up and there would commence the trials and troubles of life.

In my case it would not be quite so bad as I am of the age when I could get along anyway. I had also made up [my] mind to allow the Lady to declare herself But could not in Your case, But how much better would it have been for me had I done so I would not now have had this feeling of utter loneliness that I now have as if in a whole world full of people and I set apart without a freind or confident and see my brightest hopes shattered as if a mere nothing. But then again I think that Your letter was written at [a] time when You were worn out in mind and body, and that You would have written differently had You felt better. Now I do not aim to influence You by anything I have written, but tell You my feelings, For I beleive You are the one to Act if you are to have a happy future. And if You think I compare favorably with other men — Well and good, If not let this be the Finis upon this subject — I will await an answer in a most anxious frame of mind —

Clate wished me to enclose a clipping   will do so later

Do not allow anything you may have written me, to influence You one way or the other

For I have destroyed everything lest it should fall into the hands [of] S. outfit they pry into everything

And now my dear child I hope you will not have so much disbelief in man — ?

I remain sincerely Yours

RICHARD WETHERILL

MANCOS.

Remember me to Anna. Al hasn't rec'd her letter yet as he is in Durango —

DEAREST MARCIA:

I received Your letter a few minutes ago   Aunt Martha was in here at the time she knew who it was from without [my] telling and *smole* a knowing smile. But I was amazed to have you tell me you were only reading my letter at that late day   I suppose though you have so many that mine have to take their turn and Your correspondents are so numerous that it keeps you so busy reading their letters that you would have no time to answer more than every other one   You must feel greatly flattered to have such an immense number of admirers & lovers

You know very well that if I had realized that You would have left Denver before I did I should have kept Your photograph here and I think of sending for it anyway and would have done so long ago but there has been one here that I could see daily but I havn't seen it for a week and so you can imagine how I feel   No business to occupy my time and you so far away I could not help but think of you and your many kindnesses to me –

There has been no business owing to the mud   This is the worst town I ever was in. Crowds of men stand on the street corners watching the ladies cross the streets through the mud – Men to judge by their appearance one would mistake for Gentlemen – or if they are their opportunities have been limited and [they] are hypnotized with what the[y] see

I wouldn't live in this muddy hole for anything for I imagine there will be more sickness here in the Spring than ever was known before – Papa B [Benjamin Kite Wetherill] is still unwell but improving   I want to see him this afternoon if I can get through the mud   I will give it a trial anyway

There has been no Street Cars running for two days so you can imagine what the travel is like –

The Photos have not arrived from Chapiro [Shapiro?] yet.

But if they do not I will be taking a good many this summer and can give you all you want   But don't count on them until you see them – I have my doubts about your getting out here so soon but should you come before I leave you know how delighted I would be   But I hope to get away the last of next week   that will give you time to write me one more letter

But in the event of my not seeing you here – do or have you any Idea of coming to the Mancos   I havn't had the thought hardly that you would condescend to visit us there as you said you were so much in love with Denver

But I know you take all the enjoyment out of life that you can wherever you are and that is so different from City life there would be another kind of enjoyment and we would do what little we could. You must have your mother come at the same time and see what kind of people you had fallen in with. We are expecting a very busy season and count on all hands being kept busy –

ANASAZI   347

I will answer your questions when I find out who they were   I don't know the names myself — We have been down to the Assembly hall every day trying to work our Bill through and are now certain of success   should it fail will trade the collection for lots in Highlands and what money we can get

I have also made a sale or received a proposition for an Indian Collection and have found out many things that will help us to develop the resources of our country and when I go down and investigate I may have something to propose to you that will help you financially if you care to take it up   But don't ask me what it is now for if it proves to be anything will let you know in good season   Can't tell what a day may bring forth as one is continually learning something new and if put to use the knowledge thus gained should develop into something. I have a good many schemes on foot and they all bid fair to become something tangible. But doing business by mail is not as satisfactory to me as I should wish   It is a good deal like our [the remainder of the letter is missing].

[undated, but probably fall or winter, 1891]

My Dear Girl:

If you only knew with what feelings of Love and affection that I now have for You, You would not accuse me of being frigid. My heart is filled to overflowing with Love for You but I do not allow it to bubble over principally through will power. My natural impulse is to take you in my arms and hug and smother You almost with kisses   But from the course I have pursued heretofore I dare not and neither have you given me the right. Happily I have a conscience left, and I hope to profit even by the experience that I have had with You and in the future stick strictly to the truth. God forbid that my Dearest and best Freind should have cause to call me a liar   You little know how it cut but I accept it as just punishment for I acknowledge that I had told you many — I don't mean from this that You expect the truth as your intercourse with the world you have discovered that Lying is more Common than anything else — But I in my limited sphere even have found the truth to be the thing that will of itself raise one up in the estimation of his fellows —

Inclosed find Tally sheet of Cattle sent up by Clate —

Mrs Chapman of Durango was just in   She is stopping at the Windsor and will be there tomorrow.

Sincerely Yours in thought
Richard Wetherill

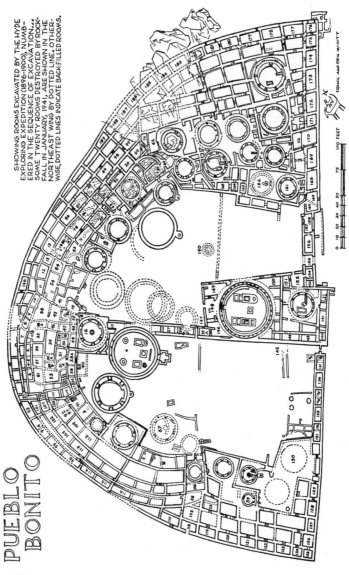

PUEBLO BONITO

SHOWING ROOMS EXCAVATED BY THE HYDE
EXPLORING EXPEDITION (1896-1900), NUMB-
ERED IN THE SEQUENCE OF EXCAVATION...
SOME TWENTY ROOMS DESTROYED BY ROCK-
FALL IN JANUARY, 1941, ARE SHOWN IN THE
NORTHEAST WING BY DOTTED LINE. OTHER-
WISE, DOTTED LINES INDICATE BACK-FILLED ROOMS.

FRANK AND DEN WHITT

0 10 20 30 40 50   75   100 FEET

350

DIAGRAM OF PUEBLO BONITO

To an uninitiated eye the honeycomb of lines diagramming Pueblo Bonito is baffling. Small wonder. The largest prehistoric ruin thus far excavated in the United States, Bonito has been the object of the most painstaking, prolonged archaeological effort ever undertaken at one site in this country. Results, even so, are neither complete nor entirely satisfactory from an archaeological standpoint. Beneath the walls shown in the diagram, buried in some places twelve feet or more below present ground level, are traces of even older walls, older rooms. The true maze of Bonito's growth never has been fully traced.

Pueblo Bonito developed from a Basket Maker pithouse village, the first small Pueblo unit rising in the north central area. The original pueblo may have numbered no more than twenty or thirty rooms. About 1000 A.D., or slightly before, the village was expanded in arcing wings. Traces of the older walls of this expansion to the east, shown by dotted lines, were found by the Hyde Exploring Expedition in 1897.

Masonry types — of which four are basic, with perhaps six variants — indicate that the present southwest wing, more humble in architectural concept and less important to the whole village in religious or clan activity, pre-dated the present imposing southeast wing. The central section dividing the pueblo into two courts, and including the largest of several Great Kivas, was built comparatively late in the period of occupation.

Not indicated in the diagram — for lack of precise information — are a Great Kiva found buried in the central area of the west court, a very early wing running eastward from a point just below the northeast section and now buried under the 1941 fall of rock, and pithouse sites found in the west court and then back-filled. All of these features of an older Bonito were discovered by the National Geographic Society expedition (1921-27) directed by Neil M. Judd.

Some of the walls shown here — notably the "keyhole" kiva (59) of the southwest wing and the whole complex of rooms rising in a tier upward from kiva 161 in the southeast wing — probably were added after the original Bonitoans had abandoned the village and left the canyon.

As rooms were abandoned, doorways were filled in with masonry. Such doorways are labeled with an "X." Open doorways marked "2" indicate doors on two-story levels, one above the other. In some instances, walls and floor features shown either no longer exist or have been covered over.

The only tree-ring dates available, obtained by Harold S. Gladwin, tell only a fragment of the story of Pueblo Bonito's growth. Gladwin's earliest date, 1026, was

ANASAZI   **351**

taken from an upper stringer found in the entrance to room 97. His latest date, 1105, was found in two beams recovered in the southeast wing.

In its general outline and compass-points of rooms, the diagram is based upon that of the National Geographic Society. In 1952 the author spent five days in Chaco Canyon measuring, mapping and photographing all of the kivas. All of the other room walls were measured and diagrammed in 1955-56 by the author and his son, Ben McNitt. Studies also were made of wall junctures in the north central and western sections. Other details for the diagram were taken from some one hundred fifty photographs made by Richard Wetherill for the Hyde Exploring Expedition.

BIBLIOGRAPHY

AMSDEN, CHARLES AVERY. *Navaho Weaving, Its Technic and History.* Albuquerque: University of New Mexico Press, 1949.

BABINGTON, S. H. *Navajos, Gods and Tom-Toms.* New York: Greenberg, 1950.

BANDELIER, ADOLPH F. A. *Hemenway Southwestern Archaeological Expedition.* Cambridge: J. Wilson & Son, 1890.

——. *Pioneers in American Anthropology: the Bandelier-Morgan Letters, 1873-1883.* Albuquerque: University of New Mexico Press, 1940.

——. *The Delight Makers.* New York: Dodd, Mead & Co., 1890. Reprinted 1954.

BAXTER, SYLVESTER. "The Old World. An Account of the Explorations of the Hemenway Southwestern Archaeological Expedition in 1887-88." Salem: Salem, Massachusetts Press, 1888. Reprinted from *Boston Herald,* April 15, 1888.

BICKFORD, F. T. "Prehistoric Cave-Dwellings." *Century Magazine,* Vol. 40, Oct., 1890.

BIRDSALL, WILLIAM RANDALL. "The Cliff Dwellings of the Canons of the Mesa Verde," *American Geographical Society Bulletin,* Dec. 31, 1891.

BLOOM, LANSING B. "The Emergence of Chaco Canyon in History." *Art and Archaeology,* Vol. 11, Nos. 1-2, 1921.

BRAND, D. D.; HAWLEY, F. M.; HIBBEN, F. C., *et al.* "Tseh So, a Small House Ruin, Chaco Canyon," *University of*

New Mexico Bulletin, Anthropological Series, Vol. 2, No. 2, 1937.

BREW, JOHN OTIS. "Archaeology of Alkali Ridge, Southeastern Utah." Papers of the Peabody Museum, Harvard University, 1946.

BROWN, E. K., with LEON EDEL. *Willa Cather.* New York: Alfred A. Knopf, 1953.

BRYAN, KIRK. "The Geology of Chaco Canyon, New Mexico." Smithsonian Miscellaneous Collections, Vol. 122, No. 7, 1954.

CATHER, WILLA. *The Professor's House.* New York: Alfred A. Knopf, 1925.

CHAPIN, F. H. "Cliff-Dwellings of the Mancos Canons." *Appalachia,* May, 1890. Also printed in *American Antiquarian,* Vol. 12, 1890.

——. *The Land of the Cliff Dwellers.* Boston: Clarke, 1892.

COWING, HERBERT. "Journal." Unpublished manuscript in the files of Mrs. Cowing at Hamden, Conn., relating a trip by horseback to the Snake Dance at Walpi with Richard Wetherill and others in 1895. Pp. 1-27.

CUMMINGS, BYRON, and WETHERILL, LOUISA WADE. "A Navajo Folk Tale of Pueblo Bonito." *Art and Archaeology,* Vol. 14, 1922.

DORSEY, GEORGE A. "The Mishongnovi Ceremonies of the Snake and Antelope Fraternities." Field Columbian Museum. Publication 66, Anthropological Series, Vol. 3, No. 3, 1902.

DOUGLASS, A. E. "The Secret of the Southwest Solved by Talkative Tree

Rings." *National Geographic Magazine,*
Vol. 56, No. 6, 1929.
——. "Dating Pueblo Bonito and Other
Ruins of the Southwest." National Geo-
graphic Society, Contributed Technical
Papers, Pueblo Bonito Series, No. 1,
1935.
DUTTON, BERTHA P. "Leyit Kin, a Small
House Ruin, Chaco Canyon," *Univer-
sity of New Mexico Bulletin,* Mono-
graph Series, Vol. 1, No. 6, 1938.
FEWKES, JESSE W. "Antiquities of the
Mesa Verde National Park: Spruce
Tree House." Bureau of American Eth-
nology, *Bulletin 41, 1909.*
——. "Preliminary Report on a Visit to
the Navajo National Monument, Ari-
zona." Bureau of American Ethnology,
Bulletin 50, 1911.
——. "Antiquities of the Mesa Verde Na-
tional Park: Cliff Palace." Bureau of
American Ethnology, *Bulletin 51, 1911.*
GILLMOR, FRANCES, and WETHERILL,
LOUISA WADE. *Traders to the Navajos.*
Boston: Houghton Mifflin Co., 1934.
Reprinted, Albuquerque: University of
New Mexico Press, 1953.
GLADWIN, HAROLD S. "The Chaco Branch
Excavations at White Mound and in
the Red Mesa Valley." Gila Pueblo:
Medallion Papers, No. 33, 1945. Pri-
vately printed at Globe, Arizona.
——. *Men Out of Asia.* New York: Whit-
tlesey House, 1947.
GREEN, C. H. "Catalogue" of prehistoric
relics from Grand Gulch, southeastern
Utah. The American Museum of Nat-
ural History. New York: Privately
printed, n.d.
GREGG, JOSIAH. *Commerce of the Prairies,
the Journal of a Santa Fe Trader.* 2
vols. New York: H. G. Langley, 1844.
Reprinted, 1 vol., Norman: University
of Oklahoma Press, 1954.

HAWLEY, FLORENCE M. "The Significance
of the Dated Prehistory of Chetro Ketl,
Chaco Canyon, New Mexico." Albu-
querque: Monograph of the University
of New Mexico and the School of American Research, 1934.
——. "The Family Tree of Chaco Can-
yon Masonry." *American Antiquity,*
Vol. 3, No. 3, 1938.
HAYDEN, F. V. "United States Geological
and Geographical Survey of the Terri-
tories for 1874." Eighth Annual Report.
Washington, D. C., 1876.
HEWETT, EDGAR L. "The Chaco Canyon
and its Ancient Monuments." *Art and
Archaeology,* Vol. 11, 1921.
——. "The Excavation of Chettro Kettle,
Chaco Canyon, 1920." *Art and Archae-
ology,* Vol. 11, 1921.
——. "The Chaco Canyon in 1921." *Art
and Archaeology,* Vol. 14, 1922.
——. "The Chaco Canyon in 1932." *Art
and Archaeology,* Vol. 33, 1932.
——. *The Chaco Canyon and Its Monu-
ments.* Albuquerque: University of
New Mexico Press, 1936.
HOLMES, W. H. "Report on the Ancient
Ruins of Southwestern Colorado, examined during the summers of 1875 and
1876. United States Geological and
Geographical Survey of the Territories.
Tenth Annual Report. Washington, D.
C., 1878.
HOLSINGER, S. J. "Report" of his investigation of the activities of the Hyde Exploring Expedition at Pueblo Bonito. National Archives, Washington, D. C.,
1901. Parts 1, 2, 3.
HYDE, BENJAMIN TALBOTT BABBITT. Letters written to Richard Wetherill, to his
other associates, and to government officials, in connection with the operations
of the Hyde Exploring Expedition. The
American Museum of Natural History,

RICHARD WETHERILL

New York. Also, National Archives, Washington, D. C.

JACKSON, CLARENCE S. *Picture Maker of the Old West: William H. Jackson.* New York: Charles Scribner's Sons, 1947.

JACKSON, WILLIAM HENRY. "Ancient Ruins in Southwestern Colorado." United States Geological and Geographical Survey of the Territories for 1874. Eighth Annual Report. Washington, D. C., 1876.

———. "Report on the Ancient Ruins Examined in 1875 and 1877." United States Geological and Geographical Survey of the Territories for 1876. Tenth Annual Report. Washington, D. C., 1878.

JAMES, GEORGE WHARTON. *Our American Wonderland.* Chicago: A. C. McClurg & Co., 1915.

———. *Indian Blankets and Their Makers.* Chicago: A. C. McClurg & Co., 1914.

JUDD, NEIL M. "Archaeological Investigations at Pueblo Bonito, New Mexico." Smithsonian Miscellaneous Collections. Vols. 72, 74, 76, 77, 78, 1922-26.

———. "Two Chaco Canyon Pit Houses." Smithsonian Institution, Annual Report for 1922. 1924.

———. "Prehistoric Pueblo Bonito, New Mexico." Explorations and Field Work of the Smithsonian Institution in 1929. Washington, D. C., 1930.

———. "The Material Culture of Pueblo Bonito." Smithsonian Institution, Washington, D. C., 1954.

KIDDER, ALFRED VINCENT, and GUERNSEY, S. J. "Archaeological Explorations in Northeastern Arizona." Bureau of American Ethnology, *Bulletin 65*, 1919.

KLUCKHOHN, CLYDE, and REITER, PAUL, et al. "Preliminary Report on the 1937 Excavations, Bc 50-51, Chaco Canyon,

New Mexico," *University of New Mexico Bulletin 345.* Anthropological Series, Vol. 3, No. 2, 1939.

LUMMIS, CHARLES F. *Some Strange Corners of Our Country.* New York: Century, 1892.

———. *The Land of Poco Tiempo.* New York: Charles Scribner's Sons, 1902. Reprinted, Albuquerque: University of New Mexico Press, 1952.

MCGREGOR, JOHN C. *Southwestern Archaeology.* New York: John Wiley & Sons, Inc., 1941.

MCLAUGHLIN, JAMES; PEAIRS, H. B., and PETERSON, W. M. "Report on their investigation of charges made in connection with the murder of Richard Wetherill at Pueblo Bonito." Records of the Bureau of Indian Affairs, Parts 1, 2. National Archives, Washington, D. C., 1910.

MCLOYD, CHARLES, and GRAHAM, C. C. "Catalogue of Cliff House and Cavern Relics." American Museum of Natural History, New York. Reviewed in *Archaeologist*, Vol. 2, 1894.

MARTIN, PAUL S.; ROYS, LAWRENCE, and VON BONIN, GERHARDT. "Lowry Ruin in Southwestern Colorado." Field Museum of Natural History, Chicago. Anthropological Series, Vol. 23, No. 1, 1936.

MARTIN, PAUL S.; LLOYD, CARL, and SPOEHR, ALEXANDER. "Archaeological Work in the Ackmen-Lowry Area." Field Museum of Natural History, Chicago. Anthropological Series, Vol. 23, No. 2, 1936.

MARTIN, PAUL S., and RINALDO, JOHN. "Modified Basket Maker Sites, Ackmen-Lowry Area, Southwestern Colorado." Field Museum of Natural History, Chicago. Anthropological Series, Vol. 23, No. 3, 1939.

MINDELEFF, VICTOR. "A Study of Pueblo Architecture: Tusayan and Cibola." Bureau of American Ethnology, Eighth Annual Report, 1891.

MONTGOMERY, HENRY. "Pre-Historic Man in Utah." *Archaeologist*, August, 1894.

MORRIS, ANN AXTELL. *Digging in the Southwest.* New York: Garden City Publishing Co., 1934.

MORRIS, EARL H. "The Aztec Ruin." American Museum of Natural History, New York. Anthropological Papers, Vol. 26, Parts 1-5, 1919-1928.

———. "Archaeological Studies in the La Plata District." Carnegie Institution of Washington, D. C., Publication 519, 1939.

———. "An Unexplored Area of the Southwest." *Natural History*, Nov.-Dec., 1922.

MORRIS, EARL H., and BURGH, R. F. "Anasazi Basketry, Basket Maker II through Pueblo III." Carnegie Institution of Washington, D. C., Publication 533, 1941.

MORRISON, LT. C. C. "Executive and Descriptive Report . . . Field Season of 1875, Appendix E to Appendix JJ to Annual Report of the Chief of Engineers." House Exec. Doc. 1, Part 2, 44th Congress, 2nd Session, Washington, D. C., 1876.

NELSON, NELS C. "Pueblo Ruins of the Galisteo Basin." American Museum of Natural History, New York. Anthropological Papers, Vol. 15, Part 1, 1914.

———. "Grand Gulch, Southeastern Utah." Unpublished manuscript, American Museum of Natural History, New York, 1920.

———. "Outline History of Early Exploration in the Southwest." Unpublished manuscript, American Museum of Natural History, New York, n.d.

NEWBERRY, J. S. "Report of the Exploring Expedition from Santa Fe, New Mexico, to the Junction of the Grand and Green Rivers of the Great Colorado of the West in 1859." United States Engineering Department, Washington, D. C., 1876.

NORDENSKIOLD, GUSTAF ERIC ADOLF. Translated by D. I. MORGAN. *The Cliff Dwellers of the Mesa Verde.* New York: Stechert, 1901.

PEPPER, GEORGE H. "The Ancient Basket Makers of Southeastern Utah." *American Museum of Natural History Journal*, Vol. 2, No. 4, Supplement, 1902.

———. "Ceremonial Objects and Ornaments from Pueblo Bonito, New Mexico." *American Anthropologist*, Vol. 7, 1905.

———. "The Exploration of a Burial Room in Pueblo Bonito." *Putnam Anniversary Volume: Anthropological Essays.* New York: Stechert, 1909.

———. "Pueblo Bonito." Anthropological Papers of the American Museum of Natural History, New York, Vol. 27, 1920.

———. Letters, 1896-99, to Richard Wetherill, B. T. B. Hyde, and associates, in connection with the work of the Hyde Exploring Expedition. American Museum of Natural History, New York.

———. Letters, 1900-10, relating to Richard Wetherill or the work of the Hyde Exploring Expedition. From the collection of her father's personal papers, owned by Mrs. James Cameron, New Rochelle, New York, and from the National Archives, Washington, D. C.

PRUDDEN, T. MITCHELL. "An Elder Brother to the Cliff Dwellers." *Harper's New Monthly Magazine*, June, 1897.

———. "The Prehistoric Ruins of the San

Juan Watershed." *American Anthropologist*, Vol. 5, No. 2, 1903.

——. *On the Great American Plateau*. New York: G. P. Putnam's Sons, 1907.

——. "The Circular Kivas of Small Ruins in the San Juan Watershed." *American Anthropologist*, Vol. 16, No. 1, 1914.

——. "A Further Study of Prehistoric Small House Ruins in the San Juan Watershed." American Anthropological Association. Memoirs, Vol. 5, No. 1, 1918.

——. *Biographical Sketches and Letters of T. Mitchell Prudden, M.D.* New Haven: Yale University Press, 1927.

——. Letters and Private Papers, Yale University Library.

ROBERTS, FRANK H. H. "Shabik'eshchee Village, a Late Basket Maker Site in Chaco Canyon, New Mexico." Bureau of American Ethnology, *Bulletin 92*, 1929.

——. "The Village of the Great Kivas on the Zuni Reservation, New Mexico." Bureau of American Ethnology, *Bulletin 111*, 1932.

SCHMEDDING, JOSEPH. *Cowboy and Indian Trader*. Caldwell: Caxton, 1951.

SIMPSON, JAMES H. "Journal of a Military Reconnaissance from Santa Fe, New Mexico, to the Navajo Country." Reports of the Secretary of War, Sen. Exec. Doc. 64, 31st Congress, 1st Session, Washington, D. C., 1850.

VIVIAN, GORDON. "Restoring Rinconada." *El Palacio*, Vol. 41, 1936.

——. "The Three-C Site, an Early Pueblo II Ruin in Chaco Canyon." Unpublished ms.

——. "The Tri-Walled Structure at Pueblo del Arroyo." Unpublished ms.

WATSON, DON. "Indians of the Mesa Verde." Mesa Verde Museum Association, 1953.

——. "Cliff Dwellings of the Mesa Verde: A Story in Pictures." Mesa Verde Museum Association, n.d.

WETHERILL, B. ALFRED. "The Wetherills of the Mesa Verde." Published in part in *Durango Herald-News*, May, 1953. Original manuscript, dated 1948, in possession of Mrs. Martha Wetherill Stewart, Tulsa, Okla.

WETHERILL, JOHN. "Keet Zeel." Supplement to the Monthly Report for the Southwestern Monuments, March, 1934.

——. "Keet Zeel." Supplement to the Monthly Report for the Southwestern Monuments, Dec., 1935.

WETHERILL, RICHARD. Letter containing a description of a painted kiva found at Snider's Ranch, Montezuma County, Colorado. *Archaeologist*, Sept., 1894.

——. "The Cliff Dwellings of the Mesa Verde." *Mancos Times*, August, 1895. Written "from data supplied by Richard Wetherill."

——. Field Notes, Grand Gulch, Utah, 1893-94. The American Museum of Natural History, New York.

——. Field Notes, Grand Gulch, Utah, 1897. The American Museum of Natural History, New York.

——. Letters, 1893-1901, to B. T. B. Hyde, F. E. Hyde, Jr., and George H. Pepper, in connection with the work of the Hyde Exploring Expedition. American Museum of Natural History, New York.

——. Letters, to Dr. T. Mitchell Prudden, Yale University Library. One, describing the find of the Basket Makers of Grand Gulch, Utah, is in the possession of Gordon Vivian, Chaco Canyon, New Mexico.

WISSLER, CLARK. "Pueblo Bonito as Made Known by the Hyde Expedition." *Natural History*, Vol. 22, 1922.

ANASAZI

INDEX

A

Abajo Mountains, Colo., 8, 72

Abbott, Judge Edmund C., 304, 305, 306, 312

Ackmen-Lowry Ruins, Colo., 130, 131, 133

Acoma Pueblo, N.M., 139

Acowitz (Ute), 22

Acowitz Canyon, Mesa Verde, 324

Agathla Needle, Ariz., 79, 160

Agovita Tensia (Navajo), 143

Alameda, N.M., 225, 234

Alamo Ranch, Colo., 16, 17, 18, 19, 20, 22, 38, 42, 43, 45, 46, 47, 53, 54, 57, 63, 72, 75, 76, 77, 78, 85, 86, 87, 96, 102, 105, 107, 140, 146, 150, 151, 153, 155, 163, 166, 173, 174, 175, 178, 179, 186, 194, 209; sold at auction, 180. *Photo* fol. p. 146

Alamosa, Colo., 15, 16

Albuquerque, N.M., 46, 112, 120, 177, 184, 187, 192, 195, 221, 222, 224, 227, 232, 234, 235, 239, 248, 252, 267, 289, 310, 314, 316

Albuquerque Journal, quoted, 305-06

Alkali Ridge Ruins, Utah, 133

Allantown Ruins, Ariz., 134

Allen, Bob, 63, 64, 71

Allen Canyon, Utah, 72, 333

American Museum of Natural History, 36, 61, 62, 73, 76, 140, 142, 146, 150, 163, 166, 167, 172, 174, 187, 188, 190, 199, 200, 250, 332, 333. *See also* Hyde Exploring Expedition

Amsden, Charles Avery, 211, 251, 255

Anasazi, 48, 56, 61, 79, 80, 81, 109, 110, 132, 135, 136, 137, 138, 144, 158, 159, 168, 187, 204, 241; contrasted with modern Hopi, 92; defined, 57; Grand Gulch–San Juan–Chaco areas, 124-25; Richard called, 164 *et seq.*

Aneth, Utah, 312

Animas River, 78, 107, 119

Antes, Howard R., 312

Antes, Samuel S., 312-13

Antiquarian, The, 332

Antiquities Act, 213

Archaeological Institute of America, 37

Archaeologist, The, 36, 67, 75, 178; Richard's letter on Grand Gulch, 329-30

Arrington, John, 255, 256, 274, 275, 276, 307, 308

Arrington, Paul, 274, 275, 276

Astor Hotel, N.Y., 218

Austin, Tex., 183

Ayers, D. W., 326

Aztec Indians, 35, 123

Aztec, N.M., 46, 230, 249, 252, 274, 287, 291, 292, 295, 296, 298, 299, 301, 304, 307

Aztec Ruin, N.M., 131, 132, 133, 134, 135, 137

Aztec Springs, Colo., 74

B

Babbitt, Benjamin, 58. *See also* Hyde, Benjamin Talbot Babbitt; Hyde, Frederick E., Jr.

Baldwin, Judge Charles Candee, 77

Bandelier, Adolph F., 37

Basket Makers, 34, 35, 132, 135, 153, 155, 157, 158, 159, 160, 163, 208, 329-30, 333; discovery and naming of, 64-66;

ANASAZI

Duff, Charles, 48
Dufur, Sheriff William F., 274, 275, 276, 277, 281, 303, 307
Durango, Colo., 20, 30, 38, 42, 43, 44, 46, 54, 55, 62, 87, 99, 107, 141, 150, 163, 165, 179, 188, 189, 192, 193, 253, 282, 294, 323
Durango Herald, quoted, 295

E

Eastwood, Alice, 85, 86
Edway, Jack, 246, 247, 261-62
El Capitan (El Jugador), *see* Pueblo Alto
El Huerfano Mesa, N.M., 108
Elmer, Sheriff James E., 249, 250, 251, 252
Escalante, Fray Silvestre Vélez de, 12, 119
Escavada Store, N.M., 195. *See also* Hyde Exploring Expedition
Escavada Wash, N.M., 5, 127, 164, 181, 192, 226, 227, 267, 274, 275
Estufas, see Kivas
Ethridge, Jim, 22, 42, 63, 105, 156, 160
Ethridge, Roe, 42

F

Fahada Butte, Chaco Canyon, 110, 125, 244, 273; refuge sites, 139
Farmer, Fred, 52
Farmington, N.M., 5, 7, 46, 107, 118, 165, 167, 173, 191, 192, 193, 195, 196, 203, 209, 211, 230, 235, 236, 243, 247, 255, 257, 263, 273, 274, 275, 276, 277, 278, 281, 282, 285, 291, 295, 296, 298, 313, 314. *Photo* fol. p. 146
Farmington Enterprise, quoted, 287, 289, 290, 294, 297
Farmington Hustler, quoted, 209, 210, 211
Farmington Times-Hustler, quoted, 281
Fay, Justice of the Peace James T., 274, 275, 276, 277, 282, 283, 284, 285, 286, 287, 289, 290, 291, 292
Fewkes, Jesse W., 28, 29, 38, 40, 91, 323

Field Columbian Museum, 56, 152, 153, 250
Finn, Bill (Joe Moody), 5, 6, 7, 229, 230, 231, 232, 265, 267, 269, 270, 271, 272, 273, 274, 275, 277, 279, 280, 282, 287, 288, 289, 290, 291, 292, 293, 296, 297, 298, 303, 304, 305, 306, 307, 308; arrested, 276; death, 316; testimony, 283-86
Flagstaff, Ariz., 113, 114
Fort Defiance, Ariz., 255
Fortified House, Mesa Verde, 31, 32, 324
Fort Larned, Kans., 100
Fort Leavenworth, Kans., 9, 10, 11, 228, 229. *See also* Wetherill, R.
Fort Lewis Canyon, Mesa Verde, 322
Fort Lewis, Colo., 18, 22, 247
Fort Wingate, N.M., 227, 272, 275, 280
Four Corners, The, 11, 46, 57, 60, 87, 254, 298. *Map,* endpapers
French, Harry, 56, 63
Frink, Charlie, 47
Frink, James, 29
Furman, Agnes, 193, 235, 255

G

Galisteo Basin, N.M., 72, 130, 139. *See also* Nelson, Nels C.
Gallegos Canyon, N.M., 279
Gallup, N.M., 5, 46, 87, 180, 181, 184, 186, 192, 193, 195, 210, 221, 239, 240, 247, 267, 274, 275, 278, 294, 298, 300, 301, 302, 317
Ganado, Ariz., 181. *See also* Hubbell, Lorenzo
Gap, The, Chaco Canyon, 5, 111, 130, 144-45, 187, 201, 235, 245, 272, 284
Gawith, Sheriff James, 300
Geological and Geographical Survey of the Territories, 13, 66
George, Carrie, 244, 245, 246, 260
George, Hostine, 244, 245, 246, 259, 260
Gila River Valley, Ariz., 38
Giles, Dick, 14

131, 136, 137, 138; Wetherill collections, 33. *See also* Cather, Willa, 28-29; Fewkes, Jesse W., 28-29; ruins: Cliff Palace, Fortified House, High House, Jug House, Kodak House, Long House, Mug House, Peabody House, Sandal House, She House, Spring House, Spruce Tree House, Square Tower House, Step House, Sun Temple, Two-Story House. *Map,* 26

Mexico City, 151

Miller, A. F., 193

Mindeleff, Cosmos, 38

Mindeleff, Victor, 38, 124

Mitchell, Henry F., 15, 47, 48, 300

Moccasin Canyon, Mesa Verde, 47, 322

Moencopi Village, Ariz., 90

Moencopi Wash, Ariz., 79, 88

Montezuma (Aztec chief), 120

Montezuma's Castle, Ariz., 113, 331-32

Montezuma Valley, Colo., 21, 74, 77, 87, 180, 208

Monticello, Utah, 117, 140

Monument Valley, Ariz., 78

Moody, Dwight, 231

Moody, Joe, *see* Finn, Bill

Moorehead, Warren K., 36, 67, 75, 178

Moqui Canyon, Utah, 160

Moqui Rock, Ariz., 160-61

Morefield, Joe, 15

Mormons, 11, 55, 60, 63, 117, 163

Morris, Earl H., 37, 118, 154, 193, 255, 256-57, 290

Morris, Milton T., 49, 50

Morris, Scott N., 118, 256; death of, 193-94

Morrison, Lt., C. C., 123

Moss, John, 13

Mug House, Mesa Verde, 32, 40, 325

Mysterious Canyon, Ariz., 160

N

Nampeyo (Hopi), 89

National Geographic Society, 128, 335, 337. *See also* Chaco Canyon

National Museum, Helsinki, Finland, 33, 43

National Museum, Washington, D.C., 31

Navajo Indians, 11, 12, 57, 60, 79, 90, 106, 108, 110, 116, 118, 123, 127, 135, 139, 160, 188, 189, 199, 218, 226, 227, 241, 244, 246, 251, 255, 256, 257, 326, *passim;* acquisitive habits, 166-68; early stronghold, 119; employed by Hyde Expedition at Chaco Canyon, 143, 145, 147, 149, 164, 165; fiesta, 185-86; trade with Hyde Expedition, 165-66, 181-84; uprising at Farmington, N.M., 194. *Photos* fol. p. 146

Navajo Canyon, Mesa Verde, 23, 25, 32, 322, 325

Navajo Mountain, Ariz., 72, 131, 160, 277

Navajo Reservation, 254-55, 261

Neilsen, J. B., 55

Nelson, Nels C., 61, 71, 72

Newberry, Prof. J. S., 13

New Mexico Highlands University, (N.M. Normal University), 188

New York, N.Y., 61, 73, 94, 140, 163, 183, 186, 190, 192, 203, 204, 207, 209, 211, 215, 218, 247; Hyde Expedition stores, 191; R. Wetherill visits, 205

Nez-begay (Navajo), 269, 276, 280, 283, 284, 287, 288, 291, 292, 293, 305, 306

Niagara Falls, N.Y., 45, 63

Nolan's Store, Utah, 95-96

Nordenskiold, Baron Gustaf Eric Adolf, 32, 38, 39, 40, 41, 42, 43, 44, 189, 326, 327, 332

Nusbaum, Jesse, 3

Nutria Canyon, N.M., 131, 133

O

Oak Creek Canyon, Ariz., 113

O'Fallon, Tom, 272, 273

Ojo Alamo, N.M., 191, 194, 195, 210, 265

Olds, Orville C., 50, 51

Oñate, Juan de, 112

Oraibi Pueblo, Ariz., 93-94, 136-37
Ormiston, Clara, 15, 16, 18, 19, 49, 50, 52
Osborn, S. E., 66

P

Pacheco, Bernardo Miera y, 119
Padilla, Thomas, 6, 169, 183, 225, 227, 272, 273, 275, 286, 291, 292
Palmer, Edna, 101
Palmer, Elizabeth Ann, 100, 104, 111, 114
Palmer, Fred, 231-32
Palmer, Marietta, see Wetherill, Marietta (Palmer)
Palmer, Sidney LaVern, 99, 100, 101, 102, 103, 104, 106, 111, 115, 118, 144
Palmer, Sidney LaVern, Jr., 100
Palmer, William A., 305
Patrick, Levi C., 27, 30, 152, 158, 323
Peabody House, Mesa Verde, 323
Peabody Museum, 36, 56, 71, 117, 140, 142, 328
Peairs, H. B., 296, 301
Pecos Pueblo, N.M., 37, 72
Peñasco Blanco, Chaco Canyon, 109, 120, 123, 124, 127, 130, 133, 337
Pepper, Alice Sophia (Hubbard), 142
Pepper, David Joline, 142
Pepper, George H., 67, 76, 141, 143, 144, 145, 146, 147, 148, 149, 159, 165, 166, 175, 176, 177, 178, 182, 184, 185, 200, 201, 250, 251, 309-10, 334, 337; nicknamed "Hostine Klish," 164; relations with R. Wetherill, 150-51, 152-53, 160, 169-72, 215-18; report on Pueblo Bonito, 151; youth and education, 142. Photos fol. p. 146
Perraly, Joe, 175
Pesh-la-ki (Navajo), 275, 284, 291, 292
Peterson, W. M., 296, 301
Philadelphia, Pa., HEE outlets, 191, 192
Phillips, "Black," 232, 265
Phoenix, Ariz., 190, 204
Pierson, Lloyd M., 129-30
Pinkney, Charles, 274, 276, 278, 289, 293,

296, 298, 303
Pithouses, 34, 123, 128, 132
Placer mining, 60, 73, 74, 85
Point Lookout, Mesa Verde, 13
Pollack, A. G., 261, 262, 263
Polyke (Polaka?), Tom (Hopi), 89, 90
Poncho House, Chinle Wash, 64, 72, 160
Pothunting, 35
Pracht, Max, 188-89, 190, 200
Price, Utah, 51
Prince, J. Bradford, 190, 198
Professor's House, The, see Cather, Willa
Prudden, Dr. T. Mitchell, 52, 66, 92, 93-94, 127, 131, 146, 150, 164, 167, 173, 174, 186, 205, 237, 239, 243, 277-78, 289, 292, 293, 294, 297, 298, 300, 301, 302, 309; calls for investigation of R. Wetherill's murder, 295-96; first visit to Alamo Ranch, 85-87; Harper's article on Cliff Dwellers, 67, 69, 70, 71. Photo fol. p. 146
Prudden, Lillian, 277, 309
Pueblo Alto, Chaco Canyon, 122, 133
Pueblo Bonito, Chaco Canyon, 5, 106, 108, 109, 111, 118, 122, 127, 128, 129, 130-31, 132, 133, 134, 135, 136, 137, 140, 143, 144, 151, 152, 159, 163, 164, 166, 168, 169, 175-76, 179, 180, 181, 182, 184, 186, 187, 194, 195, 197, 204, 205, passim; burials, 148-49, 334, 335, 336, 337, 339; described by Jackson, 123; described by Simpson, 121; first reference to in print, 118; first season of excavation, 147-51; headquarters for Hyde Expedition retail stores, 192; Hyde Expedition work halted by Washington, 188-90, 202; Holsinger investigation, 198-203; pottery cache, 148; Pracht investigation, 188-90; trading post, 173-78, passim; R. Wetherill's report on second season, 170-71. See also Chaco Canyon, Hyde Exploring Expedition; Wetherill, R. Photos fol. p. 146. Diagram, 350

Pueblo culture, 34, 123, 158, 336; contrasted with Basket Maker, 66; origin legend, 132, 134

Pueblo, Colo., 15, 30

Pueblo del Arroyo, Chaco Canyon, 109, 120, 122, 136, 137, 138, 146, 177, 178, 185, 201, 213, 236, 257, 269, 270, 284, 287, 306, 334

Pueblo de Montezuma, *see* Pueblo Pintado

Pueblo de Ratones, *see* Pueblo Pintado

Pueblo Pintado, Chaco Canyon, 109-10, 119, 120, 123, 225, 316; described by Simpson, 121

Pueblo Revolt of 1680, 139

Puerco River (of West), *see* Rio Puerco

Putnam, Esther Orne, 186

Putnam, Frederic Ward, 56, 140, 142, 144, 151, 152, 176, 188, 189, 190, 328-29; associated with Hyde Expedition, 117; visits Chaco Canyon, 186-87

Q

Quakers, 9, 10, 20, 22, 100, 223, 225, 256, 260

Quick, Eleanor, 6, 263, 264, 265, 266, 272, 275, 276, 278, 289, 290, 291, 298, 299, 304

R

Ransome, George, 274, 275

Ratliff, James, 14

Raton Springs Store, N.M., 192

Reagan, J. W., 193-94

Redrock Valley, Ariz., 95, 133

Reed, Alexander, 305, 311, 312

Richard, *see* Wetherill, R.

Richards, Reese, 15

Rico, Colo., 11, 229

Ridge Ruin, Ariz., 131

Rincon del Camino, Chaco Canyon, 5, 270, 271, 280, 287. *Photo* fol. p. 146

Rio Grande, 111, 112, 118, 119, 120, 139, 225, 234

Rio Puerco (of West), 134

Roberts, Frank H. H., Jr., 125, 132, 133, 334, 336

Rock Canyon, Mesa Verde, 32

Root, A. L., 14

Rosita, slashes Solde, 237-38

S

Sacramento, Calif., 151

Salt River Valley, Ariz., 38

San Cristóbal Ruin, N.M., 72

Sandal House, Mesa Verde, 22, 31, 324; Palmers' camp nearby, 104-07

Sanders, Ariz., 316

Sandia Mountains, 112

San Francisco, Calif., 151

San Francisco Academy of Sciences, 151

San Francisco Mountains, 114

Sangre de Cristo Mountains, 112

San Juan River, 11, 14, 21, 48, 53, 60, 61, 64, 71, 78, 107, 114-16, 119, 128, 133, 135, 137, 138, 142, 154, 160, 163, 167, 175, 191, 192, 194, 214, 223, 226, 243

San Juan Valley, N.M., 256, 257, 281, 305, 313

Santa Fe, N.M., 12, 37, 46, 59, 107, 113, 119, 122, 187, 190, 207, 212, 251, 298, 300, 301, 303, 307; as seen by R. Wetherill and Marietta Palmer, 112

Santa Fe Archaeological Society, 188, 189, 190, 198, 200

Santa Fe New Mexican, 188; quoted, 307

San Ysidro, N.M., 118, 139

Saratoga Springs, N.Y., 63

Scarf, Clint, 29

Schlatter the Healer, 113

Schmedding, Joseph, 46, 224, 225, 226, 227, 229, 230, 231, 232, 234, 238

Sellers, Col. D. K. B., 209, 289

Sells, Indian Off. Commissioner Cato, 313

Senter, Donovan, 335

Serena, Ill., 100

Seven Lakes, N.M., 181, 195

Shabik'eshchee Village, Chaco Canyon, 123, 125, 127, 128, 132, 133, 333, 334

RICHARD WETHERILL

Tso-bakis, Hostine, 6, 286, 287, 289, 290, 292, 298
Tuba City, Ariz., 114
Two Gray Hills Store, 210, 249
Two-Story House, Mesa Verde, 13

U

Una Vida, Chaco Canyon, 120, 127, 133, 316
University of California at Berkeley, 33
University of New Mexico, 127, 129, 133, 134, 335
University of Pennsylvania Museum, 33, 55, 332
Ute Indians, 8, 11, 12, 13, 18, 19, 20, 21, 22, 53, 60, 256, 322. *Photo* fol. p. 146
Ute Canyon, Mesa Verde, 322
Ute Mountain, 19

V

Valentine, Indian Office Commissioner Robert G., 219, 262, 281, 287, 288, 291, 296, 300, 301, 302, 303, 304, 310, 315
Verde Valley, Ariz., 113
Village of the Great Kivas, Nutria Canyon, N.M., 131, 133
Vivian, Gordon, 125, 135, 137, 138, 333, 334, 335, 336-37
Volk, Ernest, 56
Voth, H. R., 38

W

Waco, Texas, 183
Wade, John, 194-96, 255
Walpi Pueblo, 42; R. Wetherill's trip to Snake Dance, 87-96
Walters, Price, 299, 301
Washington, George (Navajo), 94-95
Washington, Brevet Lt.-Col. John M., 119-20
Washington, D. C., 36, 63, 122, 206, 207, 210
Weber Canyon, Colo., 55, 179
Weber Mountain, 55

Welo (Navajo), 284, 290, 291
Wetherill, Alice, 9
Wetherill, Anna, *see* Mason, Anna (Wetherill)
Wetherill, Benjamin Alfred, 9, 18, 22, 23, 28, 30, 32, 34, 36, 38, 42, 63, 74, 79, 81, 83, 84, 85, 86, 102, 103, 106, 146, 173, 174, 175, 178, 179-80, 209, 239, 240, 241, 274, 275, 276, 278, 289, 294, 317, 322, 323, 324; Gallup postmaster, 210; loses Alamo Ranch on note, 180. *Photos* fol. p. 146
Wetherill, Benjamin Kite, 9, 10, 11, 16, 20, 22, 29, 47, 53, 54, 73, 85, 102, 174, 322; death of, 178-80. *Photos* fol. p. 146
Wetherill, Clayton, 9, 22, 30, 52, 76, 77, 85, 86, 87, 92, 93-94, 103, 104, 141, 143, 146, 147, 154, 155, 156, 160, 164, 173, 174, 175, 178, 180, 186, 205, 210, 239, 243, 244, 277, 289, 294, 309, 323, 324. *Photos* fol. p. 146
Wetherill, Elizabeth Ann, 214, 215, 239, 242, 263, 269, 270, 275, 278, 283, 284, 292, 293
Wetherill, John, 9, 22, 27, 30, 31, 32, 34, 37, 39, 40, 42, 54, 55, 61, 63, 74, 84, 85, 102, 106, 160, 178, 180, 186, 193, 195, 255, 256, 277, 289, 294, 309, 324; discovery of Betatakin, 80, 83; marries Louisa Wade, 194; Kayenta trading post, 210. *Photo* fol. p. 146
Wetherill, Louisa (Wade), 20, 194
Wetherill, Marietta (Palmer), *passim*; accepts R. Wetherill's marriage proposal, 116; born, 100; called "Asthanne," 157; death of, 317; entertains guests at Pueblo Bonito, 243-44; first meeting with R. Wetherill, 103; leaves Chaco Canyon, 316; lost in St. Louis, 215; marriage, 151-52; practices home medicine, 236-38; recollections of her husband, 222-23; sues Stacher, 302-03; testifies at trial of Chis-chilling-begay, 305; troubles after husband's death,

❲